184 Self
Task

Paradox and the Prophets

Paradox and the Prophets

Hermann Cohen and the
Indirect Communication of Religion

DANIEL H. WEISS

OXFORD
UNIVERSITY PRESS

OXFORD
UNIVERSITY PRESS

Oxford University Press, Inc., publishes works that further
Oxford University's objective of excellence
in research, scholarship, and education.

Oxford   New York
Auckland   Cape Town   Dar es Salaam   Hong Kong   Karachi
Kuala Lumpur   Madrid   Melbourne   Mexico City   Nairobi
New Delhi   Shanghai   Taipei   Toronto

With offices in
Argentina   Austria   Brazil   Chile   Czech Republic   France   Greece
Guatemala   Hungary   Italy   Japan   Poland   Portugal   Singapore
South Korea   Switzerland   Thailand   Turkey   Ukraine   Vietnam

Copyright © 2012 by Oxford University Press, Inc.

Published by Oxford University Press, Inc.
198 Madison Avenue, New York, New York 10016

www.oup.com

Oxford is a registered trademark of Oxford University Press

Library of Congress Cataloging-in-Publication Data
Weiss, Daniel H.
Paradox and the prophets : Hermann Cohen and the indirect communication of
religion / Daniel H. Weiss.
p.   cm.
Includes bibliographical references and index.
ISBN 978-0-19-989590-8 (hardcover : alk. paper) — ISBN 978-0-19-989591-5 (ebook)
1. Cohen, Hermann, 1842–1918. 2. Religion—Philosophy. 3. Jewish philosophy. I. Title.
B3216.C74W45   2012
296.3—dc23   2011037437

1 3 5 7 9 8 6 4 2

Printed in the United States of America
on acid-free paper

For my parents, Eta and David Weiss

Rabbi Bunam said to his disciples:
"Everyone must have two pockets, so that he can reach into the one or the other, according to his needs. In his right pocket are to be the words: 'For my sake was the world created,' and in his left: 'I am earth and ashes.'"
—MARTIN BUBER, *Tales of the Hasidim*

אלו ואלו דברי אלהים חיים
These and these are words of the living God.
—BABYLONIAN TALMUD, *Eruvin 13b*

Contents

Acknowledgments

I WOULD LIKE to express my gratitude to the wide array of individuals and institutions who helped to nurture this book through the stages of conception, writing, and publication.

I owe much to my teachers and advisers at the University of Virginia, who provided an open and encouraging academic environment during my doctoral studies. I would especially like to thank Vanessa Ochs, Elizabeth Shanks Alexander, and Jamie Ferreira, from whom I have learned much and whose influence can be felt in various places in this book. I am also grateful to Jorge Secada for serving as the outside reader on my dissertation committee. Above all, Peter Ochs and Asher Biemann, as the two co-directors of my dissertation research, each gave generously of their time and energy throughout my graduate studies and beyond. The double-voiced character that I discerned in Cohen's text was complemented by the 'double voices' of my two advisors, with each one providing distinctive forms of crucial intellectual guidance. I hope that I can learn from their example how to mentor qualities of growth, creativity, and precision in students. In addition, I thank the Department of Religion and the Graduate School of Arts and Sciences at Virginia for funding my studies and for enabling me to devote time to the research that formed the initial core of the present study.

I have also appreciated the supportive environments in my subsequent institutional homes as I worked to complete this book. My semester at Oberlin College in Spring 2010 was truly a wonderful setting for both teaching and research, and I value the time spent with both students and colleagues. My present home at the University of Cambridge, both in the Faculty of Divinity and in Murray Edwards College, has likewise been supportive and stimulating, and I am grateful to all those who have helped to make an American from abroad feel most welcome.

I would like to thank the publication team at Oxford University Press whose professionalism and care have helped make this publication process run so smoothly. I am particularly grateful to Theo Calderara, for his initial interest in this project and for his continuing support throughout the process; to Charlotte

Steinhardt, for her guidance in navigating a range of issues from image resolutions to permission requests; to Katherine Ulrich, for her thorough copyediting, corrections, and feedback; and to Jaimee Biggins and the rest of the production crew for their timely and skillful coordination of the multiple stages and dimensions of the project as a whole. I would also like to thank Nikos Stavroulakis for his kind permission to use his striking woodcut of Jeremiah as the cover-image for this book, as well as the anonymous reviewers whose suggestions were instrumental in improving an earlier draft of the manuscript.

There are also many individuals who have contributed to this project and its ideas through conversations, suggestions, criticisms, and friendships. While this group includes many more teachers, students, and friends not named here, I would particularly like to mention Bob Gibbs, David Ford, Sarah Coakley, Randi Rashkover, Steven Kepnes, Jim Swan Tuite, Jon Levenson, Stephanie Paulsell, John Townsend, Leora Batnitzky, Jeffrey Stout, and Mark Larrimore. In addition, I am also very grateful to Omer Shaukat, Betsy Mesard, Laura Hartman, Peter Kang, Jacob Goodson, Sam Brody, Rizwan Zamir, Reuben Glick Shank Andrew Ain, Justin Jennings, Darren Frey, Jacob Rhoads, Tal Buenos, and the denizens of Cooperative Housing at the University of Virginia.

Finally, I would like to express my gratitude to my parents, David and Eta, and to my brother Jacob. The grounding provided by a warm and supportive family has been invaluable to me, before, during, and after this project.

Last but certainly not least, I cannot count the various ways in which this book would not have been possible without the encouragement, companionship, and intellectual camaraderie of Emily Filler, who read through various drafts of this manuscript and whose critiques, logical rigor, and humor have contributed directly and indirectly to shaping both this book and myself.

Cambridge, UK
January 2012

Abbreviations

RoR   Hermann Cohen, *Religion of Reason Out of the Sources of Judaism*,
       trans. Simon Kaplan (Atlanta, GA: Scholars Press, 1995).

RV   Hermann Cohen, *Religion der Vernunft aus den Quellen des Judentums*
       [1929, 2nd ed.] (Wiesbaden: Fourier Verlag, 1978).

JS   Hermann Cohen, *Hermann Cohens Jüdische Schriften,* 3 vols., ed.
       Bruno Strauss (New York: Arno Press, 1980).

CUP   Søren Kierkegaard, *Concluding Unscientific Postscript to Philosophical
       Fragments*, ed. and trans. Howard V. Hong and Edna H. Hong
       (Princeton, NJ: Princeton University Press, 1992).

Translations

WHILE I DRAW upon Simon Kaplan's English version of *Religion of Reason*, I modify his translation without comment in numerous places when such changes clarify Cohen's intent. For this reason, I include the page numbers in the original German alongside reference to the English.

In addition, while Kaplan renders Cohen's '*der Mensch*' as 'man,' I generally seek to use the gender-neutral term 'human being.' However, there are some places where 'man' is better able to convey the nuances of Cohen's use of '*Mensch*.' In such cases, accordingly, I use the term 'man' instead of 'human being,' both in directly translating and in paraphrasing Cohen's words. Likewise, I sometimes preserve Cohen's use of 'he' and 'himself' in referring to the individual human being, although I aim as a whole for a gender-balanced presentation.

Paradox and the Prophets

Introduction

I. The Continuing Relevance of Hermann Cohen and Religion of Reason

Most of us have, at some point or another, found ourselves enmeshed in an argument that seems to have no clear means of resolution. When the subject is religion, lines tend to be drawn even more sharply and inflexibly. In contemporary culture, discussions and debates about religious topics often break down into opposing camps. What one might call the 'rationalist' or 'skeptical' position tends to treat religious concepts as mere projections of the imagination or as symbolic renderings of human-derived and human-centered concepts. Conversely, a member of the 'fundamentalist' or 'dogmatist' camp is likely to insist on the objective absoluteness of the ideas of his or her particular religious tradition. One of the more unfortunate aspects of this common dichotomy is not simply the acrimonious dispute that ensues, but the fact that such disputes appear to be interminable and irresolvable. In searching for a way to bridge this conceptual gap, one begins to suspect that certain features of the common modes of communication—that is, not simply *what* they say, but *how* different sides talk about religious ideas—may be distorting the subject matter and thus not only fueling intellectual division, but also spilling over into violence among individuals, groups, and nations.

It is with the intention of addressing such conflicts that I want to reconsider the work of a figure in early twentieth-century Jewish philosophy who speaks to the fact that religious ideas are not accurately or productively communicated through either of these two adversarial positions. I argue that Hermann Cohen's *Religion of Reason out of the Sources of Judaism* (1919) simultaneously presents and performs the insight that effective communication of such ideas requires a nonstandard style that presents multiple 'voices' simultaneously, without seeking to reduce them to a theoretical unity. In contrast, attempts at direct, single-voiced communication will strip away the complexity of these ideas. This reading of Cohen's text, however, diverges from many standard scholarly accounts. While *Religion of Reason* is frequently described as one of the most, if not *the* most, significant books of Jewish philosophy of the twentieth century, Cohen has often been treated merely as a precursor to dialogical thinkers like Martin Buber, Franz Rosenzweig, and Emmanuel Levinas, whose writings have received greater attention in the field of modern Jewish thought. Likewise, with regard to general philosophy, Cohen's doctoral student and disciple Ernst Cassirer largely over-shadows his erstwhile teacher in terms of recognition and prominence. While many factors could account for this comparative neglect, I hold that one key reason may be that the genre of Cohen's final work has been fundamentally mis-understood. Combining passages and language of both scriptural commentary and technical philosophy—while also acutely conscious of the sharp methodo-logical tension between the two—*Religion of Reason* does not seem to fit smoothly into any single category of text. Previous scholarly readings that attempt to force it into a single category oversimplify and thus misconstrue that which Cohen is attempting to convey. In this study, I show that, far from being a feature that must be interpreted away, the multiplicity of Cohen's text can be viewed an essential element of his philosophical and communicative purposes.

Moreover, once the double-voiced style of *Religion of Reason* has been prop-erly understood, it may turn out that, far from being only a precursor to later Jewish thinkers, Cohen in fact also represents a *successor* to figures such as Buber, Rosenzweig, and Levinas. That is to say, while later thinkers sought to draw upon many of Cohen's basic ideas—such as his critique of totalizing modes of thought and his emphasis on the You and the particular individual—a neglect of the crucial role played by his communicative style may have resulted in a flatten-ing or distortion of some of those same ideas. By contrast, a recovery of *Religion of Reason*'s full potential may demonstrate that Cohen's thought goes 'beyond' the contributions of his inheritors and represents a fresh, relevant, and even radical voice for Jewish philosophy, as well as philosophy of religion more gener-ally, in our own day. Cohen insists that philosophy and Scripture cannot rightly be separated from one another; rather, a proper approach to philosophical thought and writing is not possible without simultaneous engagement with Scripture and its interpretation, and rationality becomes possible only by hold-ing both of the two together in their full tension. For Cohen, we might say, philosophy without Scripture is empty, while Scripture without philosophy is blind.[1] Their mutual tension, moreover, must be explicitly and performatively made manifest in the style of an author's presentation. By challenging estab-lished modes of writing about both philosophical and religious topics, *Religion of Reason* provides us with a model for overcoming the violent and seemingly inescapable dichotomies that hover above contemporary battles over religion and its relation to reason. Cohen's paradoxical style, precisely through its refusal to resolve its inherent theoretical inconsistencies, points the way toward a new mode of communication that can reopen the blocked intellectual channels that currently separate competing streams within particular religious traditions, adherents of disparate religious traditions, and religious adherents and secular critics of religion.

(a) Previous interpretations of *Religion of Reason*

Since the posthumous publication of *Religion of Reason* in 1919, readers of the text have been divided as to the nature of Cohen's final project. One early influential interpretation was put forth by Franz Rosenzweig, who claimed that Cohen broke with and moved beyond his earlier *System der Philosophie*—in which God was 'merely an idea'—to an understanding of a living, personal, relational God.[2] This position was reasserted by many (e.g., Samuel Hugo Bergman[3] and Nathan Rotenstreich[4]) in the next generation of Cohen's readers. However, a counterinterpretation also arose, whose earliest influential proponent was Alexander Altmann.[5] Leo Strauss[6] and Emil Fackenheim[7] could also be grouped under this reading. In this portrayal, Cohen never broke with his earlier neo-Kantian system, and his later work on religion is nothing other than a consistent extension and expansion of his previous understandings. These two competing accounts may be designated as the 'religious' and the 'philosophical' readings of Cohen's text. Both of these camps are able to point to passages in *Religion of Reason* that support their preferred reading, and each of the two groups, in defending its reading, tends to avoid those passages emphasized by the other group. The assumption of both groups seems to be that a convincing 'religious' portrayal of Cohen demands the downplaying or evading of the 'philosophical' voice that seems also to speak from the text, and vice versa.

In addition, one can also identify a third interpretation, which acknowledges the textual evidence for both of the other readings but attributes this to an inner conflict or vacillation within Cohen's thought and psyche. That is, despite the fact that Cohen felt drawn to a new, personal understanding of God, he could not bring himself to break fully with his old philosophical habits, and thus remained tragically torn between the old and the new. The representations of Cohen by Julius Guttmann[8] and Martin Buber[9] exemplify this third point of view. In general, the response to the two apparently contradictory tendencies within *Religion of Reason* has been either to affirm Cohen's consistency by upholding one of the poles while downplaying another, or to acknowledge the multiplicity but to accuse Cohen, the person and author, of inconsistency. The option of acknowledging the multiplicity in the text *and* affirming Cohen's consistency has not typically been raised, much less promoted.

In the context of contemporary scholarship, Cohen's work is receiving renewed attention, although many interpretations of *Religion of Reason* still adopt one of the three basic stances described above. The 'philosophical' reading of Cohen (i.e., emphasizing the aspects of his later work that are in continuity with his earlier philosophical system) has tended to dominate, while Rosenzweig's idea of a 'break' has generally been treated as a romanticizing misrepresentation; Steven Schwarzschild[10] and Norbert Samuelson[11] hold by this view. The portrait of a fractured or inwardly divided Cohen has also been maintained, as exemplified by the work of scholars such as Peter Gordon[12] and Randi Rashkover.[13]

There are some other contemporary readings of Cohen, however, that attempt to move beyond these paradigms. One of the first scholars to highlight the merits of *both* the 'philosophical' and the 'religious' readings was Dieter Adelmann. In his 1968 monograph *Einheit des Bewußtseins als Grundproblem der Philosophie Hermann Cohens*, he notes the previous polarization of Cohen scholarship and seeks to overcome it by arguing that "Rosenzweig is right" in certain regards but that "Altmann and Guttmann are also right" in other regards.[14] Specifically, he argues that Rosenzweig is correct in his claim of innovation, in that Cohen does arrive at a certain type of 'actuality' in *Religion of Reason*; however, Altmann and Guttmann are right in their claim of Cohen's continuity with his earlier system, insofar as that actuality is specifically "an actuality of the forms of reason and consciousness, legitimated by the system."[15] While I cannot fully affirm Adelmann's attempt at overcoming the earlier interpretive antinomy (since, as I will argue, the tension between the conflicting interpretations should be preserved rather than overcome), his argument marks a crucial advance in scholarship in consciously acknowledging both 'voices' within Cohen's work *while also* rejecting the idea that Cohen is simply incoherent. Moreover, I endorse Adelmann's emphasis on the essential interrelation between Cohen's account of religion and his earlier system: "[Cohen's] philosophy of religion presupposes the entire system."[16] Even if, as I will argue, Cohen's positing of the sphere of religion does ultimately conflict with the philosophical method of his system, that same philosophical method remains in full effect as a criterion for determining what can or cannot be directly or conclusively asserted about the concepts of religion.[17] Thus, when I return in chapter 3 to the tension between philosophy and religion, I will also revisit Adelmann's insistence on the significance of Cohen's system for understanding his later thought.

Following Adelmann's lead, recent decades have seen an increase in readings of Cohen that go beyond the earlier interpretive divisions. Michael Zank's detailed monograph, *The Idea of Atonement in the Philosophy of Hermann Cohen*, provides a thorough tracing-out of previous scholarly debate on the relation of *Religion of Reason* and Cohen's earlier system.[18] While acknowledging the nonidentity between the system and the ideas of *Religion of Reason*, Zank skillfully demonstrates that the latter was by no means a sudden development in Cohen's thought; rather, many of the basic concepts of *Religion of Reason* can be found in writings spanning the entire length of Cohen's career. Thus, even if some ideas in *Religion of Reason* may be new in relation to the system, this does not mean that they are new to Cohen as a thinker. If *Religion of Reason* seems to indicate that there is more to Cohen's thought than that which is contained within his system, Zank shows that there had *always* been more to Cohen than his system. This recognition can allow us to view the innovation of *Religion of Reason* not in the specific *content* of its ideas, but rather in how it juxtaposes those ideas against one another in new ways.

Zank also points out, crucially, that many of the ideas found in *Religion of Reason* can also be found in Cohen's *Der Begriff der Religion im System der Philosophie*, and he emphasizes the basic continuity between the two books.[19] This further underscores the idea that *Religion of Reason* does not simply appear in Cohen's thought as a sudden epiphany. However, Zank's account of the two books tends to blur the distinction between them. He describes them as presenting the same basic ideas within two different genres, with *Der Begriff der Religion* representing "philosophy of religion," while *Religion of Reason* represents "Jewish thought."[20] In contrast, I will argue that *Religion of Reason* represents a significant rational-philosophical advance over *Der Begriff der Religion*: while it may be true that there is little "conceptual tension" between the two,[21] an important difference between them lies in what we could call a 'stylistic tension.' While *Der Begriff der Religion* largely attempts to express its ideas within a single-voiced style typical of philosophical writing, *Religion of Reason* employs the voice of Scripture as a fundamental element in its mode of reasoning; as such, it is able to address aspects of the rational ideas of religion that are inaccessible to the monologic style. Nevertheless, Zank's argument remains crucial for emphasizing that the primary difference between the two books is *not* on the strictly conceptual level, thus pointing to the need to highlight a different type of difference.

Robert Gibbs's work represents another important step in the attempt to move beyond previous dichotomized readings of Cohen. On the one hand, he presents himself as "largely following" Altmann's account of Cohen, and thus as rejecting Rosenzweig's reading of *Religion of Reason*.[22] On the other hand, he also emphasizes that, upon carefully examining the details of the thinkers' arguments, one finds a number of close conceptual connections between Rosenzweig's 'anti-system' thinking and Cohen's 'pro-system' thinking. Both thinkers, for instance, highlight the importance of the 'I' and the 'You,' of the notion of confession, and of self-sanctification before God.[23] Importantly, from Altmann's account alone, one would not be led to expect such similarities, and Gibbs specifically notes that Altmann "neglects" these linkages.[24] While Gibbs still insists that Rosenzweig misunderstood Cohen in important ways, he accounts for these surprising connections by positing that "Cohen's desire to achieve the most radical individuality in the 'I' brings him extremely close to the efforts of his existentialist students."[25] In this account, however, the "extremely close" still retains the character of a determinate separation and distance.

In building upon Gibbs's careful philosophical analyses, I will posit that Cohen's closeness to Rosenzweig's rejection of the system is so extreme that one can no longer make the 'safe' judgment of a determine separation. Instead, we will see that Cohen's thought contains features both of a Rosenweigian break with the system, and of an Altmannian non-break. Whereas Gibbs points to the "almost paradoxical parallels" between Cohen and Rosenzweig, I take the additional step of positing that, in fact, the parallels are *truly* paradoxical.[26] This descriptive twist, though, is made possible by virtue of the substantive conceptual connections that Gibbs uncovers. By focusing on the actual details and reasoning of Cohen's text, he helps direct our attention away from the theoretical question of "Does Cohen break from his system or not?" and turns us toward an examination of what Cohen seems to be *doing* in his texts—whereupon the surprising similarities to Rosenzweig reemerge.

In his examination of the status of Cohen's *Religion*, Andrea Poma begins by confronting the previous 'camps' of readers and, rather than coming down on either one side or the other, attempts to acknowledge and account for both "the aspects of continuity and those of contrast in Cohen's thought in respect of his system."[27] By seeking carefully to weigh the various pieces of evidence, Poma initially allows the question to remain open, providing the reader with his concluding interpretation only at the end his analysis. In this way, he displays a notable sensitivity to the fact that the proper account is by no means obvious, and that one's theorizing should preserve, as much as possible, the complexity contained within Cohen's thought. Furthermore, Poma retains this complexity in his ultimate assessment, which sees Cohen's later work on religion as moving beyond the viewpoint of scientific idealism and thus of Ethics, but as remaining within the viewpoint of critical idealism, such that religion goes beyond science but not beyond reason. Religion therefore stands neither beyond nor within the limit of critical philosophy, but rather *on* the limit or border.[28] This emphasis on religion as a 'border-concept' accords in significant ways with my own reading; however, while Poma tends to present this proposal as a solution to the challenge of Cohen's complexity, I view it instead *not* as solving or resolving the problematic tension, but simply as restating it in a different form, thereby retaining the theoretical conflict. The notion of such a border turns out to be theoretically untenable and does not provide a stable place for Cohen's account to 'stand.'[29] Instead, while maintaining the neither-this-nor-that character of such a border, we need to turn to the literary qualities of Cohen's text, and look at the ways in which his double-voiced approach enables a practical communication precisely where a consistent theoretical description would fall short.

Steven Kepnes provides another important component to our understanding of *Religion of Reason* by focusing on the significance for Cohen's project of Jewish textual sources. Resisting an approach that would view Cohen's textual interpretations as an ornament to the true edifice of philosophical reasoning, Kepnes insists that it is only through attention to Cohen's treatment of textual and liturgical sources that we can comprehend his project of rational communication. In this sense, his suggestion of a Cohenian "co-priority of reason and scripture"—with a strong functional and pragmatic emphasis on the latter—helps move us away from a merely conceptual debate over a break or non-break with idealism; instead, we must follow through the reasoning implicit in Cohen's engagement with particular and concrete textual sources.[30] That is to say, Cohen's reasoning is manifested in and through this engagement and cannot be summarized abstractly apart from this engagement. Though Kepnes does not devote as much attention to the philosophical implications of this dependence on sources, his insistence on the performative and hermeneutic nature of Cohen's thought and his tracing-through of some of Cohen's scriptural-liturgical readings point toward the proper approach to *Religion of Reason*.[31] In my project, I intend likewise to focus on close readings of Cohen's textual reasonings, while also incorporating greater reflection on what this implies for the communication of religious ideas in a broader sense.

Of all contemporary readers of Cohen, Almut Bruckstein most strongly underscores the conceptual significance for Cohen's thought of textuality and literary-hermeneutical concerns. Emphasizing the philosophic import of Cohen's insistence on "the simultaneity of text and commentary," she draws structural connections between this simultaneity and the classical rabbinic conception of the relation between Written and Oral Torah.[32] Moreover, she notes the ways in which Cohen holds up scriptural commentary as a means of balancing the shortcomings of philosophy.[33] In this way, Cohen's use of Scripture not only provides a means of addressing problems of reason, but specifically serves as a conscious rational critique of purely 'autonomous' methods of philosophizing. In addition, she argues that much of the discourse in modern Jewish philosophy regarding a "polyphony of voices" can be traced back to Cohen's modes of reasoning.[34] I intend to build upon Bruckstein's basic orientation by focusing on the details and function of Cohen's literary style in *Religion of Reason*, a topic to which Bruckstein and other scholars devote less attention. The conceptual import of orality and of a multiplicity of voices, I argue, is mirrored in the polyphonic style of *Religion of Reason* itself, wherein Cohen's reasoning displays its stubborn resistance to any readerly attempts to reduce it to a single-voiced, conceptually consistent account.

This last element, however, points to ways in which these recent scholarly accounts may be subject to a different sort of danger. They have, in various important regards, been successful in 'moving beyond' the previous divisions that marked readers of Cohen. The Altmann and Rosenzweig camps one-sidedly avoided important elements in Cohen's thought, while Buber's approach recognized both 'voices,' but attributed this multiplicity to incoherence and personal indecision. In contrast, these recent scholars have sought both to acknowledge the complexity of Cohen's account *and* to insist on the coherence of Cohen's project. Such harmonizing attempts, though, run the risk of eliminating the sharp conceptual tension that, I maintain, plays a crucial role in Cohen's project. That is, it could be the case that fully 'coherent' accounts of his thought may domesticate the radical challenge that Cohen's style poses to traditional philosophical writing.

Thus, my project seeks to restore a sense of theoretical 'incoherence' to Cohen's text—yet, unlike the Buberian reading, I maintain that the incoherence represents not a personal shortcoming on Cohen's part but rather a rational and necessary feature of his intended practical communication. By challenging the assumption that a unified authorial intent must be accompanied by theoretical-conceptual consistency, this emphasis on the *paradoxical* quality of Cohen's approach can thus fruitfully draw upon the positive insights of each of the previous modes of reading *Religion of Reason*.

(b) Broader philosophical significance: Multiple voices, appropriation, and the flattening of reason

The topics addressed in this study also have relevance beyond the realm of Cohen scholarship proper. In addition to the question of "How should we understand Cohen's text?" the project of rereading *Religion of Reason* opens new avenues of exploration in broader philosophical domains as well. Cohen's attempt to communicate the concepts of religion provides suggestive responses to questions such as: How is philosophical content related to philosophical form and style? Do particular ways of writing and speaking—perhaps those common to contemporary philosophical discourse—run the risk of distorting our understanding of certain concepts and ideas? Conversely, do certain ideas intrinsically demand a nonstandard form of communication? In particular, Cohen's work raises the possibility that the desire for full theoretical consistency, while valuable for certain forms of analysis, will lead to misrepresentation and misunderstanding of key ethical and religious concepts. In this, *Religion of Reason* evokes comparisons with Wittgenstein's writings and concerns. The co-presence of multiple voices in Cohen's text can be compared to Wittgenstein's later work in *Philosophical Investigations*, in which he attempts to address various philosophical issues in a form that is deliberately non-systematic yet that does not revert to apophatic silence. And, as we shall see in chapter 3, the example of Cohen's work can likewise serve to address questions raised by the notion of Kierkegaardian indirect communication.

Cohen can also help contribute to contemporary questions regarding 'the limits of philosophy.' He does place limits on philosophy, as the discipline that seeks to contribute to theoretical knowledge; there are some areas of reality that philosophy, in the strict sense, cannot access. He does not, however, give up on the power of *reason*, which he distinguishes from philosophy. While there may be certain ideas that are impervious to impersonal or theoretical comprehension, and which will produce totalizing structures if approached in such a manner, Cohen does not dismiss the viability of such ideas entirely. Rather, he retains them, while indicating that such ideas, while still rational, may require a form of practical and personal engagement in order to be appropriated. As such, by placing limits on strictly impersonal philosophy, he broadens the concept of reason in a manner akin to the account of the rational project given by Pierre Hadot's *Philosophy as a Way of Life*.

In particular, Hadot's assertion that the 'rationality' of ancient philosophical texts was situated in a context of "spiritual exercises" can, by analogy, shed light on Cohen's project. According to Hadot, "Although every written work is a monologue, the philosophical work is always implicitly a dialogue. The dimension of the possible interlocutor is always present within it. This explains the incoherencies and contradictions which modern historians discover with astonishment in the works of ancient philosophers. In philosophical works such as these, thought cannot be expressed according to the pure, absolute necessity of a systematic order."[35] Similarly, in the case of *Religion of Reason*, the lack of full theoretical consistency both enables and forces the reader to fill the 'gap' through an ethically formative act that goes beyond a merely passive intellectual cognition.[36] However, while the non-systematicity of ancient philosophers may have been a normal and accepted feature of their cultural milieu, Cohen's modern construction of a theoretical inconsistency in the service of reason marks an innovative departure in an intellectual environment that tends to equate reason, for good or ill, with self-sufficient theoretical coherence. That is, Cohen writes with conscious awareness—stemming in part from his own previous systematizing efforts—of the failings and dangers of such a conception of reason.

In addition to presenting and performing a different approach to reason and reasoning, the themes of *Religion of Reason* are especially relevant to questions in philosophy of religion. With regard to many issues (e.g., the personality of God, the nature of prayer, the nature of divine commandment, the relative priority of reason or of revelation), Cohen's insights demonstrate that many of the various competing 'positions' that philosophers often maintain may in fact be one-sided flattenings of inherently paradoxical ideas. Likewise, Cohen's work contributes to the ongoing intellectual quest to determine the relationship between 'universal' philosophical concepts and particular religious texts (in this case, the Hebrew Bible, as well as rabbinic literature). One can view *Religion of Reason* as an exemplary attempt to preserve the particularity of a specific tradition without lapsing into sectarianism and losing sight of the wider notion of humanity. In addition, Cohen's multivoiced employment of classical Jewish sources can be of value especially for contemporary Jewish thought, which continues to struggle with questions of the particular and the universal.

II. *Situating* Religion of Reason *in its Intellectual-Historical Context*
(a) German philosophy

In order to understand Cohen's attempt to navigate the problematic relation between philosophy and religion, we must historically situate Cohen's thought within the broader trajectory of nineteenth-century neo-Kantianism, itself a philosophical reaction to the 'excesses' of earlier German Idealism. While the speculative system-building attempts of post-Kantian thinkers like Fichte, Schelling, and Hegel dominated German intellectual culture in the early decades of the 1800s, their constructions of 'pure thought' later came to be viewed as ungrounded and arbitrary. Where the post-Kantian German Idealists thought that Kant had not gone far enough and had overly restricted the scope of what can be known, their subsequent critics thought that the systematizers had gone too far, asserting claims of knowledge without legitimate warrant. While not initially focused primarily on Kant, this post-Idealist trend led to a rehabilitation of Kant's desire for a critical differentiating between what can and cannot legitimately be claimed as knowledge.

One key forerunner of this trend, which would later acquire the broad label of 'neo-Kantianism,' was Adolf Trendelenburg. Trendelenburg—under whom Cohen studied in his university days—argued that philosophy must take its cues from the sciences, including logic, mathematics, empirical science, and jurisprudence. In particular, he emphasized the importance of *method*: to the extent that a science arrives at its results according to the rigorous procedures of its governing method, to that extent will it arrive at results that have a firm basis and grounding.[37] Thus, for example, physicists may speculatively put forth any number of initial hypotheses, but they will retain only those that can pass through the crucible of methodological experimentation and testing. In this sense, the scientist submits to the scientific method in order to enact a self-imposed constraint on speculation and on assertion of claims. While the later various representatives of neo-Kantianism differed from one another in often-significant ways, they remained unified by their common commitment to "the reduction of philosophy to a learned science," as Klaus Köhnke puts it in his intellectual history of the movement.[38]

Importantly, however, this commitment to 'science' was by no means understood in the same way by all neo-Kantians, and there were no clear criteria as to what constituted a properly scientific approach to philosophy. Trendelenberg, for instance, was strongly opposed to the idea of constructing a system of philosophy; he viewed the desire for a theoretical comprehension of totality as symptomatic of the intellectual overreaching of earlier Idealism.[39] Others, however, held a less restrictive view of the limits of 'scientific' philosophy. For example, Kuno Fischer—whose thought was highly influential in the shaping of the South-West or Baden school of neo-Kantianism, which stood as the chief rival of the Cohen-led Marburg school—put forth a Fichteanized account of Kant that gave rise to a revived neo-Idealism. Far from opposing the construction of a philosophical system, Fischer sought to create a "system of pure reason" precisely by means of his Kant *redividus*.[40] This wide divergence of views indicates that the notion of a 'scientific' approach as characteristic of neo-Kantianism cannot, in itself, provide much substantive information about the movement as a whole, and one must instead examine each thinker or school on its own terms. At the same time, even without a common definition, the general *rhetorical* significance of 'science' is crucial for understanding Cohen's project in *Religion of Reason*: to approach philosophy 'scientifically' means to draw a line in the intellectual sand—while different thinkers may draw the line in very different ways, they all agree that philosophy must restrict itself only to that which lies within the limits of that line.

If we turn our attention to the Marburg school of neo-Kantianism (so designated because its chief representatives—Cohen and Paul Natorp—were professors at the University of Marburg), we can identify Cohen's place in neo-Kantianism with further precision. Cohen's immediate predecessor in the philosophy chair at Marburg was F. A. Lange (another important figure in the development of neo-Kantianism), and Lange's personal recommendation was a crucial factor in Cohen's ultimate selection for the post. Yet, while Lange clearly saw Cohen as an intellectual compatriot, the philosophical differences between the two are also illuminating. Lange represented the more skeptical wing of neo-Kantianism; his sense of 'science' was strongly shaped by experimental science's emphasis on empirical sense-data, and he sharply opposed metaphysical speculation and system-building.[41] Cohen, in contrast, viewed the construction of a system as a fundamental task of philosophy, and his deliberately titled *System der Philosophie* stands as testimony to this conviction.

However, despite Cohen's confidence that scientific philosophy could exceed Lange's more agnostic-restrictive limitations, an important factor (in addition to the socialist political leanings that they both shared) still links the two thinkers. As Ulrich Sieg puts it, "In the demand that in the positive sciences 'the *influence of the subjectivity of the researcher [is to be] neutralized*,' Lange anticipates one of the central scientific-theoretical postulates of the 'Marburg school.'"[42] Accordingly, while Cohen did seek to construct a philosophical system, he maintained a commitment to doing so through the strict use of a *method* whose impartial application guaranteed the 'objective validity' of the philosophical constructions. This concern for 'objectivity,' moreover, was specifically intended as a contrast to the *subjective* idealism of neo-Kantian thinkers like Fischer.[43] In this way, Cohen's approach coincided with Lange's opposition to metaphysics, since he retained concepts commonly viewed as 'metaphysical entities' (most famously, Kant's *ding an sich*) precisely by stripping them of their autonomous ontological status and instead reconceiving of them in terms of method, linked to the continuous task of scientific research and thought. Cohen's dual concerns in his construction of his system—his desire to go beyond the skeptical rejection of problematic concepts, while yet *not* going beyond the demands of 'objective validity'—would ultimately manifest themselves in a slightly different form in *Religion of Reason*: there, he will stake out the legitimacy of concepts rejected by his *own* system precisely because of their lack of objectivity, yet *without* directly asserting them in a way that would transgress his continued commitment to methodological objectivity. As we will see, although this latter instantiation of dual concerns will prove intractably paradoxical and will require a form of indirect communication, it nevertheless reflects Cohen's continued desire for both conceptual broadness and intellectual conscientiousness and rigor.

Both the fervor and the universal scope of Cohen's commitment to a method-driven approach to philosophy enable us as well to contextualize *Religion of Reason* in relation to the other representatives of the Marburg school itself. The intellectual collaboration of his colleague Paul Natorp was profoundly meaningful to Cohen, given the increasing spread of antisemitism within the German academic environment, as well as the intellectual isolation to which the Marburg school was subject within the broader spheres of German neo-Kantianism, general German intellectual culture, and even the University of Marburg's own philosophy department.[44] Natorp supported and followed Cohen's demand for 'scientific' criteria in philosophy, going so far as to proclaim, "[T]he *method* is everything."[45] Yet, despite such a proclamation of 'pan-methodism,' Natorp stopped short of applying the method to entirely everything: as Andrea Poma points out, he differs from Cohen in eventually coming to see *religion* as lying beyond the proper domain of the scientific method.[46] While Cohen would also arrive at an approach in which religion holds a problematic and paradoxical status vis-à-vis methodical objectivity, he never assigns religion any formal or theoretical autonomy. Cohen's stringency is thus highlighted by his refusal to allow the even the slightest assertion of independence from the method of scientific philosophy, in contrast to the ultimate willingness of another 'good Marburgian' like Natorp to make an exception for religion.

Similarly, though he was not based in the department of philosophy, the Marburg theologian Wilhelm Herrmann admired many aspects of Cohen's neo-Kantian approach and might be grouped as a 'fellow traveler' of the Marburg school. Yet, Herrmann repeatedly criticized Cohen's philosophy (with its criterion of 'objectivity') for failing to take account of the experience of the self in its particular individuality. While Cohen would later attempt to respond to Herrmann's critique (most notably in his *Der Begriff der Religion im System der Philosophie*) he was never able to do so to Herrmann's satisfaction.[47] We can understand this impasse as stemming not from any lack of desire on Cohen's part, but as an unavoidable consequence of

Cohen's commitment to the method of science. As we learn from Köhnke's account, the resistance to acknowledging the significance of individual particularity was a thread running throughout much of neo-Kantianism; most frequently, such resistance was proclaimed in the name of scientific impartiality and in reaction to earlier Romanticism's 'unscientific' championing of the individual.[48] Cohen's method-influenced incapacity to grant autonomous validity to individual particularity thus dooms his desired reconciliation with Herrmann; the mutual personal sympathy on the part of both was not sufficient. This failure helps to further characterize Cohen as one of the most uncompromising advocates of 'scientificality' within the already scientifically oriented stream of neo-Kantianism.

The above contextualization helps us to appreciate the shocking nature of Cohen's assertion, in his introduction to *Religion of Reason*, that "reason does not exhaust itself in science and philosophy."[49] While he maintains his conception of philosophy as completely determined by the method of science, he will argue that 'religion' constitutes a sphere that falls under 'reason' yet is *not* contained within philosophy. This seeming breach of his commitment to the all-embracing scope of science—and his widespread use of personal religious language throughout *Religion of Reason*—could initially make us think that Cohen has fallen back upon those very 'metaphysical' elements of earlier German Idealism that his systematic employment of 'method' had sought to eliminate. As we will see, however, he never rejects his commitment to the method of scientific philosophy; accordingly, he is ultimately able to posit the non-scientific sphere of religion only in a paradoxical and non-determinate manner. As such, while seeming to move toward certain elements of German Idealism or Romanticism, he nevertheless remains perched on the seemingly nonexistent space between the domain of method and that which lies determinately beyond it.

To give the reader a basic feel for Cohen's placement on this narrow ridge, I present below a series of general comparisons between Cohen's approach in *Religion of Reason* and the thought of major classical German Idealists. Each of the latter can be seen as going 'beyond Kant' in various regards, and it is instructive to observe the ways in which Cohen is drawn in their direction, yet refuses to abandon his commitment to what he holds to be a Kantian intellectual sobriety. While these brief comparative sketches may involve oversimplification, they helpfully illustrate the neither-this-nor-that nature of Cohen's thought and his dual conviction that his earlier neo-Kantian system and its method did not go far enough, while a determinate departure from his system would still be going too far.

Hegel

Kant maintained a sharp separation between the ideal and the actual, a position that excluded higher rational ideas (such as God and the self) from the sphere of objective theoretical knowledge. In contrast, Hegel argued that such a stance turns these ideas into lifeless abstractions; he insisted, against Kant, that one *could* have objective speculative knowledge of such ideas. Likewise, he argued for the immanence and actuality, as opposed to the transcendence, of the rational ideal.

While Cohen makes only a single and passing reference to Hegel in *Religion of Reason*,[50] his *Ethik des reinen Willens* directly cites Hegel's dictum that "what is rational is actual." Cohen then opposes this notion with his own formulation, composed in a Kantian spirit: "Here arises the enormous difference between Hegel and Kant; for Kant would say 'what is rational is not actual; rather, it ought to become actual.'"[51] This commitment to maintaining a gap between the ideal (the rational) and the actual manifests itself throughout *Religion of Reason* as well. However, despite his consistent stated opposition to Hegel, multiple commentators have raised the question of whether Cohen, especially in his later work, also displays a "neo-Hegelianism" or a "crypto-Hegelianism."[52] As we shall see, there are multiple places in *Religion of Reason* where Cohen seems to move closer to Hegel by positing the full actualization of the ideal. Even in these cases, though, Cohen asserts such fulfillment only paradoxically, in terms of the dynamic infinitesimal moment, so that there is never any static or *objective* actualization of the ideal. Likewise, when Cohen asserts the need for knowledge of God in *Religion of Reason*, this may seem like an overstepping of Kantian bounds.[53] However, whereas Hegel argues for objective knowledge of God, Cohen insists, following the biblical formulation, that knowledge of God is possible only as *love* of God: not an objective or theoretical *comprehension of* God, but rather as an engaged and passionate *relation to* God.[54] Thus, whereas one can more determinately pin down the intellectual location of Kant's and Hegel's thought, Cohen's seems to occupy a contradictory space 'between' the two.

Schelling

Schelling differed from both Kant and Hegel in emphasizing the limitations of impersonal human reason as displayed in philosophy. There are certain elements of reality, he held, that manifest themselves in the personal and non-philosophic phenomena of myth and religion. In particular, he held that the essence of human freedom cannot be grasped by reason and philosophy, but is contained in the Christian mythico-religious accounts of the crucifixion and resurrection.

While Cohen's own use of the term 'myth' in *Religion of Reason* is almost always negative and critical (myth is that from which the religion of reason must separate itself[55]), his employment of *Scripture* vis-à-vis philosophy can be fruitfully compared to Schelling's account of myth's superiority to philosophy. For Cohen, the 'primitive' sources of Judaism come to our aid precisely where the method of philosophy falls short. However, whereas Schelling sees myth as going beyond the limitations of *reason*, Cohen insists that only philosophy's limitations are in question, not those of reason. Similarly, whereas Schelling argues for the inherent value of myth, Cohen does not admit the *autonomous* validity of anything outside of the method of systematic philosophy. For Cohen, the scriptural sources considered 'in themselves' may very well be mythical—but their value is not found through considering them 'in themselves.' The sources of Judaism do not passively 'contain' truths that philosophy cannot access; rather, they lead to such truths *only when an individual actively engages them in a rational manner*. Furthermore, even when such activity leads one to areas of reason beyond philosophy, it does so only practically, and does not result in any knowledge that could subsequently be asserted impersonally in a theoretically consistent form.

Schopenhauer

Schopenhauer, while a follower of Kant in certain regards, criticized what he viewed as the overly abstract, intellectual, and externalized character of Kant's philosophy. For Schopenhauer, the world as ostensibly external to oneself is merely an illusory representation and projection from within. In particular, the moral factor in human beings comes not from an external, philosophical moral law, but from an immanent Will that manifests itself in nonintellectual impulses of compassion.

In *Religion of Reason*, Cohen refers repeatedly to Schopenhauer, and always in a critical manner. However, he also seems to move in the direction of some of Schopenhauer's criticisms of Kantian philosophy. Specifically, he agrees with Schopenhauer that, viewed in a strictly objective-intellectual manner, another person can only be viewed as another instance of myself; hence the apparent 'otherness' of the second person would have to be deemed illusory. Likewise, my moral relation to the other cannot be viewed strictly in terms of an external law, but necessarily involves compassion, a factor which involves my individual self and hence seems to have certain qualities of immanence. However, Cohen parts ways with Schopenhauer in maintaining that the other as fellowman and as You should be viewed *neither* as strictly external *nor* as strictly internal to oneself. Even though the You has no objective status and cannot be separated from my engaged relational compassion, both the You and compassion constitute rational, though not philosophical-theoretical, elements. As we will see, however, paradoxical elements such as the You (in a sense, neither external nor internal, but in another sense, both external and internal) cannot be asserted directly and instead require indirect forms of communication.

Herder

Although not a post-Kantian philosopher but rather a contemporary of Kant, Herder's ideas are also important for contextualizing Cohen's *Religion of Reason*. Herder, while one of the forerunners of modern cultural nationalism, also emphasized that every nation's culture, including its language, literature, and customs, is inherently rich and valuable. The path to truth, he maintained, is not to be found by searching for an abstract universal that is common to all humanity; rather, the members of each nation should delve more deeply into their own particular cultural heritage.

One can thus see the potential influence of Herder's thought in Cohen's decision to present his ideas through and alongside an engagement of the literary sources of his own particular religio-cultural tradition. In *Religion of Reason*, Cohen draws the religion of reason out of the sources of Judaism not because those sources are inherently superior to all other sources, but precisely because he sees them as *his own*. Furthermore, Herder's project of engaging the Hebrew Bible in his *The Spirit of Hebrew Poetry* can be viewed as an important philosophical precursor to Cohen's own reading of the same text.[56] Cohen's criticism of the method of philosophy—that it eliminates plurality and particularity in its quest for universalizing totality—also shares certain important elements with Herder's opposition to abstract universals. Thus, Cohen emphasizes that there are certain ideas that one simply cannot access through recourse to strictly 'universal' concepts; they must be drawn from particular, concrete sources. However, Cohen does not (as Herder may be inclined to do) simply reverse the priority, eliminating the quest for the universal by championing particularity as the source of truth. Instead, through his paradoxical concept of 'plurality within totality,' he seeks to present *rational* (that is to say, 'universal') ideas, even though the ideas cannot be formulated in autonomous propositions, but must remain permanently linked to—and displayed alongside of—the particularity of the sources from which they are drawn.

(b) Jewish thought

Alongside the general philosophical context of Cohen's thought, it is also important to place *Religion of Reason* in the context of earlier Jewish religious thought in particular. One of the central challenges facing Jewish thinkers in the modern period was the question of *the status of Scripture* and, more broadly, of revelation. The traditional rabbinic doctrine of *torah min ha-shamayim* assumed the divine perfection of Scripture (*torah she-bikhtav*); notably, this special status was linked to a remarkably flexible scriptural hermeneutic. In the modern period, the divine status of Scripture was no longer a given. Instead, Jewish thinkers had to respond to both rational and historical criticisms of the biblical text. The debate over Scripture's rationality can be traced back to Maimonides and Spinoza: if one associates reason with truth, then how is one to account for the passages in Scripture that appear to fall short of the criteria of rationality? Maimonides appealed to an esoteric 'inner' sense of the Bible in order to assert its complete rationality, while Spinoza, confining himself only to "what is taught by Scripture itself," concluded that the Bible has *no* inherent connection to reason.[57] Later Jewish devotees of reason were caught between their commitment to the scientific method—which made it harder to accept Maimonides' allegorical interpretations—and their desire to preserve the unique status of the Bible within the Jewish tradition—which made them hesitant to adopt Spinoza's position that the Old Testament is merely the constitution of a bygone and vanished political state. Moses Mendelssohn, who is often considered to be the first modern Jewish philosopher, took a position that can be seen as lying between Maimonides and Spinoza, although perhaps more in the direction of the latter. In his *Jerusalem*, he argues that the Bible constitutes a divinely revealed legislation—thus recovering its continuing value—but that it has no special connection to "eternal truths of reason."[58] To be sure, Mendelssohn did tend to describe the contents of the Bible as *compatible* with rational truths, but he also emphasized that these same truths could be arrived at through autonomous reflection, such that the Bible makes no *unique* contribution to the field of rational truth. Cohen, while praising Mendelssohn in other regards, criticizes him for "obscuring the concept of Judaism by limiting it to a religion of law"[59] and for equating Judaism's intellectual content solely with "natural religion."[60] In other words, Mendelssohn was able to maintain the continuing relevance of Scripture, as well as the general rationality of Judaism, but he was unable to preserve an essential relation between Scripture and reason. In *Religion of Reason*, Cohen attempts to recover such a relation, despite the apparent contradiction between the intractable particularity of Scripture and the universality of reason.

The rise of historical criticism of the Bible also posed a challenge to traditional Jewish understandings. Quite apart from the rationality or divinity of its particular content and teachings, the historical-critical method raised doubts concerning the *origin* of Scripture. Prior to such criticism, the divine origin of the Bible could more easily be viewed as a basic historical 'fact,' having occurred at a specific time and place and involving a specific human receiver: not simply *torah min ha-shamayim*, but also *moshe kibel torah mi-sinai*. The results of historical science, in contrast, seemed to indicate that the Bible did not have a unitary origin, but consisted of multiple source-texts that had been edited and put together over a long period of time. Such an account made the Bible's past seem all too human, and made it more difficult to present 'objective' evidence for the Bible's status as divine revelation. According to Gershom Scholem's narration of the effects of historical criticism, "the question in Judaism as to whether and in what sense it was still possible to speak of Revelation became inescapable. In practically all of the theologians of Judaism whose writings I know, the place which thus became vacant was filled by an attenuating and subjectivist talk of Revelation which was bound to destroy Revelation's authoritative character."[61] In this account, because evidence for the 'external' or 'transcendent' origin of the Torah has seemingly collapsed, it is assigned a purely 'internal' and 'immanent' origin. While Scholem views Cohen as a prime example of one who has taken this route, I argue in this study that Cohen's approach to Scripture seeks to sidestep the objectivist/subjectivist and internal/external dichotomies entirely. Furthermore, we can view his dependence on the literary sources of Judaism in terms of a retrieval of Scripture's "authoritative character," even though his approach also differs from traditional conceptions in significant ways.

Finally, we can also situate Cohen and *Religion of Reason* in the context of challenges not simply to particular aspects of Jewish religious thought, but to Judaism and Jewish existence more broadly. While Christian theologians had to grapple with similar questions regarding the rationality or historicity of Scripture, Jewish thinkers were confronted, in addition, by claims that the very religious and cultural distinctiveness of Jews as a minority group was incompatible with participation in modern life and society. Consider, for instance, the *Wissenschaft des Judentums* movement, which developed in early nineteenth-century Germany, and which can be seen as an extension of the earlier Haskalah movement. Whereas the latter sought, in accord with Enlightenment ideology, to encourage the broader study of secular subjects among Jews—a trend that led to increased Jewish enrollment in universities—the former adopted the academic methodology gleaned from such university studies and sought to apply it to specifically Jewish subject matter, including religion, culture, and history.[62] The movement's scholarly participants, however, did not act merely out of dispassionate academic interests. Rather, as Christian Wiese puts it, "One of Jewish Studies' [*Wissenschaft des Judentums*] essential achievements consisted in what Shulamit Volkov has called 'inventing a tradition': a modernized ethical and philosophical interpretation of Jewish traditions that aspires to prove the legitimacy of the continued existence of Jews and Jewishness within modernity, as well as its contribution to contemporary social, intellectual, and moral problems, and thus provide a basis for the intellectual and social acceptance of Judaism among both modern Jews as well as within non-Jewish society."[63] This trend paralleled the German-Jewish Reform movement, which sought to institute practical changes to Jewish religious life that would provide Jews with a way of being simultaneously Jewish and German, such that they could participate fully in broader society without feeling forced to abandon their Jewishness.[64] By the late nineteenth and early twentieth century in Germany, having established a basic scholarly construction of a modern-liberal Judaism, Jews were directly combating and responding to the negative portrayals of Judaism in contemporary Christian theological scholarship.[65]

Cohen's own scholarly trajectory is marked by repeated engagement with many of these same issues. In his early seminary days, Cohen sided with and defended his teacher Zacharias Frankel's commitment to *Wissenschaft* methodology against the criticisms of Samson Raphael Hirsch.[66] In 1880, Cohen gained notoriety for "Ein Bekenntnis in der Judenfrage," his response to Heinrich von Treitschke's antisemitic writings against the Jewish presence in Germany.[67] Later, he would publicly defend the ethics of the Talmud and assert Judaism's continuing contribution to religious progress.[68] In these writings, he displays his engagement with Protestant biblical studies, and his own emphasis on the prophets as the focal point of Judaism mirrors the portrayal by his Protestant scholarly contemporaries of the Old Testament prophets as the height of religious genius.[69] Though Cohen also has other motivations for his method of "idealizing" Jewish textual sources,[70] it cannot be denied that this method also furthered Cohen's dual goal of raising the ethical level of his fellow Jews and of defending the ethical legitimacy of Judaism to his non-Jewish contemporaries in Germany. Accordingly, in addition to *Religion of Reason*'s attention to philosophical questions, we can also note its status as a continuation of the political-apologetic side of the *Wissenschaft des Judentums* tradition: if a religion of reason can be drawn from these Jewish sources, then these sources and the religious community centered around them must likewise be worthy of preservation and ethico-cultural approbation.

In this regard, we can also take note of criticisms that have been leveled against both Cohen and the *Wissenschaft des Judentums* movement. Gershom Scholem observed that the culturally-politically situated desire to present Judaism as a rational and ethical tradition led many Jewish scholars to downplay and ignore those elements in the Jewish past that were deemed to be insufficiently rational or ethical. Consequently, the resulting portrayal of Judaism and Jewish history was distortingly one-sided; it failed to provide "a reasonably complete picture of how the Jewish organism functioned in relation to its actual environment."[71] Such a critique can be applied to *Religion of Reason*: Cohen emphasizes the rational-ethical elements of Jewish sources and, in so doing, diverges in notable ways from the results of a strictly historical-critical approach. However, as we shall see, Cohen diverges from other representatives of *Wissenschaft des Judentums* in *consciously* proclaiming the insufficiency of the historical method for his intended purposes in *Religion of Reason*.[72] Whereas Scholem criticizes the failure to provide an account of how Judaism functioned in its relation to its "actual" historical context, Cohen neither attempts nor purports to make claims about the actual or empirical status of the Jewish past. That is to say, Cohen has philosophic, and not merely apologetic, reasons for 'failing' to highlight irrational or unethical elements in the Jewish sources.

However, others have pointed out that Cohen's commitment to "idealization" may have affected his judgment in other, more negative ways. Steven Schwarzschild argues that, on one hand, Cohen was fully conscious of the irrationalities and immoralities in Jewish history, but that the point of his philosophizing was not merely to describe the past but, echoing Marx, "to change the world and, therefore, also to moralize, to 'idealize' historical Judaism."[73] On the other hand, he criticizes Cohen for failing to emphasize sufficiently that his idealized portrayal is *not* equivalent to 'the actual,' thereby leaving his readers in danger of confusing the two themselves or, conversely, of viewing Cohen's account as 'naïve.'[74] Leo Strauss, in a similar fashion, argues that Cohen's idealizing methodology led him to accuse Spinoza unjustly of malice toward the Jewish community. Cohen criticizes Spinoza for attributing to Maimonides a non-universalistic position with regard to 'salvation.' However, as Strauss points out, a closer look at actual Jewish history indicates that Spinoza's description of Maimonides did *not* contradict the Jewish consensus of Maimonides' or of Spinoza's period. As such, Cohen may be projecting his 'idealized' account of Maimonides and of Judaism back onto their actual historical counterparts; his criticism of Spinoza would then amount to the fact that Spinoza failed to perform a similar idealization![75]

Strauss then asks: "Is the right interpretation 'idealizing' interpretation, i.e., the interpretation of a teaching in light of its highest possibility regardless of whether or not that highest possibility was known to its originator, or is it historical interpretation proper, which understands a teaching as meant by its originator?"[76] This is an important question, and it is directly relevant to my central thesis in this study. Rather than answering it directly, one must first specify: the question of which method of interpretation is the 'right' one depends on the purpose and goals of the interpreter's project. It may be true, as Strauss argues, that Cohen's method, perhaps influenced by apologetic concerns, led him to an historically unjustified accusation of Spinoza. However, as I aim to show, this shortcoming does not at all detract from the *rational-philosophical* results that the same method produces in *Religion of Reason*. Indeed, it may be that Cohen's apologetic tendencies—manifested in his 'personal' (and not merely objective-historical) desire to draw ethico-rational concepts from out of the 'particular' sources of Judaism—in fact contributed positively to his discovery of the personal and paradoxical nature of religious concepts. That is to say, those qualities that made him a questionable historian of religion are precisely those that helped make him a good philosopher of religion.

(c) Development and change within Cohen's own thought

The main body of this book will focus on the way in which *Religion of Reason* presents religion and religion's relationship to philosophy and Ethics. However, in order to contextualize the positions presented in Cohen's posthumous work, I here provide a brief sketch of the development and changes regarding these topics within his previous thought, leading up to *Religion of Reason*.

At age fifteen, Cohen enrolled in the Jewish theological seminary in Breslau, with the intention of becoming a rabbi. After four years, however, he left the seminary to study philosophy, earning a doctoral degree from the University of Halle in 1865. Following a brief period in which he took a psychological-anthropological

approach to topics of religion, he soon turned to the study of Kantian philosophy, from which he appropriated the transcendental methodology that would
characterize his later systematic work during his long tenure at the University of
Marburg.[77]

Throughout this period, he sees religion in the context of a primitive and
mythical precursor to systematic philosophical Ethics. This is by no means a dero-
gation of religion; indeed, he emphasizes that many important ethical ideas have
their first historical appearances within religion. The method of Ethics is then
able to take this moral raw material and purify it through a process of idealization, transforming mythical formulations into critical philosophical accounts of
human ethical principles. Importantly, however, after the raw materials of religion's insights have been translated into the philosophically refined categories of
Ethics, the original 'mythological' forms of the ideas no longer serve any independent rational purpose. That is to say, the methodological transfer is complete
and exhaustive, so that nothing of reason has been 'left behind.' Cohen describes
this project as a "dissolving of religion into Ethics" (*Auflösung der Religion in
Ethik*).[78] While Ethics must draw upon religion for its original source-material,
religion, in turn, is dependent on Ethics for its rationalization and idealization.
Importantly, however, once Ethics has completed its transformation of religio-
mythical concepts, it no longer stands in need of its original sources. Thus, Ethics
has a rational autonomy that religion lacks.

Cohen's reluctance to assign any unique value to religion was connected, as
Helmut Holzhey has pointed out, to his fight against antisemitism.[79] If religion is
given its own independent status 'outside the bounds of Ethics,' it is likely to fos-
ter ideas that are unethical and anti-ethical, giving rise, if not to individual egoism, then to the expression of group egoism. In arguing that the particularity of
religion should be absorbed into the universality of Ethics, Cohen sought to
eliminate the self-aggrandizing of one religious group at the expense of another.[80]
As such, we ought not view Cohen's approach to 'religion' as stemming from a
negative attitude toward Judaism—indeed, he viewed his Jewish upbringing positively and nostalgically—but from his sense, based on his experience with anti-
Jewish prejudice, that the dissolution of religion's mythological particularity is
the only way to guarantee ethical and humane relations between different
groups.[81] Accordingly, if he could have discovered a way, during his earlier period,
to assign a unique value to religion without compromising the anti-egoistic firmness of Ethics, it is likely that he would have jumped at the chance.

Notably, Cohen wrote numerous essays on Judaism and Jewish topics during
this same period. Despite its focus on a particular tradition, such attention to
Judaism was not incompatible with his goal of dissolving religion into Ethics. His
point in writing about Judaism was to show that certain elements of the Jewish
tradition have important impulses in the direction of Ethics, even though they

still require methodological idealization. In accord with this project, Cohen accords rational status only to those ideas that can pass the test of the critical philosophical method. Those concepts of religion that fail to meet such criteria are consequently assigned to the category of myth. Thus, with regard to some of the traditional religious descriptions of God, Cohen writes, "[In Ethics,] God is not characterized [*bezeichnet*] as a person. God becomes a person in myth. And religion remains under the spell of myth, insofar as it applies the concept of person to the essence [*Wesen*] of God. . . . God is spirit can only mean: God is idea. Person, life, spirit are attributes that have their roots in myth."[82] While important moral insights can be gained from such concepts, their mythical attributes must be discarded as they are translated into the critical categories of Ethics.

An important intermediate point in Cohen's development prior to *Religion of Reason* can be found in *Ästhetik des reinen Gefühls*, the third and final volume of his *System*. In this work, he highlights the importance of feeling and individual subjectivity and emphasizes that these serve as an important source for religion. Many of the specific themes that will later emerge as crucial factors in *Religion of Reason*—including love, lyrical confession, longing, and compassion—already receive treatment in the *Ästhetik*.[83] One can also note that these themes did *not* play a prominent role in his *Ethik*, with its emphasis on the objectivity of duty and the moral law. As such, the fact that they required a separate volume, 'beyond' the *Ethik*, could be seen as a prefiguration of his later insistence on the shortcomings of the objectifying philosophical method itself.[84] In the *Ästhetik*, however, the insight that these aesthetic categories may be key sources of religion does not diminish the ultimate normative authority of Ethics. While 'feeling' may play an important role in 'religious experience,' it cannot serve as an autonomous ground or justification for religion.[85] Likewise, though feeling may have contributed in important ways to the historical development of religion, it cannot eliminate the mythical aspects of the latter, a task which can devolve only upon Ethics. Thus, even though religion has itself absorbed elements of art, it must, in turn, still be dissolved into Ethics.

However, as we shall see in the chapters that follow, by the time he writes *Religion of Reason*, Cohen no longer subscribes to this latter project of dissolution. He comes to see that Ethics' methodological systematization *does* leave behind an important element of reason, namely, the particularity of the individual self as an 'I' that can relate to a 'You.'[86] Religion, conversely, *is* capable of addressing this key rational category. As such, religion has an important and continuing role to play in correcting Ethics, just as Ethics must also correct religion.

At the same time, Cohen maintains his previous stance that religion has nothing objective to add to Ethics. That is to say, religion is not an autonomous sphere of knowledge alongside Ethics; instead, it is characterized only by an *Eigenart*, a distinct particularity, in relation to the latter. If Cohen were to make direct assertions involving extra-Ethical concepts (e.g., "God as person"), such claims *would* fall into the sphere of the mythological. Even his basic claim that 'there is something that Ethics leaves out' has no systematically grounded status and can only be put forth paradoxically. Accordingly, Cohen's account of religion in *Religion of Reason* is necessarily characterized by a type of *indirect* communication that presents religious concepts through the medium of scriptural interpretation, rather than through autonomous systematic propositions. This un-dissolvable dependence on sources distinguishes *Religion of Reason* from *Der Begriff der Religion im System der Philosophie*, the last book published by Cohen during his lifetime. Cohen's thought in *Der Begriff der Religion* already displays many of *Religion of Reason*'s insights regarding the relation between religion and the individual. However, whereas the former still presented religion *within* (*im*) the system of philosophy, with few references to scriptural texts, it is only in the latter that we find a heightened emphasis on the need to display the religion of reason from *out of* (*aus*) and alongside the sources of Judaism.

While Cohen's understanding of religion's status as non-systematic yet rational reached full development only in *Religion of Reason*, we should also note that this idea, while marking a significant departure from his earlier account of religion, did not arise spontaneously in the last few years of his life. In his 1901 essay, "The Style of The Prophets," Cohen already indicates his inchoate awareness of the paradoxical nature of religious concepts and their relation to 'contradictory' forms of communication. There, in his assertion that the prophets "create a style in [the] border-area between art and science," we can see him seeking out a third way between 'subjective' aesthetics and 'objective' philosophical Ethics. However, in presenting the details of the biblical prophets' "double-edged" style, he does not explicitly make the connection to the ways in which a contemporary rational-critical account of religion must also adopt an analogous type of theoretical inconsistency. As I argue in chapter 1, however, Cohen's description of the prophets' style strongly prefigures his own communicative style as displayed in *Religion of Reason*. Thus, even though Cohen continued to advocate the dissolution of religion into Ethics for a number of years after 1901, this essay shows that the seeds of his later approach were simultaneously germinating during this same period.

(d) The trajectory of *Religion of Reason* after Cohen's death

Having examined the relation of *Religion of Reason* to the past context out of which it came, we should also provide a general overview of its relation to the future that it in turned helped to produce. In terms of the German philosophical context in which he wrote, *Religion of Reason* seems to have been less influential. The rise of antisemitism in Germany, in conjunction with the perceived defeat of

Cohen's disciple Ernst Cassirer by Martin Heidegger in their Davos disputation of 1929, contributed to a turning away from Cohen's thought and from neo-Kantianism more broadly.[87] Furthermore, even where Cohen's work continued to receive philosophical attention, it was primarily his earlier system, rather than *Religion of Reason*, that was emphasized.

In Jewish circles, however, the situation was reversed: thanks in no small part to Franz Rosenzweig, *Religion of Reason* was hailed as a crucial text of Jewish philosophy, while Cohen's earlier system tended to be passed over in silence. *Religion of Reason* became a touchstone for Jewish thinkers in that it provided them with an intellectually rigorous example of an attempt to preserve commitments to both reason (the universal) and Judaism (the particular). At the same time, though *Religion of Reason* was accorded great respect, many Jewish thinkers came to view its approach to Judaism as ultimately insufficient for the post-Holocaust era. Whereas a common criticism in pre-WWII Germany was that Cohen's work was 'too Jewish,' many post-WWII Jewish thinkers tended to view Cohen's emphasis on the ideality of God as too abstract and 'not Jewish enough.'[88] For many years, Steven Schwarzschild was one of the few to have insisted on Cohen's continuing relevance to Jewish philosophy beyond his role as a historical precursor to thinkers like Buber and Rosenzweig. More recently, interest in Cohen has been renewed, although some of the same concerns that marked earlier reception of *Religion of Reason* still continue to affect contemporary discussion and debate.

III. *The Position and Contribution of This Study*
(a) Thesis and approach

While I will explore Cohen's indirect communication primarily through close readings of *Religion of Reason*, I will here directly communicate a framing overview of my own claims about Cohen and his text. My basic thesis is that Cohen's style in *Religion of Reason* can best be understood as an attempt to avoid two common distortions of religious concepts and religious language. On one hand, assigning ontological actuality to concepts such as God, the soul, and the Messiah and the messianic era, and speaking and writing of them as though they were determinate objects, can produce a dogmatic devotion to such objectified constructions and can undermine ethicality through a corresponding denigration of those who differ in their religious formulations. On the other hand, the recognition of the problems of dogmatic ontologizing can lead to an opposing tendency, in which religious concepts are seen as lacking any substantive significance of their own. While motivated by legitimate ethical concerns, this skeptical/intellectualized approach, which cleaves strictly and solely to the results of the systematic philosophical method, also contains dangers, in that the enervated concepts can lose their power to promote embodied ethical habits and practices. From Cohen's perspective, the one approach says too much, while the other says too little.[89] Furthermore, attempts at writing about religious ideas that aspire to a fully consistent and systematic presentation will tend to fall into one or the other of these extremes. Cohen's multi-voiced style (akin to Mikhail Bakhtin's notion of heteroglossia) avoids these distortions by dialogically juxtaposing the nonidentical voices of philosophy and of Scripture.[90]

A key element of my project concerns the *distinctiveness* of Cohen's use of these two voices. Merely to say that Cohen employs both philosophical concepts and scriptural sources would not be saying very much, since any number of religious, philosophical, and theological texts could be described in the same manner. Rather, the uniqueness of Cohen's approach lies in his acute consciousness of methodological rigor: he draws upon the 'voices' of both philosophy and Scripture—while simultaneously emphasizing the theoretical incompatibility between the two. In contrast, while other thinkers may draw upon or attempt to combine both realms, they typically lack Cohen's awareness of the impossibility of doing so in a theoretically consistent manner.[91] Precisely because the two *cannot* be combined, Cohen is able to *use* each as a tool for highlighting the shortcomings and limitations of the other. It is the *critical* (in a Kantian sense) nature of this approach that distinguishes his project in *Religion of Reason* and that poses a sharp challenge to many typical forms of 'philosophical theology.'

However, such talk of 'theoretical incompatibility,' alongside my use of such descriptive terms as 'inconsistent,' 'paradoxical,' and 'incoherent,' runs the risk of creating the impression that Cohen has departed from rationally grounded criteria for the concepts of religion. If Cohen is giving up on the possibility of a theoretically consistent account, doesn't this turn him into some kind of fideist? Furthermore, if a true and proper account of religion must be 'incoherent,' does this not open the door to the approval of ethically or intellectually undesirable forms of religious incoherency? Here, it must be emphasized that Cohen always insists that the concepts of religion remain firmly located within the sphere of *reason*. In contrast, there are many pseudo-religious concepts that would fall outside this sphere, and would therefore be rejected as part of a religion of unreason. Yet, it remains the case that the religion of reason requires a presentation that specifically lacks theoretical consistency. Although the concepts of religion do have an ultimate unity in reason, they display an irremediable non-unity in terms of sentential or propositional logic. Accordingly, a rational account of religion must be 'inconsistent'—such that full theoretical consistency necessarily indicates a distorted presentation—but not all inconsistent accounts of religion are thereby rational.[92]

28 PARADOX AND THE PROPHETS

Instead, as we shall see, a proper account must display a 'rational inconsistency': it must maintain the criteria of ethical universality and rigorous epistemological humility, on one hand, while simultaneously preserving the particularity of the unique human individual and the unique God, on the other. While systematic philosophical Ethics will meet the first set of conditions while failing to meet the second, the various religious forms of unreason will compromise the first in their desire to preserve the second, and will thus descend into *improper* varieties of conceptual incoherence. While Cohen maintains that the two sets of conditions cannot be combined into a single consistent account, his double-voiced account is deliberately and carefully constructed so as to convey a precisely delimited conception of religion. His account, therefore, cannot properly be called fideistic, since it is grounded on a specific set of rational criteria. It does, admittedly, differ from many common conceptions of 'reason' in calling for a paradoxical multiplicity in its form of conceptualization as well as communication.[93]

In this regard, it is also important to emphasize that the paradoxical nature of religious concepts does *not* mean that they are 'incommunicable.' Rather, it simply means that they require a distinct *type* of communication on the part of an author, as well as a distinct type of engagement on the part of a reader.[94] The 'indirect' nature of this communication, moreover, does not point to an esoteric or elitist conception of religion; the two 'voices' of Cohen's text are both completely public and open. What distinguishes his project from forms of 'direct' communication is the fact that the intended conception that lies 'between' those two voices must be *practically* appropriated by the reader and cannot be formulated in a single theoretically consistent account, either before or after the communicative act. Importantly, while I place strong emphasis on the 'noncompatibility' of the two voices, I simultaneously want to emphasize the rational-functional coherence of Cohen's communication. In everyday experience, there are any number of communicative acts that lack a conceptually systematic formulation and yet succeed unproblematically. Think, for instance, of the common practice of telling a joke. Here, the source of the humor is typically to be found in the fact that key aspects are *not* fully spelled out. Indeed, a joke that needs to be 'explained' has already lost much of its humorous effect. Often, the force of such forms of communication lies precisely in elements of unresolved conceptual tension, and attempts to restate the joke in a 'fully clear' form will generally 'miss the point' of the initial communicative act. In this sense, Cohen's approach, while innovative in its application to the realm of rational concepts, need not be seen as entirely unfamiliar or alien.

My focus on the stylistic elements of Cohen's work enables me to incorporate the diverse insights of previous scholarship, while simultaneously pointing to a path beyond their interpretive disputes and antinomies. Both the 'religious' and the 'philosophical' readings of *Religion of Reason*, by dint of their quest for a consistent reading of the text, are able to foreground different key elements in Cohen's thought. The 'religious' reading is right in its claim that Cohen's account in *Religion of Reason* accentuates the limitations of his earlier systematic writings. Given their commitment to the strict method of scientific philosophy, they were unable to do full justice to the crucial concepts of the fellowman, the unique God, and the messianic future. However, the 'philosophical' reading is correct in maintaining that Cohen never rejects his earlier system, and that he never directly asserts any content 'beyond' the limits of his system. Where both readings fall short, however, is in their common assumption that *Religion of Reason* must *either* break with *or* be in continuity with his previous system. I argue, conversely, that Cohen's account of religion is irreducibly paradoxical; it is neither 'consistent with' nor 'objectively separate from' his previous system. Anticipating later discussion, we can say that the gap between religion and philosophy is *infinitesimal*. This paradoxicality, in turn, demands a form of indirect communication on Cohen's part that cannot be reduced to either of the two 'consistent' readings.

This approach brings me closer, in certain ways, to the interpretation that sees *Religion of Reason*'s multiplicity as a symptom of an inner conflict that Cohen could never quite overcome. Such a reading is correct to observe that the text is 'wounded' and displays a certain lack of wholeness. However, against this reading, I maintain that this lack of wholeness has its roots not in any failing or shortcoming on Cohen's part but rather in the paradoxical nature of the sphere of religion itself. As such, Cohen's 'inconsistency' corresponds not to unclear thinking or vacillation, but rather to a *faithful portrayal* of his subject matter.

At this point, I also wish to state clearly that, in this project, I am *not* primarily concerned with making a definitive assertion about 'Cohen's conscious designs.' Rather, my principal claim concerns the best way to understand *Religion of Reason* considered *as a text*. In other words, I aim to provide readers today with a way of fruitfully engaging *Religion of Reason* as a coherent and rational presentation, rather than viewing it as a mere jumble of contradictory intellectual tendencies. Moreover, the argument for my proposed strategy for reading the text of *Religion of Reason* is not ultimately dependent on whether Cohen himself consciously intended for readers to employ this specific strategy. To be sure, I do try to show that Cohen's style displays a high degree of intentionality and that my claims can be justified in Cohen's own terms; however, I also leave open the possibility that Cohen had not achieved full consciousness on the matter, but was 'intuitively' led to this style by his dual commitment to philosophical rigor and to personal engagement in Judaism. Though my reading attempts to incorporate the available historical evidence regarding Cohen's understanding of his final work, the absence of a clear methodological statement on Cohen's part means that my account of *Religion of Reason* will necessarily go beyond—but should not stand in conflict with—what Cohen himself explicitly says about his aims and intentions.

That is to say, rather than create a strict dichotomy between 'Cohen' and 'the text,' my aim in this book is to give an account of 'Cohen's text,' though with the emphasis placed on the second half of this phrase.

This point is especially important with regard to my use of Kierkegaard. I draw upon Kierkegaard because his account of indirect communication can fruitfully illuminate what appears to be going on in the text of *Religion of Reason*; however, I do not intend to claim that Cohen himself had Kierkegaard in mind when he conceived his project. Thus, when I employ personalized phrases such as "Cohen's style" (which might seem to imply a primary focus on the authorial intent preceding the text), these formulations should be understood most fundamentally as claims about how one *ought to read Religion of Reason*, about the way in which patterns of reasoning are manifested on the level of the text itself. That is to say, in placing my emphasis on the *text* of *Religion of Reason*, I am primarily concerned with the *rational-philosophical* question of religious concepts and their proper communication, and only secondarily concerned with the *historical* question of Cohen's individual consciousness.

Moreover, my decision to emphasize questions of textual style over and above any attempt to provide a concise description of 'what Cohen himself thinks' is not simply a matter of scholarly selectivity. Rather, I maintain that any such attempt at reducing Cohen's account to a paraphrased description will necessarily be a distortion of his intended conceptual communication. If a straightforward account of the 'what' of religion were possible, Cohen would have provided it himself. Instead, my primary intent is to give a clear and straightforward description of Cohen's textual style, of his 'how,' which I apply to an extended close reading of his double-voiced presentation. In this manner, I aim to show *why*, according to Cohen, a single-voiced account of religion is impossible (his negative message) and also to show how Cohen overcomes this restriction by developing his source-dependent mode of reasoning and communication (his positive message). Far from abandoning the 'real content' of *Religion of Reason*, it is precisely by avoiding the impulse to formulate Cohen's single 'position' or 'opinion' that we can attain a clearer view of the rational constructions that he presents.

In this sense, my project of rereading *Religion of Reason* aims not only to demonstrate the inadequacies of previous readings of Cohen, but also to raise the possibility that such misreadings may have contributed to deficiencies in subsequent Jewish philosophy. The failure to recognize the significance of Cohen's multiform style in *Religion of Reason* has corresponded to a failure to appropriate Cohen's insight that any act of communication (including philosophizing) of such 'religious' concepts as the unique God, the You, and so on must avoid single-voicedness. While the 'what' of Cohen's dialogical thinking has ostensibly been more widely disseminated via followers of Buber, Rosenzweig, and Levinas, the 'how' of Cohen's writing has been largely neglected. Yet, since Cohen himself indicates that the two are not separable,[95] neglect of the 'how' will result in distortion of the 'what.'[96] Accordingly, attempts to write about dialogical ideas in the single-voiced style that is typical of much contemporary philosophy will likely result in misrepresentation and misinterpretation of those ideas. For this reason, in addition to its relevance for intellectual history, a study of Cohen's style can have broader methodological implications for the practice of contemporary Jewish philosophy, as well as philosophy of religion more broadly.

Taken as a whole, this study integrates three basic methodological approaches. First, I employ the method of *intellectual history*, whereby I attempt to explicate the intellectual background to Cohen's multivoiced style in *Religion of Reason*, and to construct an account of the relation between this work and his earlier essays and system of philosophy. Second, I engage in *textual analysis*, analyzing the original literary contexts of the biblical and rabbinic texts cited by Cohen, so as to more clearly understand the way that he interprets and uses them. Additionally, I analyze the textual details of the main body of Cohen's work, so as to get a clear sense of the arguments he is putting forth, while attempting to distinguish his more straightforwardly philosophical passages from those more influenced by the language of Scripture. Thirdly, I perform *philosophical analysis*: By employing the tools of rhetorical criticism and philosophy of language, I assess the links between idea-content and style and the ways in which certain concepts require a certain form of expression for successful communication. I make use of philosophy of religion and analysis of religious concepts in order to assess Cohen's account of certain key religious concepts (e.g., the relation between God and the individual, the individual's ethical task, and the ideality/actuality of religious ideas). I also apply pragmatic and performative analyses, examining the philosophical implications of Cohen's acts of text-interpretation and the ways in which Cohen's understanding of religious and philosophical ideas is displayed and performed through his juxtapositions of different genres of texts.

(b) Chapter organization

The narrative of my argument runs as follows. Chapter 1 consists of an analysis of Cohen's 1901 essay, "Der Stil der Propheten," "The Style of the Prophets."[97] In this essay, he argues for a three-way connection among method (means of discovery of ideas), idea-content, and style (means of communicating ideas). Certain ideas require a certain type of method for their discovery, and cannot be discovered through other types of method. Likewise, certain ideas require a certain type of style for their communication, and cannot be effectively conveyed by other styles. Cohen describes and distinguishes the prophets' method and style by contrasting them to those of art and of systematic philosophy. He argues that the prophetic style is characterized by a double-sidedness (or, more to the point,

an avoidance of one-sidedness), which, he implies, is necessary for the communication of their ideas. In analyzing this essay, I examine the various ways in which
this two-sidedness manifests itself in prophetic texts, as interpreted by Cohen.
Some examples include: the co-presence of tragedy and satire; the presence and
distance of the messianic future; and the sudden shifts between retribution and
consolation. In addition to identifying the presence of these stylistic heteroge-
neities, I also look at Cohen's sense of *why* such a style was necessary for the
prophetic task and message. The primary purpose of this chapter will be, by clarifying Cohen's understanding of the prophets' style, to provide a framework for
an assessment of Cohen's own style in *Religion of Reason*.

Chapters 2 and 3 center around a close reading of *Religion of Reason*'s introduction, which Cohen subtitled "Elucidation of the Title and Articulation of the
Task." By looking at Cohen's own account of his project, we can gain insight into
the proper way to read the main body of his text. In his earlier 1901 essay, Cohen
focused on the two-sidedness of the prophets' style; he did not state whether his
own ideas concerning religion demanded an analogous style. Here, he indicates
that the many of the same challenges that applied to the prophets' attempt at communication do apply to his own attempts at writing about religious ideas. It was
not simply the prophets' lack of philosophical sophistication that led to their two-
sided style; rather, the prophetic *ideas themselves*, about which Cohen also seeks to
write, demand a unique style from any conscientious expositor. In chapter 2, I
examine Cohen's account of the basic structure relating reason, philosophy, and
religion. Though his attempt to uphold both philosophy and religion as distinct
sub-realms within reason seems to lead to an irremediable contradiction, he does
not reject or deprioritize either of the two. Without resolving this contradiction,
he turns to the classical Jewish literary sources in order to highlight a mode of reasoning that encompasses theoretical multiplicity while maintaining practical unity,
thus anticipating his own methodological approach. In chapter 3, after situating
Cohen's project in relation to his earlier philosophical system, I examine his introductory, single-voiced attempt to address the conceptual content of the sphere of
religion. He emphasizes the ways in which the method of philosophical Ethics, if
systematically and thoroughly applied, will distort key ethico-religious ideas such
as the You, the unique God, and the individual self as an I. However, he does not
reject the method of Ethics, nor does he compromise its primacy. Because his twin
commitments to both religion and Ethics remain theoretically incompatible with
one another, his attempt at directly explicating the sphere of religion tends to break
down into irony and apophatic negation. Such a result, I argue, is the necessary
consequence of trying to convey religious ideas in a single consistent voice. The
communicative challenges that Cohen faces in his introduction therefore serve to
underscore the necessity of the 'inconsistent,' multivoiced style that he will subsequently adopt in the main body of his text.

Prior to examining that main body, however, chapter 4 makes use of Kierkegaardian insights in order to compensate for a deficiency on Cohen's part. While Cohen highlights the shortcomings of the method of Ethics and then performs his double-edged style, he does not provide a full self-conscious account of precisely what that style consists of and why he employs it. That is to say, while the insufficiency of Ethics and the duality of key concepts demonstrate the need for a nonconventional approach, the specific details and desired features of that approach remain unaccounted for. In contrast, Kierkegaard provides a more explicit and carefully formulated account of the problems of ethico-religious communication, especially in his *Concluding Unscientific Postscript* under the pseudonym of Johannes Climacus. Kierkegaard/Climacus emphasizes that ethico-religious concepts cannot be directly communicated and indicates practical strategies and pitfalls of which a subjective thinker must be aware in his or her attempts at indirect communication. Since Cohen's multiform style can be understood as a form of indirect communication, the application of Kierkegaard to Cohen's text can help bring Cohen's style to greater self-consciousness, enabling the reader better to see how and why his approach allows him to avoid a content-distorting one-sidedness. Although this chapter is the only one with an explicit focus on Kierkegaard, he appears repeatedly in the footnotes throughout the rest of the book, and his account of communication exerts a significant influence on my overall reading of Cohen.

Chapter 5 examines Cohen's performative presentation of three key concepts of religion: the love of God, commandedness, and repentance. For each of these, Cohen seems to display two contradictory modes of thought: At times, he speaks as though guided by the strict method of philosophy, thereby arriving at a human-centered perspective. At other times, he draws upon scriptural citations in order to describe a personal correlative engagement between the human being and God. I argue that the proper response to such inconsistencies is not to seek a theoretical mediation between them, but rather to view each of the religious concepts in question as corresponding to a practice. The multiplicity that Cohen displays can thus be viewed as the natural result of theoretical reflection on the practices that can be described as 'loving God,' 'being commanded,' and 'turning in repentance.' For all of these, an attempt to force one's thought into a fully consistent description will necessarily distort and flatten the subject matter under consideration. As such, Cohen's use of multiple perspectives and voices serves to protect the reader from the temptation to theoretize that which is ultimately paradoxical and requires a personal-practical form of appropriation.

Chapter 6 focuses on Cohen's designation of religious ideas as "infinite tasks." This notion, which involves a certain type of non-completability, is intimately connected with the notion of non-comprehensibility. While the element of infinity could make it appear as though the task can only be approached asymptotically, it turns out that Cohen's thought *does* allow for the fulfillment of the task in the infinitesimal moment of turning. However, because it has no finite duration and is both 'something' and 'nothing,' this infinitesimal moment is itself irreducibly paradoxical. Accordingly, the question of fulfillment and non-fulfillment can be given no theoretical answer and again requires a form of indirect communication. Furthermore, through Cohen's identification of the infinitesimal moment with the messianic future, the notion of the coming of the Messiah attains a paradoxical status as well. Cohen then proceeds to link his own conception of the messianic future to the messianic writings of the biblical prophets, thus pointing toward the possibility that his own philosophical conception of the infinitesimal moment may be in part drawn from his reading of those same scriptural texts. Thus, we will have come full circle: having begun with Cohen's account of the style of the prophets, we come to see that *Religion of Reason* can itself be described as the employment of a scripturally derived style for the purpose of communicating scripturally derived ideas.

(c) Avenues of further exploration

I close this introduction by indicating some of the broader questions and possibilities that this project opens up, beyond the particular focus on Cohen and *Religion of Reason*:

Can the notion of 'communicative inconsistency' be applied to the interpretation of other texts as well? Perhaps apparent contradictions in other philosophical writings may also be a reflection of the rational subject matter they address, rather than a sign of faulty reasoning. While this would not mean that *all* contradictions are 'rational' contradictions, it would demand a more subtle form of analysis beyond a mechanical 'non-consistent = non-rational.'

If certain ideas or practices resist theoretically consistent descriptions, how does this change our criteria for a 'rational account' of a given subject? It may be that a text's rationality is better measured by its ability to *avoid* one-sidedness than by its 'autonomous' theoretical coherence. As such, its rational success would derive from its practical effect on a reader, rather than from strictly internal characteristics of 'the ideas themselves.'

Might many contemporary disputes about religious topics be the result of one-sided flattening of inherently paradoxical ideas? Does Cohen's refusal to grant ultimate priory either to the 'human-centered' or to the 'divine-centered' perspective compel us to reconceive our understanding of 'secular' vis-à-vis 'religious'? While certain types of arguments and disagreements may be based on substantive differences, others may stem from a false reduction of the subject matter on the part of *both* parties. Cohen's example raises the possibility that many disputes could be ameliorated through the introduction of the notion that certain ideas are *supposed* to be 'contradictory,' and that to confine the ideas to a determinate 'position' is to categorically misrepresent them.

Do certain modes of analysis naturally give rise to bifurcated antinomies? Can Cohen's use of Scripture serve as a model for contemporary attempts at religious communication and dialogue? If 'direct' and 'autonomous' modes of writing and speaking tend to distort their subject matter, reasoning from and through textual sources—and perhaps 'non-philosophical' sources in particular—could help preserve the practical and ethical content of religious concepts, viewed specifically as concepts of reason. This corrective could apply, in different ways, to both everyday conversation and to more specialized philosophical investigations.

It is my hope that the reader will find that this book provides a good jumping-off point for engaging these various issues and, in turn, for raising new questions in the process.

A Note on Terminology

WARDING OFF SOME COMMON CONNOTATIONS

BECAUSE THIS STUDY focuses on questions of communication and miscommunication, some brief remarks on potentially misleading aspects of Cohen's terminology are in order. Cohen uses certain key words in very specific ways; in many cases, his use differs significantly from typical associations with and understandings of those same words. While Cohen's employment of these terms will be explicated in further detail in the main body of the book, I here want to provide an initial sketch, especially in order to make clear what Cohen does *not* mean. In addition, because I attempt, in my own commentary and assessment, to follow Cohen's usage, the following will also help prevent misconstruals of my own claims.

Philosophy: While this term is often used to describe 'reasoned thought' in a general sense, Cohen employs the term more narrowly. Specifically, philosophy is "the science of reason,"[1] which employs a specific critical method in order to arrive at an impersonal, clear, and distinct theoretical account of the concepts that it analyzes. For Cohen, notably, philosophy is only one mode of reasoning (alongside religion) under the broader domain of reason. I largely follow Cohen's stricter sense of the term; in instances where I want to refer to the broader sense of the concept, I use terms such as 'thought' or 'reasoning.'

Reason: Often, many would equate the terms 'reason' and 'rational' with the impersonal-objective mode of that corresponds to Cohen's sense of the term 'philosophy.' However, as noted above, the domain of reason for Cohen is broader than its sub-domain of philosophy. Thus, for Cohen, there may be concepts that are part of reason, yet cannot be grasped by impersonal thought or propositional logic. That is to say, Cohen uses the terms 'reason' and 'rational' to describe some things which others might call 'non-rational' or even 'irrational.'

Objective: This term characterizes the goal of the method of philosophy, as described above: philosophy attempts to arrive at an "objectification" (*Objektivierung*) of its concepts in order to render them clear, distinct, and theoretically consistent.[2] For the purposes of this study, the important point to keep in mind is that *'objective' is not the same as 'rational.'* For Cohen, a concept can be non-objective (or non-objectifiable) while still retaining the designation 'rational.'

Ethics, ethicality, and the ethical: Cohen's use of these terms, in particular, has given rise to much misunderstanding. For Cohen, 'Ethics' (*Ethik*) refers specifically to a sub-branch of philosophy, alongside logic and aesthetics. Ethics thus designates the results of a method that seeks an objective theoretical account of human beings and their normative duties. While its *subject matter* may involve practical action, Ethics itself is the *theoretical* science *of* that practical action. Thus, we would not speak of the 'Ethics' by which an everyday person lives; the term refers specifically to that which is constructed by the scientific philosopher. For this reason, I capitalize the term in order to distinguish it from the broader connotation that it typically enjoys.

In contrast, Cohen uses the term *Sittlichkeit* to refer to that practical, embodied pattern of action and habit that Ethics attempts to theorize. Gillian Rose argues, helpfully, that because of this connection to Ethics, Cohen's use of *Sittlichkeit* is best understood in the sense of "ethical life"; in contrast, translating it as "morality" would obscure this connection.[3] Thus, non-philosophers (including, notably, the biblical prophets) can be fully concerned with *Sittlichkeit*, even when they are not at all concerned with the theoretical-systematic discipline of *Ethik*. As we shall see, it is even possible for a one-sided philosophical concern with *Ethik* to distract one from attention to *Sittlichkeit* and to distort one's understanding of the latter. Indeed, it may be that the very method of *Ethik* itself is incapable of grasping or accounting for key elements of *Sittlichkeit*.

In addition, *Sittlichkeit* is fully rational, in accord with Cohen's expansive use of 'reason.' It is not the case that different individuals and cultures each have their own version of *Sittlichkeit*. Rather, in Cohen's use of the term, "There is only one *Sittlichkeit*."[4] As such, Cohen's use differs from the Hegelian understanding, wherein *Sittlichkeit* refers to the embodied, albeit unquestioned, customs and mores of a given culture. As unquestioned and unreflective, *Sittlichkeit* in this Hegelian sense cannot be said to be rational. While Cohen retains the embodied sense of the Hegelian usage, he also adds the elements of reflection and reasoning (though not necessarily of a philosophical variety), so that *Sittlichkeit* becomes a rationally normative term. That is, while *Sittlichkeit* can manifest itself in a variety of forms in different cultures, not every actual cultural practice—even if 'culturally approved'—qualifies as rational *Sittlichkeit*. Thus, the practical normativity of *Sittlichkeit* corresponds to the theoretical normativity of *Ethik*. I choose to render *Sittlichkeit* as 'ethicality,' in order to highlight the ideal rationality that it shares with 'Ethics.'

A related consideration involves the adjectival forms *ethisch* and *sittlich*. Cohen does not restrict *ethisch* to the strict philosophical-theoretical sense that he applies to *Ethik*. That is to say, *ethisch* is typically more or less synonymous with *sittlich*, and for this reason I translate them both as 'ethical' (in lowercase).

Finally, a crucial distinction involves the difference between the term 'Ethics' (*Ethik*), on the one hand, and the title of Cohen's book *Ethik des reinen Willens*, on the other. As stated above, I use the term 'Ethics' to refer specifically to that which results from applying the method of systematic philosophy to the realm of human duties, particularly as this method is portrayed by Cohen in *Religion of Reason*. However, this functional-methodological use of the term may not always correspond precisely to the actual content that one finds in Cohen's own earlier *Ethik*. To take one example, *Religion of Reason* indicates that the totalizing method of Ethics must eliminate all particularity and therefore cannot grasp the 'You'—yet in the *Ethik*, which ostensibly employs that method, the You is discussed prominently. While this tension will be explored in a later chapter, the main terminological point is that, in the case of any divergences between the two, my general use of the term 'Ethics' should be identified with the normative methodological concept rather than with the empirical contents of the *Ethik*.[5]

Religion: In the context of Cohen's book, 'religion' is a normative and ideal-rational concept that should not be directly equated with 'Scripture' or with 'the sources of Judaism.' Rather, religion represents that which is to be constructed *from out of* source-texts such as the Bible or rabbinic literature (see the discussion of 'Judaism' below). Likewise, in relation to my portrayal of *Religion of Reason*'s double-voiced style, the two voices in question are *not* those of religion and philosophy; rather, the two voices are those of Scripture and philosophy, and religion is that which is indirectly communicated via the juxtaposition of those two.

Judaism: The term 'Judaism' in Cohen's usage refers to an ideal concept that is rationally and ethically constructed from out of Jewish source materials.[6] However, for Cohen, it is not the case that the source materials themselves are inherently rational or ethical, although they may contain certain rational or ethical elements. Likewise, as was the case with *Sittlichkeit*, not all of the actual contemporary practices or attitudes that are commonly associated with the name 'Judaism' would be compatible with Cohen's normative ethical construction. As Andrea Poma puts it, "Judaism for Cohen is always the 'conceptual idealization' of Judaism."[7] While the precise relation between the two instances of 'Judaism' in this somewhat circular description may be complex, the main point is that the two are *not* equivalent. Martin Kavka points out that subsequent thinkers have sometimes deceived themselves by treating 'Judaism' and 'mono-theism' as naturally or inherently ethical terms, forgetting that their association with ethicality is, to a large extent, the result of Cohen's constructive labor and does not necessarily extend to other instantiations of the same terms.[8]

I

Hermann Cohen's "The Style of the Prophets"

MY GOAL IN this chapter is to provide a framework and background for my analysis of Cohen's style in *Religion of Reason*. I do so by examining what Cohen himself has to say about style—specifically, his understanding of the communicative style displayed in biblical prophetic texts—in his 1901 essay, "Der Stil der Propheten," "The Style of the Prophets." This essay's more manageable size enables me to analyze it in its entirety and to present a broader overview of Cohen's fundamental ideas, before delving into the complexities of *Religion of Reason* in subsequent chapters. I argue for a connection between this earlier essay and Cohen's later book, according to the hypothesis that when Cohen seeks to write about religious ideas (which he identifies with the ideas of the prophets), he adopts a style analogous to his earlier portrayal of the prophetic style.

Many of the religious and philosophical motifs that will appear in *Religion of Reason* as normative assertions can also be found in "The Style of the Prophets" as descriptive accounts of the biblical texts. For instance, in this essay, Cohen emphasizes the threefold connection among particular ideas, the methods required to arrive at them, and the style required to communicate them. He contrasts the style of the prophets with the styles of philosophy and of art, anticipating his later account of the methodological and stylistic differences between 'religion' and 'philosophy.' Cohen claims that the ideas that the prophets seek to communicate demand a multiform style, one that prevents any single theoretical conceptualization of their message. He thus explains apparent contradictions in the biblical text as deliberate communicative methods, designed to underscore the practical, as opposed to theoretical, nature of the prophets' ideas. As we shall see, the apparent inconsistencies of Cohen's *Religion of Reason* may turn out to have a similar rational motivation.

I. The Historicity of Prophetic Authorship: An Initial Methodological Consideration

Prior to this examination, however, I should first address a methodological point that will apply both to Cohen's reading of the prophetic sources in this 1901 essay as well as to his later approach in *Religion of Reason*. As we are about to observe, Cohen draws a link between 'style' and 'genius.' While the focus of this chapter will be on style, which relates primarily to analysis of the prophetic sources considered as texts, as literary objects, Cohen's reference to 'genius' seems also to point to the individual whose creativity initially gave rise to the artistic, scientific, or textual object in question.[1] Later in his essay, Cohen explicitly uses the term 'genius' with regard to the biblical prophets.[2] This phrasing raises a problematic concern: Does Cohen think or assume that each of the prophetic sources was produced by the 'genius' of a single individual? If so, is his analysis of the style of the sources dependent on such a presupposition? In Cohen's own day, the notion of the prophetic texts as the product of individual religious creativity was widespread among both Christian and Jewish thinkers.[3] Subsequent biblical scholarship, however, has tended to question the idea that the prophetic books in their current form are the products of single individuals. Rather, much historical evidence seems instead to indicate that each prophetic book represents a concatenation and interweaving of speeches that may have originated with multiple different individuals.[4] If such is the case, and one can no longer speak of a single individual genius lying behind the text, does this then undermine Cohen's attempt to discern a distinctive 'style' within the prophetic sources?

I maintain that Cohen's methodology is such that his stylistic analyses would *not* be undermined by a discovery of multiplicity in the historical coming-to-be of the biblical prophetic texts. That is to say, while some of his statements may indicate an assumption of a certain historical individuality, his readings of the sources are not ultimately *dependent* on that assumption: the readings themselves can still be fully maintained even if the contingent historical assumption that accompanied them later proves untenable. This methodological point is of utmost importance for Cohen's project as a whole, beyond the specific question of prophetic genius. In general, Cohen does not intend to claim that his textual readings always correspond to the 'original' conscious intentions of empirical-historical figures. That is to say, he approaches the text in his role as a *philosopher of religion*, rather than as a *historian of religion* in the strict sense.[5] To be sure, he does not reject the attempt to shed light on the historical development of the biblical sources, and, unlike some of his Jewish contemporaries, he affirmed the critical methods of modern biblical scholarship.[6] However, apparent historical multiplicity does not prevent the philosopher of religion from reading *the text as we have it* in terms of a greater degree of normative or rational unity.[7] Indeed, as we shall see in our next chapter, rather than attempting to avoid or downplay the historical multiplicity contained within the biblical sources, Cohen will explicitly highlight it and employ it as a positive feature of his non-historicist account of religion.[8]

Thus, in "The Style of the Prophets," as in *Religion of Reason*, Cohen will interpret the biblical texts in terms of a functional unity, and will frequently speak in terms of the individual prophet's intention or self-consciousness. While I sometimes follow Cohen's forms of expression in my own analysis of his interpretations, the unity in question should always be taken as a reading of the biblical *text*, and not as any sort of claim about conscious intentions of any empirical individuals who may lie in the history 'behind' the text.[9] In keeping the possibility of textual-interpretive unity independent from questions of empirical-historical unity, Cohen's approach can be seen as prefiguring, and perhaps as generating Rosenzweig's later approach to the biblical text, in which the posited sources of J, P, D, and E—hypothesized by historical-critical scholars as *ur*-texts that gave rise to the Bible as we have it today—should not prevent one from reading the present text as the unified product of 'R', signifying the text's Redactor—or more appropriately, *Rabbenu*, our teacher.[10]

II. Style, Method, and Idea-Content

Having addressed this point of methodology, let us turn back to see how, in fact, Cohen intends to read the prophetic sources. Before looking at Cohen's account of the relevance of style to the prophetic writings in particular, we can gain insight from some of his pronouncements on the significance of style more generally. Cohen's essay begins by noting the commonly-agreed-upon importance of style for aesthetic forms: "Style is the law of genius; hence the fundamental concept of Art in Aesthetics."[11] While one can easily imagine how a difference in style could significantly alter an objet d'art's effect on its observer, style is typically seen as less crucial for scientific or philosophical projects. As I indicated in my introduction, readers often think of philosophic texts in terms of the 'what' of their claims and their content, while relegating the 'how' of their form of expression to the status of an incidental vessel. In contrast to this tendency of thought, Cohen emphasizes the importance of style for *all* endeavors of the mind and spirit. Style is the law of genius "not only for the individuality of artistic genius, but also for the character in the presentation of scientific/scholarly [*wissenschaftlicher*] thought. This ought to apply generally to all scientific/scholarly disciplines [*Wissenschaften*]."[12] Thus, Cohen posits the inseparability of the 'what' and the 'how' in the communication of scientific and philosophic thought. To be sure, this significance of style may not apply in the same degree to all thought-projects; certain ideas may have greater independence from their forms of expression. In principle, though, Cohen's position demands that one give attention to style in all types of texts; a text's claim to being 'scientific' in no way exempts it in this regard.[13] By insisting that style is relevant to all scientific disciplines, Cohen thereby provides us with a theoretical warrant for examining the style of his own texts and of *Religion of Reason* in particular.

Later in his essay, Cohen links style to method (*Technik*), which he describes as the "engendering condition for theoretical content: the method of forms of thought [*Gedankenformen*], not that of poetic-musical construct-forms."[14] Here, in good Kantian fashion, Cohen draws a link between the method of investigation and the results of investigation. In terms of empirical science, the questions that researchers pose to nature, in the form of the types of experiments that they construct, will shape the conclusions at which they arrive.[15] With regard to 'philosophical' investigations, broadly construed, Cohen indicates that the methodological assumptions that are applied will affect the ideas and concepts that result. Suppose that one were to assume, for instance, that all rational judgments must be capable of expression in propositional form; or that the law of the excluded middle always applies; or that systematization is the proper goal of thought. Each of these assumptions would direct an investigator along certain paths of thought, and would correspondingly block said investigator from exploring certain other paths. When combined with his approach to style, Cohen's position here affirms the importance of the 'how' for both the 'before' and the 'after' of an idea: ideas demand certain forms of investigation for their discovery as well as certain forms of expression for their communication.

In seeking to explicate the style of the prophets, Cohen emphasizes that his task is made more difficult by the fact that the prophets do not fall into either of the two major categories of *Geist*-products. Cohen writes that the prophets "create a style in [the] border-area between art and science."[16] What precisely is the meaning of this posited border-area? Its characteristics are not immediately apparent; many readers would not even recognize the existence of such a zone. In a more dualistic mindset, 'science' is taken to be the realm of objectivity, while 'art' is the locus for subjective expression. If something is not 'science,' is not objective, then it must be subjective 'art,' and vice-versa. By proposing this border-area, Cohen aims to overcome this dichotomy. He writes, "The style of the prophets signifies, in distinction from mythology, from art, from science, the character of religion."[17] However, rather than giving a direct discursive account of this category, Cohen engages in several indirect methods. One of these is the method of contrast, which he uses to show what this border-area is *not*: the ways in which it is *not* like science, as well as the ways in which it is *not* like art. Another approach that Cohen employs is that of commentary, wherein he displays the multiform nature of prophetic style through a reading of scriptural passages. Here, I first examine Cohen's contrasts with science and art and then assess the features of his scriptural commentary.

III. *The Prophets Are Not Scientists/Philosophers*

In delineating the contrast between the prophetic style and 'science,' Cohen repeatedly points to Plato as a representative figure. In this context, Cohen uses the term 'science' to refer to scientific philosophy, and emphasizes Plato's desire to "make the *science* of ethical teaching independent of religion" and thereby "engender and establish the concept of ethicality in connection with a scientific system."[18] Plato thus provides a "grand paradigm" for future philosophic efforts and stands as "the originator of the fruitful yet fateful/fatal [*verhängnisvollen*] connection between scientific ethicality and religion."[19] In other words, by making the science of Ethics independent of religion, Plato also redefines religion by reducing it to and identifying it with the results of scientific Ethics. (In this description of Plato, Cohen anticipates his own counter-argument in *Religion of Reason*, wherein he seeks to reassert religion's distinctness from Ethics, thereby reestablishing ethicality's dependence on religion.) Though Cohen speaks explicitly only of Plato, he intends a much broader critique. Any thinker who seeks to reduce ethicality to a scientific system follows in the footsteps of Plato and is guilty of the same reduction of religion; the distinguishing feature lies not in whether or not a thinker employs 'religious' terms and concepts, but in the method used to analyze and organize those concepts. Thus, when Cohen asserts "the triumph of the religion of the prophets over the philosophy of Ethics [*der Ethik*]," he does not say ". . . over Plato."[20] Rather, he maintains that the prophets' approach to ethicality and to "the problem of man" has an advantage over philosophy as such, that is, over *any* scientifically systematic approach. When Cohen says that the prophets alone discovered the idea of humanity and that Plato failed to arrive at this idea,[21] he does not attribute this failure to any personal intellectual shortcoming on Plato's part. It is not as though Plato made a logical or procedural error in his systematizing endeavors; rather, it is precisely *because of* his conscientious application of his method that the concept did not appear. As Cohen says, "Not only did [Plato's] scientific Ethics not solve this highest problem [of the connection between nation and humanity], but he did not even once set himself the task [of solving it]."[22] Just as imaginary numbers were once thought not to exist, and indeed remain invisible within the axioms of the real number system (where the idea of a square root of a negative number has no significance), the idea of humanity cannot result from a process of strictly scientific and systematic reasoning; were such an idea suggested, it would have to be dismissed, since its systematic grounding would (rightly) appear to be insufficient.[23]

To be sure, Cohen does not give precise criteria for determining the sorts of philosophical approaches that are to be classed under the category of "the philosophy of Ethics," which stands in contrast to "the religion of the prophets." At the very least, however, given that Cohen identifies the attempt to comprehend ethicality under a scientific system as a basic feature of Plato's approach, Cohen's own philosophical *System*—which attempts to be highly scientific and systematic—would certainly be a prime candidate for the "philosophy of Ethics" category. This means that Cohen was aware of the limitations of systematic Ethics well before the publication his own systematic Ethics in 1904 as *Ethik des reinen Willens*. At first glance, this might seem senseless and strange—if Cohen already considered the method of systematic Ethics to be so limited, why would he have put such effort into such a work of his own? Furthermore, this fact also runs counter to the two dominant narratives regarding the relation of *Religion of Reason* to Cohen's earlier system: in one account, following the publication of his system, Cohen comes to realize the limitations of systematic philosophy, and thus 'breaks through' to the God of Judaism and moves away from his previous work. In the other account, Cohen's later work is seen as completely consistent with his earlier system, and so there is no need to posit any break or gap. For both accounts, Cohen's awareness of his system's limitations comes either later or not at all. In light of the 1901 essay under consideration here, I claim that Cohen realized the limitations of systematic Ethics early on, but that this did not preclude its validity within those limitations. In other words, while "the religion of the prophets" has certain important advantages over "the philosophy of Ethics," the latter also has certain important advantages over the former. While "The Style of the Prophets" primarily emphasizes Plato's and scientific philosophy's failings, other essays, such as "The Social Ideal in Plato and in the Prophets," indicate that there are places where the prophets' approach falls short and where Plato's method is superior.[24] Thus, Cohen may have held the task of writing a systematic Ethics to be worthwhile, despite his awareness that the systematic method tended inherently to obscure certain important ideas. The different methods can be compared to different tools—for certain tasks, a hammer will be of little use, and it may be more practical to use a saw instead. Yet, this does not mean that a hammer is utterly useless; it behooves a builder to learn how to use a hammer well, while simultaneously learning *when* the hammer ought to be used. The same applies to other tools as well: different tools have different uses, and the goal is not to find a single perfect tool (method) that can be used in all circumstances.[25] Cohen may thus have realized that a system of Ethics can never be 'perfect' or 'complete' (in that certain ethical concepts will always lie outside of its grasp), yet he may have deemed it a useful project to explore the results of a careful and consistent application of a systematic method to questions of ethicality. This portrayal of Cohen need not preclude the possibility of a later realization that the deficiencies of systematic Ethics run deeper than he had previously realized. As we shall see, the problems in the systematic method also deeply problematize the attempt to *write* a work of systematic Ethics—in other words, the problems in the method also create problems for style, for the form of expression. Cohen's introduction to *Religion of Reason* provides more details in this regard, but for now I will simply say that Cohen's later misgivings can be seen as a deepening of an awareness that had already been strongly expressed many years beforehand. In other words, rather than choosing between the narratives of "Cohen's views have continuity" and "Cohen's later work realizes the profound shortcomings of systematic philosophy," I claim that both are partly correct, in that the continuity of Cohen's views is exemplified precisely in his later criticisms of systematic philosophy.

While the preceding paragraphs examine Cohen's contrast between the method of the prophets and that of Plato, Cohen also emphasizes the differences in their respective styles. For Cohen, Plato's methodological approach of merging scientific ethicality and religion is outwardly manifested in his style, which is characterized by the dialogue-form and by the free use of myths.[26] According to Cohen, Plato's style "indicates" (bezeichnet) this connection[27]; in other words, one can discern the method, the way of thinking and reasoning, from the style, the way of writing and expressing. A corollary of this principle is that a certain way of reasoning will demand a characteristic form and style; likewise, the selection of a particular style will influence the content that is communicated.[28] Cohen does not provide detail as to *why* the dialogue-form and the use of myth constitute such an appropriate style for Plato's scientific systematization of ethicality. However, we can note that a written dialogue, like a system, often takes on a closed form. Any questions that are raised in a Platonic dialogue are answered within the dialogue itself.[29] Likewise, a philosophic system seeks to resolve all problematic concepts within its own framework, and only those concepts that can be comprehended by the system itself are deemed significant and meaningful. Neither the Platonic dialogue-form nor the philosophic system tends to point beyond itself.

In contrast to the Platonic style, the prophets employ the very style that Plato had explicitly rejected: rhetoric and oratory (Redekunst).[30] For the most part, they do not use the dialogue-form, except in occasional "veiled phrases."[31] Again, Cohen does not tell us explicitly why the prophets might have chosen rhetoric over dialogue. However, we can imagine why Plato, as Cohen portrays him, might not have liked rhetoric. An orator can never achieve complete systematicity, since she must constantly adapt herself to the audience before whom she stands at any given moment. Since the goal of rhetoric is to persuade, the orator might need to say one thing to one audience and another thing to another. She cannot construct a speech that will always be persuasive, once and for all. In contrast, systematic thinking does not, in principle, require revision for various types of external audiences: internal coherence of the system is the sole criterion for legitimacy. Similarly, in a dialogue-form, the speaker (Socrates) and his interlocutor are in a sense both 'Plato,' and so the problem of adapting to the audience can be sidestepped. By reclaiming rhetoric, the prophets lose the stability and constancy of systematic thought, but they gain the potential of conveying those ideas that systematic thought must pass over. While the task of addressing a particular other may be burdensome for the systematic thinker, the very non-systematicity of this task becomes the means by which the prophets are able to present their nonsystematic ideas. While the systematic ideas can be conveyed only if they are able to bypass the particular other, the prophet's ideas must be addressed to a particular audience that is not identical with the speaker himself. Thus, it may at first seem ironic that the 'dialogical' thinker Cohen would uphold the prophetic 'monologue' over the Platonic dialogue for the communication of characteristically dialogical ideas; however, it becomes clear that the latter's apparent dialogue is actually a monologue of Plato with himself, while the former's apparent monologue engenders true dialogue by leaving open a space for the listener or reader—the very absence of the second party from the text creates room for the reader/listener to become the second partner in the dialogue.[32]

IV. The Prophets Are Not Absolute Artists

While emphasizing that the prophets differ significantly from systematic philosophers, Cohen must also dispel the impression that they are mere artists. Just as many post-Kantian philosophers responded to Kant's denial of objective knowledge of God by locating the human connection to God in subjective feeling, so might a reader of the prophets, convinced by Cohen's assertion of their non-systematicity, assume that their speeches must therefore be strictly aesthetic constructions. In maintaining that the style of the prophets creates a third category, Cohen must thus carefully note the ways in which it differs from art, even while the two also share certain qualities.

This task is made more difficult by the fact that Cohen appears to lack a distinct vocabulary to characterize this third category; this difficulty may stem from the originality and newness of the very idea of such a category.[33] Thus, when contrasting the prophets to Plato, he writes, in what seems like an aesthetic portrayal, "Their eloquence is art, and poetry blossoms in them."[34] Yet, he further adds that "they are also not *mere* artists."[35] By this "mere," Cohen aims to emphasize that "[t]he prophets are not absolute artists. They do not acknowledge art as being an end in itself [*Selbstzweck*]. They want to be answerable for ethicality."[36] For an absolute artist, the purpose of her work would not depend on the response of others. While an audience may be inspired by a work of art, it would not be any less beautiful if the audience remained unmoved. In contrast, while the prophet may produce verses of great eloquence and great aesthetic beauty, their purpose is not simply to *be* beautiful but to bring the audience to lives of greater ethicality. If this aim is not accomplished, the words have failed to achieve their purpose. Indeed, one can say that their ideas—that is, the meaning of their words—have not even been *communicated* at all if this practical change fails to occur.[37]

Interestingly, this contrast with art is similar to the contrast that Cohen draws between prophetic speech and systematic philosophy. Here, the problem with art is that it becomes an end in itself, rather than finding its end in the audience. Likewise, Plato's championing of dialogue over oratory, in the quest for systematicity, also avoided dependence on a particular audience. Though in this essay Cohen applies the term *Selbstzweck* only to art, it would apply equally well to his portrayal of scientific philosophy. That is, philosophers often view the purpose of their writing as 'saying what is true' and devote less attention to the effect that their writing will have on their readers. An internally coherent argument is considered to be an end in itself. In contrast, Cohen's portrayal of the prophets as "answerable for ethicality" implies that they would be just as opposed to ethical neglect entailed by absolute philosophy as that entailed by absolute art.[38] In light of this parallel, one might say that absolute art and absolute philosophy both display an 'aesthetic' attitude toward the 'problem of man' and toward ethical life and existence.

Alongside the criticism of *Selbstzweck*, a second key characteristic of art, against which the prophets direct their objections, is its *Einseitigkeit*, its one-sidedness.[39] According to Cohen's rather Marxian portrayal, aesthetic creations are frequently among "the means by which culture sugarcoats its falsity. It is especially *art*, which indulges in luxury and which deceives through the biased showcasing [*die partielle Schaustellung*] of the beautiful over the misery and the wretchedness by which the poor are crushed."[40] Thus, the problem lies not in the presentation of the beautiful, but in the fact that *only* the beautiful is presented. It is not that the beautiful is not real or not important, but that the misery and un-beauty of the poor is also real and also important. The culture contains multiple elements, some of justice, integrity, and harmony, and some of injustice, fracture, and disunion. Rather than facing up to this heterogeneity and contradiction, the culture prefers to highlight a single part and to pretend that the other does not exist. In this criticism, one can hear an echo of Kant's criticism of philosophical dogmatists as expressed in his account of the antinomies: for each antinomy, a primary failing of the proponents of the thesis lies not in any logical inconsistency contained in the thesis, but in their ignoring of the fact that the antithesis is just as logically consistent.

Furthermore, Cohen's criticism via the prophets is not simply an attack on the personal callousness of artists or of society. Rather, there is something in the *method* of absolute art, in its internal principles, that seems to require this neglect of the non-beautiful. The prophets manifest "a deep suspicion against the one-sidedness of the aesthetic attitude, in which culture is indifferent before all ethical needs, and which makes the latter appear as a crisis that one must accept with realistic equanimity, if one wants to enjoy and not to go without the golden apples of the tree of art, which [according to this view] is the true tree of life.

The prophets identify the blindness of this one-sided attitude."[41] There is a sense in which the unbeautiful *is* incompatible with the beautiful, and so the prophet's opponents are 'right' to erase the poor from their cultural panorama. To acknowledge poverty and suffering would be to admit that society contains an unresolved conflict—in other words, there is something incomplete, which calls one beyond the beautiful. In contrast, the absolute aesthete demands that art, as a *Selbstzweck*, be complete and fully resolved within itself.[42] To the extent that non-beauty impinges on beauty, beauty is marred and is thus no longer truly beautiful. Thus, in order to create a work of beauty, one must ignore social injustice and still-incumbent ethical tasks. Such a stance is internally consistent, but only so long as the tree of art is equated with the true tree of life, an equation that Cohen and the prophets reject. For them, all elements of the sphere of 'is' must necessarily be found wanting, and so any aesthetic claims of true resolvedness and completion—and any method or style that tends to produce such claims— will be ethically deficient.[43]

V. The Multiplicity of the Prophetic Style

In contrast to the one-sidedness of art, Cohen argues that style of the prophets is most directly characterized by "its double-edgedness" (*seine Zweischneidigkeit*).[44] Through his readings of the prophetic texts, Cohen illustrates their irremediable multiplicity and more-than-oneness. While the philosophers and artists seek systematic consistency and self-contained beauty, the prophets embrace the contradictions that result from their ideas of the unique God, the individual, and humanity. Though their addresses seem to encompass mutually incompatible outlooks, their commitment to their ethical ideas (which are at the same time ethical tasks) demands the upholding of both poles in unresolved tension. In multiple examples, Cohen displays the prophets' castigation of the present, of what-is, alongside their hope for the future, for what-ought-to-be. In each case, though the competing stances of condemnation and consolation are portrayed as contradictory, they are not resolved or *aufgehoben* into an ideational synthesis.[45] Rather, the theoretical contradiction that expresses itself in the prophets' style is necessary for their communication of the practical ethical task.

For instance, Cohen points to the prophetic theme of human weakness and incapability, citing Isaiah 2:22: "Turn away from mortals, who have only breath in their nostrils, for of what account are they?" Cohen comments, "The separation of nature and man from God brings a tragic motif [*Zug*] to the style of the prophets. For that is the core-meaning of tragedy—that man is not equal to his own ethical task and composition. This is the pathological element in him, the misrelation to his composition. He is born for ethicality. But he makes a god for himself out of clay and wood."[46] Here, man is hopeless, crushed under the burden of a too-weighty task. If Isaiah's lament over human failings, which Cohen describes as a "Hamlet-style," represented the sole perspective put forth by the prophets, their style could have the consistency that can be found in despair. However, Cohen asserts that the lament does not maintain itself; rather, "[t]he tragic style of the prophets passes over . . . into satire."[47] In connection to the tragic self-debasement of human beings before idols of clay and wood, Cohen alludes to Isaiah 44:17, which he renders as: "And he says to the wood: you are my god."[48] While this verse, viewed in isolation, might seem consistent with the tragic style of Isaiah 2, the broader context of Isaiah 44:9–20 reveals it to be a satirical mockery of idol-worshipers. The passage exaggerates the practices of those who make use of idols, caricaturing a man who takes a piece of wood, bakes bread by burning part of it, roasts meat with another part, and carves the remainder into a god, before which he then bows and pleads for salvation. Such a portrait would not elicit tears from an audience, but rather jeers and laughter. Whereas tragedy presents failure—in this case, the descent into idol-worship—as the inevitable fate of humans as such, satire succeeds by portraying idol-worship as an act in which only a fool would engage. In other words, the satirist can make fun of idol-worship precisely because it is *not* inevitable. For the tragedian, the most strenuous human efforts to avoid idolatry will be futile, while for the satirist, the most rudimentary use of common sense is all that is required.[49]

While tragedy and satire both have their own theatrical worth, they are conceptually incompatible with one another. The idea of inevitability would undermine satire, while the idea of mockery—implying avoidability—would undermine tragedy. Thus, they cannot both be present at the same time. Yet, in Cohen's account, such a co-presence is precisely what occurs in and characterizes the prophetic addresses: "The art-styles [*Kunstarten*] flow into one another. The tragic motif does not mature [*ausreifen*] into drama; rather, it passes into satire. In this intermixture, their [i.e., the prophets'] style is enacted. In it lie the limits of rhetoric."[50] Importantly, this intermixture is not a synthesis in which the two styles are merged into a single view that takes both into account and overcomes the contradiction. That is, the intermixing of 'idolatry is inevitable' and 'only a fool would worship idols' does not result in a stance such as 'though avoiding idolatry is difficult, it is possible through devoted vigilance.' Rather, the two sub-styles and perspectives retain their individuality and incompatibility. In Cohen's presentation, the ethical message that the prophets attempt to convey cannot be contained in any single, one-sided perspective. The tragic perspective alone, in which there is no hope for ethical success via the overcoming of idolatry, would lead to despair and passivity. It lacks the insight of the satirical perspective, which implies that our idols are mere bits of wood that can and should be tossed away in the very next moment. On the other hand, the satirical perspective alone would not take into account the true 'impossibility' of ethical achievement—that is, it would not take into account the extent to which such achievement lies beyond the sphere of the 'possible,' beyond the realm of 'what is.' Any attempt at a single mediating position would lack the sharpness of both other perspectives; it would have neither the 'impossible' of tragedy nor the 'in the next moment' of satire. Rather, the ethical stance desired by the prophets must simultaneously be informed by both antithetical views in their fullness; such a stance will be irremediably contradictory or paradoxical in theory, although it can be embodied practically.[51]

This multiplicity can also be drawn out of Cohen's terse assertion, that in the style of the prophets lie the limits of rhetoric, of speech-art (*Redekunst*). The goal of rhetoric is to persuade the audience to adopt a certain point of view. Thus, one could attempt to convince one's audience of the truth of the tragic perspective. Conversely, one could seek to persuade them to adopt the satirical outlook. In either case, one would muster arguments for the validity of the chosen view and would show why opposing views are in error. Yet, the prophets, allegedly rhetoricians, continually undermine their own rhetorical efforts, mixing tragedy and satire, and thereby preventing any single perspective from taking hold. Their style highlights the limits of rhetoric, since any single *point of view* will be insufficient for their purposes; rather, that which they desire to engender in their audience is a single *ethical orientation*, which, viewed theoretically, will encompass multiple 'points of view.' In this context, speaking *from* a single point of view corresponds to speaking *in* a single voice; accordingly, multiple points of view cannot all be contained within a single rhetorical voice. These rhetorical limits also implicitly point to the limits of any method that seeks to arrive at or put forth an internally consistent view; the more complete the consistency, the greater the likelihood that the prophetically-demanded ethical orientation will be distorted by one-sidedness. As such, contradiction of one kind or another (though not necessarily in the form of conjoined satire and tragedy) becomes a necessary feature of a style that seeks to convey these ethical ideas.

Cohen highlights another aspect of the prophets' paradoxical multiplicity in relation to the concept of the "holy seed." The prophets castigate the entire people of Israel for their sins. Their targets are not merely the individual leaders, but "the political existence of the people, in all its civil and sacred authorities and institutions." The prophets "remorselessly place, before [their audience's] eyes and in glaring colors, the doom that is inescapably in store for the people and its great ones." In their horrific visions, "the entire people is eradicated."[52] In other words, the destruction is full and absolute; everything must be destroyed. At the same time, "a remnant of Israel remains preserved. Their hope rests in this remnant. This remnant is the new root. The root must remain. It is the holy seed. Though heaven and earth may pass away,[53] the mountains may totter, sun and moon may change their times, Israel's name and seed will remain."[54] At first

glance, this sequence might seem to lack the prophets' characteristic contradictory multiplicity. Yes, there is a *contrast* between the ruthless foretelling of
destruction and the remnant of hope, but need these be seen as *contradictory*?
However, note that Cohen presents the prophets as calling for the destruction of
"the entire people," implying that nothing is preserved. In standard logic, this
would rule out the possibility of a remnant, which requires some degree of preservation. For Cohen, though, the prophets can and must call for both, not via
compromise such as '*almost* everything is destroyed, *but* a remnant remains,' but
rather in a full-fledged both/and: everything is destroyed, *and* a remnant remains.

Cohen's account of the remnant and of the holy seed thus presents a logic of
infinitesimals.[55] In mathematics, an infinitesimal represents a magnitude that is
greater than zero and yet is smaller than every possible finite magnitude. In this
scriptural context, nothing is preserved, and a remnant is preserved—therefore,
the remnant must be a kind of 'nothing.' Everything—every thing, every finite
thing—is destroyed, and so the undestroyed remnant cannot be a finite thing.
Thus, while there is continuity, this continuity is not found in any finite element.
The remnant is the smallest possible element—or rather, even smaller than the
smallest possible element.[56] To be sure, one could also interpret the prophetic
texts in a less radical manner, but Cohen's interpretation does find support in a
plain-sense reading of a passage such as Isaiah 6:11–13 (which Cohen does not
directly cite):

> [11]Then I said, "How long, O Lord?" And he said:
> "Until cities lie waste
> without inhabitant,
> and houses without people,
> and the land is utterly desolate;
> [12]until the Lord sends everyone far away,
> and vast is the emptiness in the midst of the land.
> [13]Even if a tenth part remains in it,
> it will be burned again,
> like a terebinth or an oak
> whose stump remains standing
> when it is felled."
> The holy seed is its stump.[57]

Here, verses 11 and 12 show the full destruction: the cities have *no* inhabitants and
the houses have *no* people. *Everyone* has been sent away. Verse 13 even gives the
sense of the infinitesimal 'less than nothing,' in that after everything has been
destroyed and everyone has already been sent away, that which is left (i.e., nothing) will be burnt and destroyed *again*—and yet the holy seed will remain.[58] In

other words, the holy seed is what remains after everything that can be taken away has been taken away, and then taken away again. A seed is thus a fitting image for the remnant, since a seed is something that is exceedingly small (in comparison with the full-grown plant, it is essentially nothing) and yet provides continuity. In the mathematical theory of infinitesimals, continuity is similarly provided by infinitesimal elements which are smaller than the smallest possible distance and which remain after all finite distances have been taken away and 'destroyed.' Like the style of the prophets, the logic of infinitesimals is 'contradictory,' and yet this very contradictoriness is crucial for important mathematical concepts such as continuity, just as it is for the ethical ideas of the prophets.[59]

This paradoxical relation between complete destruction and hopeful remnant is characteristic of a repeated prophetic theme of denigrating the present while looking toward the future. According to Cohen, "[The prophet's] poetry of social compassion directs itself with all the magic of its blessedness of hope toward the yet-to-come [*einstige*] future. The present, however, with its pressing needs, with its unnatural coercion, with its glittering injustice, with its vain deceit and its ostentatious untruthfulness, deserves no compassion."[60] The destruction of *everything* thus corresponds to the present's meriting *no* compassion. Thus, it is not simply that the prophets have hope *despite* the complete destruction, but rather that their ability to proclaim hope *demands* the destruction of that-which-is. Accordingly, the holy seed can come to be only after the eradication of the present. This dynamic echoes Cohen's championing of the 'ought' over the "is," which he maps onto the prophetic championing of the ethical over idolatry. Idolatry represents placing value into something concrete, something that *is*, while the ethical places value in the relation to other persons and to the unique God, which are not static objects. Thus, the present is the realm of the is, while the future is the realm of the is-not, the not-is, the realm of the ought-to-be. The ethical orientation can be maintained only by placing all value in what ought to be, and destroying any value-connection to what is. The idea that something (in this case, the ethical mode of being) could retain continuity in the face of such a break with the present is counterintuitive. One wants to say, "But if that-which-is is completely abandoned, then there will be nothing left to provide continuity." Yet, it turns out that the contrary is the case: if anything (any thing) *remains*, there can be no continuity. Instead, nothing must remain, and this 'nothing' will provide ethical continuity. Thus, when Cohen, alluding to Isaiah 66:22, says that heaven and earth may pass away, but Israel's seed will remain,[61] the 'may' has the force of 'must': heaven and earth, the totality of that-which-is, must pass away, in order for the seed to remain. In that verse, the seed is linked to the new, the coming, heaven and earth, which come about only by the passing away of the old heaven and earth. Thus, in a verse from the previous chapter of Isaiah (65:17), the prophet had proclaimed the creation of the new heaven and new earth, while the former ones were no longer to be remembered.

Cohen cites this same verse in order to dispel a misunderstanding of the sharp prophetic contrast between present and future. In mercilessly castigating the present, the prophets may appear to be removing themselves from 'this world' and placing their hope into a far-away age, many years in the future. According to Cohen's own description of the prophetic outlook, "The 'end of days,' the 'coming time' [*das 'einst'*] overshadows all present and all actuality [*Wirklichkeit*]."[62] The prophets' visions can thus seem disconnected from 'actual' problems and matters of present concern. While one can see how such an understanding of the 'distancing from actuality' can easily arise, it greatly distorts the true meaning of the concept.[63] Cohen maintains that the prophets likely faced and responded to such criticism from their contemporaries: "Skepticism confronted [the prophets] loudly enough, saying that they were dreaming of distant days. They faced it with bold speech: 'See, I create a new heaven and a new earth.' The new heaven is the new ethicality; and the new earth, the new humanity."[64] The chief source of the misunderstanding is the equation of the prophetic messianic future with a finite, temporal future. The temporal present means this moment in time, and the temporal future indicates a finite amount of time after the present time. In principle, the temporal future could indicate any future time: one second from now would be the temporal future, as would one year from now or ten thousand years from now. However, in finite, temporal time, the near future is much more closely connected to the present than is the distant future. The further into the future one considers, the less connection there is to the present. Therefore, because the prophets insist that the present situation must be completely eradicated, so that the hoped-for future is completely dissociated from the present, such a future can only be one of an *infinitely great* distance from the present—hence, the accusation that the prophets were dreaming of distant days.

While this conclusion *would* be correct if the messianic future were a finite, temporal future, the verse from Isaiah shows the wrongness of such an understanding. The Hebrew does not say "I will create a new heaven and a new earth." Rather, the verb is a participle: *borei*, "I create" (as Cohen translates, "*ich schaffe*"). The original Hebrew intensifies the now-ness even further: while Cohen translates "*Siehe, ich schaffe . . .*," "See, I create . . ." (where "*Siehe*" is akin to the traditional "Behold"), the relevant Hebrew is *hin'ni borei*, which might be better translated as "I hereby create. . . ."[65] With this highly performative proclamation, the idea of temporal futurity is negated, since there is no determinate time-gap at all between the utterance and the enactment of a performative.[66] This appears to create a contradiction, since the hoped-for future is identified neither with the present (which remains negated) nor with any finite amount of time after the present.[67] Thus, it is not the present, but also not not-the-present, to the extent that not-the-present indicates another subsequent point in time. In other words, the hoped-for future is 'outside' of finite time altogether.[68] With his citation of

Isaiah's performative verse, Cohen indicates that it is not 'far away,' but can be here now, by striving according to the new ethical idea.[69] The new heaven is the new ethicality, the inward orientation toward the ethical, while the new earth is the new humanity, the outward and material object of this orientation, which stands in contrast to chauvinistic national divisions. The striving toward these ideas requires a break with the present, with that-which-is. Cohen presents the prophets as mapping this break with the present onto temporal language—just as the future is not the present, so the ought is not the is. However, the distance involved is not a temporal distance. Though they describe 'the future' in contrast to 'the present,' they do not desire that their audience wait patiently while maintaining their same non-ethical orientation, but rather that they adopt the ethical orientation *now*. That is, one can become infinitely removed from the present either horizontally, by waiting an infinite amount of time, or vertically, by ethically making a complete break and a complete turning away from one's previous orientation and way of being.

Since the prophets call for the latter, the challenge of conveying such an idea can help account for the characteristic two-sidedness in their style here. They must portray that which they call for as infinitely close to the present, but also as infinitely distanced from the present. Hence, one finds performative utterances of apparent immediacy alongside the talk of the "end of days," which is beyond world-historical time. Each pole plays an important role. To portray merely the closeness would risk identifying the present with the ideal, which is the opposite of what is the case, since the present must be negated; but to portray merely the distance would also distort their call for a turning and reorientation that can occur at this very moment. This paradoxical combination of infinite closeness and infinite distance with regard to ethical and religious ideals plays an important role in Cohen's own thought, especially in his later works.[70] As we shall see, his method for explicating the style of the prophets will prove very useful for deciphering his own double-sided style.

VI. *Anticipating* Religion of Reason

To provide a brief example, Cohen does not give much attention in this essay to the prophetic view of the individual. He does, toward the end of the essay, mention Ezekiel's discovery of the individual in connection with the act of repentance;[71] however, he does not provide a detailed account of how this act takes place, as he will in the chapters of *Religion of Reason* on "The Individual as I," "Atonement," and "The Day of Atonement." Yet, he prefigures these ideas in his interpretation of the prophets' dual-edged presentation of patriotism and national identity, which displays nearly the same logic as his own later understanding of the individual. That which he says about the destruction and continuity of the nation and fatherland can be mapped directly onto his account of the constant renewal of the self. On one hand, the prophets—Jeremiah above all—display a "fervent patriotism" and insist on the ultimate preservation of their people, yet, on the other hand, they simultaneously foretell the loss of their fatherland: "[Israel's] name and seed remain preserved, but the state must be destroyed."[72] This leads, in Cohen's portrayal, to "our wandering until the end of days."[73] Whereas previously, other nations were viewed as enemies, they are now united in a federation of peoples under the concept of humanity.[74] As a consequence, a new "tragic motif" arises, whereby "the prophet forfeits his fatherland, for humanity becomes his fatherland."[75]

Cohen presents this attitude as a necessary consequence of the ethical commitment to the unique God; he thus maintains a parallel conceptual structure when he applies the same ethical commitment to the problem of the individual, rather than to the nation. Just as the state must be destroyed, so must the static empirical self be destroyed in order for the ethical self of the individual (the infinitesimal seed/self and the name) to be renewed and preserved. From the perspective of the empirical self and ego, other people (read: peoples) are enemies, a threat and competition to myself. Yet, through the emergence of the ethical self, one's relation to other people becomes one of communion, as I-It relations become I-You relations. One loses one's fatherland-relation to oneself: just as fatherland all too often means 'my country, right or wrong,' so the egoistic self-relation is 'my desires, right or wrong.' By forfeiting the egoistic self-relation, one discovers the substance of ethical selfhood precisely in the act of relating to others. The ethical individual can no longer find rest in one's static (state-ic) ego or in being; rather the fate of the ethical self is that of continual and dynamic becoming, of "wandering until the end of days."[76] This opening to ethical becoming is "tragic," in that the peace and comfort of egoistic self-containment are forfeited. The ethical presentation of both international and interpersonal relations thus calls for a dual-edged character in order to account for the paradoxical destruction and preservation of the people/person.

In fact, Cohen sees this macrocosmic/microcosmic correlation as already implicit in the prophetic texts themselves. He writes, "Man exists . . . in a dual form as natural being: as individual and as tribe or nation. The prophets do not proceed from the individual in order to determine [man's] relation to God. Man is, for them, the nation, or rather, the *nations*."[77] Thus, though the prophets express their ethical concerns only in terms of the nation and nations, they do not thereby deny the relevance of the same ideas to the individual. Rather, since they conceive of 'man' as 'nation,' to speak of their ideas concerning the relations between nation and nation is to speak of their ideas concerning the relations between man and man generally. Accordingly, we might expect that their ideas could be fruitfully applied to both forms of human natural being (national and individual), and thus to relations between individual and individual. Thus, when Cohen proclaims Ezekiel as the discoverer of the individual, he does not portray him as opposing or breaking with the previous focus on the nation. Rather, his discovery comes precisely from a "mixing-together" (*Mischung*) of the earlier prophetic themes of Isaiah and Jeremiah, wherein "all prophetic motifs coalesce, in order to generate, as a new element, the solution: the *individual*."[78] Since the ethical concept of the individual is thus formed directly out of the ethical concept of the nation, it stands to reason that they might share a similar underlying structure.[79]

Cohen further emphasizes that the multiplicity of the prophetic *style* is linked to the conceptual heterogeneity contained within the *ideas* that the prophets aim to express. Given his assertions concerning the interconnections among method, idea-content, and style, this should come as no surprise. In commenting on the prophets' portrayal of God as the God of justice, he writes, "Justice is one of the two attributes around which the essence of God is centered. And it is characteristic, that, in its Hebrew expression, it contains the other attribute within itself. Beside justice stands love. And *Zedaka* signifies both . . . and just as justice is at the same time love, so is correctional-retribution related to consolation."[80] Here, a single word contains contradictory meanings, just as the style of the prophets contains contradictory themes and sub-styles. This correspondence is no mere coincidence; in proclaiming the God of *Zedaka*, the prophets must remain true to the dual nature of the idea, in both its consolatory and its retributive aspects.[81] Because this God is manifest to the human conceptual understanding in such a paradoxical way, the addresses of the prophets must necessarily lack smoothness and inner theoretical consistency. Hence, as Cohen observes, "In the prophetic speeches, insofar as they have been preserved for us, there are often unmistakable sudden leaps from the threat of punishment to sudden consolation. One cannot resist the thought that an inward contradiction must be gnawing at the consciousness of the prophets, at the self-consciousness of the prophets."[82] The passing from one theme to another occurs via a leap, which is to say, it is discontinuous; there is no way of reconciling the ideas into a single fluid synthesis. The suddenness of the leap reflects the fact that there can be no gradual transition from one to the other; because both themes are equally strong within the idea, the longer the theme of punishment has been prolonged, the more pressure there is for the theme of consolation to break forth suddenly.[83] Cohen's description of an "inward contradiction" emphasizes that the prophets do not simply choose voluntarily to express their idea in a dual-edged style, but are inwardly compelled to do so—the external multiplicity reflects an internal multiplicity. Furthermore, the inner contradiction is not a psychological idiosyncrasy unique to the prophets, as though someone else could engage the same idea without experiencing such a contradiction. Rather, the contradiction is not ultimately in the prophets but in the idea itself: the prophets are not divided *between* two mutually contradictory ideas, but rather divided *by* a single internally contradictory idea.

Cohen later describes the self-consciousness of the prophets as "the most difficult of all questions of style," asking, "Does genius know its own source?"[84] According to Cohen's reading, the prophets do not present their ideas as originating within themselves via a deliberate and conscious methodical construction, but rather as coming to them 'from without.' "Here, Isaiah . . . provides the clearest example. At his calling, he says, 'I am a man of unclean lips.' [Is. 6:6]."[85] In the continuation of this passage, which Cohen does not cite, a seraph touches Isaiah's lips with a live coal and tells him that his sin has been purged away (6:7). Immediately afterward, Isaiah hears the voice of the Lord asking, "Whom shall I send?"; he replies, "Here I am; send me" (6:8). In treating this passage as representative of the prophetic self-consciousness, Cohen seems to be reading it as follows: Isaiah, on his own, cannot produce the word of the unique God. His lips, in their 'natural' state, are unable to express the prophetic ideas. Only an external, divine intervention can make him capable this task. Thus, it is only *after* such an intervention that he can say, "Send me." In other words, while Isaiah is the one who eventually proclaims the God of justice and of humanity, the ideas that he articulates are not wholly 'his own.' Similarly, Cohen suggests that "the expression 'burden,' which is used to designate the prophetic address,[86] might be understood [as akin to Isaiah's account]. They [the prophets] feel their thoughts as a burden, which is laid upon them; the hand of God lies upon them."[87] Again, there is a separation between their thought and themselves. Even this strange self-description need not be attributed primarily to the individual prophetic psyche; it can be linked the prophetic ideas themselves, to those same characteristics that demanded a dual-edged expression. The dual quality of the ideas that prevents a uniform and systematic presentation outwardly also prevents a comprehension inwardly. That is to say, if the ideas could be cognized inwardly as determinate concepts, they could also be expressed outwardly without contradiction. Thus, it is not the prophets alone for whom the ideas are 'not their own'; because the ideas themselves transcend the comprehension of the understanding, anyone who engages the same ideas must experience a similar inward contradiction and a consequent lack of 'ownership.'[88] The multiplicity and 'non-consistency' in the prophetic style can thus be attributed to the desire that the ideas be no less paradoxical for the listeners than they are for the speakers themselves.[89]

The notion that prophets did not fully own their ideas can be linked to Cohen's presentation of the path by which they arrived at their ideas. They did not pull their ideas out of thin air; that is, they were not generated ex nihilo, either by their own ruminations or by God. Rather, Cohen points to Ezekiel in order to argue that their method involved the reworking and refining of previous 'sources.' "It appears as an irony, that the very one of the great prophets [i.e.,

Ezekiel] who was devoted to the restoration of the temple and the sacrifice should at the same time be the one who most deeply succeeded in the discovery of the ethical individual. One can detect, in fact, an ambivalence of which the others are free."[90] This ambivalence involves the positive portrayal of the sacrifice, whereas other prophets sharply criticized the sacrificial cult, which they viewed as ethically corrupt. However, according to Cohen, not only does this positive view of the sacrifice not diminish Ezekiel's commitment to the prophetic call for ethicality, but it even serves to "intensify" (*verstärken*) this call.[91] That which seemed primitive and inimical to ethicality in fact allowed Ezekiel to reach a higher ethical level than that of his prophetic predecessors. However, this higher level did not result from an uncritical acceptance of the sacrifice (the other prophets were correct to reject this attitude), but from the sacrifice having been "interpreted and idealized" by Ezekiel.[92] Thus, Ezekiel avoids a mode of thinking in which the sacrifice must be judged as 'good' or 'bad' purely in itself; rather, he maintains that the sacrifice *can be* evaluated positively, not 'in itself,' but rather through an ethical reinterpretation.[93] Furthermore, his retention of the recast sacrifice need not be understood merely as an exercise in apologetics or nostalgia.[94] Because the prophetic ideas cannot be conceptually comprehended or 'owned' by an individual, an approach that attempted to rationally derive them from first principles would fail; such deductive ratiocination works only for concrete determinate concepts that are fully comprehensible to the understanding. Instead, Ezekiel's use of the sacrifice as a received and preexisting source (which in itself is neither good nor bad, but ethically indeterminate and vague) provides him with the necessary raw materials for interpretatively uncovering the ethical individual.[95] Along these same lines, Cohen cites and comments on Jeremiah 15:9: "'If you bring forth the precious from the vile, you shall be as My mouth.' The prophet is an analytical chemist [*Scheidekünstler*][96], who sorts out and separates the pearls of the ethical calling from the base human world [*der gemeinen Menschenwelt*]; the analytical chemist of the eternal ideal from out of base actuality."[97] The prophet is not called merely to bring forth the precious, but specifically to bring it forth *from* the vile and the base.[98] Just as aluminum cannot be found in nature in its free form but must be separated out from bauxite ore, so the prophet requires ambivalent or problematic sources in order to derive the ethical ideals. Additionally, just as the method requires the use of sources, so too the style: even after its derivation, the idea cannot be detached from its unrefined source; the latter must be presented alongside the former. Hence, along with the call to the ethical individual, Ezekiel's prophetic addresses retain a detailed description of the sacrificial rites and implements.[99] This source-dependence corresponds to the internally contradictory character of the ideas: both qualities shield the ideas from conceptual consistency and theoretical systematization.

VII. *The Primacy of the Practical*

Cohen also emphasizes that the multiplicity in the prophets' style corresponds to the fact that their desired effect is not theoretical or merely intellectual, but rather practical and active. In other words, the practical nature of their ideas produces a natural multiplicity when mapped onto the sphere of theoretical, and thus requires an active avoidance of conceptual consistency and one-sidedness in verbal expression. Conversely, if there were (or could be) a unity in the theoretical expression, then the idea would itself be theoretical and not practical.[100] Thus, different types of communicative content demand and require different communicative styles: the proper expression and communication of a theoretical concept calls for a unity in verbal presentation and would be undermined by a lack of consistency, while the proper expression and communication of the prophets' active-practical ideas would be distorted by an overly consistent theoretical description, and therefore specifically require a non-unity in verbal presentation. This theoretical incompleteness serves to underscore the fact that the communication itself cannot be 'completed' through mere intellectual comprehension but requires, in addition, engaged practical enactment.

In some cases, as we have seen, the prophets avoid theorizability by oscillating between two contradictory perspectives. Though a given perspective can be taken in a theoretical manner, the co-present of contradictory perspectives cancel each other out and prevent full theoretical comprehensibility. In other cases, the prophets emphasize the non-theoretical by avoiding any 'perspective' at all. Regarding the temptation to despair of human ethical improvement, Cohen notes, "The style of the prophets resists such pessimism. Initially, however, pessimism is countered not by optimism, but by a *tragic pathos*."[101] Both pessimism and optimism (like any ism) would be too one-sided and too intellectual, whereas pathos goes beyond the theoretically cognizable. The prophets' employment of pathos does not mean that their ideas should be identified with 'mere feeling'; rather, it serves a useful negative purpose in preventing the identification of their ethical ideas—which draw upon the whole individual—with mere intellect.

The prophets' theme of the love of God also serves to counter the tendency toward intellectualization. In the prophetic writings, "To know God means: to love God. Love is his essence. Love becomes a basic motif in the style of the prophets, because it is a basic affect of their human emotion. And the emotional power of this thought has overflowed the prophet with all the magic of poetry. 'I drew them with the cords of a man, with the bands of love' [Hos. 11:4]."[102] Note that Cohen does not say that the prophets emphasize love of God in addition to knowledge of God. Rather, he maintains that whenever they say knowledge, they mean love, a relation that involves an active engagement of all the parts of the self. Accordingly, since there can be no knowledge of God that is not at the same time love, there is no possibility of theoretical or objective knowledge of God.[103] For this reason, it is not 'assent' that the prophets seek from their audience, but rather a practical self-commitment and reorientation. The emotional and poetic elements of their style thus function as reminders of the ways in which their message "overflows" the bounds of the theoretical.

At the same time, this emotional transcendence of the theoretical runs the risk of being taken purely aesthetically. As was stated earlier, Cohen views the prophetic style as creating a border-area between art and science. If it therefore exists between two commonly recognized genres, its acknowledged non-identity with one can lead to its being wholly identified with the other. Cohen maintains that the prophets themselves had to respond to such a misperception: "The prophets are wise men [i.e., akin to scientists] and poets [i.e., akin to artists]. However, they are not called poets. And they later struggled against being taken for poets. Ezekiel scoffs that to his people his word is like a love song, sung with a beautiful voice with mellifluous accompaniment."[104] Here, Cohen alludes to Ezekiel 33:32, which reads in full, "To them you are like a singer of love songs, one who has a beautiful voice and plays well on an instrument; they hear what you say, but they will not do it."[105] Here, the people's fault is not primarily disobedience, but rather a type of genre-misrecognition. The prophet's audience eagerly listens to his words (see Ezek. 33:30–31), but feels no obligation to change their own actions and orientation. If the prophet's words actually were an aesthetic product, such a response would be wholly acceptable. Both aesthetic and intellectual-theoretical utterances can be appreciated and affirmed without requiring anything of the listener's will.[106] However, if the prophet's ideas are of a practical nature, to hear and not to do is in reality not to hear; the words have not been conveyed if they do not result in a change in practice and habit (or, at the least, a willful refusal to change).

Furthermore, in order to distinguish this change from a mere change of feeling or of thought, Cohen highlights passages where the knowledge of God (which risks being taken theoretically) is identified with particular external ethical tasks. For example, he cites and comments on Jeremiah 22:16, which criticizes king Shallum for not following in the footsteps of his father Josiah: "He [the king's father] upheld the rights of the poor and the needy. Verily, this is—to know me.' The knowledge of God is here equated with social justice as such."[107] The knowledge of God is thus less of a knowing, in the conventional sense, and more of an interpersonal doing and acting.[108] Note too that Jeremiah does not say that the knowledge of God (internally) will result in just action (externally), but that the just action *is* knowledge of God. This should not be understood as mechanical or behavioristic action; the point is not that there is no internal component, but rather that there is no internal competent that could be conceptualized or identified apart from the outward action and habit. Similarly, commenting on

Isaiah's vision of messianic harmony in which nation no longer lifts up sword against nation, Cohen asserts, "The knowledge of God signifies this peace of humanity."[109] In this case, the practical behavior that is equated with the knowledge of God—that is, world peace—goes beyond anything that an individual can accomplish on his or her own. This makes it clear that the knowledge of God is not a static or finished state of mind, but rather an infinite task. Thus, in enjoining their listeners to actively and continually strive toward bringing about this peace, the prophets must avoid conveying anything finished, which is to say, they must avoid conveying anything theoretically comprehensible. A concept that can be fully grasped is complete and determined unto itself, whereas the prophetic ideas must contain an incompleteness that impels the listener to practical actualization. Hence, the idealized visions of the messianic future, combined with castigation of the present, serve to reinforce this incompleteness and not-yet-ness of that which 'is' and can currently be grasped. While the prophets cannot force their listeners into the reorientation of the self that they demand, they can encourage this negatively through a style that closes off graspability in the realm of the theoretical.

Because this anti-theoretical bent and emphasis on practical willing could make it seem as though the prophets enjoined passionate and arbitrary acts of will without rational justification, Cohen also goes out of his way to emphasize that "[e]thicality has knowledge as its precondition. The knowledge of God is, first and foremost, knowledge."[110] A self-driven, capricious willing is thus ruled out; the term 'knowledge' indicates a firm connection to something outside of oneself. However, because objective and theoretical knowledge have already been precluded, the meaning of Cohen's insistence on 'knowledge' is not immediately apparent. This difficulty again reflects the marginality that he attributes to the prophetic style; possessing neither the objectivity of science nor the subjectiveness of art, its status resists intuitive classification. Thus, Cohen articulates the questions that many readers of the prophets would ask: "Are [the prophetic ideas of ethicality] only figments of the imagination, deformed products of a divine madness? Or should a truth be ascribed to them, even though they lack scientific grounding?"[111] Cohen comes down on the side of the latter, but faces the challenge of explicating the meaning of a truth that is not scientific truth, corresponding to a knowledge that is not objective knowledge. His answer seems to lie in a truth and a knowing that demand the self-engagement of the knower.[112] Thus, not only do the prophets proclaim ideas that demand a practical self-engagement from their listeners, but they themselves arrived at the ideas only through the same engagement of self. In other words, their practical ideas resulted from a practical method. Cohen states that the prophets' "fundamental idea"—that is, the unique God—proved its "methodological power" by enabling the discovery of the ethical idea of humanity, a victory that the method of scientific philosophy could not achieve.[113] However, it was not merely by reflecting on the *concept* of the unique God that prophets made their discovery, but rather by active and engaged devotion *to* the unique God.[114] "The love of God [*Die Liebe Gottes*] signifies love for humanity; it is the love by whose power humanity arises. Without it, it [i.e., humanity] does not exist [*vorhanden*]. The love of God calls it forth and authenticates it and will bring it into actuality."[115] While *die Liebe Gottes* can mean God's love (i.e., love that comes from God), it is connected, in this context, to love for God. As stated above, Cohen maintains that "to know God means: to love God."[116] Thus, it is through the prophets' active and practical love of the unique God that the idea of humanity is generated within them; mere self-contained reflection and speculation would have been insufficient. Furthermore, even after arriving at the idea of humanity, they must continue their active love; were they to cease or become passive, the idea would leave them and would no longer be "at hand" (*vorhanden*). For this reason, while their ideas have the firmness and reliability of truth and knowledge, they can never be scientifically grounded, since this would require the prophets to approach their ideas from an objectified, detached, and dispassionate perspective, in whose light the ideas would disappear.

Cohen's presentation of the style of the prophets provides examples of the ways in which a text can communicate a specific message through a lack of theoretical consistency. Though the prophets were not philosophers, this was not a defect, but rather provided important advantages (although it possesses drawbacks as well), since a fully systematic philosophy is incapable of properly addressing certain ideas. In the case of Cohen's own writing in *Religion of Reason*, the situation is a bit more complicated. Because Cohen also attempts to convey many of the same ideas that he finds in the biblical prophetic writings, *Religion of Reason* cannot be a purely philosophical text. However, unlike the prophets, Cohen himself is a philosopher. Thus, in *Religion of Reason*, he will *make use of* philosophy, but he will also employ 'other voices,' especially those displayed by the sources of Judaism, in order to convey his ideas.

The subsequent chapters will thus show in detail how the ideas that Cohen addresses in *Religion of Reason* contain a multiplicity akin to the one that he identifies in the prophetic style. We first turn to Cohen's introduction to *Religion of Reason*, where he criticizes the one-sidedness of systematic philosophical Ethics. He emphasizes that Ethics stands in need of supplementation by what Cohen calls 'religion,' a mode of reasoning that is capable of addressing key ideas such as the I, the You, and the God of the individual. We will then examine the main body of his text, exploring the various ways in which Cohen intermixes and alternates scriptural and philosophical language in order to convey the ideas—contradictory from a theoretical perspective, but unified from a practical perspective—that form the basis of the religion of reason.

The Sources of Multiplicity

COHEN'S PROJECT IN ITS OWN TERMS

THIS STUDY WILL ultimately seek to read *Religion of Reason* as a work that employs multiple 'incompatible' voices in order to convey ideas that would be distorted by a direct, linear style of writing. Ideally, in addition to serving as an exercise in creative interpretation, my reading of the book would also accord with Cohen's own understanding of his project. Unfortunately, Cohen himself is not explicit about his choice of style. He does not tell us *why* he writes in the way that he does, nor does he provide guidelines for *how* we ought to interpret his text. However, a clearer sense of *what* he considers his overall project to be can aid us in answering these other two questions. Cohen subtitles his introduction "Elucidation of the Title and Articulation of the Task." In other words, he finds it necessary to explain the meaning of each of the components in "Religion of Reason out of the Sources of Judaism." Each of the words in the title contains a level of ambiguity; one's understanding of Cohen's project might vary greatly, depending on how one conceives of "reason," "religion," "sources," "Judaism," or even "out of." As noted earlier, Cohen intends these terms in very specific ways that may sometimes diverge significantly from their popular connotations. I argue that if we can more clearly comprehend the fine details of his title and its parts, we will understand why Cohen's task could not be carried out in a consistent, single-voiced style.

Accordingly, this chapter and the next one examine Cohen's introduction, with an eye toward elements that could prove relevant to questions of communication and style. In this chapter, I first look at Cohen's description of his general hermeneutical approach to historical sources. I then trace through his account of the basic structural relation of philosophy and religion within the encompassing sphere of reason. Finally, I highlight the ways in which his exposition of the development of the traditional Jewish sources anticipates elements of the stylistic multiplicity that he will later employ in the main body of *Religion of Reason*. Each of these three components pertains to aspects of Cohen's project that can be stated directly. However, Cohen's introduction also includes a section in which he attempts to exposit the paradoxical conceptual content of the sphere of religion. I deliberately omit discussion of this section from this chapter, in order to emphasize the unresolved contradictions in Cohen's architectonic. I return to this section in the next chapter, in which I highlight the insufficiencies of Cohen's initial attempt to address these contradictions.

I. 'Aus'

Cohen's overarching aim is to construct a religion of reason *from out of* (*aus*) the sources of Judaism. This project takes the sources of Judaism as its starting material and eventually ends up with a religion of reason. But *how* exactly does one move from the former to the latter, from sources to religion? What are the criteria and principles of interpretation through which one reads the source texts? Does the proper understanding of religion "fall out" naturally from the sources? Or does deriving something *from* the sources also require that one bring something *to* the sources? In answering these questions, Cohen's argues that the proper interpretive method depends equally upon a priori concepts *and* empirical historical data. Accordingly, he criticizes other methods that omit one or the other of these two elements.

Cohen first argues that a strictly historical approach to the sources, based upon the method of induction, is insufficient for the project of constructing and discovering the religion of reason.[1] In Cohen's portrayal, scholars in the field of "history of religion" [*Religionsgeschichte*], faced by the overwhelming variety of historical forms, attempt to construct a unitary concept by seeking out the 'lowest common denominator' among different instances of what is often called 'religion.' They therefore cast aside 'inessential' differences and search for the common core that supposedly lies at the center of every historical manifestation of religion. However, Cohen considers this attempt to be doomed to failure: "There is no opposition to reason and understanding, no opposition to human ethicality in the broadest sense, which has not become the center of gravity of a so-called [*angeblichen*] religion."[2] Thus, after eliminating all irrational elements from various 'religions,' one will be left with a common denominator of—nothing. In light of this, "the prejudices that deny to religion not only conceptuality/intelligibility [*Begrifflichkeit*], but also spiritual/intellectual [*geistigen*] value generally, become understandable."[3] That is, *if* one assumes that the inductive method is the proper one for this problem, then one *ought* to come to the conclusion that 'religion' is devoid of intellectual and conceptual content. One should not criticize the conclusion in itself; the problem lies in the choice of method. Indeed, those who reach such a negative conclusion are more correct and more honest than those who also employ the method of induction and yet claim to have 'discovered' a positive content for the concept of religion.

Cohen does not himself believe that religion is an empty concept, but rather that its content is invisible to the method of induction, as employed by the scholarly field of historical science: "History of religion [*Religionsgeschichte*] has no means whatever of securing the legitimacy of religion; according to its methodological concepts, there is no legitimacy [*Recht*] other than that which takes place and exists [*sich vollzieht und besteht*] in historical fact."[4] Because, in this case, the data set of historical fact produces no inductive unity, the history of religion is at a loss.[5] If another method is to succeed, it must be one which does not limit itself to past historical actualities. For Cohen, while induction treats the concept of religion as the *result* [*Fazit*] of historical development, one should instead view the concept as the antetype [*Vorbild*] and the preparatory-sketch [*Vorzeichnung*] of the historical development that we examine.[6] That is to say, we must first begin with the concept of religion, and then examine the historical sources in light of that concept.

In this section, Cohen does not define the concept of religion, nor—apart from a vague "the concept of reason must engender the concept of religion"— does he give an account of precisely *how* we are to arrive at this concept of religion.[7] (As we shall see, the absence of a precise definition of religion may not be mere oversight on Cohen's part; it may be the case that the concept of religion *cannot* be given a clear and consistent definition.) Instead, his primary point here is a negative one, namely, to highlight the insufficiency of the purely inductive method of the history of religion.

After discussing the concept of religion, Cohen moves on to examine the concept of Judaism in particular. At first, it may appear that one *can* employ the method of induction in the case of Judaism. Whereas the historical data in the case of religion contained an almost infinite variety, the literary sources of Judaism are more narrowly delimited and finite in scope. As such, discovering a common essence among them may seem more feasible. Cohen warns, however, that this is in fact not possible; the same methodological issues raised by the concept of religion also apply to the concept of Judaism: "One can never succeed in educing [*entwickeln*] a unifying concept of Judaism out of the literary sources, unless this [the concept of Judaism] itself, following the analogy of the organism, is anticipated [*vorwegg-enommen*] as the ideal objective."[8] One must anticipate the concept *before* seeking to interpret the sources.[9] Again, Cohen does not spell out the content of the concept of Judaism, nor does he say what it means to "anticipate" it. He merely emphasizes that, methodologically speaking, *some* sort of concept must be presupposed.

Cohen does not mean to dismiss the importance of the literary sources, and he affirms that history, and literary history in particular, is an essential factor in the development of the concept of Judaism.[10] Thus, on one hand, he can say that the literary sources contain the development of the concept of Judaism. On the other hand, though, one cannot *discern* that development without an independently obtained concept. That is to say, the concept of Judaism and its development are not self-evident from the sources alone: a person could be thoroughly familiar with the sources and yet have a completely misguided understanding of what Judaism consists in. In arguing for the insufficiency of the literary sources, Cohen maintains that "in the course of history up to now, the concept may not yet have been brought forth and fulfilled."[11] Irrational and unethical elements are intertwined with previous historical instantiations, up to the present day, and one therefore needs an additional interpretive criterion beyond the sources themselves. Considered as a potential data set for induction, the written sources are 'incomplete'; they outwardly display only *part* of the concept of Judaism, namely, that part that has unfolded in history thus far. Any act of induction performed on them will therefore result in an incomplete understanding of the concept.

Cohen thus draws a link among transcendental concepts, a teleological account of history, and the method of induction. The concept is in the process of displaying itself in history, but this process is not yet complete—nor will the process ever be completed: it is infinite. To say that we must use the ideal concept as the criterion for examining the actual historical sources[12] is equivalent to saying that we must use the future (the concept as it will unfold in its infinite future development) to determine and to understand the past and the present (the concept as it has unfolded up to now). The method of induction fails not simply because *this particular* set of historical facts is incomplete, but because any such set (containing only the past but not yet the future) will necessarily be incomplete.[13] By applying this principle to Cohen's own writing, we can already anticipate his structural need for a form of indirect communication. Just as the historical literary sources of Judaism do not 'directly' display the ideal concept, so too Cohen's own literary production would have misrepresented the religion of reason if he had sought to convey a content that could be directly or inductively appropriated. Indeed, it may be that previous readers of *Religion of Reason* were stymied precisely because they sought to apply the same inductive approach for which Cohen criticized the scholars of *Religionsgeschichte*.

Having argued for the shortcomings of induction, Cohen acknowledges that his proposed alternative contains difficulties of its own. The idea that one should approach the literary sources with a concept already in hand raises such questions as: "But how can the ideal-concept of the matter in question be anticipated beforehand? . . . How is it possible to start with the allegedly finished, completed concept of religion or of Judaism, and from this supposition consider the literary sources as material to be tested by this concept?"[14] While induction may be problematic, Cohen's approach does not even seem *feasible*. Even if one did use a previously obtained concept as the criterion by which to read the sources, wouldn't one simply get out of the sources that which one put into them?[15] Wouldn't this be mere eisegesis, turning Scripture into a wax nose by reading our own biases and presuppositions into the text, rather than exegesis, trying to see what 'the texts themselves' have to say?

Rather than directly answering the question of "How is it possible?" Cohen turns the challenge back on his interlocutors, asking, in essence, "How can one do otherwise?" According to Cohen, the sources remain "mute and blind" if one does not first "approach them with a concept."[16] The method of induction, which seeks to work from 'the texts themselves,' *can*, to be sure, extract a wide variety of historical observations from the sources, but it cannot draw any conclusions about *religion* or about *Judaism*, considered as concepts of reason. At the same time, Cohen also repudiates an approach that would presume to base its account of religion and Judaism *only* on an independent concept, without reference to the concrete details of the textual sources. For Cohen, in contrast, having the concept ahead of time does not mean 'knowing everything' ahead of time. The 'anticipated concept' does *not* provide content by itself; it only supplies a basic guideline and rule for reading and filtering the raw material provided by the particular text. While Cohen upholds the concept in order to avoid being "simply conducted [*geleitet*] by the authority" of the literary sources, he "certainly" wants to be "instructed [*belehrt*] by them."[17] While rejecting the traditionalist or historicist tendency that assigns sole "authority" to the texts, he also distances himself from those who would construct a theology or a philosophy of religion without doing justice to 'the way the words run.'

Thus, Cohen's titular *aus*—by which he moves from the sources of Judaism to the religion of reason—is neither induction from the texts alone, nor deduction from the concept alone.[18] However, though Cohen asserts that "the question regarding the concept of Judaism does not hover wholly in the air, not exclusively in the antithesis of induction and deduction," he does not provide a label for his proposed method, which constitutes a third alternative beyond such an antithesis.[19] To fill in this gap, I borrow a term from C. S. Peirce and describe Cohen's approach as a logic of *abduction*.[20] Unlike the other two modes of reasoning, abduction is able to produce something new and original which is not inherently 'given' in its starting components (the latter, in Cohen's case, are the text and the concept). At the same time, compared with induction and deduction, abduction is less 'secure'; it does not have the same level of assurance as a deductive syllogism, or even of a well-argued historical-inductive argument. Instead, it simply posits something that *may* account for the observed data: Cohen seeks to provide a reading that fits the basic criteria of the anticipated concept, and also takes the textual data into account. However, because this reading does not fellow directly or automatically from the observed data, and in fact goes 'beyond' it, the reading need not be historically (i.e., inductively) probable, and may even be 'historically implausible.' Indeed, the logic of abduction is very similar to what Cohen himself calls the method of idealization, and it is precisely the 'unhistoricity' of this method that Cohen's critics have criticized.[21] Nevertheless, Cohen here insists that his non-inductive, non-deductive approach is the only one capable of accessing and constructing the religion of reason.

Accordingly, we can say that Cohen views the concept of Judaism as neither strictly empirical (corresponding to the method of induction) nor dogmatic/rationalistic (corresponding to deduction), but rather as transcendental.[22] Although the details will become clearer later, we can begin to discern further parallels between Cohen's textual hermeneutic and his communicative style in the main body of *Religion of Reason*. The former upholds the equal significance of both text and concept, preventing a reduction of meaning to a single one of the two, while the latter's apparent inconsistency and multiplicity will prevent the reader from securing a reductively consistent theoretical account of the ideas of religion.

II. *What Religion Is Not*

Having argued for the necessity and legitimacy of his non-inductive textual hermeneutic, Cohen next attempts to map out the basic structural relationship between reason, religion, and philosophy. In accord with the title of his book, he seeks to carve out a spot within the realm of "reason" for what he calls "religion." However, rather than provide a direct definition for religion, he instead provides an extended account of the many things that religion—because of its connection to reason—is *not*. In so doing, he opposes other philosophical accounts that deny the rational character of religion. Thus, according to Cohen, religion is not based on the senses; it is not based on an obscurantist instinct; it is not based on the eudaemonistic desire for pleasure and avoidance of pain; it does not have its source in the contingent sphere of the imagination; it is not a mere product of sociological forces; it is not the illusory invention of priestly or privileged classes for the purpose of maintaining power. Importantly, Cohen does not deny the reality of such human phenomena, nor does he deny that these descriptions may very well be applicable to *what often goes under the name of 'religion.'* Rather, his point is to emphasize that religion, in the sense of the religion of reason, is to be understood as *something else* and must not be identified with these non-rational manifestations.[23]

In addition, he also emphasizes that religion is not merely a less sophisticated form of philosophy. He opposes the view that treats religion as something for 'simple folk' who lack the intellectual capability to grasp philosophy's higher abstractions. Rather, religion is just as necessary for the wise as for the simple. Furthermore, Cohen—perhaps alluding to and opposing Hegel's account of philosophy and religion[24]—denies that religion can be seen as a 'subset' of philosophy: "Nor is it the case that he who has a share in science and philosophy thereby and therein possesses religion."[25] Such an approach would acknowledge that religion is necessary for everybody, but would say that the wise can access religion simply by being versed in philosophy, and would therefore have no need for a *separate* engagement with anything outside of philosophy. Cohen's opposition to this view implies that there are certain aspects of reason that philosophy and science cannot access: even if someone had attained to the supreme heights of philosophy, a remnant of reason would still remain untouched. As Cohen puts it, "reason does not exhaust itself in science and philosophy."[26] Ultimately, then, we are left with a structure wherein "reason," in Irene Kajon's formulation, "takes on . . . a double aspect": it divides into two sub-realms, namely "philosophy" and "religion," such that neither of these two sub-realms are identical with one another.[27] While this structure will later reveal itself to be 'theoretically impossible,' Cohen here simply presents it casually, without immediately drawing out its paradoxical implications.

Cohen next seeks to show how the connection of religion with reason affects its connection with the multiplicity of particular historical religious forms. Because reason is, by definition, common to all human beings *qua* human beings, the fact that religion has its basis in reason means that the religion of reason must also be a universal human phenomenon.[28] The universalizing aspect of reason means that one cannot hold religion to be confined to a particular sect, culture, civilization, or era. All human beings, across time and space, "even those in the most primitive conditions of culture," have a share in the religion of reason.[29] Cohen indicates, in addition, that all cultures have something *unique* to offer to our understanding of the religion of reason. It is not the case that one who studies 'more advanced' cultures has nothing to learn from 'less advanced' cultures. Rather, each culture offers a manifestation of reason that no other culture can reproduce. Because reason can never be captured directly in any one manifestation, the study of a wide range of cultures is crucial for gaining a proper understanding of the religion of reason.[30] Notably, when Cohen asserts that "in no particular people's consciousness is the religion of reason exhausted," he employs the same term (*erschöpft*) as he did a few sentences earlier in his claim that reason does not exhaust itself in philosophy.[31] In both cases, he emphasizes that any single point of view—whether that of philosophy or of a particular culture, be it ancient Israel or nineteenth-century Prussia—is insufficient: one *must* approach reason from a multiplicity of cultural perspectives if one is to avoid a one-sided distortion and flattening.[32]

However, after granting the religion of reason such a broad, inclusive scope, Cohen then turns around and offers some qualifying restrictions. It is not the case that *every* element in the present form of a given culture's 'religion' qualifies as a manifestation of the religion of reason. There may very well be religio-cultural elements that retain quite irrational aspects. For Cohen, "philosophy and science" are required by every culture in order to critically engage its received myths and traditions, thereby enabling it to achieve a fuller actualization of the religion of reason.[33] As such, reason (and hence the religion of reason) is universal, but not necessarily *uniform*, across different cultures.

Unlike Hegel, though, Cohen does not rank various cultures on a scale of comparative rationality. He does not see later cultures as necessarily superior to earlier ones, nor does he portray 'primitive cultures' as necessarily less rational than 'advanced cultures.' While every culture must seek to become more rational, relative to its own current state, it is also the case that each culture contains important facets of reason not found in other cultures. Thus, Cohen endows every culture with a 'relative superiority' over every other culture. Furthermore, a given culture's lack of rationality in a particular area should not be viewed as permanent state or an essential feature. Rather, once a culture has "gained command of science and philosophy," it is capable of engaging in self-correction, thereby attaining a rational status on par with that of any other culture.[34] Cohen maintains that all cultures contain the raw material for reason; they need only to shape that material by scientifically criticizing their received myths and traditions. Accordingly, rather than saying, "Reason does not manifest itself to as high a degree in this culture," one ought at most to say, "Reason does not *yet* manifest itself to as high a degree in this culture."

While Cohen's general pluralistic approach is notable in its own right, we can also detect an implicit connection to Cohen's personal desire to present the rational promise of the Jewish sources. If the religion of reason is universal by definition, then it can also be found in a not-so-obviously-rational source like the Hebrew Bible. Furthermore, the Jewish sources, including later rabbinic texts, can (again, by definition) display unique aspects of the religion of reason that are not to be found in other Christian or Western sources. In this way, Cohen can claim that his project is not merely of parochial Jewish interest, but rather contains a universal significance.[35]

As we shall see, Cohen also holds an intellectual allegiance to both 'Hebrew' and 'Greek' modes of thought. Rather than seeking to champion one over the other, Cohen's pluralism allows him to uphold both, without erasing the differences between them. Indeed, it may be the case that each mode of thought has advantages that the other lacks and that both are necessary in order to attain to a more complete understanding of reason and its complexities. Thus, recalling Cohen's earlier account of the relation between idea-content and style, we can draw a link between his assertion here, that a multiplicity of *cultures* is required for the *understanding* of the religion of reason, and his employment, in the subsequent chapters of his book, of a multiplicity of *styles* in the *communication* of the religion of reason.

Having defended universality as "the fundamental condition of the religion of reason," Cohen feels the need to justify the fact that his own book is devoted specifically to the particular sources of Judaism. Since his account of the religion of reason deals only with Jewish sources, a reader could conclude that Cohen views these sources as the exclusive origin of the religion of reason.[36] If this were true, and the religion of reason could not also originate elsewhere, "the criterion of universality would be compromised."[37] While Cohen insists that this is not the case, and that he does not restrict the religion of reason to these particular sources, he has good grounds for supposing that many readers would see universality and particularity as mutually exclusive. Historically, attempts to ground religion in particular texts or sources *have* often resulted in triumphalist, exclusivist, or chauvinistic accounts of religion. Conversely, accounts of religion that aspire to universality have typically grounded themselves on presumptively universal principles. Cohen, counterintuitively, claims to draw the universal from out of the particular. That is, he assumes that reason (i.e., the universal) is attempting, "in spite of all social obstructions and all obstacles," to "wrestle its way" into the history of particular cultures.[38] Even though a particular culture may contain many impediments to universality, one can uncover its glimmerings if one approaches that culture's sources in the right way.[39] In other words, rather than looking for the universal *directly*, one can find it precisely *within* a culture's non-universalistic elements. To be sure, Cohen has not yet explained *why* one should go to all the trouble of 'excavating' non-universalist elements, rather than taking a direct route to the universal.[40] At this point, he has simply emphasized that his working from a set of particular Jewish sources does not inherently *preclude* a universalist account of religion.[41]

III. Judaism and Philosophy

Having designated the Jewish sources as a resource for the religion of reason, Cohen then seeks to determine the relation between the Jewish sources and *philosophy*. Here, we begin to see the first signs of the *problematic* nature of this relationship. At first, Cohen simply states baldly, "Judaism, to be sure, has no share in philosophy."[42] However, immediately afterward, he asserts that his first statement stands in contradiction to the previously stipulated universality of reason. Both religion *and* philosophy, as sub-domains of reason, must accordingly be just as universal as reason itself. Thus, Cohen states both that the sources of Judaism have no share in philosophy and that they *must* have a share in philosophy.

Cohen responds to the dilemma by stating, "Here, too, the riddle is solved by the distinction between *primary-originality* and derivative actuality. And here, unmistakably, the distinguishing mark [*Merkmal*] of a methodological *characteristic-feature* [*methodischen Eigenart*] supervenes on the primary-originality, which objectively distinguishes [the primary-originality] from all qualities of indefinite-ness with which gradual-progression is afflicted."[43] This means that all cultures, including Judaism, have an original drive toward speculation. However, the ways in which this core element is developed may vary from culture to culture. Thus, we must distinguish between a loose, general sense of the term 'philosophy' and the stricter, methodological sense of the term. According to Cohen, the latter refers specifically to the path developed by the culture of ancient Greece: "The Greeks bestowed on philosophy a characteristic-feature, which likewise distin-guishes it from all speculation—be it ever so profound—of other peoples."[44] This "characteristic-feature" entailed the application of the *method of science* to ques-tions of reason and speculation; as Cohen stated earlier in his introduction, "Phi-losophy is the science of reason."[45] Thus, Cohen's initial statement, that Judaism has no share in philosophy, simply refers to the uncontroversial observation that the classical Jewish sources do not employ a scientific philosophical methodology.

However, because the Jewish sources *do* share in the primary-originality of reason, we should also be able to find elements in them that correspond to some form of rational thought, that is, to 'philosophy' in the general sense. As Cohen puts it, "The Jews indeed resisted their [i.e., the Greeks'] science; however, they could not furnish any resistance to their philosophy ... the universal character of reason, even if science is excluded, connects religion with philosophy."[46] Here, when Cohen says that the Jews could not resist "their philosophy," we should *not* take this to mean that the Jews were unable to resist the Greeks' scientific method of doing philosophy; on the contrary, they *did* resist this method, which Cohen indicates by saying that the Jews resisted "their science." Rather, Cohen is saying that although the Jews resisted the Greeks' scientific method of speculation, they did engage in their own, different type of rational speculation.[47] Furthermore, as Cohen subsequently makes clear, the development of this form of reasoning took place prior to and independently of the direct Greek influence on later Jewish history; the connection to philosophical reason is native to the "*ur*-thought" (*Urgedanken*) of the Jewish biblical sources.[48]

Having argued for the a priori necessity of a connection between 'philosophy' and the Jewish sources, Cohen is thereby able to justify the basic project of *Reli-gion of Reason*: "Therefore it will be our task to investigate in the sources of Juda-ism the philosophic *ur*-motifs in which, and by virtue of which, the religion of reason is able to push its way through."[49] In other words, the philosophic ele-ments latent in the Jewish sources are only "*ur*-motifs," not fully developed philo-sophical concepts. In their current form, their rational potential does not always present itself with full clarity. However, when *Cohen approaches the sources* with his philosophical methods and tools, he will be able to 'clear away the dust' so as to display the underlying forms and patterns of reasoning whose consistent appli-cation gives rise to the religion of reason.

However, although the Jewish sources contain 'philosophical elements' in a general sense, it is incorrect and misleading to describe them as 'having their own philosophy' or as 'philosophical' in their own right. As Cohen emphasizes, "We should not resist the fact that the concept of philosophy is changed and distorted [*entstellt*] if it is not practiced as scientific philosophy."[50] Cohen's point in linking the sources to philosophy is simply to emphasize that, when *approached through scientific philosophy*, the sources *are capable of* giving rise to concepts of greater philosophical clarity—not that they already or inherently do so.

The above description, notably, would also be in keeping with Cohen's earlier project of dissolving religion into philosophical Ethics. In that project, one would apply the philosophical method to the sources in order to eliminate their mythological vagueness and thereby display their underlying philosophical *ur*-motifs. In *Religion of Reason*, conversely, while Cohen still calls for the sources to be *further* clarified through philosophical analysis, he no longer insists on their *complete* philosophization. As we shall see, the lack of full conceptual clarity in the sources of Judaism is not *merely* a sign of their philosophical underdevelopment. Rather, their very 'vagueness' may also be a sign that they have *preserved* something that would necessarily be absent from a fully philosophical account. However, this proposed 'something' remains problematic; while Cohen does not call for complete elimination of unclarity through philosophy, he also never says that one should 'stop short' in one's task of philosophically clarifying the sources. Thus, Cohen is faced with a thorny dilemma: without full philosophical development, the sources will retain mythical, and hence ethically problematic, elements. However, a full elimination of mythical sources will lead to an equally problematic totalization. As we shall see, there is no theoretical or static alternative to this unappealing forced choice between mythology and totalization.

IV. Religion and Ethics in Conflict

Cohen explores the dynamics of this predicament through a renewed examination of the relationship between philosophy and religion. Up to this point, it has seemed as if religion and philosophy might be able to 'play nicely' together: both were legitimate and necessary sub-spheres of reason. Because reason does not exhaust itself in either of them, religion is able to address aspects of reason that philosophy cannot, and vice versa. However, it now becomes evident that the relation between the two is not quite so harmonious.

Cohen has set up the concept of 'religion' and has distinguished it from 'philosophy', without yet clarifying *what* religion consists in. He now tells us, "Since religion has been defined as the religion of reason, *man* is established as its sphere as well as its content."[51] Thus, religion will provide some sort of knowledge about the character of human beings. This claim seems innocuous enough. However, when we inquire about the particular *content* of that knowledge, we find that that content may in fact be empty. "It may appear as if all contributions, which are comprised under the scientific knowledge of man, are already exhausted . . . Ethics, as a branch in the system of philosophy, confronts us with the claim that it governs all affairs of man and that it must therefore deny a similar share in the knowledge of man to every other mode of knowing and thus also to religion, insofar as it claims to be one such [mode of knowing]."[52] Cohen thus presents Ethics as a 'jealous god': Ethics claims to be able to provide everything there is to know about man. Other modes of knowing may produce knowledge about other topics, or they may address aspects of man besides knowledge, but they cannot provide any *knowledge* about *man*. Put negatively, anything that falls outside the grasp of Ethics is either not knowledge or it is not about man. The presumption on the part of religion to provide unique knowledge of man thus directly assaults Ethics' self-presentation as the sole source of such knowledge.

As a result of Ethics' refusal to "share" the knowledge of man, Cohen's carefully balanced conceptual structure of the previous section is called into question. There, he had posited religion simply as a formal entity: let X designate a mode of knowledge that has a share in reason (and thus contributes to knowledge) yet is distinct from philosophy. Now Ethics, as a branch of philosophy, comes along and says: there can be no such thing. While Cohen is certainly entitled to posit such an X, it may turn out that X is empty, just as if he had said: let X be a rational number such that $X^2 = 2$. This challenge to Cohen's account of religion raises the possibility that Cohen's philosophical opponents from the previous section—who viewed religion as arising from animal instincts, the imagination, or various other non-rational sources—were not necessarily prejudiced despisers of religion. Rather, their refusal to acknowledge religion's share in reason may have been the natural consequence of their faithful commitment to the method of philosophy and Ethics. In other words, once they recognized that religion differed from philosophy and yet appeared to deal with the concept of man, they were *obligated* to deny religion any unique contribution to rational knowledge.[53]

In contrast to this quite 'logical' conclusion, Cohen is determined to maintain religion's share in reason. However, he can see only two possible options, both of which "seem equally disastrous for the problem of the religion of reason."[54] The first option, reminiscent of Cohen's own earlier project of *Auflösung*,[55] would be to locate religion within the domain of Ethics. In this case, religion does provide rational knowledge of man, but it no longer retains its own distinctiveness (*Eigenart*). It becomes simply an idiosyncratic name for a particular sub-branch of Ethics and contributes no *unique* knowledge of its own. The *distinct* problem of a religion of reason is thus "invalidated" (*hinfällig*), thereby undermining Cohen's stated project.[56]

The second option, which would preserve both the rationality and the distinctness of religion, is predicated on the insufficiency of Ethics: "Contrary to all expectations, it might turn out that Ethics, as a branch in systematic philosophy, having heretofore been described as one such [branch], is not sufficiently capable of mastering the entire content of man and that religion, for its part, might be able to provide a supplementation, a filling-in of this lacuna."[57] This approach, though, would undermine the coherency of the method of Ethics, to which Cohen is also committed. If there were a sector of knowledge that only religion could access, then religion would have to enter into the system of philosophy (understood as the science of reason, which produces knowledge), alongside logic, Ethics, and aesthetics. In this case, however, "the methodological concept of Ethics would become ambiguous . . . the danger would arise of a methodological conflict within the domain of philosophy. There cannot be two self-sufficient methods, side by side, for the problem of man."[58] If there were two independent, non-identical methods within the same system, they would inevitably give different accounts of the content of the concept of man.[59] Ethics would say: *this* is what is true of man, while religion would say: no, *this* is what is true of man. Thus, the system would be rendered inconsistent. Because Cohen remains committed to the consistency of the system of philosophy, he does not support bringing religion into the system, and he upholds Ethics' claim to unique governance of knowledge of the concept of man. In this, he differs from other thinkers who would do away with systematic Ethics or with the philosophical system itself because of its failure to accommodate religion, as well as from those who would grant religion autonomous content.

Cohen is therefore, by his own admission, left at a true impasse. His proposed notion of religion and philosophy as dual, non-identical domains of reason leads to contradiction and cannot be consistently maintained. Religion must be rational and distinct from Ethics, yet Ethics cannot and should not share its systematic role with religion.[60] He has, in effect, constructed an elegant *reductio ad absurdum* refutation of the possibility of a religion of reason—but this in itself should indicate to the reader the paradoxical direction of Cohen's argument. While his introduction will subsequently (attempt to) describe the unique content that religion contributes, we deliberately postpone our examination of those passages until the next chapter. For now, we leave the contradiction hanging, in order to underscore the fact that Cohen never overcomes, nor claims to overcome, the theoretical 'impossibility' of his project.

Instead, we turn to Cohen's discussion of the sources of Judaism. In Cohen's portrayal, these sources are characterized by a fundamental *multiplicity*. This multiplicity, furthermore, displays a structural similarity to the multiplicity that we have already observed within reason, namely, that of philosophy and religion. The latter multiplicity, to be sure, turned out to be contradictory. However, by examining the different functions of multiplicity within the Jewish textual tradition,

Cohen accustoms the reader to the notion that conceptual 'inconsistencies' can coexist alongside a functional unity. In his account of the tradition, particularity and universality; theory and praxis; and preservation and innovation remain inextricably bound to one another in a creative tension. Outwardly, he does not directly present the Jewish sources as a normative model for the presentation of the religion of reason, but merely puts forth a descriptive account of a particular historical tradition. Yet, as we shall see, this 'innocent' historical account is not quite so innocent, as he will later appropriate the structure of these sources for the communicative style of his own book.[61]

V. Biblical Multiplicity

According to Cohen, the sources of Judaism are predicated on the basic-idea of the unique God. Yet, despite the practical unity and coherence of this idea, its literary manifestations lack a corresponding theoretical unity: "The products of this basic-idea are manifold [*mannigfaltig*], as they traverse a long distance. And even the first beginnings do not lack a great multiplicity [*Mannigfaltigkeit*], an apparent contradictoriness [*Gegensätzlichkeit*]."[62] Cohen's reference to "the first beginnings" (*die ersten Anfänge*), is likely an allusion to the creation account(s) in the opening chapters of Genesis. While much interpretative ink has been spilled in trying to reconcile the two accounts, Cohen treats the multiplicity as an expected and perhaps even necessary feature of any attempt to convey the idea of the unique God.[63] Though Cohen does not say so explicitly, the implication seems to be that if an interpretation *were* to achieve true harmony and consistency, the practical idea would be flattened and distorted.[64]

Cohen highlights Deuteronomy as another example of practical unity alongside conceptual multiplicity. He notes the peculiar formulation of Deuteronomy 4:5–6, in which "statutes and ordinances" are described as the Israelites' "wisdom." While one might normally be inclined to think of 'wisdom' in terms of intellectual or theoretical capabilities, it is here applied to a corpus of specific concrete laws and regulations. For Cohen, this oddity reveals an essential feature of biblical thought: "Deuteronomy posits a reciprocal relationship [*Wechselwirkung*] between religious theory and ethical practice ... This connection between theory and practice remains definitive for Judaism and therefore for its literary sources as well. The whole Pentateuch has this consistent double-character [*einheitlichen Doppelcharakter*]."[65] Theory is thus not a fully independent domain, separate from practice; rather, it is always grounded in practical tasks and actions. That is to say, with regard to Jewish religion, there is no autonomous theoretical content: all ostensible 'theory' points beyond itself to embodiment in action. Accordingly, we can begin to ask whether this practical nature of religious theory acts to prevent full systematic consistency in its presentation.[66]

Examining the prophetic texts, Cohen locates another type of multiplicity in their approach to received authority and tradition. He identifies the sources' "duality" (*Doppeltheit*) as their "greatest riddle": "In all other religious traditions there is only one origin, and only one kind of source. Israel also constitutes an exception here, and this exception continues to uninterruptedly bring forth ever-new exceptions. The prophets are independent bearers of the tradition alongside Moses, who lies far from them, in deep darkness, so that they themselves have to lift the veil of myth from off of him."[67] Normally, there would be a single original source of authority, to which all later figures would trace themselves back. Here, however, the prophets proclaim their own authority, yet without denigrating or rejecting Moses' authority. They present their teaching neither as analytically derived from what came before nor as completely separate and different.[68] Their reception of the past is a demythologizing interpretative act: they must base themselves on their Mosaic sources, but must not simply pass them on unchanged. Cohen's assertion of an inner-biblical correlation of *traditio* and *traditum* has been also been corroborated by more recent biblical scholars.[69] For our purposes here, we can note that Cohen does not seem to attribute the prophetic re-origination of the tradition to this or that shortcoming in the particular details of Moses' words. Rather, the very act of *having received* the ideas of religion creates the need for renewed 'demythologizing' and dynamic reappropriation. While some ideas may be able to be passed on unchanged, there is something in the idea of the unique God that requires a continuous re-origination. Thus, Cohen may view his own relation to the prophets (and to the sources generally) as analogous to the relation of the prophets to Moses.

VI. *Multiplicity, Orality, and Interpretation in Rabbinic Literature*

Moving beyond the biblical canon, Cohen applies this same conception of religious transmission and communication to post-biblical Judaism as well. He describes the scribes, the *sofrim*, as "new bearers of the old word" and argues that their very name carries an historical contradiction, "since they were, on the contrary, speakers, as of old only the prophets and singers were."[70] While we might tend to think of writing as separate from speaking, Cohen emphasizes that the two were not separable for the scribes.[71] Thus, their transmission of the fixed written canon was interwoven with their handing down of the more fluid "oral teaching" that accompanied it.[72] In ascribing equal significance to the oral teaching, the scribes were not egoistically seeking "to match themselves against the authority of the Bible"; rather, the concept of the oral teaching sprang from "the fundamental-power of the nation-spirit . . . which also recognized its right even with regard to the original teaching, and which wanted to and had to assert itself in its homogenous development of the original teaching."[73] Here, the oral teaching refers not to a fixed corpus, but rather to each scribe's prerogative to provide a performative explanation of the written material that he passed down. As in the case of the prophets, the original teaching could be successfully transmitted *only* by being orally (re-)shaped by those doing the transmitting.[74] They "had to" assert their independent power, not in order to supersede the Torah, but precisely in order to transmit it.[75] As such, the Talmud and the midrashic collections must be viewed as equally valid sources of Judaism; their chronological distance from a 'first origin' does not diminish their authority, since the ideas of religion, by their nature, are subject to a continual re-origination. The oral is not subordinated to the written; rather, the two stand in a correlation to one another.

The "duality" (*Doppeltheit*) of the sphere of religion also manifests itself within the oral teaching itself. Just as Cohen pointed to Deuteronomy's correlation of practice and theory, so the oral teaching consists of the apparent disjunction of halakhah and aggadah. In this case, halakhah seems associated with the particular and the concrete, while aggadah connotes non-concrete teachings, principles, and stories. Despite their formal differences, Cohen traces out the underlying unity that joins the two together. The collections of midrash, for example, employ the same method to produce both halakhic midrash and aggadic midrash; the one Torah gives rise to both to both equally. Likewise, the Talmud consists not only of halakhah; rather, "in the middle of juridical discussion, a homily suddenly entwines itself with comfortable edification. It is characteristic of this duality that it does not place two separate style-forms next to each other, but places these like branches growing out of the same tree."[76] Here, as with the other correlations produced by the primary origin, neither of the two components have an autonomous significance. One does not understand the first in isolation and then move on to understand the second. Instead, each is the necessary complement of the other: the aggadah illuminates more general ethical and religious significance of the specific laws, while the halakhah clarifies the particular practical implications of the edifying stories and teachings.[77] Accordingly, as one finds in the Talmud, an attempt to communicate the ideas of religion requires a continuous back-and-forth movement between the two.[78] This stylistic alternation is strikingly similar to Cohen's own alternation between "scriptural" and "philosophical" passages in the main body of *Religion of Reason,* and it seems likely that he may have drawn some inspiration for his style from its talmudic counterpart. In both cases, the nature of the ideas under consideration gives rise to a non-consistency of style that conveys a practical unity. Using Cohen's metaphor, the "tree" itself cannot be displayed directly, and one can communicate its features only by swinging back and forth between its apparently incongruous "branches."

Returning to the theme of the oral and written teachings, Cohen now draws a sharp distinction (though not a separation) between them. The oral teaching, with its unity that underlies the duality of halakhah and aggadah, "is spontaneous [*unmittelbar*], as the 'fruit of the lips,' whereas the written teaching is stamped on brazen tablets."[79] Cohen's use of the phrase 'fruit of the lips' alludes to Isaiah 57:19, where God declares, *borei niv sefataim*, "I create the fruit of the lips." While the plain sense of 'fruit of lips' in this verse is simply 'speech,' later Jewish interpreters have associated it with prophetic speech in particular, linking *niv* (fruit) with *nevuah* (prophecy).[80] In this reading, since God says, "I create the fruit of the lips," then 'fruit of the lips' must mean speech created by God, that is, prophecy. By drawing upon this tradition, Cohen implies that the oral teaching is itself akin to prophecy, in the sense of an independent origination of the teaching of religion. As we have seen, Cohen had already indicated that *every* teaching of religion can be communicated only through independent re-origination; he now makes the link to prophecy more explicit. (Indeed, given that Cohen is about to expound his own teaching of religion, he even seems to be placing *himself* in the role of prophet!) In addition, the appearance in Isaiah of the word *borei*, 'create,' further underscores Cohen's view of the oral teaching as a new origination. In a view consonant with much of earlier Jewish tradition, Cohen associates 'creation' precisely with a new and independent event that is not merely the product of a previous cause (cf. 'creation from nothing'). Thus, the acts of speech that constitute the oral teaching are not analytically derived or determined from received tradition; they are new, synthetic creations, whose unity is established by the primary originality, by God.[81]

Cohen does not confine this re-origination to the corpus of classical rabbinic literature: the oral teaching "is not a production that is finished at once [*ein unmittelbares Erzeugnis*], but rather one that is not closed, one that unceasingly begets itself. The book is closed; the mouth remains open."[82] The connection with the primary originality leads to ever-new reshaping of the written teaching, and any attempted closure of the oral teaching would be a flattening devitalization. Every new act of teaching qualifies as a new origination of the oral teaching, which cannot, as religion, be confined to any determinate group or time period. This portrayal of the oral teaching helps Cohen make sense of the "otherwise paradoxical" rabbinic idea of "halakhah to Moses from Sinai," *halakhah le-moshe mi-sinai*. While it may seem strange that the rabbis would claim that their own innovations were given with the ostensibly long-past Mosaic revelation, Cohen's account of religion and re-origination also contravenes typical conceptions of temporal sequentiality. There is only one primary origin, but it manifests itself equally in each of its re-originations, so that every later teaching is also an/the 'original' teaching. Thus, the teaching put forth by the rabbis is also the teaching that was handed down to Moses at Sinai.[83] In a sense, one can say that it was not handed down *then* until it was proclaimed *now*.[84] This 'now' extends beyond the early rabbis to the teaching of religion at every point in time: to the extent that something is a teaching of religion, it too shares in the 'originality' of the earliest teaching.[85] There can therefore be no second-hand teaching of religion.[86]

Cohen further asserts that the idea of "halakhah from Sinai" arises specifically from "a critical self-consciousness with regard to the written law." There is something inherently lacking in the written text considered in itself. A written text has a static existence outside of any particular individual; in contrast, each instance of the oral teaching cannot be separated from the performative interpretation of a particular individual at a particular time. As such, it corresponds to religion's lack of theoretical autonomy. Thus, it was not simply the case that the oral teaching contained 'additional content' that *happened* to fall outside the bounds of the written canon; rather, because of its practical, non-autonomous nature, the transmitted teaching *could not* be confined to a fixed, objective written form.[87] Cohen links this non-objectivity with inwardness: "The critical *ur*-feeling of Deuteronomy, 'the Torah is not in heaven, but in your heart' [Deut. 30:12, 14], remains living in this idea and in the courage and clearness of this assertion [of halakhah from Sinai]."[88] Just as the teaching of religion did not originate only at one determinate point in past time, so too it cannot be located in space in any determinate location outside of oneself. One can identify something as separated from oneself only by objectifying it. Thus, the written teaching becomes the source of religion only by an individual appropriative act of interpretation: the Torah "should not remain only the written Torah: it is in *your* heart and *your* mouth; thus it *had to* become to oral teaching."[89] Cohen's use of the second person (preserving the language of the biblical text) underscores the relational nature of religion: the Torah is in "your heart," not in "one's heart." While an objective teaching could be comprehended by 'one' from a written text and would not require the equivalent of an oral transformation, the teaching of the unique God requires engagement from 'you.' As we shall see, part of the challenge that Cohen faces in the main body of his book is how to preserve the essentially oral quality of religion in a written form of communication.

Cohen asserts that the correlation between orality and writing in the rabbinic teaching of religion gives rise to a specific form of biblical hermeneutics. In explicating this mode of exegesis, he distinguishes it from two competing ways of understanding the rabbinic method. Though the external stylistic forms of classical rabbinic literature may vary, "[t]hey are all supported by the basis of *one* logic, one methodological deduction."[90] This accords with what we have already seen: the single logic of the primary origin and the teaching of the unique God, while unified in practice, produces a plurality of aggadic and halakhic forms in the theoretical sphere. However, while the terms "logic" and "deduction" could seem to connote a strictly analytic or deductive mode of reasoning, this is not so: "One misunderstands the talmudic exegesis of the Bible if one wants to understand it merely from out of the formalism of this logical deduction."[91] That is, the logic of the rabbinic hermeneutics does display an outward formalism as *one* of its aspects, but this not is its sole or determining feature. The rabbis do not move from the biblical text to their interpretation by means of a formal deductive logic, though their rhetoric may often create the illusion of their doing so.[92] The Bible does not constitute a set of axioms through whose application theorems may be analytically or mechanically derived. "The opposite is the case. The thought is thought—whether in aggadah as an ethical thought in the imaginative form of poetry or in halakhah as a law—for which one will find authorization in the biblical word after the fact."[93] While a formalistic understanding of rabbinic hermeneutics reduces the interpreter to a mere applier of mechanical rules, Cohen's description here seems to eliminate the significance of the biblical text, turning it into a mere 'wax nose' that will automatically validate whatever thought arises in the mind of the interpreter. In this portrayal, the justificatory biblical verses that are ultimately cited would be nothing more than inessential *ex post facto* prooftexts.

Both the 'formalistic' and the 'prooftext' accounts are one-sided: for both, the true source of the interpretation ultimately lies *either* in the text *or* in the reader.[94] Cohen's subsequent sentences show, however, that his understanding of the midrashic method cannot be reduced to either of these options: "Through this psychological form of thought, the title of the oral teaching becomes all the more understandable. Otherwise, it would be almost inconceivable that the memory of the Talmudist could have searched out the analogy for the directly present case from among the great treasure of the biblical word and its sentence structure. In the opposite case, the imagination becomes comprehensible."[95] One does not start with the verse and then derive the thought, nor does one start with a completely independent thought and then seek out a supporting verse: rather, the thought and the verse arise together in the imagination of the interpreter.[96] If the verse were *only* after the fact, we could not understand how the interpreter was able to find a verse whose very syntactic structure meshed so specifically with his thought. Instead, the verse must be both before *and* after the fact. The interpreter's previous engagement with and study of the biblical text shapes her thinking, so that the thought arises out of and through the raw material of the verses, but not deductively so: the particular interpreter adds something new in the new thought.[97] In this correlation, the thought cannot be separated either from the text or from the interpreter.

In this portrayal, it is not the case that the oral teaching is dynamic while the written teaching is static. Rather, the written Torah (in conjunction with the interpreters) plays an active role in the production of new thoughts beyond its initial plain sense: "Just as the problem is alive, so is the word. The written teaching itself becomes an oral one."[98] The livingness of the scriptural word is linked to the nature of ideas of religion: unlike theoretically autonomous concepts, they are not self-sufficient and cannot be statically comprehended by an individual thinker. Instead, they have their life and their continued existence *between* the thinker and the sources. As such, the written text cannot simply speak once and then 'die,' but must continue to speak. Similarly, the ideas of religion also demand the use of a faculty of thought that is not engaged by strictly deductive reasoning: "Logic attaches a seriousness to the *imagination*, because the imagination is carried and supported by the substantive seriousness of a problem."[99] If the midrashic interpreter were able to simply deduce his ideas from the text, imagination would be superfluous, but the ideas of religion cannot be derived deductively from an objectively external text. Rather, the interpreter must employ his imagination to form a 'hypothesis' that is based upon yet goes beyond that which is objectively given. In this abductive logic, the imagination does not run wild arbitrarily, since it is guided by a problem that, while not 'objective,' has a substantive reality outside of the interpreter himself.[100] That is, the interpreter's imaginative readings of Scripture are grounded in his pre-existing practical relation to the primary origin, to the unique God, and to his fellowman as You. If Cohen intends for his own account of religion to be interpreted according to a similar logic, he will have to find a way to encourage the reader to go imaginatively beyond the 'written teaching' that Cohen presents. As we shall see, Cohen's use of multiple voices may function precisely in this way, in that it staves off a merely 'formalistic' reading of his text.[101]

VII. *Judaism's Encounter with Philosophy*

Moving beyond the classical rabbinic sources, Cohen finds in medieval Jewish philosophy a precursor to his own philosophical-religious project. Although the classical sources displayed "traces" of philosophical reflection, they did not achieve the methodological objectivity that a scientific approach demands. In the Middle Ages, however, Jewish participation in the surrounding general culture led Jews to compose works of "autonomous [*selbständigen*] philosophy." This developing interest in the philosophical method was eventually applied to the traditional sources themselves: "[N]ow autonomous science establishes itself in the exegesis of the Bible, as of the Talmud. Often, it is the same authors who, alongside autonomous philosophy, devote themselves to Bible-exegesis."[102] At first glance, this development does not appear problematic: here is a method, here is a text—why not apply the one to the other? Given Cohen's previous account of religion and philosophy, however, we can detect a potential tension in the quest for a scientific reading of the Bible. Previous midrashic interpretation had *not* been scientific. For this reason, many of the traditional Jewish readings can seem fancifully distant from the apparent plain sense of Scripture.

However, this same non-objectivity enabled the preservation of crucial religious ideas that would disappear under a strictly scientific and objective mode of interpretation.

An actual example from the medieval *peshat* tradition of plain-sense exegesis can help clarify this dilemma. Commenting on the binding of Isaac, Abraham ibn Ezra writes,

> Our rabbis of blessed memory have said that Isaac was thirty-seven years old when he was bound. And if these are the words of received tradition, we will accept them. But from the perspective of reason [*mi-derekh sevara*], this is not valid, because [if this were the case,] it would have been fitting for Isaac's righteousness to have been revealed [in Scripture], and his reward would have been double his father's reward, because he willingly handed himself over to be slaughtered. But there is nothing said in Scripture about Isaac [receiving such a reward]. And others have said that he was five years old, but this too is not valid, because he was able to carry the wood for the burnt offering. The closest to reason [*ha-karov el ha-da'at*] is that he was around thirteen years old, and that his father bound him by force, against his will.[103]

Here, ibn Ezra explicitly places the two competing approaches to Scripture alongside one another. If we go by autonomous reason, we would say that Isaac was thirteen, but if we go by our received traditional sources, we would say that he was thirty-seven (or five). Thus, ibn Ezra recognizes two distinct methods, without seeking to assess which one is 'really correct': if we use this method, we get this result, but if we use that method, we get that result. The method of tradition (or what we might call non-autonomous reason) contains multiplicity (Isaac is both thirty-seven and five years old), while the method of autonomous reason produces a single best reading. One advantage of the method of autonomous reason lies in its ability to adjudicate between different readings. Under the traditional midrashic method, there are no substantial grounds for prioritizing the "five-years-old" reading over the "thirty-seven-years-old" reading. In contrast, the method of autonomous reason uses ostensibly universal criteria for eliminating invalid readings: 'everyone' should agree that a boy of five cannot carry wood, and that a willing sacrifice by a man of thirty-seven would have received greater scriptural mention. At the same time as it achieves this interpretive objectivity, though, the method of autonomous reason also eliminates the religious notion of Isaac's voluntary submission to God's will. While this loss might not, in itself, seem like a completely ruinous adjustment, it is a harbinger of the broader depersonalizing totalization that would result from a fully scientific reading of the biblical text.

Although it is possible to read ibn Ezra as paying mere lip service to tradition before going on to assert what he *really* thinks, we can also interpret him in a manner that places him closer to Cohen. It may be that ibn Ezra does not want to denigrate the traditional reading, but simply to emphasize the contrast with an objective reading. In other words, he may be saying, "It is fine and even good to uphold the traditional reading—but do not make the mistake of treating it like an objective or obvious reading. Do not *assert* such a traditional reading over against other readings, as though it had an objective ground." Thus, placing the methodologically objective reading alongside the non-objective reading can help a reader to see *how* (or how not to) understand the latter. Without this corrective, one is likely to slip into dogmatic assertion of the traditionally received readings, leading to interminable conflict with no means for its resolution. With the corrective, one can better recognize the traditional readings *as* traditional. In the case of *Religion of Reason*, Cohen will present source-derived and source-dependent formulations alongside formulations that accord with the method of Ethics. If the former were treated objectively or constitutively, they would conflict with the latter and thereby give rise to a logical contradiction.[104] In order to avoid this conflict, the reader is compelled to approach the 'religious' statements non-objectively—in other words, practically, regulatively, and appropriatively. The tension between the two modes of reason remains, but it becomes a fruitful rather than a destructive tension.

Cohen argues that the later course of Jewish philosophy reveals just such an attempt to maintain religion and philosophy together. Indeed, because religion is an ever-developing and never-completed ideal, philosophy even comes to play an active role in the production of the religion of reason: "The claim to be a source now inheres all the more in autonomous philosophical work, since the latter is the mother-soil of exegesis."[105] Philosophical work becomes a source of religion because the development of philosophic skill enables one to interpret religious sources properly. Because one's interpretations must accord with the universality of reason, the method of abstract philosophy can serve as a helpful guide, even though the particularity of the religious ideas must simultaneously resist expression in an objective or fully consistent form. Cohen represents this dynamic as "a hot battle at the border of religion and philosophy" that can never "be brought to complete extinguishment," and he identifies Maimonides as "the focal point of these unceasing agitations [*Bewegungen*]."[106] The controversy generated by Maimonides' work shows that the relation between philosophy and religion continued to remain in question: some Jewish thinkers rejected philosophy for its apparently destructive effect on traditional religious notions, while others came to view the traditional midrashic approach as non-rational and at best merely poetic. While Cohen insists that this "hot battle" must persist in some form, he wants to shift its locale to the inwardness of the particular individual. Instead of producing partisan camps, the 'incompatibility' of religion and philosophy should be the source of ethical energy that strives to put into practice that which cannot be brought to a theoretical resolution. He views Maimonides' successors as moving in precisely this direction: "Their efficacy passed over into devotional and educational literature. The title 'books of discipline [i.e., *musar*],' under which these books of ethical teaching were collected, settles the practical character of these writings and makes their value as religious sources indubitable."[107] By addressing themselves beyond their own borders toward a reader whom they sought to instruct, these texts were able to avoid the theoretization and totalization that otherwise characterizes many philosophical texts. They employed aspects of the philosophical method, but were also able to preserve the practical nature of the sphere of religion.[108] From his praise of such texts, we can hypothesize that Cohen's own book might reproduce a similar relation to philosophy, such that any apparently theoretical statements must be evaluated in the context of the ultimately practical nature of his project.

VIII. From Religion and Ethics to Philosophy of Religion

Toward the concluding pages of his introduction, Cohen provides an important key for interpreting the main body of his text. In the context of the apparent conflict between "prophetism" and "nomism," Cohen makes passing reference to the question of whether "a contradiction in principles must not also be a contradiction in the consciousness of the persons." He then answers this question in the negative: "The opposition in principles [*prinzipielle Gegensatz*] between intellectualism and mysticism already provides an analogy here; this contradiction, however, came to the most fruitful counterbalance in the most profound representatives of mysticism."[109] In other words, one should not gloss over the opposition in principles, that is, the theoretical contradiction. This contradiction is real, but it is also a necessary component in the generation of certain profound truths. Note, however, that the fruitful counterbalance did not manifest itself in a mystical *account* of human beings and God, but rather in the individual *persons* who inwardly negotiated the opposing principles.[110] In this description, Cohen seems to be giving us warrant to place his own work alongside that of the mystical rationalists and rational mystics.[111] Though *Religion of Reason* may or must contain an "opposition in principles" between the voices of Scripture and of philosophy, it may be that the two were held in fruitful harmony in the person of Cohen himself. Likewise, if a reader wants to appropriate Cohen's communication successfully, she should not look for a theoretical harmonization but must allow the competing principles to form a counterbalance in her own person.

Given this distinction between "principles" and "persons," we can better understand Cohen's opposition to what he considers a wrong type of distinction: "Commonly, a distinction is made between religion [*Religion*] and ethicality

[*Sittlichkeit*], not only between religion [*Religion*] and Ethics [*Ethik*]."[112] According to Cohen, even the latter distinction consists *only* in "the methodological distinction between Ethics and religion." In other words, Ethics and religion will produce teachings that *look* different, because they apply different methods (objective and non-objective) and thereby refract their shared subject matters of human beings and God in different ways. However, this difference is limited to the theoretical and semantic level. Apart from this, the religion of reason "can no longer recognize any distinction in content between religion and ethical teaching [*Sittenlehre*], between Jewish religion and Jewish ethical teaching . . . There is no separation in the Jewish consciousness between religion and ethicality [*Sittlichkeit*]."[113] As such, the individual embodied person will not be faced by conflicting duties or commands. He will not be told to do one thing by religion and another thing by ethicality. He will, however, have to perform his uniform ethical obligations without full theoretical comprehension thereof: when he *reflects on* his duty, it will divide itself into the two equally valid and equally necessary perspectives of religion and Ethics. When re-translated back into the practical sphere of existential duty, these two theoretical perspectives should again converge in a uniform imperative.

In contrast, a view that affirms a distinction between religion and ethicality will lead to ethically problematic results. Within such a split, religion will tend to become associated with duties toward God, while ethicality will become associated with duties toward one's fellow human beings. If duty is divided into two spheres, the possibility arises that one's obligations toward God might conflict with one's obligations toward human beings. At the very least, one might be compelled to make decisions as to which sphere is more deserving of one's time and energy. Those who rightly care about God will be led to neglect man, and those who rightly care about man will be led to neglect God.

In Cohen's assessment, the classical Jewish sources do not fall victim to this objective separation between man and God and therefore do not distinguish between religion and ethicality. Instead, they uphold the correlation of the divine and the human: "The concept of the unique God belongs to Jewish ethical teaching. The Jewish sources make it unmistakably clear that it was in the teaching of man, not merely of man as individual but also of peoples and humanity, that the unique God came to be discovered. And all the particulars in the wide manifoldness of statues and ordinances, every ethical regulation, every ethical precept, all are rooted in 'Hear O Israel.'"[114] That which *appears* to be 'about God' turns out to be also 'about man,' and vice versa. According to Cohen, the idea of the unique God came not from speculation about heavenly realms, but from pondering the proper relations between individuals and peoples: to treat others as equal representatives of humanity while still upholding their particularity *is* to treat them as correlates of the unique God. Likewise, a commitment to the unique God leads

directly to the various ethical obligations that constitute one's relation to one's
fellow human beings. In a sense, if all theology is 'actually' anthropology, so too
all anthropology is 'actually' theology: no prioritization of one over the other is
possible.

Because man and God are not separable, there can be no special duties to God
alone.[115] As representative of the biblical view, Cohen cites the beginning of
Micah 6:8: "It has been told to you, O man, what is good...."[116] The verse continues: "... and what the Lord requires you: only to do justice and to love mercy and
to walk humbly with your God." This set of commands functions negatively as a
rejection of the proposal of the preceding two verses, namely, that God desires
sacrifices of calves, rams, oil, and one's first-born and that these will bring one
closer to God. Instead, Micah proclaims that one pleases *God* by acting justly and
mercifully toward one's fellow *human beings*. These ethical relations with other
humans are the *only* thing that God desires. However, the rejection of special
duties to God does not preclude the idea of a special *relation* to God, as indicated
by "walk humbly with your God." Thus, Cohen will speak of relation to God in
prayer, love, and ritual. At the same time, these actions are not isolated from ethicality; they serve to shape the ethical self and therefore also strengthen one's relations with other human beings. There is only one ethicality, but in *describing* it
one speaks sometimes in terms of relation to God and sometimes in terms of relation to human beings. If we apply this approach to the main body of Cohen's own
text, we find that Cohen sometimes speaks from a 'mundane' human-focused
perspective, and sometimes from a 'divine' God-focused perspective. A debate
over which one represents Cohen's 'true convictions' is beside the point, since
each perspective represents only one part of a correlation and must be understood as the equal and necessary counterpart of the other perspective.

Cohen closes his introduction with a discussion of the relationship between
different historical religious traditions. Just as objective separation of God and
man can lead to a conflict of duties, so too a certain type of focus on distinctive
objective features in a given religious tradition can create conflict with and
unwarranted rejection of other traditions. Cohen emphasizes that it is only the
concept of reason that endows Judaism with its "true unity." Because reason is
common to all people, this judgment prevents the identification of Judaism's
unity with any empirical elements particular to the Jewish tradition: "All material
factors, no matter how much one continually tries to transfigure them, remain
material, as long as they cling to a community of blood. They also make spiritual
analogies, which are found *in other* blood-communities, difficult to understand
and suspicious."[117] Thus, while other thinkers might exalt particular practices or
Jewish bodily kinship as the unifying essence of Judaism, Cohen argues that these
"material factors" do not meet reason's criterion of universality and therefore cannot be *rationally* defended as providing Judaism's unity. While Cohen does value

the particularity of Judaism as a source for the religion of reason, this particularity is not an end in itself but must be critically shaped and interpreted in accord with non-particular criteria. Without this process of idealization, any glorification of the material factors remains on the side of egoism. Additionally, identifying any particularly Jewish factors with the essence of Judaism will inevitably place other traditions or "blood communities" at a disadvantage, since they obviously lack these 'essential' Jewish elements. In particular, since Judaism presents itself as a teaching about the unique God, a "material" understanding of Judaism will also attach material criteria to the God-human relation. Thus, even if the patterns of reasoning about God and human beings in other traditions may seem similar to those in Judaism, the difference in material factors will lead to the conclusion that other traditions must have a lesser connection to the unique God.

In contrast, the enthronement of reason as the "guiding principle" establishes a criterion that "calls forth and secures the community of spirit. From out of this community, the particularity of a specific religion does not become a barrier that might exclude the possibility of other religions."[118] While some might think that affirming the legitimacy of one's own religion excludes the feasibility of others, Cohen denies that this must be the case. If one is committed to one's own tradition *as a religion of reason*, differences in particularity will not qualify as grounds for exclusion. Importantly, though, Cohen does *not* assert the existence of a 'general' religion of reason that could be formulated apart from all traditions. Rather, the religion of reason always and only has its meaning in relation to *particular sources* of one kind or another.[119] As such, one is able to discern "spiritual analogies" only through familiarity with one's own tradition: through habituation in the exercise of drawing the religion of reason from out of one's own sources, one becomes skilled in recognizing the basic patterns of reason, and one is then able to recognize those same patterns when others find them in *their* sources. Like other concepts in the sphere of religion, these unifying patterns cannot be expressed in direct or objective terms, but only through performative movements that remain tied to particularity. Thus, as was the case with the plurality of religion and Ethics, there is no *theoretical* unity to the plurality of different religious traditions. However, a *philosophy of religion (Religionsphilosophie)*, by exhibiting the movement between source and critical interpretation, can illuminate the underlying patterns that connect the different manifestations of the religion of reason.[120] Such an endeavor would ideally be able to display universality, in accord with its philosophical approach, yet do so in a form that does not wrest away the particularity of religion.

Looking back at what has been presented thus far, we are left with two distinct intellectual constructions, separated by a persistent theoretical gap. On one hand, we have Cohen's account of the basic structural relation of philosophy and religion, wherein each occupies a distinct sphere under the broader domain of reason. This same account, however, eventually led to the conclusion that this proposed structure was conceptually contradictory, thus rendering the project of a religion of reason unfeasible. On the other hand, Cohen's account of the sources of Judaism raised the possibility that theoretical multiplicity or contradiction need not obviate a functional or practical type of unity and coherence. This *historical* example, though, does not answer the *philosophical* question concerning the religion of reason. While biblical or rabbinic sources may happen to display varying degrees of rationality, they were not explicitly composed with reason as a determining methodological criterion. As such, their multiplicity or inconsistency may sometimes reflect an insufficient degree of critical conceptual analysis. In contrast, *Religion of Reason* does intend to hold itself to the standards of critical philosophy, and so it cannot simply put forth rationally ungrounded assertions. Despite the suggestiveness of the Jewish sources, the 'impossibility' of the religion of reason still looms.

I argue that, as Cohen has presented it, there truly is no theoretical solution to this problem. Accordingly, instead of attempting to produce an unsatisfactory solution, he instead lets the contradiction stand and dives into an examination of the specific conceptual content that the method of Ethics claims to comprehend. There, he will performatively seek to display the shortcomings of this method, even though he still cannot assert that any 'knowledge of man' lies beyond its reach. At first, he attempts to do so directly, in a single voice. The failures and deficiencies of this direct analysis will then underscore the need for an indirect style, at which point the multiplicity that he has highlighted in the sources of Judaism will re-emerge as a primary model for his own textual style.[121] For the moment, though, we turn to Cohen's initial attempt to adjudicate the incompatibility of religion and Ethics.

3

Resisting Auflösung

A SINGLE-VOICED ATTEMPT

WHEN WE LAST left religion and Ethics, they were locked in what appeared to be a fight to the death. One either had to subsume religion under the domain of Ethics, in which case peace would be attained at the expense of religion's distinctness, or one could assert that the sphere of religion was needed to address conceptual content that Ethics cannot master, in which case the autonomy of Ethics would be compromised. Both options have the effect of undermining Cohen's project of a religion of reason. Whereas many thinkers, faced with this dilemma, would give up in despair, Cohen instead forges on, deliberately bracketing the methodological incompatibility of his dual commitment to religion and Ethics.[1] In this chapter, we examine Cohen's attempt to establish a place for religion within reason while resisting the dissolution (*Auflösung*) of religion into Ethics.

Whereas the previous chapter confined itself to those elements of his project that posed no significant challenge to communication, we here begin to address the inherent paradoxicality of the sphere of religion itself. Accordingly, although Cohen valiantly attempts to demonstrate the insufficiency of the method of Ethics, we also find that the ostensibly bracketed contradictions still prevent Cohen from consistently asserting religion's distinct rational status. Because, in his introduction, he attempts to communicate the conceptual content of religion by means of his own voice (as is typical of most philosophical writing), without relying on the additional voice of Scripture, he is forced to resort to irony and vagueness in his attempt to convey that which cannot be directly asserted. The communicative limitations of this approach thus highlight the need for a different communicative style and set the stage for the multi-voiced style that he will adopt in the main body of his book.

I. Religion and System in Cohen's Thought

Before examining the details of Cohen's attempt to negotiate the conflict between religion and philosophical Ethics, it is important first to situate this conflict in relation to Cohen's earlier thought. We noted in the previous chapter that Cohen does not provide a positive definition for 'religion.' However, he is similarly circumspect about what he means by 'philosophy.' Instead, he treats both terms in a highly formal manner, presenting them as non-identical sub-domains of reason. A reader of Cohen's previous writings, however, will associate the term 'philosophy' with Cohen's tripartite *System der Philosophie*, as well as his subsequent *Der Begriff der Religion im System der Philosophie*. I maintain that such an association is precisely what Cohen intends; as such, his discussion of the tension between 'religion' and 'philosophy' (or between 'religion' and 'Ethics,' where Ethics forms a sub-branch of philosophy) represents an important retrospective judgment on his earlier work. That is to say, the potential conflict between 'religion' and 'philosophy' corresponds to Cohen's attempt at assessing the potential conflict between his current thinking in *Religion of Reason* and his previous thinking in his *System der Philosophie*. Thus, while the main part of the present chapter will explore this conflict via a close reading of the text of *Religion of Reason*, I will begin here with a brief historical overview of key issues concerning Cohen's previous approaches to his *System* and its relation to the notion of 'religion.' In this way, a reader of *Religion of Reason* will be better able to appreciate precisely what is new and different in Cohen's final construal of the problem.

First, we should note the significance of the term 'system' for Cohen's thought. In the previous chapter, we noted Cohen's assertion that the "concept of philosophy is changed and distorted if it is not practiced as scientific philosophy."[2] Cohen's own *System* represented his attempt to practice philosophy in its proper, scientific form. Specifically, he seeks to produce a philosophical construction based on specific methodological criteria: only those concepts that satisfy such strict criteria can be included within his systematic account, while concepts that fail to meet these criteria must be excluded. In this way, as we saw in our introduction, his approach is characteristic of the neo-Kantian turn to 'science' as a means of avoiding the metaphysical excesses that characterized earlier German Idealism. By cleaving strictly to this method, Cohen aims to construct a unified conceptual account that corresponds to the unity of consciousness, the ultimate goal of the philosophical endeavor.[3] A central criterion of his philosophical method, and one that will lead to much tension with the concept of religion, is that of generality or universality. In order to qualify as a proper concept of systematic philosophy, a notion must be 'purified' of any non-general particularity. As such, the concept of the particular human individual—which Cohen associates with the category of religion—will take on a problematic status vis-à-vis the method of Cohen's philosophical *System*.

However, if we examine Cohen's earlier writings, we find that the problem of religion's questionable legitimacy may not immediately stand out in its full clarity. For instance, Dieter Adelmann points out that Cohen's concern with religion was not an entirely new development in his thought; rather, from very early on,

Cohen viewed an account of religion as a necessary and important counterpart to his philosophical system, wherein religion, by uniting the three branches of the system (Logic, Ethics, Aesthetics), would help the latter to achieve its goal of unity.[4] In this sense, the mere positing in *Religion of Reason* of 'religion alongside systematic philosophy' does not in itself represent a break from his earlier systematic thinking, since it is possible to view it as the enactment of a component that had long accompanied his plans for his system. Furthermore, argues Adelmann, it is not merely the case that Cohen's emphasis on religion is compatible with a non-rejection of his system. In addition, for Cohen, religion itself is crucially *dependent* on systematic philosophy, as only the latter can establish the ethical autonomy that serves as a necessary foundation for a proper conception of God.[5] In this sense, if religion *were* to break with the system, the rational foundation of religion would be undermined. For these historical and conceptual reasons, Adelmann maintains, the relation in Cohen's thought between religion and system should be seen as one of complementarity, rather than as one of conflict.

Here, however, a crucial point to consider is that while Cohen may have previously anticipated a role for religion, his sense of *what is signified by the term 'religion'* changes in important ways in *Religion of Reason*. In his earlier thinking, as Adelmann notes, Cohen sought to propound a "scientific concept of religion."[6] Such a concept could indeed complement his goal of constructing a scientific system of philosophy. However, in *Religion of Reason*, his concept of religion changes to include a focus on the individual's irreducible *particularity*, such that religion can no longer be equated with the method of science.[7] This change, however, also throws into question the relation between religion and the system. Cohen still insists upon the importance of the system, but the stubborn non-generality of the particular individual means that religion must necessarily stand in conflict with the requirements of systematic philosophy.[8] As we shall see, this is precisely the paradox that Cohen must try to maintain: religion is both dependent on the system, which must therefore be preserved (as Adelmann correctly maintained) *and also* undermines the unity of the system (as readers like Rosenzweig suggested). Cohen's refusal to drop either side of this contradictory pair of ideas means that an interpreter of Cohen's thought is likewise prevented from asserting either continuity or non-continuity between his final work and his earlier writings.

Another key point for appreciating the relation between *Religion of Reason* and Cohen's previous work concerns the particular *content* of religion. Michael Zank emphasizes that many of the key concepts in *Religion of Reason*, and precisely those that could most seem to indicate a break from his previous system, had in fact already been put forth by Cohen in earlier writings. For instance, as we shall see, Cohen places great emphasis in *Religion of Reason* on the idea of atonement as a crucial factor in distinguishing the I as a unique individual in relation

to the unique God. Yet, Zank's study demonstrates that Cohen began to highlight the importance of atonement as early as the 1890s and continued to develop
this theme throughout the period in which he constructed his philosophical system.[9] Likewise, while *Religion of Reason* marks out the particularity of the You as
a core distinguishing feature of the sphere of religion, Zank reminds us that
Cohen had already discussed the relation between the I and the You in his *Ethik
des reinen Willens*, that is to say, precisely in the heart of his philosophical system![10] Given these lines of connection, one could argue that even the focus on
individual particularity in *Religion of Reason* should be viewed merely in terms of
a stronger emphasis, rather than as a departure from a previous position.

In this regard, I posit that what is new in *Religion of Reason* is not the content of religion per se, but rather *Cohen's view of* the status of that content vis-à-
vis his systematic work. Though Zank is correct in showing the influence of the
idea of atonement in Cohen's *System*, it is also the case that in *Religion of Reason*, Cohen opens his chapter on atonement by emphasizing philosophical Ethics' task of "dissolving" the particular individual into totality.[11] Thus, the
implication is that the idea of atonement is incompatible with the method of
systematic philosophy; if traces of this idea did in fact remain in Cohen's system, this would indicate that he had failed to apply the philosophical method
with full and proper scientific rigor.[12] Likewise, while the correlation of the I
and the You does appear in his *Ethik*, Cohen's introduction to *Religion of Reason* (as we shall see presently) insists that Ethics' methodological goals of totality and of a unified systematic conception are incompatible with and must
eliminate the non-totalizable particularity of You.[13] While in the *Ethik* the goal
of totality was an unproblematic and straightforward good, it now takes on a
problematic and ominous character.

Thus, while the You *did* appear in the *Ethik*, Cohen here seems to indicate
that, methodologically speaking, it *should not have*—the strict process of conceptual totalizing ought to have 'dissolved' the You from the pages of that book prior
to its publication.[14] The historical and textual continuity of *Religion of Reason*
with his earlier *System*, as rightly pointed out by Zank, should therefore be distinguished from the conceptual *dis*continuity between religion and the systematic
method that Cohen highlights here. In a sense, one could say that by rigorously
developing certain concepts that he had included within his system, he came to
realize that those concepts stood in sharp tension with the method of that same
system.[15] As such, the 'break' from his earlier system should not be seen as going
'beyond' the system; rather, the break emerges from within the system itself.
And, once again, the story is even more complicated, since Cohen himself also
will still insist on a conceptual continuity with his system—but this claim of continuity is now, paradoxically, maintained simultaneously alongside his new claim
of discontinuity.

In addition to questions of continuity with regard to the content of *Religion of Reason*, there may also be key elements of continuity with regard to its method. As we shall see, and as is indicated by the full title of his book, Cohen aims to present a rational account of religion specifically by reasoning "out of the sources of Judaism," by interpretive engagement with Jewish textual sources. Yet, quite similar modes of such Jewish textual reasoning are also to be found in Cohen's earlier systematic work, particularly in his *Ethik*.[16] One can, therefore, plausibly trace back elements of Cohen's double-voicedness, his counterbalancing of Scripture and philosophy, to his earlier systematic work.[17] Here again, however, an element of discontinuity must also be noted: in the *Ethik*, while Cohen draws upon Jewish sources as 'raw material' and views them as highly important in this regard, he is methodologically committed to the notion that those sources can enter into the sphere of Reason only to the extent that they have been 'filtered' through the method of systematic philosophy. In contrast, in *Religion of Reason*, the Jewish sources are according rational significance precisely for their contribution of a 'remnant' or 'excess' that *cannot* be absorbed by the method of philosophy. Thus, as was the case with the conceptual content, while the actual employment of the method of text-reasoning can appear as an element of continuity with his earlier work, Cohen's assessment of the *status and significance* of that method stands in discontinuity with his previous approach.

However, while such elements of discontinuity play a crucial role in *Religion of Reason*, the elements of continuity are equally noteworthy and can help us to ward off a faulty understanding of the relation between the *System* and *Religion of Reason*. Cohen's presentation in *Religion of Reason* of the abstracting, totalizing 'method of philosophy' could easily lead a person to imagine that Cohen's earlier *System* must have been quite dissimilar to *Religion of Reason*'s 'Jewish' and 'religious' content and approach.[18] Yet, as we have seen, when one actually examines the *System*, one finds that it contains many of those very same 'Jewish' and 'religious' elements! In other words, the account of 'systematic philosophy' and 'Ethics' given in *Religion of Reason* does not provide a fully accurate picture of Cohen's own *System* and his *Ethik*. Instead, we can view his earlier *System* as already reinventing what 'doing philosophy' means, moving toward a more text-based and hermeneutic approach, and incorporating concepts such as atonement and the I-You relation—albeit in an partial manner, and without yet consciously theorizing the shortcomings of the totalizing tendencies of the method of philosophy. Thus, the present study focuses specifically on Cohen's description of the relation between 'Ethics' and 'religion' *as presented in Religion of Reason*; however, one should not simply assume that *Religion of Reason*'s account of 'Ethics' is fully identical with the content and method of his own earlier *Ethik*. Instead, the various elements of similarity or dissimilarity should be carefully examined in their own right.[19]

One final point that can illuminate this issue is to consider the similarities and differences between *Religion of Reason* and the work immediately preceding it, *Der Begriff der Religion im System der Philosophie*. This latter book was motivated in large part by Cohen's desire to respond to the critiques put forth his Marburg colleague Wilhelm Herrmann, who argued, notably, that Cohen's *System* was unable to account properly for the particular individual.[20] Herrmann maintained that in order to account fully for the religious experience of the individual, one needed to depart from the systematic method of scientific philosophy. In *Der Begriff der Religion*, Cohen attempted to show that it was possible to account for the individual without having to reject his system's method, thus seeking to find common ground with Herrmann while maintaining his commitment to scientific philosophy.[21] In the process, he goes so far as to admit that his account of the human being in the *Ethik* was incomplete and stands in need of a specific treatment of the particular individual, which is to be provided by religion.[22] And, broadly speaking, the characteristics of the sphere of religion in *Der Begriff der Religion*, especially with regard to the particularity of the individual, are essentially the same as those assigned to religion in *Religion of Reason*. However, while recognizing the need for the distinct sphere of religion, Cohen *does not yet admit any fundamental conflict* between religion and systematic philosophy, and it is this point that separates *Der Begriff der Religion* from *Religion of Reason*. He does acknowledge that, at first glance, it might *seem* as though philosophical Ethics demands the destruction of the particular individual—yet he quickly insists that to draw such a conclusion is an "error" that "misunderstands" Ethics and its method.[23] Instead, he argues that religion can preserve the particular individual while still functioning as a "homogeneous supplement [*Ergänzung*] to Ethics' conception of the human being: a supplement as continuation [*Fortsetzung*]."[24]

In *Religion of Reason*, by contrast, the claim of simple homogeneity is dropped, and he finally asserts that the method of Ethics *does* demand the elimination of the particular individual.[25] The totality at which the method of Ethics aims, previously treated as a fully praiseworthy goal of rational thought, is now critiqued as representing a harmful threat to uniqueness and individuality. Once again, though, Cohen simultaneously insists that religion must still function as a "supplement" [*Ergänzung*] to the method of Ethics, which remains unshaken.[26] In this way, he differs *both* from his previous approach in *Der Begriff der Religion* (which upheld the systematic method while maintaining that it does not demand the elimination of the individual) *and* from Herrmann's position (which called for a break from the systematic method, because it demanded the elimination of the individual): instead, he says that (1) the particular individual must be preserved, (2) the method of Ethics does in fact demand the elimination of the individual, and (3) the method of Ethics, with its systematic goal of unity of consciousness, must also be maintained in its full authority. One can easily imagine how an attempt to present such a position in a fully consistent single voice might prove challenging—to put it mildly. Yet, this is precisely what Cohen attempts in his introduction, albeit without ultimate success. And, within the framing background of the above comparison to his earlier writings, it is to the details of this attempt that I now turn.

II. Objectification and the Method of Ethics

Cohen proposes that we first examine the method that characterizes and constitutes the philosophical domain of Ethics, without immediate comparison to religion. When we do so, "we become aware of a deficiency that appears directly out of the deepest depth of the ethical concept of man."[27] Rather than declaring by external fiat that religion *must* stand alongside Ethics as a distinct sphere of reason, Cohen instead decides to look *within* Ethics itself for evidence that points to the need for such a supplement. With this goal in mind, he observes in the method of Ethics the following crucial features:

> Ethics, due to its methodological opposition to everything sensual and everything empirical in man, arrives at the powerful [*gewaltigen*] consequence that it must first and foremost wrest away the I of man [*das Ich des Menschen*] from *individuality* as such [*überhaupt*], in order to give it [i.e., individuality] back to him from a higher pinnacle in a not only elevated but also a purified form. In it [i.e., in this form] the I of the human being becomes the I of humanity [*Menschheit*]. Only in humanity is the true objectification achieved, which is able to ethically secure the human subject. As long as man is not capable of this objectification of his self, just that long does he remain ensnared in the vagueness of the empirical, and the purity, which Ethics in accordance with its fundamental method has as its task, does not come into being.[28]

Ethics seeks firm *knowledge* about man: it wants to discover truths that are *always* true of man. It does not want to say what is true of this or that particular human being, since one is true of one human being may not be true of another. Ethics must always search for general truths (things true of all human beings, of human beings in general), not particular truths (truths whose validity is restricted to a single particular individual). That is, if person A has red hair, one can certainly say, "Person A has red hair," but one cannot say, "Man has red hair," since this is not true of all human beings. Consequently, in its quest for the content of the universal concept of man, Ethics must treat "red hair" as indifferent and insignificant: it is not part of the *Ethics'* concept of man.

Furthermore, the truths that Ethics seeks must not simply be true of all human beings *at the time of the investigation*, but must also be true of all human beings *at all times*. That is to say, it seeks truths that will *always* be true of man and are thus time-independent. Thus, even if there were only one person in the world, and that person had red hair, one could not say, "Man has red hair," since that same person's hair might someday turn gray. In general, because everything empirical is subject to change over time, Ethics must eliminate everything empirical in its quest for the essential content of the concept of man.

Thus, when the method of Ethics turns its gaze upon the human self, upon the I, it is doubly compelled to strip away the I of man—that is, the I of the *particular* individual—from individuality. On one hand, the I, the empirical self of any given person, is different from the particular self of others: the distinctive facets of a given person's character and the bare fact of being this *particular* individual stand in the way of discovering truths about man in *general*. Furthermore, any single person's character—that person's I—may change and develop over time; things that are true of a given person at this point in time may not be true at another point in time. As such, the I of man, of a particular man, cannot be generalized. Since Ethics seeks only general truths, it cannot assimilate the empirical I of man and must discard it as inessential.

Instead of looking at the I of the particular individual, Ethics looks at the I of humanity, of *Menschheit*, of human-ness. Humanity designates precisely those qualities that are true of all human beings at all times, of man in general. Once we have abstracted away everything empirical and accidental, we are left with an abstract philosophical construct which, when examined, will provide the content for Ethics. From the perspective of the method of Ethics, the particular I that is discarded in the process of abstraction is counted merely as rubbish; its loss is of no significance, since it could contribute nothing to Ethics' quest for general truths. Indeed, the inconsistent, shifting I of the particular person *must* be abandoned, as one discards the rind of a pomegranate, in order for the purified and refined individuality of man-in-general to "come into being." Anything empirical retains an inherent vagueness, since it is subject to change and thus is not *always* true; accordingly, all empirical knowledge of man, however apparently consistent, remains uncertain and insecure. In contrast, the abstracted concept of humanity is no longer subject to change and can be judged confidently and securely. In Cohen's terms, the human subject has been 'objectified,' has been made into an object about which pure, objective knowledge can be obtained. Such objective knowledge is the task of philosophy generally; the method of objectification is applied to every topic that it examines, and the human self can be no exception. To be sure, the objectification of one's self may be more difficult than the objectification of other things, but the true philosopher will not shirk from this noble task.[29]

In presenting his description of the method of Ethics, Cohen attempts to speak from the perspective of method of Ethics itself. Every method of evaluation implies a certain value-system, in which certain things are deemed meaningful and significant, while other things are deemed insignificant and indifferent. Thus, the method of Ethics (and of scientific philosophy generally) treats everything empirical and contingent as insignificant, and accords value only to that which is unchanging and objectified. Cohen therefore speaks repeatedly of the "purity" that the refining and abstracting method of Ethics provides to its subject matter. As Cohen uses it, the term 'purity' has a distinctly positive connotation, implying not simply uniformity and consistency, but a freedom from undesirable 'impurities.' By describing the I of humanity as "purified," Cohen's description takes a specific stance that assigns undesirability to empirical individuality. Importantly, we should not impute this valuation to Cohen himself; rather, we can view Cohen as *playing a role* in order to bring out more clearly the implications of the method of Ethics.[30] The same can be said of many of the other valuational formulations in the above citation: from the perspective of the method of Ethics, the abstracted I of humanity is positively "elevated" and "secure"; the method of Ethics "achieves" the "true" objectification of the self. In contrast, if man is "not capable" of this objectification, then man remains negatively "ensnared" in the "vagueness" of the I of individuality.[31]

As we shall see, Cohen intends these valuations somewhat ironically. However, in another sense, he affirms them as the proper consequences of the method of Ethics. He does not criticize the method of Ethics for viewing matters in this way; on the contrary, this is what the method of Ethics is *supposed* to do. Since its task is to arrive at general, universally valid truths, it *must* wrest away empirical aspects of individuality. We can view the method of Ethics as an abstracting machine: put in messy, empirical matter at one end, and receive refined and abstracted generalities at the other end. The blame for any undesirable results rests not with the machine itself, but with *people* who use this machine exclusively for all problems.[32]

For the next several paragraphs, Cohen continues to speak in the voice of the method of Ethics. This rhetorical move affords him several advantages. First, he can continue to display the resulting products and valuations of the method of Ethics, so that his readers can better understand how it functions. Rather than attempting to define what the method of Ethics 'actually is' from a neutral perspective, he gives his readers a pair of colored glasses, showing them what things look like when viewed from the perspective of Ethics. Secondly, he is able to suspend his own *judgment* on the validity and relevance of the method of Ethics. Does he think it should never be used? Used with reservations? All we know is that the unqualifiedly glowing praise of method of Ethics is probably not identical with Cohen's own perspective, but we do not yet know whether the latter is wholly opposed to, or whether it simply differs slightly from, the perspective from which he speaks here. Furthermore, as we shall see, it may be that Cohen *never* passes judgment on the method of Ethics in a wholly direct manner, so that his judgment is not merely temporarily but rather permanently suspended.[33]

Thus, Cohen goes on to proclaim, in his best stage voice, that "Ethics can discern and acknowledge [*erkennen und anerkennen*] the human being only [*sch-lechterdings nur*] as humanity. As an individual, he can only be a bearer [*Träger*] of humanity. And as this bearer of humanity, he does not lose the character of the individual, when he thus becomes the symbol of humanity. Humanity alone con-fers upon him true individuality in this symbol."[34] In comparison with the previ-ous citation, Cohen has changed slightly his description of the relation among the method of Ethics, man as humanity, and man in his individuality. Before, Cohen spoke of the method of Ethics as performing an active and violent altera-tion, "wresting away" the I of man from individuality, in order to make man con-form to the criteria of general and objective knowledge. Here, by contrast the image is one of more passive discernment: Ethics can perceive man only as humanity; man as a particular individual is *invisible* when viewed through the method of Ethics. While the imagery of wresting away may seem to imply a deliberate and active choice on the part of the method of Ethics, the imagery of discernment emphasizes that the method is unable to do otherwise. Since Ethics cannot grant any significance to what it cannot see, the I of the particular individual can play no role in the concept of man within Ethics.

Thus, when Ethics considers an individual human being, it can only think of her as a representative example of the general and abstract concept of human-ness. Considered in her own particularity, the individual has no significance; for Ethics, she is only a token of the type of humanity, only a symbol that points away from itself and toward the higher universal form. Cohen's language of symbol and of 'discerning as' indicates the ways in which the method of Ethics can also be understood as a mode of hermeneutics: the particular human being is the text, which, when interpreted, is shown to signify humanity.[35] When one reads a text in this way, one does not accord significance to particular details of its word order, rhythm, imagery, and so on, but only to the general propositions and truths that the text symbolizes and 'points to.' Or, in a different metaphor, the method of Ethics performs an allegorical and symbolic reading of man-as-text: although the apparent or 'fleshly' sense of the text (the empirical individual) seems devoid of meaning, the purifying technique of allegoresis is able to access the spiritual sense that constitutes the text's 'true' significance.[36]

As an example of the fruits of the method of Ethics, Cohen next describes the relation between individuality and the concept of the state: "Humanity, however, is not the only symbol for the individuality of man that wrests him from his empirical ambiguity [*Zweideutigkeit*]. The abstraction of humanity actualizes itself in history in the *state*. The state is the transitional-link from individual man to humanity."[37] The term *Zweideutigkeit*—literally, "having two meanings, two interpretations"—aptly characterizes the problem with empirical individual man. Any two individuals, or any one individual at two different times, differ from one another and thus represent two different answers to the question of what 'man' is. Viewed empirically, 'man' appears to have not only two, but many different meanings, thus frustrating and precluding the single universal meaning that Ethics demands for knowledge. In response to this dilemma, the concept of the state steps in to provide the social-political means for achieving Ethics' requisite one-ness and *Eindeutigkeit*. It enables multiple human beings to place their identity in a single structure, thus coordinating and creating unity out of previously chaotic and variegated individuals. In addition, the various states are themselves to be coordinated in a federation of states: like the individual of the human being, the individuality of the state must also be purified and combined in a higher unity.

The constructive solution of the state and the federation of states allows Cohen to declare: "All methodological danger is now eliminated from Ethics. The individuality of man, which it [i.e., Ethics] grounds in humanity, is freed of any semblance of paradox: the state forms the mediation between the empirical individual and the idea of humanity, whose bearer man becomes."[38] The "danger" referred to consisted in any remaining individual particularity that would impair objectification and thereby prevent knowledge. Accordingly, the apparent paradox consisted in the fact that, while the idea of humanity in theory generates a unified concept of man, the actual lives of human beings continued to display non-unity. The state removes this paradox through its system of laws that coordinate all the actions of its individual citizens, eliminating disunity in practice as well as theory. Furthermore, the state not only governs outward behavior but also purifies any remaining inward deviance from unity: "In the individuality of the state, in which the empirical man participates with every fiber of his heart, in accordance with whose rhythms his own pulse beats, the miracle is actualized, which appears to lie in the ethical teaching of humanity as the fulfillment of man. The state, particularly in this age, makes it clear beyond every doubt that man circulates his higher metabolism in the organism of his state."[39] While the idea of pure human-ness, stripped of particularity, may have seemed like an unattainable hope, the state, wondrously, can bring it about. The state demands not simply legal conformity, but complete absorption into the social unity. Every last bit of each citizen's particular individuality is transferred to an identification with the individuality of the state. No connection remains to empirical individuality. The citizen's heart, his most inward yearnings, pulse in harmony with the state; there is no longer any individual will that could egoistically rebel against the universal directives and one-ness of the state. While his physical metabolism remains distinct from that of others, the higher metabolism of his mind and spirit have left behind all divisiveness of particularity.[40]

If the above description recalls the conclusion of George Orwell's *1984*—"He loved Big Brother"—this is no coincidence. Cohen aims to make clear that the method of Ethics, if consistently applied and carried to its logical conclusions, results in a fully totalitarian society, with no place for individual dissent, critical thought, or diversity. Anything connected to particularity must be smoothed away. Again, however, we should not view this panegyric to the state as representative of Cohen's own convictions. In contrast to the sentiment of this passage, we can be confident that Cohen himself would *not* describe the elimination of particularity as a "miracle," and that he would *not* agree with the wisdom of "this age" that finds man's highest calling in a total identification with his state. Likewise, he might say that the "paradox" of individual particularity that the state seeks to eliminate is in fact *not* something that should be eliminated: the paradox should be preserved and perhaps even embraced, despite the "methodological danger" that it poses to Ethics.[41]

In spite of their unpalatability, Cohen does not flinch from or attempt to mitigate the consequences of the method of Ethics. To anyone who claimed to have constructed a system of Ethics that left room for diversity and did *not* eliminate particularity and the I of man, Cohen would say: you have not properly applied the method of Ethics. While the desire to preserve particularity may be commendable on many other grounds, a strict devotee of the method of Ethics would have to attribute it either to unclear thinking or to a sentimental weakness of the will and a failure to pursue truly objective knowledge. In many ways, however, Cohen's over-the-top presentation of Ethics is puzzling. If his ultimate aim were to undermine the validity of the method of Ethics and its quest for objective knowledge, this lurid exposé would make sense: "We must rid ourselves of this inhuman method—look at the horrors to which it leads!" Yet, Cohen does *not* reject or condemn the method of Ethics. Indeed, in many of his other essays, as well as in the main body of *Religion of Reason*, Cohen earnestly praises, without any hint of the irony displayed here, the ideals of humanity and of the federation of states.[42]

In fact, even though I have highlighted the ways in which the current passages display indirect or ironic criticism of the method of Ethics, there are *also* ways in which we can view Cohen as sincerely affirming what he says here regarding the method of Ethics. The method of Ethics overcomes egoism, both on an individual and a group level. One person may often treat others as less-than-human, simply because those others are viewed as 'different' with regard to some aspect of particularity. This can take the form of individual egoism, wherein I treat others as less significant simply because they are not me, or of group egoism, wherein I treat others as less significant because they do not share my gender, ethnicity, economic class, state citizenship, and so on. The method of Ethics says: do not discriminate in this manner; rather, treat all others simply as representatives of a common universal humanity. By ignoring empirical particularity, the method of Ethics eliminates the risk of egoism on the individual and group levels. Because Cohen does oppose these forms of self-centeredness, it is possible to read the current passages as honestly championing a vision of the world in which bigotry and selfish greed are no more.[43]

Thus, these passages give rise to two contradictory readings, one of sincere praise and one of ironic denigration. I argue that we can view Cohen as intending both perspectives simultaneously, without privileging one over the other. It is not that he puts forth one perspective outwardly or exoterically, while esoterically hinting that the other represents his true opinion.[44] He does not say one thing for one audience, and another thing for another audience: he says both *himself*. We need not read this bi-valence as stemming merely from an ambivalence or vacillation on Cohen's part; he may have strong rational motivations for avoiding a single determinate response to the problem. For instance, Cohen is about to detail a "shortcoming" in Ethics' concept of man—namely, its inability to account for the You—for which religion provides a supplement. This could make it sound as if Ethics were 'mostly fine' in itself, but simply needed a little extra help from religion. In contrast, he wants to show that, consistently applied, Ethics is not simply slightly limited but radically destructive, completely dissolving particularity in its totalitarian uniformity. Yet, his commitment to Ethics' anti-egoistic universality prevents him from imposing any restrictions to the scope and validity of its method. He seeks both to wholeheartedly affirm and to wholeheartedly oppose the method of Ethics, without any compromise or middle ground. While a direct approach would have to choose one or the other of these attachments, his ironic-yet-sincere, sincere-yet-ironic presentation allows him, paradoxically, to maintain both together. We thus see that even Cohen's general overview of his project cannot completely avoid the stylistic indirectness that characterizes the main body of *Religion of Reason*. At the same time, an important difference between the two forms of indirection is that while the main body employs a back-and-forth alternation between more distinctly discrete voices, the introduction attempts to use a *single voice* throughout. Thus, while the main body can present each separate perspective 'sincerely,' since they are presented in succession, and not at the same time, Cohen's introduction must display two distinct perspectives *simultaneously*. His use of irony may thus be necessitated by his attempt to say two different things with only one voice.

III. *The Unconvincing Discovery of the You: Further Challenges for Communication*

The objectifying method of Ethics, if applied consistently, will decisively shape the status of one's relation to others. Drawing upon grammatical pronouns, Cohen asks whether the He, the other-person-in-general, is "only another example of the I."[45] Ethics must answer in the affirmative, since, once it has wrested away the I of the particular individual and replaced it the I of humanity, there remains no criteria for distinguishing between two people, between myself and another. Considered as individuals, both I and the other person are nothing other than identical bearers of the same general humanity.[46] Cohen, conversely, resists the conclusion, and responds, "Speech [*Die Sprache*] already protects us from this error: it [i.e., speech] sets up the You before the He."[47] Speech maintains the sharp distinction between the terms "You" and "He." The two are not interchangeable: We say, "You are," but not "He are," and "He is," but not "You is." While the third-person generality of the He could potentially be assimilated to the totalizing unity of Ethics, the particularity of the You resists this assimilation and thus exemplifies the conceptual characteristics of the sphere of religion. By virtue of this same particularity, the individuality of my I, as distinct from the You and therefore also from the He, can be reinstated. Because the I of religion arises in and cannot be separated from the engaged relation to the You, it cannot achieve the impersonal autonomy that the method of Ethics demands.[48]

However, the particularity of speech is by no means a convincing proof in the eyes of the method of Ethics. The "error" of identifying the I as merely another example of the He, and thus of neglecting the You, is no miscalculation or oversight on the part of Ethics. Rather, the generalizing stems from an inherent and systemic characteristic of the method of Ethics and cannot be 'fixed.'[49] Accordingly, after having raised the possibility of the You as distinct from the I, Cohen then asks, "Can [Ethics], in accordance with its concept of man, as humanity, be responsive to this classification of individuals [i.e., the You in its particularity], does it have the methodological means for establishing it, if its only goal is the *totality* [*Allheit*] that is fulfilled only in humanity? Must it not presume the task of such a division and gradation, the problem in general of plurality [*Mehrheit*], to be an aberration from its unitary [*einheitlichen*] goal of totality?"[50] Cohen's implied but unstated answer to these rhetorical questions is that no, Ethics cannot establish the You, and yes, it must view the problem of plurality as raised by the You, as an aberration. He refrains from stating this answer directly, since to do so would force a confrontation with Ethics. If Ethics were to be explicitly consulted, the more-than-oneness entailed by the irreducible difference of the You would have to be eliminated, thereby undermining his project of a religion of reason. For the same reason, he can gesture to the observed fact of speech, but he cannot directly assert the legitimacy of the You, since to do so would undermine the authority of Ethics. This persisting contradiction between religion and Ethics means that the You remains problematic and conceptually unstable.

Despite this instability, Cohen attempts to argue anew for the necessity of the You. When he does so, however, his argument contains a number of gaping holes. Here, I attempt to explicate both the argument and the holes, with the awareness that the latter may be inescapable and that Cohen may also be conscious of this. Cohen asserts that the You represents "a classification within humanity," even though "humanity itself is not capable of carrying out this classification."[51] The You is not a separate concept outside of humanity; it is a sub-concept *within* humanity. Therefore, it does not correspond to a separate branch of objective knowledge, apart from that which is governed by the method of Ethics. As a sub-concept, what is true of general humanity must also be true of the You, although there may be things that apply to the You that do not apply to general humanity. Thus, it seems that nothing that religion teaches should be in conflict with the teachings of the method of Ethics—religion simply *adds* things that the method of Ethics (necessarily) overlooks. However, because Ethics claims to provide all objective knowledge about man, that which religion adds must somehow be non-objective. Given this portrayal of religion, "the authority of Ethics remains intact. But its supplementation is no contradiction to unity of its method: for this method breaks down, must break down, before the new problem of the You, while on the other hand the concept of the individual demands this You."[52] There seems to be a bit of circular reasoning here. Yes, *if* we insist on having the concept of the particular individual, then we need the You, which the method of Ethics cannot provide, and so we need a supplementary method. But, on what grounds is this concept of the individual even necessary in the first place? From the perspective of Ethics, the particular individual was an unnecessary and even undesirable element that was supposed to be *removed*. Yes, the dissolution of the individual creates a totalitarian and depersonalized conception of humanity, but this is precisely the goal of Ethics and does not constitute a problem from its point of view. Thus, there can be *no reason from within Ethics* as to why we should treat the individual as significant. Ethics only "breaks down" from a perspective outside of Ethics.[53] Furthermore, because Ethics governs all objective knowledge of man, this means that there may be no objective grounds for the significance of the individual. One cannot give an objective answer for why a purely objective method is insufficient. Thus, while Cohen provides no grounds for his upholding of the individual, this may be due to the fact that *there are no grounds* that can be stated in the direct, single-voiced style that he attempts to maintain in his introduction.[54] Accordingly, Cohen's argument contains an unavoidable hole that can only be filled by the reader. Cohen can *point to* the disturbing consequences of the loss of the individual, and to the salutary aspects of the preservation of individuality, but the reader herself, as an existing individual, must decide whether the former are truly negative and whether the latter are truly salutary. Given Cohen's sensitivity to the limitations of a single-voiced style of communication (as evidenced by his sophisticated use of multiple voices in the main body of his text), we can surmise that he would not have been surprised by the presence of this type of gap in his own single-voiced argument.

Thus, Cohen's attempt to maintain plurality *while also* maintaining the totality and unity of humanity must result in paradox. If one focuses on the differences between individuals, unity disappears. If one maintains unity, difference disappears. Cohen's claim to maintain the You as a classification of humanity, to maintain plurality "within totality [*innerhalb der Allheit*]"[55] contains a tension that cannot be translated into a consistent, unified argument.[56] Thus, we can draw a connection between idea-content and style: the communication of a concept that goes beyond yet remains within the unity of Ethics demands a style that goes beyond systematic consistency and yet does not result in sheer contradiction and senseless discordance. If one attempts to present a concept containing plurality via a unified, consistent argument, one reenacts the method of Ethics, and thereby eliminates the particular and the You, turning the concept into an abstracted something-else. Anything that *can* be presented in a fully consistent manner falls within the boundary of Ethics. As Cohen stated previously, the particular individual, before particularity has been wrested away, is characterized by vagueness, ambiguity, *Zweideutigkeit*: in other words, by two-meanings, by more-than-one-ness. In order to attain unity, the method of Ethics must wrest away this multiplicity. Conversely, if one wants to maintain this multiplicity and plurality, one *must avoid unity in one's presentation*. The conceptual multiplicity and non-oneness must correspond to a multiplicity, a non-oneness, in presentational style. If a presentation of the You is fully consistent, it will give a one-sided and distorted account of the You. If it is to avoid one-sidedness, it must necessarily be non-consistent.

We can also express this situation in terms of voices. There are certain subject matters which *can* be communicated in a clear and consistent single voice. These subject matters—such as the concepts of general humanity or of impersonal moral duty—are those that correspond to Ethics and are suited to its method of objectification. Other subject matters (such as the You) are not suited to objectification and require an alternative to the direct single voice. This alternative can take many different forms; the crucial requirement is that one must break with the totality and oneness *somewhere*. For instance, one could do this by writing in a single voice, but eliminating clarity, so that each sentence is vague, poetic, inconsistent, or paradoxical in itself. Even an individual sentence, if it comes across as clear and self-consistent, will distort the non-objectifiable subject matter. Thus, one employs cryptic, non-concrete, elusive, or metaphorical language throughout.[57] Or, one could write in a *deliberately* one-sided single voice, so that one displays a particular aspect of one's topic clearly, even though it leaves out or distorts other aspects. In this case, one might then compose a second work that also speaks in a single voice, but from a different perspective. In this way, one could learn different things from the different compositions, even though both would also distort the subject matter in different ways.[58]

Or, one could employ multiple distinct voices within a single work. Each individual voice could be basically 'consistent,' and the break with totality would come from the 'incompatible' combination of different voices. It is precisely this approach, I will argue, that characterizes the textual style of the main body of *Religion of Reason*. In the three examples highlighted here, the break with determinate unity occurs at the level of the sentence, in the oeuvre, and in the single work, respectively. In contrast, if someone attempts to write a completely consistent, single-voiced work on, for instance, 'man as individual,' one will end up—even if involuntarily or unconsciously—distorting and reducing one's subject matter. Furthermore, even if a work on this topic *claims* to be consistent, a closer examination will inevitably turn up holes or inconsistencies that can never be completely eliminated.[59]

Additionally, we can draw a link between these communicative stipulations and Cohen's attention to language and grammatical pronouns. Both the He and the You have a share in language, just as Ethics and religion both have a share in reason. However, the He and the You correspond to different grammatical persons, to the third person and the second person, respectively. Just as the method of the He is not capable of attaining the You, we can also say that third-person language cannot adequately grasp or convey second-person content. That is, there is something contradictory in trying to talk about the You in third-person language; the second person cannot be properly translated into the third person. Even the phrase 'the You' already constitutes an abstraction from second-person to third-person language. The term 'the' indicates something general, determinate, and objectified, whereas, as Cohen has shown, the referent of a second-person address is not general but particular, and therefore non-objectifiable. Thus, while Cohen's formulation of "Ethics cannot discover the You" is problematic, it would also be strange had he written "Ethics cannot discover you"; there is no good solution to this dilemma. Thus, *to speak in the third person is to eliminate the You*, in a manner equivalent to the method of Ethics. This elimination occurs both in form (the word 'you' does not appear in third-person sentences) and in idea-content (one has turned the You into an objectified something-else). Thus, third-person accounts that claim to speak about the You (and other concepts of religion), even if they provide plentiful servings of 'religious' terminology, are likely to have unknowingly replaced their subject matter with an abstracted simulacrum. As we shall see, the insight of *Religion of Reason* is that one may be better able to convey the second person through a *doubling* of the third person, that is, by presenting more than one third-person voice.

IV. Broader Implications of the (Still Ungrounded) Sphere of Religion

Despite the 'objectively ungrounded' nature of the You and of the notion of 'plurality within totality,' Cohen proceeds to adumbrate further conceptual content in the sphere of religion. Thus, he examines various philosophical rejections of the notions of suffering and compassion. The ancient Greek Stoics, for example, "proclaim suffering as indifferent (*adiaphoron*) and accordingly exclude it from the domain of the ethical [*Sittlichen*]."[60] In contrast, Cohen insists that the other's suffering and my compassionate response are precisely that which generate the You and, correspondingly, the individuality of my ethical I. Cohen does not disagree with the Stoic position per se; because suffering 'merely' affects the sensual aspects of a person, a consistent application of the totalizing method of Ethics, stripping away empirical individuality, *would* rightly remove suffering from its sphere of concern. In contrast, the introduction of the You, which preserves the particularity of the individual, not only allows but demands compassion for suffering.[61]

Cohen presents a similar critique of more recent philosophical accounts of compassion. Even in cases where there is a desire to retain compassion within a philosophical construction of human relations, the method of Ethics makes it impossible to assign compassion any *rational* status. Thus, an approach that Cohen labels as "pragmatism" is able to retain compassion only by viewing it as a "useful illusion, through which suffering is lessened by being shared."[62] It cannot be anything more this, since the otherness of the You can be given no objective grounding. In light of this half-hearted preservation of compassion, Cohen acknowledges the logical consistency by which "metaphysics rejects this affect, because it presupposes only an illusion."[63] For Spinoza, according to Cohen, "compassion is of the same breed as envy," since both involve sensual passion, and both must be sacrificed in the construction of a fully objectified self. In this view, compassion is a "worthless illusion," not a useful one.[64] Despite this difference, both camps, as adherents of the method of Ethics, are at one in insisting upon the non-rationality of compassion and therefore of the You.

The acknowledgement of the place of compassion within reason, conversely, would lead to a reevaluation of corporeality and embodiment. The You arises precisely out of compassion for the *empirical, physical-emotional* suffering of the other. As such, the You is constituted by and cannot be separated from the particularity of physical embodiment; to detach such qualities from the You would be a reversion to the objectified human-being-in-general. The I that arises as the correlate of the You is equally bound to embodiment: "Bodiliness belongs precisely to the soul of the individual, and the soul is neglected if the plight of the body is neglected."[65] This approach stands in contrast to the body-soul dualism that is part and parcel of the method of Ethics. Because all empirical individuality must be wrested away, the conception of the soul and the self in Ethics can have no connection whatsoever to the un-totalizable particularity of the body. Any concern for one's own embodiment, accordingly, must therefore be classed as un-ethical egoism. The sphere of religion, on the other hand, opens up a conception of the self that (perhaps paradoxically) retains embodiment without thereby lapsing into egoism. Thus, just as the I of the religion has its life neither in self alone or in other alone, but in the relation *between* self and other, between I and You, it equally has its life neither in body alone nor in soul alone, but in the relation between body and soul.[66]

This discovery of the embodied self of religion subsequently leads Cohen to reevaluate other traditional concepts. Just as the I is distinct from the You, and is not merely another instance of the same general 'humanity,' so too 'my sin' is sharply differentiated from 'the sin of another person.' From the perspective of the sphere of religion, I can talk only about my own sin; there can be no such thing as 'sin' in a general sense.[67] Thus, Cohen states, "I should study sin in myself, and through sin I should learn to know myself. If others sin is of less interest to me than that I only learn to have insight into how I myself in my inmost being am afflicted with sin."[68] Cohen's first-person expression in this passage is crucial to the idea that he seeks to convey. He cannot say "a person should learn that he is afflicted by sin," since through this statement he would be attributing sin to "a person," when in truth he can only attribute it to "I myself."[69] He is thus forced to break with the third-person, single-voiced style that he otherwise attempts to maintain throughout his introduction.[70] If the concept of sin is tied to myself, I cannot make statements about sin that do not also include myself. The use of the first person makes the connection to self explicit. However, in other ways, first-person formulations can also convey the wrong idea about sin and other concepts of religion. Cohen does not want his reader to conclude that sin applies *only to Cohen*; he wants each reader to apply the idea also to herself. At the same time, Cohen cannot explicitly assert to the reader "You are a sinner" or "All people are sinners," since this would be a reversion to 'sin in general' and would undermine the particularity of the religious concept of sin. In a sense, the second- and third-person formulations are 'too general' and say too much, while the first-person formulation is 'not general enough' and says too little. The lack of a solution to this dilemma underscores the impossibility of a single-voiced communication of concept of religion, and sets the stage for Cohen's later use of multiple voices.

Like the concepts of the self and the other, the concept of God is also affected by the totalizing method of Ethics. Cohen acknowledges that many philosophical systems *do* incorporate a certain concept of God, but emphasizes that this concept, like that of the self, must necessarily be an objectified one. Holding up his own *Ethik des reinen Willens* as an example, he writes,

> If we remain with our own Ethics, which, more decisively than every previous one, incorporates the God-idea into the teaching-content of Ethics, its meaning [i.e., the meaning of the God-idea] still completely corresponds to the concept of man in general within Ethics. Just as man here [in Ethics] signifies humanity/human-ness [*Menschheit*], so too God provides only the completion of the doctrine of humanity. Just as man in Ethics is only an example of humanity, so too is God the only guarantor of humanity. Humanity is the subject of *general* ethicality [*Sittlichkeit*].[71]

Thus, we see that just as there is a correlation between self and other, so too there is a correlation between man and God. With regard to the former correlation, the method of Ethics produces and must produce a general objectified self that corresponds to a general objectified other (the He). Likewise, God corresponds to man in both Ethics and religion, but the God that correlates to Ethics' general, abstracted man can only be a general, abstracted God. In contrast to the unique God of religion, there can be no personal God in Ethics, since man as generalized humanity does not participate in *any* personal relations, not even with other human beings or with himself.[72] There can be no 'God of the individual' when there are no distinct individuals in the first place.

This objectification has nothing to do with God or with human beings specifically; rather, *every concept* in the "general ethicality" that Ethics produces must be general and objectified. Regardless of private piety, every philosopher who is faithful to the proper method of Ethics will arrive at such a depersonalized God. While it has been common since Pascal to contrast the God of Abraham, Isaac, and Jacob with the God of the philosophers, the proper contrast is with the God of the *method of* philosophy. That is, the root of the difference lies not so much in different kinds of people (e.g., *homo sapiens, homo faber, homo religiosus*), but in different kinds of method. Thus, even Cohen's own *Ethik*, which, he indicates, is more God-centered than any previous Ethics, had to present a generalized God of humanity. One gets the impression that Cohen would have very much liked to incorporate a personal God into his system, but that such desire and will were irrelevant: the method would not allow it.[73]

In exposing and criticizing these limitations of the method of Ethics, Cohen still confines himself to a primarily negative delimitation of the sphere of religion. Religion is presented as that which does *not* wrest away individuality, which does *not* insist on the identity of self and other, which does *not* eliminate compassion, and which does *not* objectify and depersonalize the concept of God. This underlying circumspectness may stem from his continuing awareness that the entire sphere of religion retains a problematic character vis-à-vis Ethics. He is able to say: *if* the sphere of religion were shown to have legitimate status within reason, here is what its concepts would look like. However, because he is unable to assert that initial 'if' in a direct manner, his further elaborations of religion retain an air of hesitancy. In striving to speak in his own voice, without the aid of Scripture, his statements end up taking on the form of a simultaneous saying and not-saying.

Cohen indicates his awareness of these matters when he describes the failure of Ethics to account for the particularity of the suffering other as the "border-point [*Grenzpunkt*] at which religion arises."[74] Thus, the content of religion is not something separate from Ethics, but neither is it contained within Ethics: it stands precisely *at* the border-point of Ethics, neither inside nor outside. For this same reason, though, religion's content cannot be stated directly. If it were outside of Ethics, it could be stated directly (although it would also outside of reason, and thus invalid), and it were inside of Ethics, it could also be stated directly (although then it would be subsumed under Ethics and would no longer be religion proper). This border-quality of the sphere of religion also means that its concepts cannot attain any theoretical stability. Thus, Cohen writes that "the interest in suffering and in compassion is henceforth recognized as an ethical [*ethische*]—in distinction from a theoretical—world-explanation."[75] In contrast to Ethics, which *does* produce theoretical explanations,[76] the religious concept of suffering can have meaning for practical ethicality, but can have no purely theoretical value; as such, one cannot make any direct, autonomously consistent assertion regarding compassion. Likewise, "[t]he God of religion is never a theoretical concept, never a concept that should merely broaden and clear up the knowledge and the understanding [*das Wissen und die Erkenntnis*] of man."[77] That is to say, the concept of the God of religion adds no theoretical content to a person's knowledge, in contrast to the concept of the God of Ethics, which does contribute to such knowledge.[78] Because Ethics must govern all theoretical knowledge concerning the human being, any presumed theoretical content on the part of religion would constitute an affront to Ethics' sole sovereignty. As such, any stable, concrete statements that would *seem* to follow from Cohen's account (e.g., "The You is uncovered via the rational factor of compassion"; "My ethical self is inseparable from embodiment"; "My own sin is different from the sin of others"; "The God of religion relates to the particular individual") cannot be defended in a 'consistent' manner: if pressed, he would have to admit the groundlessness of such 'assertions' *qua* direct, univocal propositions.

We have highlighted the tensions that crop up when Cohen excavates the contested sphere of religion. Without claiming to have solved the basic contradiction inherent in the idea of a rational sphere of religion alongside Ethics, he attempts to document the ways in which religion can supplement the inherent limitations of the method of Ethics. Yet, his attempt falls short; as I have demonstrated, his language takes on a tortured quality as he resorts to ironic formulations, circular arguments, and varieties of half-saying. These difficulties, I argue, expose the insufficiency of the single-voiced form of writing that Cohen employs in his introduction and point to the need for a different communicative style. While Cohen does not explicitly describe what such a style would look like, we can anticipate that it will bring together the three primary sections of his introduction: namely, it will (1) appropriate elements of the multiplicity displayed by the sources of Judaism in order to (2) address the structural contradiction between religion and philosophy/Ethics, yet (3) without devolving into the snarls of a single-voiced account of religion. At this point, the successful combination of these three elements may very well appear to be a supremely difficult if not impossible task. Nevertheless, I will shortly argue that the main body of *Religion of Reason* breaks free from the contortions of the introduction to display a style that enables Cohen to uphold both religion and Ethics through a form of indirect communication that carefully juxtaposes the voices of Scripture and philosophy. Prior to this, however, we must first map out some key elements of a theory of indirect communication. For this clarification, a figure who might initially seem like an unlikely counterpart to Hermann Cohen comes to our aid: namely, the Danish philosopher Søren Kierkegaard.

4

Making Cohen's Style Explicit

A KIERKEGAARDIAN INTERLUDE

THIS CHAPTER AIMS to correct for an omission in Cohen's own account of his project. In his introduction, he lays out differences between 'religion,' on one hand, and 'philosophy' and 'Ethics,' on the other. While the latter employ an objective and objectifying method, the concepts of the former preserve particularity and plurality, and consequently cannot be strictly objective. Despite its distinctiveness (*Eigenart*), Cohen indicates the sphere of religion cannot be presented directly, for it would then come into conflict with, rather than simply supplementing, the method of Ethics. Additionally, a presentation that attained full theoretical consistency would inevitably flatten and objectify the concepts of religion. Instead, the desired presentation of 'plurality within totality' demands a form whose multiplicity and theoretical non-consistency can preserve religion's characteristic conceptual features.

The main body of Cohen's book employs precisely such a non-direct style of communication in order to present an account of various religious concepts, including the unique God, the fellowman, atonement, and the messianic age. However, while Cohen's introduction indicates some general criteria for any communication of religion, we are not informed of the rationale behind his specific approach. He never provides the reader with an explicit account of what his style consists in and how it functions: he performs and displays this style, but does not describe it. Here, I seek to supplement Cohen's project by making the style of his text explicit, with a particular focus on the interaction in his writing between Scripture and philosophy. Although much of what follows is an extrapolation from Cohen's text, I consider it to be the hypothesis that can best take account of (a) what Cohen says in his introduction about the relation of religion, philosophy, and sources; and (b) what Cohen actually does with his source material in the remainder of *Religion of Reason*.

In order to provide a theoretical background for my hypothesis about Cohen's style, I draw upon Søren Kierkegaard's account of indirect communication. This account provides us with conceptual categories for the stylistic elements that operate only implicitly in Cohen's text. In particular, I focus on Kierkegaard's *Concluding Unscientific Postscript* (pseudonymously authored by Johannes Climacus) as well as, to a lesser extent, his *Practice in Christianity* (pseudonymously authored by Anti-Climacus).[1] Although Kierkegaard indicates that many of his pseudonymous works are themselves examples or performances of indirect communication, I utilize these two here specifically for their more direct account of a *theory of* indirect communication. That is, I seek their answers to such questions as: What is it about ethico-religious concepts that makes their communication so difficult? What are some stylistic guidelines for a thinker who wishes to communicate such concepts while avoiding distortion? What should be the communicator's own relation to her subject matter? While the pseudonymous authors Climacus and Anti-Climacus may potentially diverge from one another—as indicated by their different names— in many significant ways, I argue that with regard to the present questions they are largely in agreement.[2] Therefore, I use both of them interchangeably in my depiction of Cohen's style as an example of 'Kierkegaardian' indirect communication.

I. Cohen and Kierkegaard

At this point, the question might arise of why Kierkegaard would be helpful for illuminating Cohen. What has Copenhagen to do with Marburg? Since Cohen is typically viewed as a neo-Kantian rationalist, while Kierkegaard tends to be portrayed as an existentialist opponent of rationalism, it might seem as though the two would have little in common. I argue, however, that although their writings often *appear* very different, and although they often express themselves in divergent ways, the two have a fundamentally similar understanding of the personal and non-theoretical nature of religious concepts. Here, in order to contextualize this claim, I briefly survey previous scholarly assessments of the relation between Cohen and Kierkegaard.

As it turns out, Cohen and Kierkegaard appear to been placed in direct juxtaposition only infrequently, a lacuna that already serves to indicate that they have not been viewed as comparable, much less compatible, thinkers. When they *have* been juxtaposed, the comparison has frequently been one of contrast. Furthermore, these negative comparisons typically appear as brief remarks without further explanation or substantiation, as though the gulf and opposition between Cohen and Kierkegaard were obvious and self-evident. Thus, we find comments such as Michael Zank's: "In contrast to Kierkegaard and those close to Cohen who were influenced by Kierkegaardian faith beyond culture, Cohen affirmed the rationalism of religious faith."[3] Or, in Steven Schwarzschild's words, "God is for Hermann Cohen always the source of ethical freedom—thus ethically distinguished in his protest against Hegel from Kierkegaard's."[4] Likewise, according to Eugene Borowitz, "Rabbi [Joseph] Soloveitchik's philosophical content and method are more like Sören [*sic*] Kierkegaard than Hermann Cohen."[5] As might be expected, it is usually over questions of the rational and the ethical that the two are presented as mutual foils to one another.

In light of my examination of Cohen's conception of reason, philosophy, Ethics, and religion (as displayed in his introduction to *Religion of Reason*), I would argue that such perceived contrasts rest on a misunderstanding of both philosophers. While Cohen, to be sure, continues to uphold the primacy of 'the ethical'[6] (as distinguished from 'Ethics'), Kierkegaard, especially when writing in Climacus' voice in the *Postscript*, also upholds the importance of 'the ethical' as a task of inwardness and subjectivity, characterizing it as "the essential stronghold of individual existence."[7] Climacus' treatment of 'the ethical' stands in sharp contrast to Johannes de Silentio's account of 'the ethical' in *Fear and Trembling*. In the latter, de Silentio criticizes the limitations of 'the ethical,' which (in his use of the term) corresponds to the objective, non-existential, Hegelian universal. This account of 'the ethical' is commonly attributed to 'Kierkegaard,' thus giving rise to the apparent contrast with Cohen.[8] However, Cohen's own critique of the limitations of 'philosophy' and 'Ethics' could easily be reformulated in quite 'Kierkegaardian'—or rather 'Silentian'—terms.[9] Thus, one can argue both that Cohen is compatible with de Silentio and also that Climacus is compatible with Cohen. While such argumentation demands a much more extensive exposition, I hope that this brief indication can serve, at the very least, to call into question the 'obviousness' of a Cohen-Kierkegaard opposition.[10] If Cohen turns out to be similar to Kierkegaard, the view of Cohen as an abstract rationalist would have to be revised; conversely, if Kierkegaard turns out to be similar to Cohen, one would be compelled to reassess Kierkegaard's alleged opposition to 'reason.'

When we turn to the few scholars who *do* affirm similarities between the two thinkers, these are usually confined to a specific aspect of their philosophy, without assessment of broader overarching correspondences. Thus, for instance, Martin Yaffe compares Cohen's and Kierkegaard's analyses of Mozart's *Don Giovanni*.[11] Or, as Sylvain Zac briefly remarks, "Cohen holds, like Kierkegaard, that the individual does not exist empirically and that it is 'before God' that he traces the stages of his being-constituted."[12] In their treatment of Judeo-Christian historiography, Robert Jan Van Pelt and Carroll William Westfall transition from Cohen to Kierkegaard by noting, "Cohen's interpretation of the future-directedness of Hebrew historiography might seem like an echo of some of the ideas formulated by the Danish philosopher Søren Kierkegaard (1813–55). Like Cohen, Kierkegaard thought about history as a prophetic challenge."[13] Pierfrancesco Fiorato links Cohen's account of the messianic future to Kierkegaard's concept of repetition.[14] In a somewhat more extensive comparison spanning several paragraphs,

Katil Bonaunet argues that Cohen and Kierkegaard both present the concrete I as being formed in stages and that both locate sin outside of the domain of Ethics.[15] If one were to combine all of these isolated points of similarity, a more extensive and integral picture of Cohen and Kierkegaard's complementarity might start to come into view. The only example that I have found of such a suggestion comes from Samuel Hugo Bergman, who remarks, in a parenthetical aside, "It is outside the scope of this essay to draw a parallel between Kierkegaard and Cohen. Kierkegaard's struggle against Hegel, his transition from the ethical to the religious phase, from 'the general' to 'the individual,' exhibits many features similar to Cohen's, although, of course, the Protestant Kierkegaard and the Jew Cohen move in different intellectual climates."[16] It may be that differences in their "intellectual climates," combined with the outward differences in their mode of presentation, have played a role in obscuring a deeper underlying affinity in their ideas.

Although direct links between Cohen and Kierkegaard may be harder to come by, a consideration of the intellectual-historical streams shared by both thinkers can make the notion of their mutual compatibility seem less implausible. For instance, as noted by Bergman, sharp resistance to Hegelian modes of thought represents their most immediately shared connection. While Kierkegaard's criticism of Hegel is well known, scholars have also argued that a reaction against Hegel functions as a central motivating factor in Cohen's reasoning as well.[17] As mentioned above, both thinkers' emphasis on the preservation of the particular individual can be linked directly to Hegelian notions of the totalizing task of philosophical Ethics. Similarly, both thinkers objected to Hegel's attempts to close the 'gaps' to which he himself had objected in Kant's philosophy. Cohen rejects Hegel's identification of the 'is' with the 'ought,' of *Sein* with *Sollen*, of the actual with the ideal, and seeks to maintain the gap between the two.[18] This fundamental intellectual orientation manifests itself in heightened form in *Religion of Reason*'s emphasis on the conceptual and stylistic non-identity of religion and philosophy and in its corresponding refusal to dissolve the particular individual into totality. Likewise, in the context of a discussion of Hegel, Kierkegaard/Climacus emphasizes that ethical existence, in contrast to the Hegelian system, entails the constant maintenance of a similar gap: "Existence is the spacing that holds apart; the systematic is the conclusiveness that combines."[19] Their shared opposition to such systematic-theoretical closure—which applies just as, if not more, strongly to each thinker's general attitude and orientation as to their more specific philosophical assertions—thus represents a crucial common intellectual patrimony for Cohen and Kierkegaard.

Moving further back in history, we can also point to the two thinkers' connection to Kantian thought. Here, Cohen's share in this historical stream is more obvious, while Kierkegaard might initially seem a less likely candidate for the 'Kantian' mantle. Yet, recent scholarship has unearthed greater connections between Kant and Kierkegaard, in terms of both historical influence and conceptual commonality.[20] In particular, Ulrich Knappe has highlighted Kantian structural elements in Kierkegaard's conceptions of ethics, of the will, and of the relation between the theoretical and the practical.[21] While Kierkegaard does certainly depart in important ways from Kantian assumptions, the same is true of Cohen as well, particularly in *Religion of Reason*. As such, recognition of Kierkegaard's Kantian aspects can strengthen my general claims of his ability to illuminate Cohen, while his departures from Kant can help us better to understand the new and distinctive elements that characterize Cohen's final book.

In addition, we can find important intellectual-historical connections between the two thinkers by locating them in streams of thought issuing from the ideas of Moses Mendelssohn and G. E. Lessing, whose attention to the ethically formative potential of the aesthetic sphere, beyond the realm of mere intellectual cognition, can be seen as re-emerging in Kierkegaard and Cohen's attention to style and communication. Mendelssohn develops a conception of 'mixed sentiments'; for example, he points to the fact that a sympathetic observation of another's suffering arouses both pleasure and displeasure: pleasure in connection with one's love for the sufferer, but displeasure in connection with the suffering that the other experiences.[22] Mendelssohn emphasizes that this type of phenomenon, precisely because of its inner tension, can have unique moral-pedagogical value, and his friend Lessing also reaffirmed and expanded upon this notion. Here, I follow the recent scholarship of Willi Goetschel, who emphasizes that, rather than viewing such mixed sentiments (or 'affects,' in Goetchel's descriptive terminology) merely as a hindrance to rational thought, Mendelssohn "possesses a highly developed sensitivity for the affects' constitutive role in the formation of reason and the will."[23] In this regard, intellectual competence and scientific rigor may be necessary factors in this formation, but they are not, in themselves, sufficient.[24] As such, the affects not only differ from 'mere' passions, but they play a crucial role, alongside cognitive thought, in the quest to overcome unreasoned domination by the passions.[25] Building upon Mendelssohn's approach, and through direct dialogue with him, Lessing not only emphasizes the ethical and formative importance of the affects, but highlights, in particular, the central role played by *Mitleid*, compassion. For Lessing, although *Mitleid* is bound to the particular individual who experiences the affect, it can play a key role in generating a universal orientation toward humanity as a whole.[26] In response to such a prioritizing of *Mitleid*, however, Mendelssohn urges Lessing to remember that *Mitleid* does not automatically lead to proper moral and rational formation, and that, if not properly shaped by reason, it also has the potential to lead to quite undesirable effects.[27] As such, it does not have a purely autonomous value; it plays a crucial role in providing a means for going beyond the insufficiency of mere intellectual reflection, but its proper functioning consists of its integration with the restraining criteria of reason.[28]

Before tracing out important echoes of this Lessing-Mendelssohn dialogue within *Religion of Reason*, we should also note that these thinkers make an explicit appearance in Cohen's earlier *Ästhetik des reinen Gefühls*. Referring to the "intimate connection" between Mendelssohn and Lessing, he notes that Lessing's work points to the possibility that aesthetic experience may in fact call forth "a new, distinctive type of consciousness."[29] Likewise, he highlights the significance of Mendelssohn's phrase "the perfection of all powers of the soul" (*die Vollkommenheit aller Seelkräfte*), which points beyond "knowledge" (*Erkenntnis*) and "desire" (*Begehren*) to the affects as a third crucial "faculty of the soul" (*Seelenvermögen*).[30] Subsequently, Cohen explicitly affirms the positions of Mendelssohn and Lessing, asserting, in his own voice, that the affects are to be "distinguished from knowledge [*Erkenntnis*] and desire [*Begierde*]" and that, through the affects, there emerges "a new type of consciousness . . . the new soul-faculty of feeling."[31] In other words, Cohen here puts forth the possibility of a spiritual-psychological faculty that is not identical with 'objective knowledge' and yet is also not to be identified with 'merely individual' passions. Furthermore, this discussion is found in a section of the *Ästhetik* entitled "The Subjective Psychological Qualities [*Die subjectiven seelischen Qualitäten*]."[32] Here, then, the term 'subjective' is used not in a derogatory sense (as in 'merely subjective'), but rather designates the connection between subjectivity and a crucial and distinct component of perfected human consciousness.

Though Cohen does not restate the explicit connection to Mendelssohn and Lessing in his *Religion*, the structural continuity is apparent. In his introduction, as we have seen, Cohen emphasizes that the sphere of religion is distinct from the sphere of philosophy, with the latter characterized by the quest for 'knowledge' and for 'objectification.' Yet, despite its distinctness from philosophy, religion is also not to be identified with non-rational egoism and base passions. Thus, religion mirrors the role assigned by Cohen in his *Ästhetik* to the affects, which were likewise distinguished from both knowledge and desire. Moreover, Cohen explicitly applies the term 'affect' to compassion, *Mitleid*, the central mode of human relation within the sphere of religion.[33] Even while acknowledging that previous philosophers have rejected the rational value of compassion precisely because of its subjective nature, Cohen nevertheless insists on upholding its share in reason.[34] In other words, not only does a connection to subjectivity not exclude a connection to truth, but it can even be constitutive of the proper human relation to the truth and truthfulness of reason.

The relation between subjectivity and truth can also point us to the influence on Kierkegaard's conceptual framework of the Mendelssohn-Lessing intellectual stream. Of the two, Kierkegaard explicitly cites only Lessing in this regard, and not Mendelssohn, but the same basic emphasis on subjectivity and passionate striving as key elements of human perfection comes across quite clearly. In the *Concluding Unscientific Postscript*, which will serve as my primary Kierkegaardian text for illuminating Cohen's style, Kierkegaard/Climacus includes a lengthy section consisting of "An Expression of Gratitude to Lessing" and "Possible and Actual Theses by Lessing."[35] Here, as for Mendelssohn and Lessing, objective intellectual reflection is not rejected outright; rather, the emphasis lies on its limitations and insufficiencies with regard to the will and the affective engagement of the existing individual. Thus, we can view Kierkegaard as quite consciously locating himself within an earlier line of thought that is also picked up, perhaps independently, by Cohen.[36] As such, when the additional heritage found in relation to Kant and Hegel is added to that of Mendelssohn and Lessing, we can begin to discern a broader pattern of factors that could ultimately have given rise to a convergent evolution of thought in Cohen and Kierkegaard.

In addition to such shared influences, another potential indicator of compatibility between the two can be found in the number of later thinkers who were in turn significantly influenced by both Kierkegaard and Cohen. Looking at twentieth-century Jewish philosophy, one can point to Martin Buber, Franz Rosenzweig, Emmanuel Levinas, Joseph Soloveitchik, and Abraham Joshua Heschel as examples of those who either explicitly acknowledged their debt to, or whose thought displays clear influence by, both Cohen and Kierkegaard. Another prominent example, and perhaps one of the earliest to directly juxtapose Cohen and Kierkegaard as joint influences, is Karl Barth, who asks himself, in the opening paragraph of his preface to the fifth edition (1926) of his *Epistle to the Romans*, whether his readers have simply "been presented with what is really no more than a rehash, resurrected out of Nietzsche and Kierkegaard and Cohen."[37] To be sure, these subsequent thinkers may not all have consciously viewed Cohen and Kierkegaard as *similar* influences; however, if each of these thinkers was able to produce a coherent philosophy from out of the intersection of these two influences, this should at least raise the possibility that the two influences themselves might also substantially intersect with one another.

In arguing that *Religion of Reason* can be illuminated by Kierkegaard's account of indirect communication, I am not claiming that Cohen himself had Kierkegaard in mind in developing his communicative style. As far as I have been able to determine, there is no definitive evidence that Cohen ever read any of Kierkegaard's works at all.[38] While Cohen's intellectual milieu may have provided some stimulus for Kierkegaard-inflected modes of thought,[39] I go no further than a mere observation of a convergence of their ideas as displayed in their respective texts. Accordingly, I try to highlight some of the ways in which Kierkegaard's linking of communication with multiplicity, personal relation, the dynamics of possibility and actuality, and the confusion of conceptual spheres can aid us in our reading of Cohen's complex blending of Scripture and philosophy.

II. Multiplicity and Communication

In the previous chapter, we examined Cohen's claim that the concepts of religion, as exemplified in the correlation of the I and the You, contain an inherent plurality (*Mehrheit*) and multiplicity that resist the objectifying-unifying demands of the method of Ethics. There, I suggested that the communication of such concepts might also require a corresponding stylistic multiplicity. Climacus illuminates this possibility through his insistence that a proper communication of ethical or religious concepts (i.e., of "essential knowing" and "essential truth"[40]) will necessarily contain elements of irreducible ambiguity and multiplicity. Accordingly, he states that the existing subjective thinker is just as negative as positive and that, furthermore, such a thinker's form of communication must correspond to his (multifaceted) form of existence.[41] Because the existing thinker is constantly striving and has no static positive results of his own, he must not present positive results in his communication, "lest by being overly communicative he transform a learner's existence into something other than what human existence is on the whole."[42] This "something other" will frequently be an objectification of a properly subjective concept. Importantly, while employing various forms of negativity can help prevent objectification, the communication must *also* contain just as much of the positive as the negative. A genuine communication does take place, even though it cannot be consciously cognized or systematically stated by either the communicator or the receiver. If the communication were wholly negative, then the sphere of the religious would be empty rather than "invisible."[43]

Climacus also describes the subjective existing thinker by saying that he—and thus his form of expression—has just as much of the comic as of pathos.[44] Here, the comic corresponds to an orientation of jest, humorousness, or non-credulity as applied to an utterance or an idea, while pathos represents an orientation of earnestness and sincere assertion. Because these two modes are contradictory, no consistent, unified result can be gleaned from such a communication. Yet, if either of the two modes were absent, a one-sided distortion would occur: "The proportion provides an interdependent safeguard. The pathos that is not safeguarded by the comic is an illusion; the comic that is not safeguarded by pathos is immaturity."[45] While each of these one-sided presentations has the virtue of consistency and comprehensibility, the former says too much while the latter says too little. Climacus indicates that, despite their contradictoriness, pathos and the comic are both necessary in order to portray the contradictions that do in fact characterize human existence, especially in relation to ethical and religious concepts:

The subjectively existing thinker is therefore just as bifrontal as the existence-situation itself. The interpretation of the misrelation, viewed with
the idea ahead, is pathos; the interpretation of the misrelation, viewed
with the idea behind, is the comic. When the subjective existing thinker
turns his face toward the idea, his interpretation of the misrelation is
pathos-filled; when he turns his back to the idea, allowing it to shine from
behind into the same misrelation, his interpretation is comic. Thus it is the
infinite pathos of religiousness to say *Du* to God; it is infinitely comic
when I turn my back and now within the finite look at that which from
behind falls into the finite. If I have not exhausted the comic in its entirety,
I do not have the pathos of the infinite; if I have the pathos of the infinite,
I immediately have the comic also.[46]

Thus, a person who is inclined to affirm the notion of a personal God must also
be able to recognize the 'other side' of the existence-situation, namely, that such a
notion has no grounding in objective thought and should not be asserted as
though it did. Accordingly, one must simultaneously present God in personal
terms (with the idea ahead) and in non-personal or even anti-personal terms
(with the idea behind). Both "interpretations" must be given *equal* emphasis, so
that neither is able to gain a stable foothold in the receiver's consciousness.[47]

In the case of Cohen's text and style, I argue that a similar multiplicity can
be found in the ways that Cohen employs Scripture and philosophy. In general, Cohen's style consists of citing a passage from Scripture and then providing his own interpretive commentary. Cohen's movement from verse to
interpretation is shaped by the philosophical method and the criterion of
universality. However, the degree to which he shapes his text varies from
example to example. In some cases, he remains close to the language of Scripture, and reshapes the text only slightly. In other cases, he presents a more
abstract-philosophical perspective that reshapes the text to a greater degree.
Thus, the various interpretations fall along a spectrum. On one end, we have
the scriptural citation itself, before any interpretation has been applied. This
citation contains many non-objective elements, such as personality, particularity, and interpersonal relation. At the same time, the citation itself remains
vague and unclear, and has the potential to be interpreted in many different
ways. On the other extreme, we have an interpretation which has been fully
reshaped according to the philosophical method, so that all non-objective elements have been abstracted away. In this case, the interpretation is clear and
has been purified of vagueness. Thus, one end of the spectrum is vague but
rich in particularity and personality, while the other end is clear but flattened
and depersonalized. Each pole contains important features that are lacking in
the other. In practice, Cohen's interpretations generally fall somewhere

between these two extremes. Thus, depending on the degree of reshaping, his various interpretations may look very different from one another and may be 'logically inconsistent.' (In the next chapter, we will examine some of these 'inconsistencies' in detail, for example, God as idea versus God as loving and personal; autonomy versus a commanding God; and self-purification versus God's forgiveness.)

This multiplicity is necessary, though, for Cohen's stated task of communicating the religion of reason. Any *single* interpretation will lie at a given point on the spectrum and will necessarily be lacking in rational clarity or particularity-personality, or both.[48] If Cohen's interpretations cleaved only to the language of Scripture, they would remain vague and could be compatible with unethical and irrational understandings of religion. In contrast, if his interpretations consistently leaned toward a highly abstract-philosophical presentation, the personal-particular features that characterize religion would be lost, and a reader would come away with an overly objectified understanding. In order to avoid such distortions, Cohen's text must present interpretations from varying points along the interpretive spectrum.

Linking Cohen's style to Kierkegaard's account of the subjective thinker's indirect communication, we can say that Cohen's more philosophically slanted formulations correspond to the comic, while his more scripturally slanted formulations correspond to pathos. As Climacus says, pathos involves saying *Du*, You, to God—in other words, addressing and relating to God personally. Similarly, we have seen that Cohen locates the You in the personal-particular sphere of religion, a sphere which is displayed especially by Scripture. In contrast, the comic arises "when I turn my back," breaking with the personal relation and assessing the relevant concepts indifferently and objectively. Likewise, for Cohen, the method of philosophy produces an objectified and impersonal interpretation of its subject matter. To truly approach the religious concepts in their fullness, a "bifrontal" approach is needed that can encompass both contradictory perspectives together, without eliminating their contradictoriness.

An interpretation of Scripture that described God solely in personal terms would thus run the risk of "illusion" and of saying too much: thinking that the personality of God is something that could be directly stated and asserted. In contrast, an interpretation of Scripture that completely depersonalized God would be guilty of "immaturity" and of saying too little: turning God into a theoretical and intellectual concept, without acknowledging the additional importance of personal relation. Importantly, as Climacus points out, each of the two modes must be asserted in their entirety, and neither should be granted priority over the other. One must fully engage in pathos and in personal-particular interpretation of scriptural concepts, and also fully engage in the comic and in depersonalized-objective interpretation.

Each individual person is likely to be inclined toward one type of lopsided-ness or another. Some may be inclined to describe God in personal terms and may be disturbed by and dissatisfied with accounts that describe God impersonally, as an idea or as the moral ideal. (Such people are likely to criticize impersonal accounts for 'reducing' God to a 'mere' idea.) Others are inclined to describe God in impersonal terms and may consider personal descriptions of God to be unjusti-fied and worryingly anthropomorphic. In terms of the foregoing discussion, we might say that the first type has too much of pathos and needs more of the comic, while the second has too much of the comic and needs more pathos. Cohen's style, as displayed in *Religion of Reason*, serves to offend as well as correct both types. A reader who wants to think of God as a person must train himself to rec-ognize that God can be *equally* regarded as an idea. A reader who wants to think of God as an idea must train herself to recognize that God can be *equally* regarded as a person.[49] Indeed, since the notion of an equal awareness of both perspectives is an ideal that can never be perfectly attained, one can say that someone who views God ultimately as a person should attempt to turn himself into someone who views God ultimately as an idea—but once this is achieved, he should then work to turn himself into someone who views God ultimately as a person, and so on. In certain ways, Cohen's style should have a fundamentally destabilizing effect on the reader—whenever someone feels too comfortable with either direc-tion, his or her comfortability should be taken away.[50]

This instability is linked to the irreducible cognitive vagueness of religious concepts. Because they are strictly practical, and not theoretical, concepts, they can never be consciously comprehended, even by a person who appropriates and actualizes them. For this reason, one who seeks to communicate must avoid giv-ing the impression that the communication *could* be received as something fixed or determinate. Thus, Climacus praises Lessing for his skillful style that deprives his readers of any objective results. A complacent or theoretically oriented reader might be inclined to ask, "Has [Lessing] accepted Christianity, has he rejected it, has he defended it, has he attacked it?—so that I, too, may accept the same opin-ion."[51] However, because Lessing "had enough skeptical ataraxia and religious sense to discern the category of the religious," he refrained from giving even "the slightest trace of any result" that could be parroted by rote.[52] The implication is that giving a determine result or opinion would lead the receiver to misunder-stand the category of the religious and its concepts. In a positive sense, the *absence* of determinate results can guide a receiver to the realization that the significance of ethical and religious concepts is to be found in *something other than* conscious intellectual comprehension.

In Cohen's case, it is particularly the *hermeneutic* nature of his style that plays a significant role in preventing 'results.' A reader might come to Cohen's book asking, "Should God be thought of as personal or as impersonal?" or "Does

Cohen think of God as personal or as impersonal?" Such a reader assumes that there *is* a single answer to the question, and she will seek to find that answer in Cohen's words. However, because he works from and reasons from Scripture, from a source-text, Cohen is better able to neutralize this desire. In some instances, he interprets and comments on passages about God, the soul, the messianic age, and so on, in personal, substantive terms. In others, he interprets Scripture in a more impersonal, abstract-philosophic manner. Thus, Cohen has shifted the question from "*Is* God personal or *is* God impersonal?" to "*Do I interpret* this verse about God in personal or in impersonal terms?" Even the reader who initially seeks a single answer to the first question can more easily recognize, in the case of the second, that there is no single 'correct' reading of the verse, since a text can certainly be *interpreted* in multiple ways.

That same reader, though, might also feel that Cohen is ignoring the more important issue: "Yes, yes, I see that you can interpret this *verse* personally as well as impersonally—but what I want to know is whether *God* is *really* personal or impersonal!" Cohen's move to a hermeneutic style, however, is not an avoidance of philosophical questions; rather, such a move serves to indicate that the philosophical questions *have the same shape* as the hermeneutic ones: just as the scriptural verse leaves us with an irresolvable interpretive multiplicity, so religious concepts leave us with an irresolvable cognitive multiplicity. This multiplicity might appear frightening to some: if we cannot know what is really the case concerning God, does this not lead to chaos and relativism? Cohen's response to this concern would be twofold: first, the lack of theoretical or conceptual unity does not entail a lack of practical unity. There are things that can be *done* even though they cannot be *thought*. Thus, one can still attain a form of security and assurance, but it will not be of the theoretical variety. Second, if Cohen is correct about the irremediable multiplicity of religious concepts, then one could arrive at a single unified answer only by distorting the concepts themselves. That is, one could answer the question "Is God personal or impersonal?" only by objectifying the concept 'God,' in which case one would end up providing an answer about something other than that which originally gave rise to the question. In contrast, Cohen's conceptual multiplicity and his hermeneutic approach may provide a more faithful picture of the concepts in question. As such, seeking too much clarity may actually lead to unclarity, while preserving multiplicity and vagueness may contribute to a clearer understanding.

The style of *Religion of Reason* can thus be viewed as a form of exercise or training for Cohen's readers. Rather than directly insisting on the multiplicity and non-comprehensibility of various religious concepts (an approach that would raise resistance in readers), Cohen is able to accustom his readers to multiplicity through the process of scriptural interpretation. By means of the scriptural buffer, readers can gradually become habituated to a mode of reasoning in which theoretical oneness is not an overarching goal. By coming to realize the futility inherent in a quest to determine the single 'right' interpretation of a passage, they can more easily recognize the equivalent futility in seeking 'results' and objectively determinate accounts with regard to religious concepts generally.

III. Personal Relation and Communication

Another key element affecting the communication of religious concepts involves the communicator's personal relation to the subject matter. As Climacus emphasizes, "In order to study the ethical, every human being is assigned to himself. In that regard, he himself is more than enough for himself; indeed, he is the only place where *he* can with certainty study it."[53] That is to say, he cannot study it in general, but only in relation to himself. Thus, "for me, *my* dying is by no means something general . . . Nor am *I* for myself some such thing in general."[54] 'Dying' (in general) is something different from *my* dying, and 'the self' (in general) is something different from *my*self. Likewise, the question of the immortality of the soul (in general) is something different from the question of whether *I* am immortal.[55] In each of these instances, the transposition from the personal to the general will distort the concept and turn it into something illusory. It will also lead to interminable dispute and contention among those who have varying 'opinions' about the generalized-distorted concepts.[56] Thus, the attempt to communicate ethical or religious matters using a non-personal third-person voice is problematic.[57] However, using a fully personal first-person voice has its own dangers, in that it can seem to apply only to the communicator himself, and not to the receiver. Likewise, a second-person address has other shortcomings; I cannot talk about 'your immortality,' 'your dying,' and so on, since only *you* have access to those matters. If *I* could talk about them, then everybody could talk about them, and hence they would be general. Since all three of the standard voices have aspects that tend to mislead, none of them is fully sufficient for a communication of essential truth.[58] Instead, a form of non-direct exposition is necessary.

Cohen's account of religion in distinction from Ethics, as presented in the previous chapter, indicates that *all* concepts in the sphere of religion are inherently bound up with personal relation and individuality, precisely in the sense that Climacus describes here. The I of religion is precisely *my* I in its particularity, and is not equivalent to the I of humanity in general. Likewise, the You cannot be assimilated to the He, to the general other; the You is *my* other, the other that confronts and constitutes *me*. The God of religion is no longer merely the God of humanity in general, but rather, as the God of the individual, is specifically *my* God.[59] Additionally, Cohen distinguishes sharply between my sinfulness and the sinfulness of others, that is, between *my* sin and sin in general.[60] As such, we must look for ways in which Cohen's style aids in preserving and conveying the personal nature of the concepts that he discusses. In a negative sense, Cohen's style should *prevent* the concepts from being taken as "something general," while, in a positive sense, his style should *prompt* or even *compel* the reader to relate personally and actively to those same concepts.

One useful conceptual tool for analyzing this aspect of Cohen's style can be found in Anti-Climacus' account of a "sign of contradiction," which he describes as "a sign that contains a contradiction in its composition . . . But the contradictory parts must not annul each other in such a way that the sign comes to mean nothing or in such a way that it becomes the opposite of a sign, an unconditional concealment."[61] In other words, although such a sign facilitates a significant communication, one cannot state the content of the communication in consistent, objective terms. This contradictory form of representation is distinguished from another type of contradiction, in which the contradictory elements simply negate one another, leaving *no* meaning to be gleaned from the sign. Thus, not every contradiction is a meaningful contradiction. However, in the case of the sign of contradiction, there *is* meaning, but no objective or theoretical meaning.

Anti-Climacus suggests that a "communication that is the unity of jest and earnestness" is an example of such a sign.[62] If a communication were simply one of jest, or simply one of earnestness, one could objectively and impersonally comprehend and state the content of the communication. The unity of jest and earnestness precludes this possibility, because jest and earnestness cannot be consciously held together: they contradict one another. The two elements cannot be objectively unified by the understanding: only an active and practical (not simply speculative) appropriation by the recipient can grasp them simultaneously. Thus, the communication must "mak[e] the recipient self-active."[63] Similarly, anti-Climacus later says that with regard to a unity of jest and earnestness, "[i]f anyone wants to have anything to do with this kind of communication, he will have to untie the knot himself."[64] That is, the contradictory communication cannot be grasped by the theoretical understanding, but requires the active engagement of the personal self (i.e., "himself"). The contradiction thus serves to repel a theoretical approach: because one cannot find any meaning in *this* way, one is forced to take a *different* approach.

In this type of communication, no objectively separable meaning is intended. If, however, readers are determined to derive an objective meaning from the communication, its contradictory nature means that it can be just as easily and plausibly interpreted in terms of a communication of jest as in terms of a communication of earnestness. Thus, if one presents faith in this manner (as a sign of contradiction), "the most orthodox sees it as a defense of the faith and the atheist sees it as an attack."[65] The former interprets it as a communication of earnestness, ardently commending faith, while the latter sees it as a communication of jest, sneeringly mocking faith. Both of these positions put forth consistent interpretations and "form a judgment about what is presented." In reality, though, the presentation is "is neither attack nor defense."[66] In order to dispassionately judge something to be an attack or a defense, one need not relate oneself personally to that which is presented. However, in the case of a sign of contradiction, one can judge it to be an attack only by ignoring crucial elements that seem to point to a defense, and vice versa. If one takes seriously all of its elements, one cannot form a consistent dispassionate judgment about the communication at all. One can only approach the communication through passionate engagement of one's self, and even then, one will *still* be unable to form a consistent judgment about the nature of the communication.

Working from the hypothesis that *Religion of Reason* constitutes such a "sign of contradiction," the persistent scholarly dispute over the book becomes more understandable. Typically, intellectual historians and historical philosophers seek to form an objective, impersonal judgment about what is presented in a given text in order to clarify the author's philosophical and ideological stance. Though certain texts may initially appear vague and confusing, the scholar's task is to remove that vagueness. When one approaches Cohen's text in this manner, however, it can easily appear to contain contradictory 'positions' in roughly 'equal' proportion. Consequently, in order to form a consistent judgment about the book as a whole, scholars are led to downplay or ignore certain passages. Thus, some read Cohen's text as a "defense" of a personal-existential view of religion, representing a return to a traditional conception of faith, while others see his text as an "attack" on (or at least a non-embrace of) such a view. Often, as in Anti-Climacus' description, readers construct Cohen's text in their own image: those who would themselves put forth a "defense" find such a position in *Religion of Reason*, while those would put forth an "attack" see Cohen as doing the same. In some cases, though, the opposite is the case, as, for example, when 'defenders of the faith' see Cohen's account of religion as too abstract and impersonal.

While these interpretations differ from one another, they all tend to share a particular methodological assumption: namely, that *if* we assume that a past historical author sought to convey a specific communication, we can best understand that communication by constructing a theoretically consistent hypothesis about his text. In other words, we seek the hypothesis that best accounts for the given text, but this hypothesis should itself be clear and free of vagueness. If we cannot successfully construct such an hypothesis, we are forced to conclude that the historical author was guilty of unclear thinking or internal contradiction. Thus, if the text appears vague, we must either eliminate the vagueness or transfer the vagueness to the person of the author himself.

However, there is another alternative: if we find that we cannot construct an objective and impersonal hypothesis, perhaps we need to approach the text in a personal and engaged manner.[67] It may be the case that the different parts of

Cohen's text cannot be 'held together' in an objective, theoretical, or static manner, but only through a form of practical and active relation that involves the reader's self as an existing person. As such, we can view the various types of interpretation found in *Religion of Reason* as projections of a non-theoretical subject matter onto various theoretical planes, in a manner analogous to the projection from different angles of a three-dimensional object onto a two-dimensional plane. That is, Cohen seeks to communicate a transcendental X which, when projected in one way (via a strongly philosophic reshaping), produces interpretation Y, but which also, when projected in another way (via a reading that retains more of the personal elements of Scripture), produces interpretation Z. Cohen only presents Y and Z, leaving it to the reader to reconstruct X. Because Y and Z remain contradictory in impersonal thought, this fact should serve to elicit personal engagement from the reader who seeks to read the text in a coherent manner.[68]

This indirect approach is no mere idiosyncrasy of Cohen's; rather, it is essential for communication, since the X *cannot* be presented directly, but only by various projections in the form of scriptural interpretations. This situation is analogous to the traditional Jewish idea of "attributes of action," as designated by Maimonides and expounded by Cohen in chapter 4 of *Religion of Reason*. Just as God does not reveal his essence, but only the effects of his essence,[69] so an essentially personal religious concept cannot be presented directly, but only via its various effects on the reader of Scripture. With regard to Cohen's style, the force of 'cannot' is primarily practical-communicative, not ontological: *if* one tries to present the concepts directly, the reader is likely to receive them in a distorted form, and the communication will not succeed.

IV. *"Were it not written in Scripture, it would be impossible to say it."*

Another important aspect of Cohen's style can be brought out through an intriguing statement of Anti-Climacus': "Indirect communication can be an art of communication in redoubling the communication; the art consists in making oneself, the communicator, into a nobody, purely objective, and then continually placing the qualitative opposites in a unity."[70] Thus far, we have focused on the ways in which Cohen places qualitative opposites in a unity—but what does it mean to say that the communicator makes himself into a nobody, purely objective? I argue that, in *Religion of Reason*, Cohen does so by using Scripture to say things that he could not say on his own. In other words, he makes his independent voice into a nobody and 'lets Scripture speak' in his stead—albeit with his own interpretive shaping. It is typical, with regard to most books, to attribute the statements found in the text to 'the author himself,' to the author as a subject. Here, however, because the interpretive statements have their origin in Scripture, none of them can attributed simply to 'Cohen himself'; as such, Cohen as communicator can be considered more object than subject.

In examining the various ways in which this is the case, I want to frame the discussion through a phrase that occurs repeatedly in classical rabbinic literature: *ilmalei mikra katuv, i efshar le-omro*, "Were it not written in Scripture, it would be impossible to say it." This phrase most frequently accompanies midrashic interpretations of Scripture that humanize and anthropomorphize God in striking or daring ways.[71] In its classical usage, the sense of "impossible" in the phrase seems to shade more toward notions of permissibility or propriety: without the authority and backing of the written scriptural text, such a bold theological statement would be presumptuous. With regard to Cohen's text and style, however, the phrase applies even more literally: there are things that Cohen is *unable* to say without the help of Scripture. Were he to attempt to 'say things on his own,' his efforts would be not simply impious, but unsuccessful: the desired communication (and hence the 'saying') would fail to occur.

(a) Personal relation and general statability

Recall Climacus' insistence (discussed above) that religious concepts are inherently connected to one's personal self and are "by no means something general."[72] As such, a direct, third-person statement will distort the concept by leaving out this personal relation.[73] If a statement can be expressed in a general, impersonal form, then it can be grasped in a general, impersonal manner, in which case it is no longer essentially personal, and hence no longer a religious concept. This situation stands in contrast to the communication of objective concepts, wherein one person can state something in third-person terms and the receiver can straightforwardly agree (or disagree), without giving rise to distortion. As Climacus writes, "Ordinary communication between one human being and another is entirely immediate, because people ordinarily exist in immediacy. When one person states something and another acknowledges the same thing verbatim, they are assumed to be in agreement and to have understood each other."[74] Such agreement, however, depends upon on a shared object of thought that both parties have in common. In the case of religious concepts, the two parties cannot have an object of thought in common, because the concepts are particular to each individual and are not general.

For this reason, Cohen cannot express third-person statements such as "God loves" or "God is the creator of the world" in his own voice. The concepts to which such statements refer would have validity only in connection to Cohen's individual ethico-religious striving and actions; when expressed in general sentences that are grammatically complete unto themselves, they are cut off from that personal and active connection. In the case of a written text on a printed page, the speaker/author as individual is even further removed from the statements, which appear to the reader as disembodied and self-sufficient. However, while Cohen himself cannot directly make statements that describe God in personal terms, he *can* cite and interpret scriptural passages that do so. By doing so, he is able to say, as it were, "Do not attribute the content of these interpretative statements to *me*. I am simply the messenger, interpreting what Scripture has said." Thus, the statements in *Religion of Reason* that seem to come 'from Cohen' are in fact not independent or self-sufficient, but remain tied to their scriptural source. Because they do not have meaning apart from this source, they cannot be received as objectively grounded propositions. Their dependence on Scripture prevents their 'generalization' and points to their analogous dependence on the active, personal relation of the particular individual. By speaking through the voice of Scripture rather than his own, Cohen can indirectly put forth positive-sounding statements without having to abstract misleadingly from his own relation to the concepts involved.

(b) Respecting the limits of philosophy

In a similar fashion, Cohen's use of Scripture enables him to preserve his commitment to the scientific austerity of the method of philosophy and of Ethics. As I discussed in my previous two chapters, Cohen does not view religion as an independent sphere of knowledge, and he will not positively assert anything that goes beyond the method of philosophy.[75] Were he to do so, such assertions would come into conflict with the results of philosophy and would ultimately undermine ethicality by promoting allegiance to objectified, unreal entities.[76] For this reason, Cohen, when speaking in his own voice, is unable to say anything more than philosophy warrants. At the same time, if he *only* said that which philosophy warrants, he would remain in the sphere of Ethics, and his project of presenting a religion of reason would collapse, along with the concepts of the You, the fellow-man, and the unique God. Thus, he cannot say more, and yet he *must* say more.

This is where Scripture steps in to help. If Scripture speaks, and Cohen merely provides interpretation, he himself has not transgressed the limits of philosophy. That is, if Cohen himself asserted, "God is a personal You," he could be asked, "On what grounds are you saying this?" He would then be at a loss, since he would not have any objective grounds to which to point. Yet, he does not want to say, "God is not a personal You," since this would be saying too little. However, if Scripture addresses God in personal terms and says, for example, "For You, Lord, are good, and ready to pardon" (Ps. 86:5), Cohen can then cite this verse and comment on it.[77] If he is questioned about residual personal elements in his commentary, he can point to the source material that he has been given, without having to make any positive or negative declarations as to his own view of God's personality. Furthermore, his use of Scripture also helps prevent his readers from drawing philosophically unwarranted conclusions about God and other religious concepts. Because his statements are interpretations of Scripture, their ontological status remains open. To be sure, a reader *could* read Cohen's statements and say, "These are propositions that describe *what is really the case* with regard to God's personality." While such a reading cannot be fully prevented, the hermeneutic nature of Cohen's style might be more likely to prompt a response such as, "These interpretations describe the ways that God appears in these texts." The mode of reasoning exemplified by the latter response can enable a person to approach the religious concepts as regulative and practical,[78] without feeling the pressure to finalize them in a constitutive or ontological manner, which would in turn lead to philosophical illusions and over-sayings.

(c) Saying two things at once

Scripture's ability to, as it were, say two things at once also helps enable Cohen to speak. If he speaks on his own, any single sentence of Cohen's will distort the relevant religious concepts. That is, any complete sentence that is internally consistent will say either too much (e.g., by suggesting God's personality) or too little (e.g., by failing to suggest God's personality). Even if, as discussed earlier, he were to counterbalance the one-sidedness of a given statement by elsewhere putting forth a 'contradictory' statement, he would still face the problem that *both* of the statements are 'inaccurate' misrepresentations. The religious concepts contain an internal duality or multiplicity that is incompatible with the closed subject-predicate unity of third-person propositions. In order to avoid misrepresentations completely, Cohen would have to keep silent.

According to classical rabbinic conceptions, however, Scripture is not bound by such restrictions. As the Talmudic interpretation of Psalm 62:12 expounds, "'One thing God has spoken, but twice I have heard, that strength belongs to God': One verse of Scripture will produce multiple meanings."[79] While finite human beings can only say one thing at a time, God—and hence God's word—has the power to say and intend two (potentially 'inconsistent') things in a single statement. For this reason, Scripture is especially suited to expressing the internal heterogeneity of religious concepts. Accordingly, when Cohen comments on Scripture, he can (and often does) provide different interpretations of the same verse and is thus invested with Scripture's ability to say two things 'at once.'[80] By remaining tied to the scriptural verses, with the ever-present potential for re-interpretation, his interpretative statements stay 'open' and are able to avoid the reductive one-sidedness and finality that would result from speaking 'on his own.'

(d) Religious concepts as continual tasks, never static actualities

Cohen is also prevented from speaking on his own by the fact that, for an existing human being, religious concepts represent continual tasks, and never static actualities.[81] Were Cohen directly to assert, for example, "God is unique," such a statement would wrongly appear as a constative 'fact' and as static knowledge over which Cohen has control and possession. To the contrary, the idea of God's uniqueness is not independently or objectively actual; rather, it remains incumbent upon Cohen to actual*ize* this idea. That is to say, although "God is unique" has the outward form of an 'is' statement, it is, properly speaking, a statement of 'ought.' Because the idea represents a still-pending and continually pending imperative, Cohen cannot state it in terms that omit the imperative element.

Yet, to leave the matter merely in terms of an 'ought' would be saying 'too little': there is also a sense in which Cohen *does* want to affirm the actuality of God's uniqueness and of other religious ideas. As we will see in chapter 6, although religious ideas lack objective or autonomous actuality, they can gain actuality in the moment of active subjective engagement.[82] However, the transition to saying and reporting breaks with the active engagement and moves into a detached mode in which the ideas are *not* actual (or: are no longer actual) and in which their actuality cannot be asserted.

Scripture, by way of contrast, can and does present religious matters—God's uniqueness, God's forgiveness, God's role as creator, revealer, and redeemer—in direct, straightforward description. While an existing human being, who is in time and is always becoming, must view these ideas in relation to incumbent tasks and ideals, Scripture presents them, from the perspective of eternity, as concrete actualities.[83] Thus, when he cites and comments on scriptural passages, Cohen can flesh out the inner relations of various religious concepts without having to assert their actuality in his own voice. His interpretations remain formally dependent on Scripture, mirroring the ways in which the actuality of religious ideas is not a factual given, but remains dependent on the existing individual's active engagement and striving.

In addition to opening his lips and enabling him to speak, the use of Scripture also facilitates proper communication between Cohen and his audience. Because the religious ideas are not static actualities for Cohen himself, he must also prevent them from being received *as* static actualities by his readers. As Climacus puts it, "Existence-actuality cannot be communicated, and the subjective thinker has his own actuality in his own ethical existence. If actuality is to be understood by a third party, it must be understood as possibility, and a communicator who is

conscious of this will therefore see to it, precisely in order to be oriented to existence, that his existence-communication is in the form of possibility."[84] That is to
say, even if the religious ideas have actuality for *Cohen* by virtue of his active existential engagement, their actuality must not be presented to his readers as something already given. For example, if Cohen were to assert directly that "God is
unique" or that "the world was created by God," the reader could easily come to
think of these ideas simply as objective facts whose truth, like that of "the earth is
round"[85] or "the Iliad was written by Homer," is independent of any inward striving on his part. Instead, the religious ideas must be presented in terms of a *possibility* whose potential actuality for an individual reader depends on that reader's
own subjective engagement.[86]

Cohen's use of Scripture aids in accomplishing this possibility-presentation
by placing a hermeneutic buffer between the religious ideas and the reader's
objectifying tendencies. The significance of Cohen's readings lies not in the verse
itself, nor in the commentary itself, but in the movement from the verse to the
commentary and in the relation between them. When a reader encounters the
commentary, her attention is simultaneously directed back toward the source
text. In this way, she is able to see that the meaning that Cohen draws out of the
passage is not an immediate given, but only one *possible* reading of the text. The
meaning comes into actuality *only when* Cohen reads the passage in this way.
Prior to and apart from such engagement, the verse is vague and its meaning is
merely potential. Furthermore, in order to apprehend the significance of Cohen's
commentary, the reader must herself reenact and reconstruct the interpretive
movement from verse to commentary. By educing this dynamic re-actualization
of meaning, Cohen's style differs qualitatively from a static 'giving' of religious
assertions. By encouraging his readers to engage religious concepts as hermeneutical tasks, he is habituating them into engaging such concepts also as ethical-
existential tasks, and not as objective actualities.

V. Cohen's Communicative Goals

Kierkegaard's writings can also lead us to a better understanding of Cohen's overall authorial goals. That is, given *Religion of Reason*'s unique philosophical-scriptural
style, what is it that Cohen wants his readers to take away from the book? I argue
that Cohen may only be secondarily concerned with the specific *content* of the
religious concepts that he discusses—in other words, the characteristics of the
unique God, the nature of the messianic age, God's love for the poor, and so on.[87]
While these details are undoubtedly important, his primary focus may be more
methodological: *How* does one approach and reason about religious concepts?
More specifically, how does reasoning about religious concepts, which are non-
objective, *differ* from reasoning about objective, non-personal concepts? Cohen

must show that there is not simply one rational method (i.e., that of strict phi-losophy and science) but rather two distinct modes of reasoning, which employ different methods and produce different results.

Like Cohen, Climacus addresses the challenge of keeping different realms distinct. He emphasizes that one can approach ethical or religious topics from different perspectives or with different methods. Some notions may have legiti-macy in one domain, but not in the other. For example, he contends that the unity of truth and being holds true in abstraction, but not for an existing per-son.[88] Or, if one understands the term 'being' abstractly, then one can define truth as something finished—but this is not the case if one looks at 'being' from the perspective of an existing spirit.[89] Conversely, "Viewed world-historically, a thesis becomes untrue that viewed ethically is true and is the vital force in the ethical, namely, that every existing individuality has a possibility-relationship with God."[90] Likewise, "it is entirely correct that there is something true for an existing person that is not true in abstraction."[91] In each of these cases, no error need occur. A person is entirely warranted, for instance, in asserting the unity of truth and being, as long as he (1) specifies that this claim is made in the sphere of abstraction and (2) acknowledges that the claim is *not* true for an existing individual. Likewise, a person can emphasize every existing individual's possibility-relationship with God, provided that he is aware that this thesis is *not* true, viewed world-historically. As long as the two spheres are kept distinct, there is no problem.[92]

Problems arise, however, when one thinks, writes, or speaks without the proper categorical distinctions between the two. Consider Climacus' presenta-tion of the acrimonious debate between thinkers who defend the notion "that there is an either/or" and Hegelian thinkers who seek to cancel the either/or. The two parties argue back and forth, and though the Hegelians often claim to have triumphed, "there may be a misunderstanding at the root of the conflict and the victory."[93] On one hand, "Hegel is perfectly and absolutely right in maintaining that, looked at eternally, *sub specie aeterni*, there is no *aut/aut* [either/or] in the language of abstraction, in pure thought and pure being."[94] Thus, the defenders of the *aut/aut* are in the wrong if they seek to criticize Hegel in that sphere. On the other hand, "Hegel is just as much in the wrong when he, forgetting the abstrac-tion, plunges from it down into existence in order by hook or by crook to cancel the double *aut*."[95] Thus, both parties make absolute and undifferentiated claims, neglecting the distinction between the two spheres. As such, both distort the notions of the *aut/aut* and of the unity between being and thinking.[96]

Apparently, Climacus thinks that this type of error is all too easy to make. That is, a person can easily slip into the habit of talking about a given topic *without realizing* that she has entered into the sphere of abstraction.[97] When this occurs, one can easily be guilty of "making a transition from the ethical to something other than the ethical," of "confus[ing] God with something else," and of "confus[ing] myself with something else."[98] In these instances, the likely consequence will be a distorting objectification of the ethical, God, and myself. Furthermore, Climacus implies that many people do not even have a clear sense of the distinction between the two spheres in the first place: "people have entirely forgotten what it means to exist and what inwardness is."[99] That is, they have no conception of the subjective sphere of existence and inwardness and accordingly treat *everything* objectively.[100] Their blurring of the categorical spheres is not an occasional error, but rather a systemic and all-pervasive one. In terms of communication, this danger is doubled: if *either* the communicator *or* the receiver neglects the distinction between the spheres, the communication will tend to become objectified.

Applying Climacus' account to *Religion of Reason*, we can view Cohen as addressing an audience that may not have a clear conception of the non-objective sphere of religion. Accordingly, he seeks to illustrate the relevant features of this sphere through an extended performance that displays the fruits and products of a non-objectifying mode of reasoning. If one were able to apply the method of philosophy (corresponding to Climacus' "abstraction") to the question of man in a full systematic manner, one would produce a consistent theoretical account, albeit one lacking the concepts of the You, the unique God, the fellowman, and the individual as I. In contrast, Cohen shows that the application of a different method (corresponding to Climacus' "existence") will produce an account that lacks theoretical consistency, but encompasses a richer array of ethico-religious concepts. As Climacus argues, these two spheres have different standards for valid reasoning: while theoretical non-consistency in the sphere of strict philosophy would betoken faulty reasoning, its presence in the sphere of religion can instead prompt the recognition that a different *type* of concept is being addressed.

Similarly, while the communicative goal that corresponds to the method of philosophy is the conveyance of sound theoretical knowledge about its subject matter, this is not the communicative goal with regard to the sphere of religion. Indeed, this *could not* be the goal, because the concepts in the sphere of religion have no objective or theoretical content about which one could have such knowledge. Thus, we can view one aspect of Cohen's communicative goal in negative terms: namely, that the reader should come away from the book with a *lack* of autonomous theoretical knowledge about the religious concepts. If the reader comes to the book with pretended knowledge about the subject matter, then the effect of Cohen's contradictory style should be (as Climacus puts it) to *take knowledge away* from the reader.[101] If a reader comes to the text with a determinate position, one of Cohen's interpretive passages may seem to affirm it, but another will undermine it. This second passage, however, cannot itself become a source of knowledge, since the first passage remains to undermine *it*.

In positive terms, this inability to extract theoretical knowledge from *Religion of Reason* would ideally lead the reader to the conscious *recognition that* there is no theoretical knowledge to be gained about the concepts and that one should instead approach them with a different end in mind. This recognition characterizes what Climacus calls "the simple wise person," who refrains from claiming comprehension of essential truth itself, saying instead, "[A]t most I comprehend that it cannot be otherwise, that it must be incomprehensible."[102] Additionally, this awareness should also strengthen the reader's ability to identify the category-confusions that often occur in expositions or disputes concerning religious concepts: if others treat religious matters as though they involved objective concepts and theoretical assertions, a reader habituated by Cohen's account should be able to recognize the presence of an improper mode of reasoning and a wrongly applied method.

It is true that, although there can be no *theoretical* knowledge with regard to religious concepts, Cohen does want to retain another sense of the term 'knowledge' in connection to the sphere of religion. That is, while he insists on the importance of 'knowledge of God,' this does not refer to impersonal, objective knowledge. Rather, Cohen draws upon the biblical sense of the term, which connotes an engaged personal relation.[103] Because he recognizes that the modern use of the term 'knowledge' is quite different from its biblical use, he stresses that 'knowledge of God' should be understood specifically as "active devotion to, and acknowledgement of God."[104] Cohen's retention of the term 'knowledge' may be intended to ward off a misunderstanding of his account of religion as merely emotive and anti-intellectual. He emphasizes that the concepts of religion *do* have a substantive content with a cognitive component, even though this content is neither objective nor theoretical.[105]

Because the 'knowledge' that corresponds to religious concepts is of a personal and individual sort, Cohen's communicative goal cannot consist of the direct conveyance of such knowledge. Instead, through his various and often-contradictory interpretations, he illustrates the *effects* of such knowledge. It remains to the reader to 'put the pieces together' and to discern that which lies behind the various interpretations, an act of transcendental reconstruction that can only be performed in an engaged and personal manner. Cohen's role in this process is simply to provide the occasion and opportunity for this 'self-activity' on the part of the reader, which in turn becomes the source for the practical knowledge that characterizes the sphere of religion.[106]

This practical knowledge further differs from theoretical knowledge in that the former represents a dynamic capability or habit which is not permanent and may be present in various degrees at different times. If one learns from a history book that "the Iliad was written by Homer," there is not a pressing need for a continuous relearning of this piece of theoretical knowledge. In this case, one's knowledge is essentially an either/or affair: either one knows this fact, or one does not. In contrast, because a religious idea such "God is unique" is not a theoretical matter, it cannot be learned 'once and for all.' Rather, one's practical knowledge in this regard will manifest itself in life in the form of stronger or weaker ethical habits. If the habits corresponding to the practical acknowledgement of God's uniqueness are not reinforced, they will atrophy, and other habits, corresponding to an objectified conception of God, will become dominant.

Thus, when a reader engages in a self-active reconstruction that 'transcends' Cohen's presentation of the theoretical contradictions, this act can *strengthen* her practical knowledge and habits; however, this represents only one moment in what must be a continual process. If those strengthened habits are to be further strengthened and preserved, the reader must also continue to engage in other practices. Now, it is possible that one example of such a practice could be a re-reading of Cohen's own book: a re-engagement of the contraries, even if they have already been 'seen' before, can have a renewed de-objectifying effect. However, *Religion of Reason* can also be understood as providing the reader with a guidebook containing numerous examples of how to move *from* Scripture *to* practical-rational understandings of religious concepts. By following Cohen's lead, the reader can learn how to directly engage Scripture herself. In this sense, each reader will be able to re-derive the religion of reason from out of the sources of Judaism, not in order to produce a theoretical account of religion, but as a repeated practice of ethically formative reading. Because Scripture continually remains 'rough' and 'vague,' each instance of re-reading provides a renewed opportunity for a dynamic reconstruction and recreation of the personal-practical religious concepts. A single reading, in contrast, will provide only a temporary effect and a temporary attainment of practical knowledge. In this sense, even Cohen's own written interpretations do not represent conclusive 'results'; they are merely illustrative snapshots culled from what must be a continuous process of re-origination.

This might also be an opportune moment to raise the question of why Cohen employs *Scripture* to convey his ideas. While the hermeneutic approach of reasoning-from-sources is essential to Cohen's communicative style, couldn't other texts have played the role of the source from which to reason? Cohen himself points to this possibility in the introduction of his book, when he states that other religious traditions have the duty to construct a religion of reason from out of *their* sources.[107] Thus, one reason for Cohen's choice is that he views the Hebrew Bible as the primary source-text for the tradition with which he himself identifies. However, there may be also internal aspects of Hebrew Bible's content and style that particularly lend themselves to the type of rational reading that Cohen presents. For instance, as Cohen points out, the Hebrew Bible is not the product of a strictly philosophical mode of reasoning.[108] Rather, its style is characterized by a fundamental "naïveté."[109] As such, its concepts may lack full conceptual clarity, but they also preserve many of the personal-relational qualities of the sphere of religion. While its presentation of God and man may, in its plain sense, sometimes fall short of reason's criterion of universality, it has the advantage of not objectifying and flattening those crucial concepts.[110] Thus, the Hebrew Bible provides Cohen with rich raw material that he can reshape, preserving its correlational properties while drawing out an understanding that accords with the universal demands of ethicality. In contrast, a more refined source-text, whose content is already more in accordance with the criterion of universality, is likely to have also flattened and objectified the personal-relational aspects of its subject matter. While such a text could be used for deriving a theoretically consistent philosophical or theological system, it might less suited to Cohen's theoretically contradictory presentation of religion. That is, since Cohen seeks an understanding of religion that is both rational and non-objective, it might be easier for him to work with a text whose concepts are non-objective but not-yet-rational, rather than with a text whose concepts are more rational but objectified.[111]

Another advantage to the Hebrew Bible's 'primitivity' concerns the dynamic and personal nature of religious concepts, which cannot be communicated directly, in a general and impersonal manner, but must be actively engaged and reconstructed by each individual. The fact that the biblical text is 'rough' and 'unfinished,' that it *requires* its reader to engage and shape it, constitutes a positive advantage for the practice of formational reading. If a text directly puts forth refined spiritual ideas, it might be harder to draw the meaning out of the text through personal engagement, since the drawing-out has 'already been done' for the reader. Furthermore, if such refined ideas were given directly in the plain sense of the text, this could create the impression that they *can* be given directly, in other words, that they are something general. This in turn would mean that they could be impersonally comprehended, with no inherent connection to embodied ethical habits. In contrast, the Hebrew Bible's vagueness necessarily turns the process of reading into a 'do it yourself' endeavor, creating a stronger link between the meaning that is drawn from the text and the individual's *act* of interpretation.

Finally, as a qualification of the preceding discussion of Cohen's communicative style, it should be emphasized that the link between assertoric expression of ideas and conceptual distortion is not an inherently necessary one. It is not the case, for instance, that a third-person style must *always* lead to objectification of religious ideas. Instead, we should say that in certain circumstances, a third-person style *can tend to* or *is likely to* lead to objectification. Climacus also indicates that his guidelines for indirect communication need not be understood as universally applicable theses about all human communication; rather, his warnings are linked to *culturally specific and culturally contingent* associations with language. He repeatedly notes that the category-confusions that he seeks to combat are characteristic of "our day," "our age," "this age," and so forth. He also indicates that other cultures (e.g., Greeks and Jews in antiquity) might have been less guilty of confusing the spheres and of misunderstanding the categories of inwardness and subjectivity.[112] Thus, it is entirely possible that there could be a culture in which people could speak about ethico-religious matters in what could seem like a more direct, straightforward manner, without giving rise to distortion and confusion. That is, the receiver of the communication could recognize that, even though a statement has the *form* of an impersonal 'is,' one should not treat the subject matter as though it were a theoretical topic. In such a case, the receiver would contribute the 'repersonalization' and 'deobjectification' himself. The main point, though, is that "this age" tends *not* to respond in this way and therefore requires a different form of communication.

Even within a given culture, in a particular time and place, there could be a wide range of responses to a communication that is more direct. Some individuals might be more able than others to speak and hear about religious concepts without objectifying them. Thus, the style of *Religion of Reason*, which makes explicit the non-theorizable and non-objectifiable nature of religious concepts, may be more necessary and beneficial for those who would otherwise be prone to theoretization and objectification. In some ways, those who consider themselves to be philosophers or intellectuals could be more at risk than less theoretically inclined individuals. As Climacus puts it, this can be a situation in which "the wise person" could be at a disadvantage to "the simple person."[113] A "simple" person could be intuitively capable of employing and speaking about religious concepts without objectifying them, even if that person were not *consciously aware* that the concepts were 'non-objectifiable' and that they lacked 'theoretical content.' In practice, however, the lack of such conscious awareness could make a person—including one with fewer intellectualizing tendencies of his own—more susceptible to being led astray by seductive objectifying arguments; a greater conscious awareness can be useful both for correcting *and* for preventing such errors. Thus, the training in the practical-relational nature of religious concepts that Cohen's text provides can strengthen the ability of *all* readers to avoid ethically and intellectually deleterious confusions of categories.

5

Communicating through Contradiction

COHEN'S PERFORMANCE OF RELIGIOUS CONCEPTS

THIS CHAPTER EXAMINES Cohen's presentation of three key concepts, namely, the love of God, commandedness, and repentance. For each of these, readers who attempt to construct a consistent theoretical account of 'Cohen's position' will likely find themselves frustrated. While Cohen sometimes seems to reject the notion of God as personal agent, there are other places where he appears to speak freely of a personal and active God. Thus, while he sometimes speaks of the love of God as love for an idea, he elsewhere presents the individual's love for God in terms of an intimately personal relation. In some places, the ethical imperative arises autonomously from within, while in other places it appears to be a result of God's command from without. Similarly, purification from sin is sometimes presented as the result of self-sanctification, while elsewhere it is God alone who purifies. For each of these concepts, we encounter what seem to be two distinct perspectives: one is human-centered and is shaped by the method of philosophy, while the other is centered in the personal correlation between God and the human being and is strongly influenced by scriptural formulations.

Faced with these challenges, an interpreter's initial instinct may be to 'make sense of' these contradictions by searching for a third perspective that could mediate between the other two. In this case, though, there may be no single theoretical perspective that could mediate between Cohen's disparate statements concerning love of God, commandedness, and reconciliation. Instead, a reader of *Religion of Reason* may be better served by viewing each of these concepts as corresponding to a *practice*. That is to say, there is a distinct practice, a doing, in which a human being can engage and which can be described as 'love of God' or 'loving God.' When we *reflect on* this practice, however, we find that it cannot be conceived of as a theoretical unity; instead, it 'splits' into two contradictory ways of conceiving it. One must emphasize both of these in order to communicate the practice properly; if one of them is given primacy, this distortion of one-sidedness will fail to convey the proper concept, and will in turn lead to a different and distorted practice. That is, an account that sought to achieve consistency by presenting the love of God either by upholding 'love of a person' and rejecting 'love of an idea,' or by upholding 'love of an idea' while rejecting 'love of a person,' would convey a flattened concept and would produce a deficient practice. The same could be said with regard to the practices of 'being commanded' and 'purifying oneself/being forgiven.' In each case, the practice can be learned or conveyed in various ways (e.g., by means of story, ritual, or lived example), but it cannot be thought or described in a theoretically consistent manner. As we shall see, Cohen's use of distinct 'voices'—each of which corrects for the one-sidedness that would otherwise result from the dominance of the other—enables *Religion of Reason* to avoid such theoretical flattening and distortion. With regard to these concepts of religion, then, that which has unity in practice requires multiplicity in theory, while that which may be contradictory in theory can 'work' in practice.

I. Loving God
(a) Love of a person and love of an idea

That Cohen recognizes potential pitfalls in the notions of God's love and love for God is indicated by his devoting an entire chapter not simply to "Religious Love," but to "The *Problem* of Religious Love" (my emphasis). Before turning to this chapter, though, let us first examine a number of passages in *Religion of Reason* that describe the love between God and human beings in starkly and unqualifiedly personal terms. In these passages, there are no indications that applying such personal language to God is at all 'problematic.' In some of them, notably, Cohen's personality-infused descriptions are directly juxtaposed with scriptural citations, indicating that he has 'carried over' the language of the Bible in his own formulations. For instance, he describes "the fundamental commandment of *love* for God," which he links both to Deuteronomy 6:4–5 (the *shema* and *ve-ahavta*) and to Deuteronomy 11:1 ("Love, therefore, the Lord your God, and always keep his charge, his laws, his rules, and his commandments").[1] Here, Cohen does not restrict or qualify the apparently personal nature of this love. His main point in this passage is to emphasize the link between the commandment of love for God and the commandment of following God's laws; in so doing, he appears simply to take for granted the use of the term 'love' in its scriptural setting, a setting which certainly has no qualms about personifying the divine.

In a later passage, Cohen indicates another dimension of divine-human love, stating, "God loves the stranger."[2] He links this assertion to Deuteronomy 10:18–19, where it says of God that "he executes justice for the orphan and the widow, and he loves the stranger, giving him food and clothing. Therefore you shall love the stranger, for you were strangers in the land of Egypt." Cohen's own statement

is taken directly from the biblical formulation, but again, he does not treat the
fact that God loves or that God can love as remarkable; rather, his emphasis is on
the fact that God loves *the stranger*, and therefore you ought to as well. Furthermore, the same verb (*a-h-v*) is used in verses 18 and 19 to describe both God's love
for the stranger and the love that is commanded of the addressees ("you") of the
speech. Thus, if your love for the human stranger is clearly a personal love, a love
between persons, the plain sense of the verse—which Cohen does not reject or
even qualify here—would seem to imply that God's love (designated by the same
term) is likewise personal.

Elsewhere, we find that Cohen presents the relationship between God and
human beings in even more strongly personal language, quite apart from an
explicit connection to any particular scriptural verse (although his portrayal of
this relationship is clearly drawn from and influenced by Scripture as a whole).
For instance, the love for God is no mere staid intellectual orientation, but rather
a fervently personal devotion: "This love for God, which has all the strength of a
passion, laments and wails and rejoices and feels jubilation; it moistens with its
tears the resting place, and it makes the intestines burn."[3] In addition, God's love
for the human being and the human being's love for God are not separate and
self-sustaining attitudes. Rather, like the mutuality of inter-human love, they constitute a "reciprocal relationship [*Wechselwirkung*] between God and man" in
which "God loves man. And man loves God."[4] Within this relationship, both
parties are 'interested parties' and seek out one another: having identified God's
love with his goodness, Cohen declares (prefiguring the title of Abraham Joshua
Heschel's *God in Search of Man*), "When man seeks God with his love, God seeks
him with his goodness."[5] This personal intimacy and mutuality extends so far that
Cohen even describes the relationship between God and the human being as one
of "friendship," linked to "the brotherhood of the covenant."[6]

All of these descriptions can be viewed as constituting the voice of 'pathos'
and 'the positive,' as described in the previous chapter. God and the human
being's relation to God are portrayed in personal, and indeed very 'human,'
terms—perhaps a little *too* human, one could easily think. To be sure, in an
important sense, it is Scripture that says these things (and Scripture is known to
'speak in human language'), but Cohen also seems to say them, beyond the
boundaries of the quotation marks that delimit his scriptural citations. Furthermore, apart from the personal-*sounding* language of his descriptions, Cohen
explicitly identifies the personality, the person-hood of God, as that which separates religion (as derived from the sources of Judaism) from "Greek speculation,"
that is, from the method of philosophy. The distinction of the former from the
latter consists in "the transformation of the neuter into a person," a shift that
Cohen also expresses, a few sentences later, as "the transformation of an abstraction into a person."[7] (This description parallels Cohen's introductory account of

the distinction between philosophy and religion, wherein the fellowman is discovered via a similar transformation of the He into the You.) Thus, since Cohen's aim in his book is to put forth a presentation of *religion*, his person-centric accounts of God's love and of love for God need come as no surprise.

Immediately after asserting this transformation, though, Cohen also points out, "As a result of this, admittedly, anthropomorphism becomes unavoidable."[8] For Cohen, the term 'anthropomorphism' designates a uniformly negative error that is to be avoided and opposed. We must distinguish, however, between anthropomorph*ism* and anthropomorph*ic* forms of expression. In Cohen's use, the former refers to the conceptual application of qualities to God that ought properly to be applied only to humans, that is, conceiving of God in terms that are *too* humanized. This is not to be equated with using 'human' *language* in describing relation with God, something that Cohen himself does, as we have seen, in many places.[9] Such language is a legitimate tool for communication, so long as it does not result in a distorted form of conceiving and (since the concepts of religion are practical concepts) of action.

If we again recall Cohen's efforts in his introduction to avoid both egoism and totalizing objectification, we can say that problem of the former consisted in 'too much' of the particular individual, while the problem of the latter consisted in 'not enough' of the particular individual. These ethical dangers are paralleled in the present context by anthropomorphism, in which God is 'too much of a person,' and the approach of Greek speculation, in which God is a neuter abstraction and thus 'not enough of a person.' Importantly, Cohen does not say that religion's "transformation of the neuter into a person" *itself* constitutes an example of anthropomorphism, but rather that anthropomorphism becomes unavoidable *as a result* of this transformation.[10] Thus, there seems to be a sense in which the dynamic act of moving *from* abstract neuter *to* person is legitimate and desirable, but where dwelling upon 'person' as a static concept can also turn 'person' into its own type of abstraction and thereby lead to illegitimate and undesirable consequences. 'Neuter' appears to say too little, but 'person' seems to say too much. In other words, Cohen does not want to *conceive of* God as either neuter or person; rather, he seems to be seeking out the paradoxical space between the two.

Consequently, having initially looked at 'positive' passages that convey a strongly personal account of God, we should now examine 'negative' passages that seem to present God in more abstract terms. While Cohen speaks freely throughout his book of God's love and of love for God, he acknowledges, in the opening paragraph of his chapter on "The Problem of Religious Love," that "it is neither in itself clear, nor psychologically settled, what love means with regard to God, neither God's love nor love for God."[11] While typical connotations of the term 'love' do involve a relation between persons, they also frequently include elements of eros and sensual, if not sexual, qualities. If love of God is portrayed in personal terms, does this then mean that it must encompass some form of sensuality as well? Cohen adamantly rejects this notion and insists that religious love, as love of God (and fellowman), "is a new concept of religion, which is not identical with sexual love, and not with eros, and hence also not with aesthetic love."[12] At the same time, he also emphasizes that love of God is not merely intellectual love, in the sense of Spinoza's *amor intellectualis*, a love in which "love is knowledge only" and is consequently only a theoretical attitude.[13] While each of these other two types of love (aesthetic and intellectual) could be easily and directly conveyed, religious love "is not something self-evident [*Selbstverständlichkeit*]. It must be explicated and penetrated at every point of religion."[14] In other words, because of a natural tendency to turn it into one or the other of the two more easily comprehended types of love, great care must be taken in thinking about religious love. Aesthetic love encompasses personality but also eros, while intellectual love removes eros but also personality. In contrast, religious love can be said to remove eros while retaining personality, thus placing it on the border between aesthetic and intellectual love. This dynamic recalls Cohen's earlier account of the prophets, who "create a style in [the] border-area between art and science."[15] As in that case, a dualistic mindset can make it appear as though there could be no category 'between' aesthetic and intellectual love.[16] Consequently, accounts of religious love that rightly recognize its lack of eros will also tend to remove the element of personality, thus assimilating it to intellectual love, while accounts that rightly recognize the element of personality will also tend to incorporate sensual categories (even if not explicitly), thus assimilating it to aesthetic love and giving rise to anthropomorphism. Because religious love "is not something self-evident"—a situation which can be linked to the theoretically-contradictory nature of religious concepts—Cohen finds a greater value in demarcating the love of God negatively: it is *not* intellectual love and it is also *not* aesthetic love. If one can successfully avoid both of those categories—no easy task—then one is more likely to find oneself on the right track.

Cohen continues his negative approach by denying to God many of the qualities that one would usually associate with the object or subject of personal love. For instance, he denies that the notion of existence (*Dasein*)—as distinguished from being (*Sein*)—can be applied to the unique God,[17] and he refers derisively to "the so-called existence of God."[18] Cohen also insists that the unique God "can have no actuality [*Wirklichkeit*]." The notion of God having actuality could apply only to "reverence for a God imagined as human-esque," but it can play no role in the love of the unique God.[19] While 'denying the existence of God' and 'denying God's actuality' (or even 'God's reality,' another possible translation of *Wirklichkeit*[20]) might seem like surprising positions to find alongside other passages that affirm the love of God,[21] one must be attuned to the specific meaning that Cohen assigns to these terms. His denial of the existence of God is predicated on the fact that "existence is attested by the senses, by perception."[22] Likewise, "actuality is a concept relating thought to sensation."[23] The removal of sensibility from God, he argues, has constituted a long-standing and prominent (though not exclusive) trend in Jewish religious thought, from Onkelos to Maimonides: "From the very beginning Jewish speculation combats the anthropomorphism in the Bible."[24] Consequently, his own similar denial of the sense-related attributes of existence and actuality ought not, he indicates, place him outside the mainstream of Jewish tradition.

At the same time, even if Cohen is able to find historical precedents for his position, its uncompromising negativity appears to preclude the notion of personal love: how can love be possible if the object of love neither exists nor is actual? In addressing this difficulty, we should first note that the absence of these features *would* eliminate love with regard to a human being: one cannot love a human being who is not (and has never been) actual and who lacks any sensible qualities. Cohen's negative position therefore serves, at the least, to counteract any potential anthropomorphisms that a reader might have inadvertently acquired from Cohen's 'positive' descriptions of God's love. If a reader thinks that lack of actuality would eliminate love for and from God, this indicates that such a god was overly "human-esque" in the first place. Secondly, though Cohen denies actuality and existence to God, we do *not* find any instances in which he says, "God is not a person." Thus, we are apparently faced with the odd situation in which God is not actual and yet loves and can be loved as a person. If such a combination seems like an impossibility, this may be because it *is* impossible from an objective-theoretical point of view. In a sense, Cohen's negative denials seem to take away everything that was posited through his positive descriptions, leaving nothing behind—but this 'nothing' is a special, personal type of nothing, whose theoretical emptiness does not preclude a rich practical and regulative content. Hence, one cannot *conceive of* relating personally to a non-existent, non-actual God—yet one can *do* so in practice. Accordingly, Cohen does not 'solve' the problem of religious love directly, within in the theoretical framework of his text; instead, he remains just as negative as positive, presenting both scriptural positivity and anti-anthropomorphic negativity, and leaving it to the reader to respond to the problem of love through the act of love.

A slightly different variation on negativity can be found in Cohen's discussion of the significance of the idea of God and of God as idea. Here, the negativity takes the grammatical form of positivity: rather than saying that God *is not* actual, Cohen seems to indicate that God *is* an idea and that, therefore, love for God is love for an idea.[25] From this, multiple commentators have concluded that, for Cohen, God is abstract, depersonalized, and falls short of 'the living God of the Jewish tradition.'[26] If God is 'only' an idea, they argue, a reciprocal, interpersonal relation of love is ruled out and rendered unthinkable.

Such a conclusion, though, falls into the trap of one-sidedness and neglects the paradoxicality of Cohen's understanding of religious concepts. First of all, these commentators often make the mistake of conflating Cohen's technical use of the term 'idea' (*Idee*) with everyday uses of the term as synonymous with concepts such as 'concept' or 'notion.' Thus, they would argue that just as one's thirst would remain unquenched if one attempted to drink the concept of water rather than water itself, so too love for the God-idea cannot compare to love for God Godself.[27] It may indeed be the case that one cannot personally love and be loved by a 'concept' or a 'notion,' but Cohen never says that the love for God is love for a concept. In contrast, the term 'idea,' as Cohen uses it, designates something qualitatively different. Cohen is strongly influenced by Kant, who (himself influenced by Plato) defines 'idea' as "a necessary concept of reason for which no corresponding object can be given in sense-experience."[28] Thus, while the concept of water differs sharply from actual water as an object of sense-experience—such that the 'mere concept' could be deficient in comparison—an idea of reason is dissociated from sense-experience as such, and so has no corresponding object of sense-experience in comparison to which it might 'fall short.' As we shall see, it is the latter part of this definition—the categorical separation from sensuous attributes—that is most relevant for Cohen's description of God as an idea. Let me now illustrate some further details of Cohen's sense of 'idea' through the explication of one of *Religion of Reason*'s most frequently misunderstood passages.

Recognizing that 'love for an idea' might strike many readers as bizarre, Cohen raises the question, "How can one love an idea?" He then responds, "How can one love anything other than an idea? One loves, even in the case of sensuous love, only the idealized person, only the idea of the person."[29] At first glance, this assertion makes it seem as though Cohen is only digging a deeper philosophical hole for himself—having already turned God into a depersonalized abstraction, he now wants to do the same to other human beings as well. Martin Buber's reaction to Cohen on this point typifies an understandable resistance: "Yet even if it were correct that in the love of 'the senses' (or more correctly, in the love that comprehends sensuality) one loves only the idealized person, that does not at all mean that nothing more than the idea of the person is loved; even the idealized person remains a person and has not been transformed into an idea."[30] Here, 'idea' and 'person' are treated as mutually exclusive: if the person *had* been transformed into an idea, then he or she would no longer remain a person. Cohen, on Buber's reading, has forgotten or distorted this basic fact of human personality.

Instead of criticizing Cohen on such grounds, however, the very strangeness of his assertion should perhaps instead lead the reader to wonder whether, in fact, something else is going on. It should be clear—as evidenced by his emphasis on relating to the fellowman as a 'you'—that Cohen knows full well that the love of another human being is a personal love, and is love for a person. Therefore, if he says that one loves "only the idea of the person," this must mean that such love is *not* exclusive of loving the other as a person, as a 'you.' Indeed, it may mean that one loves the other as a 'you' *precisely by* loving only the idea of the person. Cohen never says that one loves the idea of the person *instead of* the person himself: rather, to love the idea of the person *is* to love the person himself. In other words, although the human being has many sensuous attributes, one does not direct one's love at any of these. Rather, the person whom one loves—in other words, the 'you'—is *not* sensuous, is invisible to the senses, and hence is 'only' an idea.[31]

If we apply this analysis to the case of God, we can see that loving 'the idea of God' need not be incompatible with, but may actually be constitutive of loving God as a person.[32] It is true that the situation is slightly different, in that the human being *also* has sensuous attributes, even though these are not the object of one's love, whereas in the love of God there are no sensuous attributes involved at all. In both cases, however, the fact that that which one loves is 'only' an idea does not detract from the depth, reality, or personal nature of the relationship.[33] In fact, as was the case with God's actuality, the desire to assert that God is 'more than' an idea will result in the introduction of sensuous categories into one's understanding of God, thereby engendering an ethically problematic anthropomorphism.[34]

In spite of the functional equivalence that they may share, however, it cannot be denied that the notion of 'idea' *sounds* and *feels* very different from that of 'person.' Speaking of God as an idea gives the impression that God is subordinate to, dependent upon, and found only within the human psyche. Buber's opposition to the notion of God as idea may thus stem from his desire to prevent the reduction of God to a mere product of fantasy and imagination.[35] Conversely, speaking of God as a person gives the impression of God's independence from and externality to the human being. In relation to oneself, an idea would ostensibly be immanent while a person would be transcendent. In Cohen's account, however, and in accord with his concept of correlation, neither immanence nor transcendence properly accounts for the relation between God and the human being. Each of these options would be representable by the objective method of philosophy, whereas Cohen, in contrast, emphasizes that "there is only a *subjective* dividing wall (*mechitza*) between God and man."[36] Because the "dividing wall" is only subjective, there can be no single theoretical account that properly conveys the nature of the relation: God is neither strictly internal nor strictly external to the human being.[37] Thus, the fact that 'idea' *seems* different from 'person' may correspond to the multiplicity of voices that is required to communicate religious concepts. While one can speak in personal terms when commenting on Scripture, it may be that 'idea' is all that one can say when reflecting abstractly on the God-human relation (as Cohen is doing in this section). In other words,

God's personal love is not something that can be asserted philosophically as an objective general truth; it holds true only for the individual who is engaged in the relationship.

The implications of Cohen's allegiance to this philosophical austerity are fittingly (though perhaps inadvertently) illustrated by a somewhat critical statement of Martin Buber's, who writes, "[T]hough Cohen indeed thought of God as an idea, Cohen too loved him as—God."[38] Here, Buber portrays Cohen as torn between his intellectual commitments and his religious sentiment. Though Cohen subconsciously desires to love God as a person (i.e., "as—God"), he is 'blinded' by his philosophical method and is unable to consciously affirm what his heart is telling him. Accordingly, in Buber's depiction, a more self-conscious Cohen who was less in thrall to his philosophical prejudices would cease to hop between two ideas and would come finally to think of God as God, leaving behind the notion of God as idea. In my portrayal, conversely, 'idea' is not something that should be overcome and rejected—especially not in thought.[39] That is, while Buber's account of Cohen is equivalent to "He thought of God as an idea *but* he loved God as a person," a better description could be attained by changing the conjunction: "He thought of God as an idea *and* he loved God as a person."[40] While one may actively and dynamically relate to God as a person, there is an important sense in which one ought not *think of* God as a person. In Climacus' terms, one must keep the sphere of speculative abstraction separate from the sphere of ethical existence and subjectivity: what is valid and true in one sphere is false in another. The necessary act of abstraction involved in reflecting *on* God means that the descriptive term ('person') that is highly appropriate in the context of relating *to* God becomes highly inappropriate in the context of impersonal speculative thought, and thinkers err when they falsely remove the division between these two spheres in a quest for a single universal description. By contrast, Cohen's style in *Religion of Reason* helps maintain this distinction by displaying the love of God both from the perspective of (general) thought and from the perspective of the particular individual's dynamic relationship.

(b) The psalm as literary manifestation of religious love

Another way of approaching Cohen's understanding and presentation of the love of God is to examine his account of the biblical psalms. According to Cohen, the psalm represents "the style-form of religious love, of the love of God."[41] As we saw in his discussion of "The Style of the Prophets," he views idea-content and style as intimately bound to one another.[42] A particular idea-content (the 'what') calls for a particular style and form (the 'how') for its proper communication. Put differently, a particular idea-content will display its effects by giving rise naturally to a certain type of literary expression. As Cohen puts it, "The particular character

[*Eigenart*] of monotheism determines the particular character of the psalms."[43] Thus, one can gain an understanding of different types of concepts not only by examining them directly as abstract notions, but also indirectly, by examining and comparing the different textual forms in which they manifest themselves.[44] In the case of religious concepts, which resist direct theoretical analysis, the turn to indirect textual manifestation is all the more necessary. Thus, as part of his strategy for conveying the unique features of religious love, Cohen focuses on the psalm (as the style-form of religious love), seeking to differentiate it from other, ostensibly similar literary forms. Specifically, he compares the psalm both with the hymn of praise to the hero or deity and with the lyric love poem. Thus, he approaches the concept of religious love through two layers of indirection, first by looking at its literary form, and then by employing an indirect, contrastive method in order to bring out that form's essential features.

Cohen acknowledges that "[t]he psalm . . . has its analogy in the Greek, as well as the Babylonian hymn," a literary form that he characterizes as "a paean to the deity or a dithyramb to the god, who helped a hero to victory, or even a song of victory for the hero himself and for his ancestors, like such songs as Pindar sang."[45] A key characteristic of such hymns consists of an absence of personal relation between the praiser and the praised, between the singer and the god or hero. In contrast, the distinguishing feature of the psalm involves "the transformation of the hymn, as praise of God, into the longing of love, which drives the soul to God."[46] The change is one from respectful and grateful praise from afar, in which God is assumed to be transcendent and distant, to intimate desire, in which one seeks a God who is immanent and near. In the psalm, it is not this or that gift or mighty act of God which is the focus, but rather the personal nearness of God Godself; as stated by Psalm 73:28, which Cohen cites, "The nearness of God is my good."[47] Importantly, Cohen emphasizes God's closeness and immanence not in an absolute sense, but only *relative to* and *in contrast to* the impersonal distance of the hymn of praise. Elsewhere, for instance, he wards off a *too* immanent understanding of the love of God, asserting, "God himself is not desired. Mythological love directs itself toward God himself. In contrast, monotheistic love yearns only for the nearness of God, the nearness of God to man, the nearness of man to God."[48] Thus, in one place, he emphasizes nearness in contrast to distance, whereas in another place he emphasizes *merely* nearness, in contrast to possession or union. Accordingly, in relation to Cohen's primary goal of avoiding one-sidedness and imbalance, his contrast of the psalm to the hymn of praise indicates the *direction* in which one needs to move: *if* one is currently positioned at the hymn of praise, then one needs *more* immanence and closeness.[49] This relative contrast does not, however, make an assertion about the static nature of the psalm, which, like the concept of religious love of which it is the literary manifestation, remains ungraspable by the theoretical understanding.

Additionally, while Cohen seeks to differentiate the psalm from the hymn of praise, he admits that the two share "external similarities."[50] In acknowledging such similarity, Cohen may especially have in mind such psalms as Psalm 29, which begins, "Ascribe unto the Lord, O you sons of gods, ascribe unto the Lord glory and strength / Ascribe unto the Lord the glory due to his name, bow to the Lord in holy splendor," and which goes on to praise God's vanquishing mastery over the various forces of nature, concluding with a call for God to use this strength to protect and bless "his people." With a simple replacement of Marduk for YHVH, such a composition might be at home in an ancient Babylonian hymnal. However, Cohen does not want to 'prove' from the psalm itself that it is different from the hymn of praise, a task that might easily devolve into tendentious hair-splitting. Rather, while granting *external* similarity, he insists that the psalm contains an "*inward* difference from the so-called Babylonian psalm. That which does not become immediately clear with regard to the psalm itself [*am Psalm selbst*], in its style-form, becomes distinct in it from the viewpoint of prayer."[51] In pointing to this "inward" difference, Cohen distinguishes between "the psalm itself" and the psalm considered "from the viewpoint of prayer." According to Cohen, the general form of prayer is found when a people "expresses in language its relation to a deity. The first stammering of man in a direct address to God can be nothing other than prayer."[52] Thus, the distinguishing characteristic of the psalm reveals itself *only* when one views it as a direct address to God. In contrast, "the psalm itself"—apart from the viewpoint of prayer—does *not* inherently display religious love, and could just as easily be taken as a non-relational hymn of praise.

This corresponds to Cohen's approach to Scripture more broadly, in that the literary sources become sources of *religion* only when engaged through the proper personal-practical orientation. Here, his hermeneutics and his conceptual analysis reinforce one another; in both cases, the engagement of the individual is the determining factor: just as 'the love of God' does not have general, theoretical significance, but takes on meaning only for the practically engaged individual, so too the significance of the psalm, as the literary manifestation of that love, cannot be discerned through a objective-historical method, which can only reconstruct the historical social setting of the psalm, but cannot judge whether any historical singer of the psalm inwardly intended it as prayer, as a direct and personal address to God. Only the hermeneutic intention of the individual interpreter of the psalm can enable one to approach it from the viewpoint of prayer.

Cohen maintains this distinction in the continuation of his treatment of the psalm, repeatedly referring not simply to "the psalm" but to the psalm "considered as prayer [*als Gebet betrachtet*]."[53] When approached in this way, the psalm's distinctiveness comes into view: "the I itself, the subject, becomes the object. Not the singer as such is the subject; rather, he must first bring it forth from out of himself."[54] In a hymn of praise, the speaker lauds the god, but the description is objective: it is simply a description of what the god has done. As such, anyone could say it, since it does not require any special relation to the object of praise; the orientation of the speaker is not relevant. In contrast, in the psalm considered as prayer, the speaker is not a given. Only the I of the unique individual can love the unique God, can directly address the unique God as 'you.'[55] The act of speaking therefore requires something of the speaker: it requires an inward and active striving in order to be able to speak.[56] In other words, the speaker, as subject, becomes object, because the speaker must not only strive toward God, but must also and simultaneously strive toward becoming a speaker who can strive toward and directly address the unique God. In accord with the concept of correlation, these two strivings are actually equivalent, and God does not cease to be the object of striving when the I itself also becomes the object.[57] As Cohen states, the psalms "sing neither of God alone, nor of man alone."[58] However, God does cease to be a *separable* object, an object separable from the speaker—a separation that would correspond to the psalmist being able to sing "of God alone." Lacking this separation, the psalm's love of God loses the general-objective conceivability that the hymn's praise of God still retains. The subject-as-object transformation also accounts for Cohen's need to present the love of God both as love of a person *and* as love of an idea, since a one-sided account (in either direction) would correspond only to a situation in which the subject is a given and the object is directly conceivable.

Cohen also emphasizes that having the I as object, as goal, does not entail a directedness toward 'oneself,' in the sense of one's ego. He writes, "The shaft of [the singer's] own inwardness [*Inneren*] must be unearthed, if the I in a new free self-sufficiency and purity is to arise. But for this the dialogue [*Zwiegespräch*] with God is necessary. And this dialogue is constituted by the monologue [*Monolog*] of prayer."[59] In other words, again in accord with correlation, one brings forth the I precisely by directing oneself to the 'you,' who, in the case of the biblical psalms, is the unique God.[60] The speaker cannot unearth the shaft of her inwardness on her own, by digging within her empirical self, but only by going beyond herself in dialogue.[61] In a sense, her inwardness is not something that exists simply 'in herself'; rather, it is found in the relation between herself and God. However, by the same token, God cannot be said simply to exist 'outside of' the singer of the psalm.[62] This strange relation is underscored by Cohen's description of the prayer as both monologue and dialogue. Dialogue implies an exchange between two persons, while monologue involves only a single person. Thus, the question of whether prayer involves 'another person,' apart from the singer of the psalm, lacks an unambiguous answer. Neither 'dialogue' nor 'monologue' (cf. 'person' vs. 'idea') can accurately represent the paradoxicality that hovers, as with all religious concepts, over the love of God.

Having emphasized the difference between the heroic hymn and the psalm as a transformation of praise into the longing of love, Cohen next compares the psalm to a literary form that is undeniably awash in love's longing. He maintains that the psalm has an "analogy" in lyric poetry (*die Lyrik*), the latter being "the confession that the soul itself utters of its own most inward and intimate experience. This most intimate experience is love."[63] Cohen insists that this basic definition also applies to the psalm's love of God, as the psalms "are written in the style-form of lyric poetry."[64] At the same time, though, the psalm differs sharply from most lyric poetry, in that the latter typically takes the form of erotic love for another human being, while the psalm removes all sensuality from its still-passionate desire.[65] While the hymn, in relation to the psalm, required a move to greater immanence and closeness of relation, the lyric poem demands a movement toward greater transcendence. If one begins with the lyric poem, one must 'take away' a certain sensual immediacy and givenness in order to reach the psalm.

Again, though, this taking-away must be seen only in terms of a direction of movement, and not in terms of a static condition. Simply to eliminate or negate sensuality would seem to undermine the psalm's claim to be an expression of passionate desire. As Cohen asks, "Does the psalm lack something of the fundamental power of love, because the love for God removes itself from eroticism with all its secrets?"[66] Here, the assumption is that love without sensuality and without the erotic is an insubstantial, feeble relation, not worthy of the name 'love.' While Cohen ultimately affirms the full passion of the non-sensual love of God, he acknowledges the validity of the question's suspicion. In the case of typical lyric poetry, a non-sensual love *would* be no love at all: "lyric love cannot and may not detach [the] idealization of the beloved person from the sexual *ur*-desire."[67] Because the lyric poem only represents an *analogy* for the psalm, the latter is not subject to this same limitation; it can embody robust love in the absence of sensuality. Yet, since the love of God is a paradoxical concept, there can be no *closer* or *better* analogy than the lyric poem. That is, while the lyric poem's sensual and erotic nature ultimately differentiates it from the psalm, a strictly non-sensual literary form would be unable to account for the psalm's passionate longing. As such, the psalm's love cannot be sensual, but it also cannot be non-sensual in a theoretically comprehensible sense. In a sense, while one can *love* without sensuality (i.e., this is a practice in which one can engage), to *conceive of* this love as non-sensual would lead to a distortion of one-sidedness. Cohen indicates this 'liminal' quality of religious love in his claims that "[the] all-powerfulness of the longing for God presumes to go right up to the *border* of sensuality"[68] and that it "goes up to the *border* of aesthetic love [*Kunstliebe*]."[69] This notion of 'border' or 'limit' (*Grenze*) again recalls Cohen's placement of the style of the prophets in the border-area between art and science. In this geographical-spatial metaphor, a border lies 'between' two regions, and falls neither on this side nor that side. At the same time, the border is infinitely close to *both* sides—yet it has no 'thickness' of its own. In this sense, the psalm represents a borderline literary form, which is distinct from both the too-distant praise of the hymn and the too-immediate eroticism of the lyric poem. Yet, despite its distinctiveness, it has no theoretical content of its own and gains its substance only in the practical and regulative engagement of the praying individual.

(c) The wonder of the psalm

While asserting this border-form, Cohen also seeks to emphasize that there are important ways in which his own assertion does not 'make sense.' That is, the direct linguistic assertion of a paradoxical, non-theoretical concept runs the risk of being inadvertently theoretized by the reader, thereby turning the concept into something categorically different. In order to avoid this result, Cohen attempts to underscore the 'strangeness' of the love of God: "One cannot love the unique God as a man or a woman. And yet one loves him and seeks him, and confesses this desire, because it is a true experience of the soul. This is indeed a wonder in the history of the soul, but monotheism itself is such a wonder."[70] Here, the "and yet" (*und doch*) represents the paradox. In theoretically consistent thought, there cannot be a love in which the object of love in not loved as a man or a woman, that is, as a sensual human being.[71] But, in practice, one does love and seek out the unique God. Cohen specifically omits any indication as to how one moves from the former statement to the latter: there is no logical-theoretical ground that could account for such a leap. Thus, Cohen describes the soul's love of God as a "wonder" or "miracle" (*Wunder*). Such love is miraculous not so much in the sense of something out of the ordinary, but rather as something that transcends the grasp of the theoretical understanding and is therefore 'supernatural.'[72] Yet, the love of God is not unique in this regard, since all of monotheism (as the service of the unique God), and hence all religious concepts, also transcend theoretical comprehension. While such concepts and the practices to which they correspond may be everyday occurrences and therefore 'familiar,' Cohen's description aims to emphasize that they remain eternally 'strange' when reflected upon abstractly.[73]

In the continuation of his description, Cohen further emphasizes the personal-practical nature of religious love: "And the literary expression of this wonder is the psalm, the highest creation of monotheism. For the prophet only admonishes one toward the love of God. But the psalm confesses this love as an actual experience of the soul. And this confession of the soul's experience is the psalm, as prayer."[74] A number of important points flow out of this pronouncement. First, in literary-textual terms, Cohen contrasts the psalm with the prophetic writings. While both the psalm and the prophetic admonition have as their object the worship and loving service of the unique God, there is something about the *form* and *style* of the admonition that makes it less ideal for communicating and conveying the love of God. As Cohen subsequently writes, "One recognizes ever more clearly the origin of prayer in the psalm and, within the latter, in the dialogue [*Zwiesprache*], which repentance conducts between the I and God. Prophetic rhetoric could not awaken this dialogical monologue [*dialogischen Monolog*]: it could be created only by lyric poetry, which is the original-form of love in longing."[75] While Cohen does not say so explicitly here, it seems that the most pertinent difference between psalmic lyricism and prophetic rhetoric involves the distinction between God as second-person object of address and as third-person object of description.[76] In a text of prophetic admonition, the prophet (1) encourages his audience (2) to love and serve God (3).[77] By its very style and structure, this form of communication can seem to imply that God has third-person existence, that is to say, a general and theoretical status, quite apart from the audience's own active engagement and current service, or lack thereof. While there may potentially be some positive value in such direct exhortation, it can also have the inadvertent affect of objectifying the specifically personal relation of love for God. In Climacus' terms, such an admonisher risks becoming a counterproductive "barker of inwardness."[78]

In contrast, the psalm, in the form of the lyric poem, consists of a second-person address, in which God is longed for as 'you.' The shift of God from the third person to the second corresponds to the deepening of a general-social responsibility into a personal-individual relation. Similarly, the observation that, literarily speaking, God appears in the second person and not in the third person mirrors the fact that, conceptually speaking, God 'appears' only regulatively-practically and not theoretically-constituitively. Cohen further accentuates the psalm's personal nature by arguing that it not only omits *third-person* reference to God but even, in a sense, omits *all* predicative description of the addressee. In the psalm, he maintains,

> Longing penetrates body and soul, and its expression knows no borders. But only it itself, only this anguish itself and this upsurge of the soul does the psalm describe and sing of; God, however, remains outside of this description. Whereas lyric poetry usually describes the beloved person, toward whom the longing draws it, here only the heart which feels the longing is described, but its object, God, is invoked not so much in his beauty, but rather exclusively only in his goodness, thus only as the archetype of ethical action.[79]

In other words, textually speaking, the psalmist's addressee remains 'invisible' to the reader of the psalms. God's love has its reality only for the one who is actively engaged in prayer; if I observe or read about such a person, I can see only her longing itself, but not its object.[80] From the reader's perspective, it can (and perhaps should) appear as though the psalmist is talking to 'nobody.' In typical lyric poetry, by contrast, the ability to provide description of the beloved corresponds to the actual-sensual existence of another human being, whose reality is *not* wholly dependent on personal engagement.[81] The psalm's absence of description, furthermore, is not simply for the sake of a potential reader of the psalms, but applies also to the pray-er herself: because the personality of the relationship exists only in the dynamic act of engagement, she possesses no descriptive terms that she could grasp through impersonal, abstract thought. In this sense, the pray-er's faculty of theoretical understanding stands in the same relation to the pray-er's action as does the reader of the psalm to the engaged psalmist. In each relation-pair, that which is powerfully present and real to the first party must remain absent and invisible to the first.

In this regard, it is significant that, in his paragraph on the wondrous nature of the love of God and of the psalm, Cohen four times repeats the phrase "the soul's experience" or close variants thereof.[82] It is specifically the *soul* that experiences and participates in the love of God—a term which Cohen, drawing upon Ezekiel, associates specifically with the ethically integrated and responsible individual, and not simply with the human as a living empirical being.[83] In other words, the soul, and not the faculty of the theoretical understanding, is the aspect of the human being that is active in the passionate and ethical act of loving God. In addition, it should be noted that Cohen renders 'experience' not by the term *Erfahrung*, which refers specifically to empirical-sensual experience that leads to theoretical knowledge, but by the term *Erlebnis*, whose root-meaning of 'life' can allow for a broader, more holistic meaning.[84]

If *Erfahrung* is that which gives rise to *Erkenntnis*, knowledge, it seems, in Cohen's presentation, that the *Erlebnis der Seele* of religious love gives rise instead to *Bekenntnis,* confession, a term which also appears four times in that same paragraph.[85] Earlier, Cohen had described reason's share in religion as bringing about "the transformation of knowledge [*Erkenntnis*] into love."[86] In this formulation, it may appear as though the relation toward God, having been transformed into one of love, is *no longer* one of knowledge. However, like the tension between 'idea' and 'person,' the static replacement of knowledge by love would be one-sidedly distorting. While knowledge sounds too impersonal and abstract, love can seem 'too personal' and emotion-based, lacking substantive content: each single term, to the extent that it represents a theoretically consistent concept, will mislead in one direction or another. In his effort to avoid both egoistic subjectification as well as totalizing objectification, he seems to seek a concept that can somehow fill the paradoxical gap 'between' love and knowledge. Thus, while he notes that "love is not knowledge," he insists that "Scripture demands knowledge as well as love." Yet, he does not want to view this as two separate demands; rather, "knowledge is demanded only as love," even though the two "are not identical with one another."[87] Here, Cohen's struggles to express himself may appear self-contradictory, but it may be the case that his very inconsistency in the theoretical-reflective act of writing represents an accurate reflection of the internal theoretical inconsistency of the religious concepts themselves. That is, an honest reflection on these concepts will produce contradictory forms of expression.

Cohen uses the term 'confession' in an attempt to convey this paradoxicality. While *Bekenntnis* shares an etymological root with *Erkenntnis*, it differs in that "*Bekenntnis* signifies an *action of the will*, in distinction from purely theoretical *Erkenntnis*."[88] As acknowledgment of another, *Bekenntnis* has substance apart from one's own ego, yet it has no objective substance: its content is found only in the personal and dynamic *act* of confession. Since the confession is inseparable from the engaged address to God, it not static knowledge that one possesses for oneself, and therefore it cannot be grasped by the theoretical understanding.[89] Rather than a generally valid propositional assertion, it can instead be viewed as a type of performative speech-act.[90] As confession, the utterance of the psalm as prayer brings about and actualizes the very relation to which it refers. The relation cannot be asserted prior to the act of confession—but, unlike some other forms of speech-acts (e.g., a pronouncement of marriage), it also cannot be asserted *after* the act of confession. In accord with its strictly personal-practical, non-general nature, it is only *in* the act of prayer that the relation holds true.[91] Hence, in the realms of reflective thought and of writing, which exist outside of the act of prayer, one must take care—as Cohen does through his indirect communication—to avoid the impression of direct assertibility as regards the personal love of God.

Cohen provides a good illustration of the performative nature of prayer in his treatment of the connection between prayer and faith. He writes,

[P]rayer is dependent on faith/belief [*Glauben*] in the good God, who wants to help and can help the individual human being. Whether he does it [i.e., whether God *does* help], does not concern me in the duty of my need [i.e., the duty of prayer]. With regard to my duty, I have nowhere to ask about the outcome. But if faith in the outcome is necessary for the magic power of my devotion, then no poison of skepticism refutes me. My heart achieves the innocence of faith in God, the good one. Therefore I pray to him. My prayer becomes for me faith. So intimately does the prayer now connect my individuality with my God, with the God who in this prayer more than ever becomes my God.[92]

Here, although there is no place to "ask" about the outcome of one's prayer, *faith* in the outcome is necessary. 'Asking' corresponds to the desire for a theoretical assurance or knowledge. Such theoretical confidence, however, would in turn be subject to the doubt of skepticism. In contrast, Cohen does not 'think' or 'claim' that God will help him; indeed, he prays in the complete absence of any probable indication of help. In Climacus' terms, Cohen's faith in the good God represents "an objective uncertainty": with regard to objective knowledge, he has no certainty whatsoever.[93] Instead, his confidence in God is inseparable from the relationship created by the personal act of prayer itself. It is not simply the case that he *first* attains confidence and *then* prays. On the other hand, it is also not the case that he *first* prays and *then* attains confidence. The first sequence is ruled out by the lack of objective, impersonal grounds for faith, so that it seems that prayer must precede faith. The second sequence, however, is ruled out by the pointlessness of petitioning an addressee in whom one has no confidence, so that it seems that faith must precede prayer. This antinomy has no solution in thought, and can only be overcome in the *practice* of prayer, whereby the faith and prayer arise simultaneously and are indistinguishable from one another: "My prayer becomes for me faith."[94] Thus, since faith neither precedes nor succeeds the practice, there is no place for a direct statement of faith in a personal God: to turn from the engaged practice to the reflective act of writing removes the ground for that which can be said only in prayer.

In addition, the passage underscores the ways in which faith is connected not simply to the practice of prayer, but specifically to the *personal-individual* practice of prayer. Throughout the paragraph, Cohen speaks in the first person: "*my* heart," "*I* pray," "*My* prayer." These phrasings are crucial to Cohen's communication of the nature of the love of God: in an important sense, it is *not* the case that "*one* prays to God" or that "*One's* prayer becomes *one's* faith." Here, the first-person phrasing corresponds to *Bekenntnis*, whereas a third-person formulation would correspond to *Erkenntnis*. The final sentence of the passage makes this especially clear: it is the act of prayer that connects "my individuality" not simply to "God" but to "my God." Grammatically, "God" can appear to be an impersonal term, whereas "my God" explicitly indicates the personal relation that is inherent to the concept of religion's unique God.[95] As Cohen states in his *Der Begriff der Religion*, "Totality, in whose terms humanity is to be conceived, does not guarantee individuality, *as such*. For this I need God, as *my* God. *My own God is the God of religion*."[96] In other words, without the "my," God is not the God of religion. In the present context of the psalm, Cohen states that God *becomes* my God through the act of prayer. Apart from the engaged act of prayer, God is not (yet) my God. Thus, in order to remain faithful to this dynamic, if one is outside of the act of prayer, one must *avoid* conveying the notion of God's personal reality. It may very well be that Cohen is drawing upon Jewish liturgical tradition, which refers to God using different terms in prayer and outside of prayer. In the act of liturgical performance, the name of God is pronounced as *adonai*, "my Lord." When referring to God outside of the act of prayer, even in a direct citation from the liturgy, the name of God is pronounced as *hashem*, "the name." Here, the first-person nature of "my" is literally built into the term of direct address, while the term of referential description is abstract and impersonal. Echoing the last sentence of Cohen's passage, we can say that *hashem* becomes *adonai*, becomes "my Lord," only in prayer. In this sense, Cohen's tendency to describe God as "an idea" when speaking in third-person philosophical language could be viewed as analogous to the use of *hashem* when referring to God outside of prayer. In both cases, a non-engaged mode of speech demands a non-personal form of designation.

Finally, we should note that communicative concerns may also influence the fact that, in the context of prayer, Cohen often speaks of religious love in terms of love for God, from the human perspective, but does not always refer explicitly to God's love for the human being. While this is not an absolute trend (see the examples cited earlier in this chapter, where Cohen speaks of divine-human love as a "reciprocal relationship"), it may be that Cohen tends to avoid describing God's love since, like the psalmist, he can speak only of his own longing, and thus only from the human perspective. However, another reason why Cohen may not separately describe God's love is that, in important ways, it is *not* a separate love. As Cohen writes, "The fundamental form of religion, whose logical expression is the correlation of God and man, is, as it were psychologically, the love for God."[97] Here, "the correlation of God and man" mentions both parties and implies an inherent mutuality, while "the love for God" appears to indicate only the human's loving and longing. According to Cohen, though, the two alternatives are both different expressions of the same "fundamental form of religion." Thus, when the act of prayer is said to express man's love and longing for God, it can also be said to contain God's love for man, even when the latter is not explicitly mentioned. In fact, the absence of a separate description (in writing) may actually correspond to the presence and intimacy of the personal reality. In contrast, the inclusion of a separate description of God's love could imply an objectified relation between the two parties. Thus, Cohen writes,

> The psalm has the lyric style-form. It confesses the love of the soul for God. It feels this love as longing for God. This lyrical confession has to sing a monologue [*Monolog*] in the dialogue [*Dialog*]. The soul unites both persons of the dialogue; for the soul is in itself [*an sich*] given by God, and is therefore not exclusively the human-soul. Hence, it can seek God and speak to God and with God.[98]

Because both persons of the dialogue are united in the soul, the love must be expressed in a monologue, which *appears* to involve only one person. In contrast, a form of expression involving two categorically separated parties would imply a disunity of the soul. Thus, it is precisely thorough the monologue that the speaker can speak not only to but also with God. Again, Cohen's paradoxical and mystical-sounding formulation should be understood as stemming from the impossibility of accurately representing religion's practical concepts in theoretical terms. "Monologue" is one-sidedly misleading, but so is "dialogue," just as mentioning only the human love for God appears to say too little, while also mentioning God's love says too much. Consequently, the responsibility must ultimately rest with the reader to 'correct for' the illusive one-sidedness that will inhere in any given instance of Cohen's forms of communicative expression.

II. Being Commanded

"Says who?" This question characterizes what is often taken to be a fundamental contradiction between the notions of human autonomy and God's command.[99] In debates over the source of normative action, God's command is frequently portrayed as 'external' and thus heteronomous, while autonomy, in contrast, provides the moral law with an 'internal' origin.[100] As Cohen portrays commandedness, though, while there can be a *practice* of aligning one's will with a normative mode of being and action, *reflection on* that practice will give rise to contradictory representations. Accordingly, the source of normativity cannot be said to be either 'within' or 'without': each of these corresponds to a one-sided account. Here, in explicating Cohen's presentation, I highlight the ways in which he undermines a consistent theoretical understanding by calling into question both the 'externality' of God's command and the 'internality' of the moral law.

In many places in *Religion of Reason*, Cohen's language does seem to call up an image of an external God who issues commands to human beings from without. For instance, with regard to the Sabbath commandment of Deuteronomy 5:11–14, which states that the children of Israel should observe the Sabbath "in order that your male servant and your female servant shall rest like you [*kamocha*]," Cohen writes, "In the Sabbath, the God of love showed himself as the unique God of love for man. We asked, what meaning could God's love have? The answer is now found. Compassion for the poor, which God has awakened in us through his commandments, has become the intelligible basis for the meaning of God's love."[101] Here, if the ethical imperative of compassion for the poor had to be "awakened" in us through God's commandments, it would appear as though we would *not* have been aware of this imperative 'on our own.' In other words, our internal autonomous capabilities were insufficient, and we stood in need of an external commandment and commander. As a qualification to this apparent heteronomy, two points should be emphasized. First, Cohen's own statement is a re-echoing and repetition of the language of Scripture, which clearly represents the Sabbath commandment as something that its recipients learned specifically from the personal divine injunction. In the words of Deuteronomy 5:14, "therefore [i.e., for the sake of compassion for the poor] the Lord God commanded you to keep the Sabbath day."[102] Thus, when Cohen speaks of the compassionate imperative as springing from God's command, it remains somewhat unclear whether he would also use that same language when speaking 'in his own voice,' or whether he is simply providing a paraphrase of the scriptural passage. This 'unclarity,' however, may be rationally motivated, since it allows Cohen to point to the notion of personal commandedness while avoiding the danger of heteronomy that would accompany an impersonal philosophical assertion. Secondly, Cohen is not speaking about ethical imperatives generally, but specifically about the need for compassion for the fellowman, as exemplified by the poor man. The autonomous method of theoretical Ethics does *not* recognize this particular imperative of compassion; the latter gains its substance only through the engaged personal relations of love of God and love of the fellowman. As such, it would seem to require a source 'external' to Ethics. At the same time, while religion is not internal to Ethics, it also cannot be strictly external: rather, it arises on the "border-point" of Ethics.[103] Thus, we should already be attuned to the fact that the 'externality' that Cohen's language seems to assign to God's commandment may actually be an unconventional 'non-external externality.'

Indeed, some of Cohen's statements can even make it appear to be an 'internal externality.' Cohen writes, "[The] commandment of God is clarified [*klargestellt*] in man's heart, in man's spirit of holiness."[104] The reference to "man's heart" alludes to Deuteronomy 30:14, which states that God's commandment is not in heaven or beyond the sea; rather, "the word is very close to you; it is in your heart and in your mouth, to do it."[105] Cohen comments on this verse, "Thus the teaching is no longer in heaven, and it has not come from heaven; rather, its origin is apparently made wholly subjective: in your heart and in your mouth."[106] This account, though, may seem to go too far: if the notion of an external command seemed heteronomous, the notion of a purely subjective origin in the human being would eliminate God's role entirely. Cohen's description of the commandment's origin as "*apparently* subjective" is thus crucial: because there is indeed no longer any *objectively* separate origin for the commandment, it can very easily appear to be merely subjective, especially in a dualistic framework in which the only alternative to 'objective' is 'subjective.' In order to avoid this interpretation, Cohen draws upon the first part of Deuteronomy 30:14 to emphasize that the commandment "is not far from the spirit of man, but near to it."[107] That is to say, it is not *identical* with the spirit of man, but only *near* to it, just as, elsewhere, it is only nearness to God, and not union with God, that is desired.[108] However, the notion of nearness raises anew the problem of heteronomy: even if the commandment is *very* near to the spirit of man, 'near' still seems to imply 'outside of.' Thus, we are faced again with the contradictory dynamic we saw with the love of God: here, 'in your heart' is too internal, while 'very near' is too external. While one way of approaching this situation would be to say that the commandment is *infinitesimally* near, this only redescribes the non-theorizability of the concept of commandedness but does not overcome it. Ultimately, both 'internal' and 'external' are insufficient to describe the correlative nature of God's commandment. We should thus view the main point of Cohen's presentation of "in your heart" as a *movement away from* a one-sided 'external' understanding of commandment; he does not, however, seek to replace this with an equally one-sided 'internal' understanding.[109]

Indeed, Cohen indicates that the very question of and quest for the 'true' source of normative action stem from a confused theoretization of a properly practical concept. He writes, "The origin of the ethical law stands beyond all question with regard to the particular task of the ethical will."[110] For the existing individual engaged in a particular ethical task, there no place for asking whether the obligation comes from the moral law within or from God's command without.[111] The theoretical distinction between internal and external commandedness arises only when one reflects upon the practice of heeding the ethical obligation. Precisely because, in the doing, it cannot rightly be said to be *either* internal *or* external, it can seem, upon reflection, to be internal (because not external) or, alternatively, to be external (because not internal). Both are equally 'accurate,' and equally inaccurate, as a description of "the soul's experience" of commandedness. It is not that 'we do not know' the source of the command, but rather that the paradoxical practical concept has no theoretical correlate. It is not a matter of 'uncertainty': we know that there is no question of 'knowing.' Instead, one must act in a state of not-knowing, striving to eliminate any inclinations toward theoretical one-sidedness: if a person is inclined to think of the command as external, she should learn to push her way of thinking more toward internality, and vice versa.[112]

Furthermore, the fact that the commandment's origin is 'unknown' does not mean that God's command is a mysterious event. While the term 'revelation' (*Offenbarung*) may otherwise have otherworldly connotations, Cohen emphasizes that this term is not traditionally found in the Jewish sources. Rather,

> [t]he technical expression is "the giving of the Torah" (*matan torah*). This giving harbors no mysteries within itself. In all benedictions over the Torah, it says, "who has given the Torah," and God is named "giver of the Torah" in the liturgical formulation. Here nothing is said of a mystery, nor of an unveiling (*revelatio*). God gives the Torah, as he gives everything, life and bread, as well as death. Revelation [*die Offenbarung*] is the testimony

of reason, which is not animal sensuality, but comes from God and connects [one] with God.[113]

Because God's giving of the Torah is not an objectively distinguishable or anoma-
lous event, God's command is also not a heteronomous order. It *is*, in an important sense, a 'miracle,' a *Wunder*, and it will and should remain strange to the
theoretical understanding. But, practically speaking, it is simply another element
of everyday life, as is bread—which, for its own part, should also been seen a
miracle. There can be no question of whether bread 'actually' comes from God or
from the sun, rain, earth, and the farmer's labor. The same goes, analogously, for
God's command.[114] In both cases, the practical obligation, whether to gratitude or
ethical action, is not dependent on a theoretically consistent account of origin.

   We can also approach the issue of autonomy and commandedness by emphasizing the difference between the *method* of Ethics and that of religion. Cohen
writes, "If Ethics demands that the will fulfill the ethical-law as the law of ethical
reason, then it can be only a methodological distinction when the religion of
reason teaches [one] to think the will of reason as the command of God."[115] Similarly, he later states, "We already have mentioned that God's law does not contradict the autonomy of the ethical will. The difference lies only in the method of
formulating the concept, which is the difference between Ethics and religion."[116]
Thus, while Ethics—with its objectifying method that wrests away personality—
formulates ethical obligation without the notion of personal commandedness, of
being commanded by another person, religion, based on the notion of correlation, formulates ethical obligation in terms of a personal and commanding God.
Presented in this way, the 'problem' of autonomy seems to disappear, since the
presence or absence of a commanding God simply concerns various ways of
expressing the same thing. Looking at ethical obligation from this perspective, we
see a commanding God; looking at it from that perspective, we do not see a commanding God. Note too that Cohen does not prioritize one or the other of the
two perspectives: while one could say that religion 'reinterprets' the abstract ethical law in terms of a divine command, one could just as easily say that Ethics
'reinterprets' God's personal command as an abstract law of duty. There are no
grounds for saying that one or the other representation is more 'metaphorical'
than the other.

   At the same time, though Cohen's claims of the methodological-perspectival
compatibility of religion and Ethics may be valid and important, they also run the
risk of glossing over and obscuring the fundamental theoretical *in*compatibility of
the two approaches. That is, it may be the case that the salient differences with
regard to the question of commandedness are simply a reflection of the more basic
difference between Ethics and religion, but this latter difference is itself rather
contentious. As Cohen emphasizes in his introduction, Ethics must deny that any

other approach, including that of religion, can contribute to knowledge about man.[117] In particular, religion's preservation of particularity and personality stands as a sharp offense to the method of Ethics, which insists that knowledge about man must consist only of general-universal elements. Ethics would thus reject and oppose the notion of a personal commanding God, just as it objects to the notion of the You as other than the I. Thus, while the method of Ethics "is based on the autonomy of the will [*Autonomie des Willens*]," this same basis is bound up with the "dissolution [*Auflösung*] of the individual" in totality.[118] Accordingly, it would seem that the preservation of the individual as I requires a softening of the rigor of autonomy—for example, through the notion of an I who is commanded by a You. Yet, Cohen also states that "the autonomy of the will [*Autonomie des Willens*] must remain inviolably in power," and that, furthermore, "the human being as I" will be lost "at the outset, if autonomy [*Selbständigkeit*] is not absolute."[119] In other words, both autonomy and lack of autonomy will cause the individual to be lost! Again, this contradictory situation parallels Cohen's approach in his introduction, where his continued commitment to the sole autonomous authority of the method of Ethics seemed to conflict with his call for a supplementation through religion. Just as his 'solution' of 'plurality within totality' remained theoretically contradictory, so too his asserted 'compatibility' of autonomy and commandedness must be understood specifically as a paradoxical-practical compatibility. That is to say, because they are *not* compatible, except in the individual's engaged act of ethical willing, Cohen's written-theoretical account must present them as both compatible *and* non-compatible.[120]

In presenting the paradoxical nature of commandedness, Cohen draws upon a number of rabbinic passages that seem to display a similar awareness of that paradoxicality. In so doing, he points to the possibility that his practice-oriented de-theoretizing of commandedness is not simply a modern innovation, but has also roots in the core sources of ancient rabbinic Judaism. For example, in connection with Exodus 24:7, Cohen notes,

> The Talmud has already pointed to the order of the words with which the reception of revelation was affirmed: "we will do and we will hear." First the doing was taken on [*aufgenommen*], and only subsequently the hearing and the understanding. This is no offense against the fundamental demand for knowledge of God. For this knowledge is at the same time love for God; it is therefore ethical knowledge, knowledge of practical reason.[121]

Here, Cohen most likely has in mind BT Shabbat 88a–b, where the Israelites are praised multiple times for having said *na'aseh*, "we will do," prior to *nishma*, "we will hear/understand." At first, this seems like heteronomy par excellence.[122] If I am given a command, do I not need to analyze and understand it first, so that I can see whether the commanded action is ethical or unethical, rational or irrational? If I commit to the doing prior to understanding, will this not constitute blind obedience? According to Cohen, though, the priority of doing over understanding does not indicate heteronomous action, but rather serves to specify the unique type of 'understanding' and 'knowing' that is involved. In the case of an empirical command from another human being, doing before understanding *would* constitute heteronomy. God's command, however, contains no objective or theoretical content. Hence, it is not simply the case that one acts prior to understanding, but that there is no separate understanding to be had at all. Instead, the 'understanding,' as love, is of a practical nature and is inseparably bound up with the doing.[123] Although, in a sense, one can be said to gain knowledge and understanding through the doing, it never becomes theoretical understanding.[124] Even after the doing, one is still not in possession of any knowledge that could be objectively stated or communicated. As Cohen says, "[T]he verse states, 'All that the Eternal has spoken, we will do and understand [lit., hear],' [Ex. 24:7] but one must interpret 'understanding' more precisely, in the usual sense of obeying, so that it signifies only the inward spiritual hearing that has doing as its consequence."[125] In other words, it is *not* the type of understanding that could be separated from doing. That *na'aseh ve-nishma*—acting without prior understanding—does not entail a *deficiency* of understanding is indicated by the following Talmudic account:

> R. Eleazar said: When the Israelites placed *na'aseh* before *nishma*, a heavenly voice went forth and said to them: Who has revealed to my children this secret, which the ministering angels make use of? As it is written (Ps. 103:20), "Bless the Lord, O his angels, you who are mighty in strength, doers [*osei*] of his word, hearkening [*lishmoa*] to the sound of his word": First *osei*, then *lishmoa*.[126]

In other words, *na'aseh ve-nishma* is not the result of human ignorance or degraded submissiveness. If even the ministering angels, who are frequently portrayed as possessing great knowledge and understanding,[127] are governed by *na'aseh ve-nishma*, this may imply that there simply is no purely theoretical knowledge to be had with regard to God's command.

As such, it is true, in a sense, that one acts and obeys in the absence of 'knowledge' and 'understanding'; however, this absence is not the sort that would constitute heteronomy. In fact, one can even say that it is precisely this absence—in which action is motivated not by any theoretical or objective factor but solely by love—that is the determining factor for moral *autonomy*! As Cohen writes,

If love arouses action, then no external [*fremder*] object is its motivating cause. The love for ethicality is the love for God. This principle means for religion, what the following principle means for Ethics: action does not result from an external motivating cause, nor from an external directive [*Befehl*]. It is the result of the will, to which autonomy belongs. Love has to exclude everything external as a motivating cause.[128]

Thus, to obey God's command out of love for God means to exclude the influence of any other motivation—the influence, one might say, of 'foreign gods.' While most forms of submission to another being would destroy autonomy, the submission to the unique God, as a non-objective relation, is actually constitutive of autonomy. Drawing upon the rabbinic interpretation of Exodus 32:16 ("And the tablets were the work of God, and the writing was the writing of God, engraved on the tablets."), Cohen writes,

> The spirit of the revelation does not consist in the transcription on the tablets. The Mishnah (Sayings of the Fathers [6:2]) is correct: "Do not read 'engraved' but rather 'freedom on the tablets' (*al tikra harut ela herut*)." To be sure, the wording does not easily lend itself to this interpretation, but the meaning of this interpretation is correct, and the purity of monotheism depends on this meaning.[129]

Here, in Cohen's reading, that same word which seems to entail heteronomy ends up being transformed into freedom, that is to say, autonomy. If one thinks of the command of God as something external and objective—in other words, engraved—this *would* constitute heteronomy. Thus, in addition to saying, "Read 'freedom,'" the Mishnah also says, "Do *not* read 'engraved'": in order for the word of God to be equivalent to freedom, 'engraved' must be reread and opposed. Interestingly, the hermeneutic process by which 'engraved' becomes 'freedom' has the same shape as the de-objectification of God's word, which the mishnaic text describes. The written verse—in its plain sense, akin to an 'objective' meaning— still says 'engraved'; it becomes 'freedom' only when *you* actively read it as such. Likewise, objectively or impersonally understood, the notion of God's command sounds like an external injunction; it becomes freedom and autonomy only when the existing individual engages it personally.[130]

Up to this point, we have focused primarily on the ways in which Cohen seeks to save the notion of God's command from the charge of heteronomy. Without saying that it is strictly internal, he attempts to show that it is *more* internal that it may initially appear. At the same time, he also seeks to show that the requirement of the autonomous ethical-law (*das Sittengesetz*), as viewed from the perspective of Ethics, is less internal and more external than *it* may appear to be. He writes,

"The ethical-law is the law of ethical reason. If it should be applicable to the psychological nature, to the soul-concept [*Seelenbegriff*] of man, it must be formulated as the law of duty."[131] While the ethical-law must remain 'autonomous,' this does not mean that each person is free to give herself her own individual code of action. Instead, there is a single, universal law to which each individual must submit, and which often stands in opposition to individual desire. Thus, from the perspective of "the psychological nature," the autonomous law of reason can often seem quite heteronomous and imposed. Thus, when Cohen cites the rabbinic maxim, "Better is he who acts as one commanded than he who is not commanded and acts,"[132] he acknowledges that "through the command [*Befehl*], the action is apparently de-autonomized [*entselbstet*], and its ultimate origin is placed only in God's command [*Gebote*]."[133] That the loss of autonomy may be only apparent, however, can be seen from the similarity of this maxim to the familiar Kantian maxim, that one should act not only in accord with duty but also out of duty.[134] Both 'not commanded and acts' and 'in accord with duty' allow for the possibility of egoistic or other extraneous motivations, while 'commanded and acts' and 'out of duty' remove such motivations and thus ensure autonomy of the will precisely through their demand for strict compliance. Thus, the command of God need be no more or less 'coercive' than the imperatives generated by the method of Ethics. As Cohen notes, "Even according to Kant's teaching, the human being is not a volunteer of the ethical law, but has to subjugate himself to duty."[135] Both Ethics and religion therefore present a form of freedom through subjugation; the main difference is whether one submits to an impersonal duty or a personal command. Likewise, for both, the ethical imperative can be equally portrayed as external or internal to myself.[136] Cohen's presentation of all of these different possibilities (personal-internal; personal-external; impersonal-internal; impersonal-external) serves to underscore the theoretical multiplicity that results from reflecting on the practice of aligning one's will with ethical demands. At any given point in time, an emphasis on one or another of these possibilities may be needed to correct a one-sidedness in thought (which would manifest itself as a one-sidedness in practice), but none of them should be given absolute primacy.

Finally, it should be emphasized that, in Cohen's model, the *practical* problem of the role of 'outside authority' does not depend on whether ethical obligation is presented as originating in God's command or in the autonomous will of reason. Even if the autonomy of reason is emphasized, one may still need training or guidance from other people in order to learn to recognize its demands. Conversely, to say that God commands does not mean that one is necessarily bound by what *another person claims* to be the command of God. Even the notion that the Torah is the word of God need not undermine practical autonomy, since the written word always requires and is subject to renewed interpretation: "the book is closed; the mouth remains open."[137] Likewise, neither Ethics nor religion is inherently opposed to the notion of traditional practices, but they would both oppose the claim that a practice should be accepted *simply because* it is tradition. That is, there may be good reasons to preserve traditions, or even to treat certain people as functional authorities, but in any case, one must *make the decision* to do so (in accordance with the criteria of reason, using Cohen's broad definition of the term), so the choice is still ultimately bound up with oneself.[138] Cohen's project, in *Religion of Reason*, is not to produce a determinate or authoritative code of action, but rather to *display and perform a method* for reasoning through and about received sources and traditions. His main point is to teach his reader how to work with religious concepts without falling prey to one-sided distortion, an error which, in the case of God's command, can equally take the theoretical forms of over-internalization or of over-externalization.

III. *Purifying Oneself and Being Forgiven*

In this section, I examine Cohen's presentation of repentance, with a focus on the potential conflict between divine and human agency. Does God act to purify the human being from sin, or is it solely an act of the individual's self-purification? Or, alternatively, are these two actions equivalent? Throughout, in order to uphold ethical autonomy, Cohen presents a consistent opposition to any mediating action in repentance—but would God's involvement also constitute such a mediation? As was the case with love and commandedness, Cohen gives no determinate answer to these questions: the method of philosophy pulls him in one direction, while Scripture pulls him in another. However, whereas my treatment of love and commandedness examined the contradictory nature of these concepts by drawing upon various non-consecutive parts of *Religion of Reason*, this section focuses specifically on the vacillations in Cohen's sequential narrative. Rather than gathering all of Cohen's statements concerning repentance into a comprehensive analysis, I present three shorter and distinct accounts, examining, in turn, sections from his chapters on "The Holy Spirit," "Reconciliation," and "The Day of Atonement." In each, I follow the path of his narrative through a series of constant reversals on the issue of God's involvement in repentance and self-sanctification. I argue that his inability to reach a static conclusion corresponds to the dynamic and non-theoretizable character of religious concepts such as repentance. Accordingly, a reader of *Religion of Reason* who has followed along through Cohen's chain of argumentation, having been buffeted and tossed about by his reversals, will likewise be left with no stable theoretical account; she can retain the various divergent elements in Cohen's narrative of repentance only through a practical and personally engaged appropriation.[139]

(a) The Holy Spirit

At the beginning of the passage under consideration, Cohen comments on Psalm 51, reading it as a prayer for forgiveness of sin. Introducing verses 9–11, he states, "And now forgiveness is called upon." He then cites from the verses themselves: "[Purge me with hyssop, and I shall be pure.] Wash me, that I might become white as snow.... Hide not your face from my sins."[140] He then comments, "Along with sin, as an intrinsic attribute of human beings, we here also anticipate *forgiveness*, as an intrinsic attribute of God, which, up to now, we had not developed from God's uniqueness, nor from creation and revelation, nor from holiness."[141] In his presentation here, Cohen derives the notion of God's forgiveness not as a necessary conclusion of the philosophic method, nor as an analytic deduction from other religious concepts, but specifically from the fact of the scriptural text: because the psalmist addresses God and asks for forgiveness and purification, this indicates that God must be one who forgives and purifies. While strictly philosophical considerations might otherwise preclude such a notion, Cohen does not (for the present moment) seem concerned to address such objections. Instead, he simply reasons from the basic structure of the text in order to construct his concept. Later, Cohen cites verse 13, "Cast me not away from your presence, and take not your holy spirit from me." He then comments: "I have your holy spirit. Sin cannot frustrate it in me. And you cannot take your holy spirit from me because of my sin."[142] Here, Cohen draws upon the fact that the psalmist asks God not to *take away* God's holy spirit, in order to arrive at the notion that the individual person currently *has* God's holy spirit. Furthermore, Cohen himself formulates this statement in the first person, addressed to the second person: "*I* have *your* holy spirit." We could view this as a simple paraphrase of the biblical text's form of expression, but we could also view it as displaying Cohen's awareness that the concept of the holy spirit belongs specifically to the particular individual's relation with God, and does not belong to 'the human being in general.'[143] As such, it is most properly expressed in confessional form, rather than as a third-person assertion.

Throughout Cohen's discussion of Psalm 51—as well as in the text of the psalm itself—the agency for forgiveness, purification, and sanctification appears to rest with God. No qualifications are given that would either mitigate God's role or even assert the human being's active role in the process. While we might have expected a proviso such as, "Although the psalm *seems* to speak of God as the one who washes and purifies, it is actually the human being's act of self-purification that accomplishes this," Cohen's language instead cleaves to the God-centered viewpoint of the psalm.[144] When he moves away from the psalm, however, and turns to a discussion of holiness and sanctification, his language shifts and incorporates a more philosophically-governed perspective. Although he still draws upon scriptural verses, he now makes sure to counterbalance God's agency with human agency. Thus, while he does invoke God's repeated statement that "I, the Lord, sanctify you," (Ex. 31:13, Lev. 22:32, and elsewhere)[145] he also emphasizes the command of Leviticus 11:44, which enjoins, "And you should *yourselves* sanctify yourselves, and you will be holy."[146] Here, while the *hitpa'el* form of Leviticus 11:44 could be read simply as a command to remain holy and avoid impurity, Cohen reads the verse strongly, emphasizing the reflexive action: *you yourselves* are the ones who sanctify yourselves, with the implication that the sanctification of the human being is not merely the result of *God's* action. He writes, "Self-sanctification [*die Selbstheiligung*] corresponds to [or even 'is equivalent to,' *entspricht*] the bestowal of holiness [*der Verleihung der Heiligkeit*] by God."[147] Here, the viewpoint seems more evenly balanced between God and the human being. Whereas the psalm represented the petitioner's act of repentantly pleading for forgiveness as the prelude to God's subsequent purification and preservation of God's holy spirit, the two parties' actions now seem simultaneous, or even equivalent. Although God sanctifies man, and man also sanctifies himself, the two events cannot be separated into objectively distinct actions.[148]

While this parity already seems like a departure from the psalm's God-centered viewpoint, Cohen immediately adds a qualification that further heightens the contrast: "[The bestowal of holiness by God] is not some sort of transference of a fragment of salvation [*Heilsstückes*], but only the demand, therefore the encharging to this task of self-sanctification."[149] The two actions now seem more separate; God participates only by giving the commandment that serves as a necessary prelude, while the act of sanctification proper is accomplished by man himself—a seeming reversal of the psalmic portrayal of agency. It is true that Scripture and rabbinic tradition connect sanctification with the human being's performance of commandments,[150] but Cohen appears to be taking an extra step in asserting that God's role in sanctification is *only* in the act of commanding. This step seems to be motivated more by philosophical concerns regarding human ethical autonomy than by the language of the sources themselves. This human-centered portrayal of sanctification accords with my overall claim regarding Cohen's indirect communication, namely, that when he departs from the language of Scripture and speaks 'in his own voice' as a philosopher, he is more likely to downplay God's role as an active personal agent.

Though Cohen's God-centered and human-centered portrayals of sanctification do appear different from one another, one need not subordinate one to the other. Furthermore, while one could attempt to construct a third account that would 'reconcile' them, it may be more fruitful, and more faithful to the practice of repentance, to preserve the separateness of the two 'contradictory' accounts. Cohen himself points in this direction when he states, "The holy spirit can neither be God alone" (in which case, God would be the ultimate agent of sanctification), "nor man alone" (in which case, man would be the ultimate agent of sanctification), "but neither can it somehow be man and God at the same time [*zugleich*]" (thereby 'reconciling' the question of competing agency), "rather it is an attribute of both concepts, or rather the connection of both."[151] Each of the three rejected approaches would create oneness (either by eliminating the agency of one of the parties or by proposing a single joint agency), whereas Cohen's proposed approach maintains a conceptual two-ness. The 'incompatibility' of Cohen's portrayals of sanctification can thus be seen as the communicative correlate of this lack of one-ness. This theoretical 'wound,' however, is not an end in itself; rather, it enables practical unity through relation: "God and man must remain separate [*getrennt*], insofar as they are to be united [*vereinigt*]."[152] One must avoid the temptation to satisfy the (in itself legitimate) desire for unity by seeking to achieve the latter in thought; a false unity in thought would remove the separation required for a relational unity between persons in practice.

At the same time, Cohen also emphasizes that the unification (*Vereinigung*) of God and man is not a connection (*Verbindung*), and that the unification excludes mediation (*Vermittlung*).[153] Here, he is concerned to emphasize that the crucial separation between God and man is not an *objective* separation. While unity in thought does not provide *enough* distance, and thereby eliminates the possibility of relation between two persons, the notion of an objective separation would create *too much* distance and would create the need for a mediator in order to connect them.[154] In terms of the indirect communication of Cohen's text, this means that his presentation of contradictory accounts of sanctification cannot be a final end; the accounts cannot remain permanently or objectively separated. Rather, while preserving the *theoretical* separation of the God-centered and human-centered accounts, the reader should also be led to the *practice* of repentance, in which the two accounts are 'united.' This last movement, however, can be achieved *only* by the reader; Cohen's responsibility is to preserve the apparent/theoretical contradictoriness of the concept of sanctification, which he accomplishes by moving 'inconsistently' between different perspectives and different 'voices.' In other words, he must maintain the semblance of separation for the sake of unification. Cohen notes that the notion of the holy spirit inevitably carries with it "the appearance, the illusion of mediation."[155] Viewed purely theoretically, God and man *do* appear objectively separate and in need of mediation by the holy spirit as a third entity; likewise, the contradictory accounts of sanctification *should* seem as though they stand in need of a theoretical synthesis. Despite such illusive appearances, however, God and man do stand in direct relation to one another, and the holy spirit is not a third entity but merely the "function, which designates the correlation" between the two.[156] Accordingly, the two contradictory accounts do not require a third mediating account; rather, they are to be related functionally by way of the individual's engaged act of repentance.

(b) Reconciliation

Initially, Cohen's chapter on "Reconciliation" (*Versöhnung*) does not oppose the notion of God as redeemer from sin, but simply emphasizes that reconciliation *also* involves the action and unification of the individual human self. Sin has not only separated man from God, but it has also separated man from himself, from his ideal self as an ethical I. Thus, "[t]he reconciliation that the human being has to bring about with himself finds its conclusion, its solution, in redemption by God, which is reconciliation with God. This is the goal. This is the task for the ethicality of the I, in distinction from all social-, from all totality-ethicality [*von aller sozialen, von aller Allheits-Sittlichkeit*]."[157] In order to become an I, the individual must strive for reconciliation with God, but God's role as redeemer is not presented as a problem. Cohen underscores this notion through his comparison of Jeremiah and Ezekiel. In his reading, both prophets agree that, in order to do good, man is in need of a new heart and a new spirit. However, Jeremiah holds that God will give these to man,[158] whereas Ezekiel makes the new heart and new spirit a task for the individual human being. Cohen cites Ezekiel 18:31: "*Cast away from you* all of your transgressions, wherein you have transgressed, and *make yourselves a new heart and a new spirit*."[159] According to Cohen, Ezekiel "excelled all his predecessors" by calling upon man himself, as individual, to make himself a new heart—and thus become an individual—by actively casting away and turning from his past transgressions.[160] Because ought implies can, the prophetic imperative indicates that the individual human being is able to play an active role in the making of his new heart and new spirit. Importantly, though, the significance of the human being's self-renewal is not to free him from the need for God, but rather to free him from fate (*Verhängnis*), so that he thereby becomes "an individual, who is not absolutely dependent on the relations of social plurality [*Mehrheit*], in which he is enmeshed. He is an autonomously spiritual [unity], because he is an ethical unity."[161] Here, the attainment of autonomy does not mean that *God* has no role in redemption from sin, but rather that no *objective social circumstances or forces* can prevent the individual's ethical turning.

Similarly, when Cohen introduces the notion that reconciliation and purification (the latter being "the symbolic expression for reconciliation") take place "before God," his point is not to deny that God actively brings these about, in which case the emphasis would have been on '*before* God,' in contrast to '*by* God.' Rather, he intends to assert that that it is God, and not the priest or any other mediator, who brings about reconciliation and purification, so that the emphasis is on 'before *God*,' in contrast to 'before the *priest*.'[162] Thus, he is quite willing to say that God "effects" (*bewirken*) reconciliation,[163] and that God

is the unique redeemer. He alone brings redemption, which consists in the
reconciliation of man with God, and, thorough this, in the reconciliation
of man with himself, in himself, and indeed to himself. As the uniqueness
of God means first and foremost his oneness, so reconciliation and redemption proceed solely from him, without collaboration of any kind.[164]

At the same time, while the priest and other mediators are excluded, the penitent
human being himself is by no means excluded. Hence, Cohen refers to "the purification that the individual has to accomplish in himself by a repentance that cul-
minates in confession. But this 'in himself' is included [*eingefügt*] in the
correlation with God."[165] Because both are included in the correlation, the individual's action cannot be objectively separated from God's action. As such, the
former does not fall under the proscribed category of collaboration.

Up to this point in Cohen's narrative of reconciliation, then, we have the following picture: the individual plays an active role in his or her own purification,
but God also plays an active role. However, it is not said that God and the individual 'divide' the task or that they 'work together'; in some places it may sound
like the individual is the fundamental agent (as in Cohen's contrast of Ezekiel to
Jeremiah), while in other cases it may sound like God is the fundamental agent.
At the same time, there is no indication of a *conflict* between the agency of God
and that of the individual. Cohen's primary point is to exclude additional influences or agents, such as the social forces that may appear to impinge upon the
individual's autonomous ethical agency, or the priest who may appear to impinge
upon God's unique agency as redeemer. The question of the compatibility or
incompatibility of God's agency with that of the individual simply does not seem
to arise and is not addressed.

Immediately after this 'peaceful' account, though, Cohen begins to muddy
the waters. If we move away from the biblical view, which holds man and God
together in correlation, and examine the issue of repentance and reconciliation
from a more human-centered philosophical perspective, the notion of God's
involvement starts to take on an ominous tinge. Cohen writes,

> We still need to worry about the individual as I and therefore to examine
> more precisely the work of repentance that is incumbent upon him. For
> this, his own proper work, the collaboration of God is to be excluded [*aus-
> zuschließen*]. It says [e.g., in Lev. 16:30] "before God," not through [*durch*]
> God, nor even with [*mit*] God, but absolutely only before [*vor*] God.[166]

Now, the emphasis has changed from "before *God*" to "*before* God." The notion
that God would be the primary agent (*durch*) or even a co-agent (*mit*) is forcibly
rejected. The primary problem lies in the fact that, if the act of repentance is

constitutive of the transformation of the individual into an I, into an ethical agent, then it must be the individual herself who does the turning-away from and breaking with sin:

> Any assistance [*Beistand*], any collaboration [*Mitwirkung*] in repentance would make the turning [*Umkehr*] into a being-turned [*Umführung*], and would thwart the autonomous achievement and task of man . . . [repentance] should be a real, a real-izing action of the will, which elevates the human being to an I-individual. Therefore it can only be an action of his own achievement.[167]

Had we looked only at this passage, we could very easily have concluded that Cohen sees no role for God's agency in the process of repentance. The tone here is quite different, and much less scripturally oriented, then that of the previous passage, where he sought simply to exclude the collaboration of the priest. Rather than attempting to reconcile the two passages, we may be better served in viewing them as truly 'contradictory.'

Indeed, no sooner has Cohen positively asserted God's exclusion from the act of repentance, when he begins to backtrack again. In his conclusion to the current section (§43), he writes,

> The conscience cannot accept any joint-knowledge by another [*Mitwissen Anderer*], and thus cannot accept any assistants or accomplices [in the work of repentance]. But is God too thereby excluded [*ausgeschaltet*]? This question can no longer arise. Repentance must take place "before God" . . . for now, it is essential only to make clear that the bringing about of redemption is man's autonomous action.[168]

Based on the foregoing part of the section, we would have expected him to answer the question "Is God thereby excluded from the work of repentance?" with a resounding "Yes!"—especially since he himself had explicitly indicated as much a few paragraphs earlier (see above). Instead, he gives a non-answer: "This question can no longer arise." Thus, whereas previously the exclusion of God seemed necessary in order to secure man's autonomy, he is now willing to pass over the former matter in silence, so long as the latter is still guaranteed. Note, though, that he still cannot bring himself to say that God is *not* excluded: from the philosophical perspective from which this section is oriented, a positive revocation of exclusion *would* shatter the fragile autonomy that he seeks to preserve. In Cohen's strained formulations, we can perhaps discern his desire to reintroduce the scriptural notion of God's purifying forgiveness. Yet, he maintains his strict self-discipline, recognizing that this notion is theoretically incompatible with that of autonomy.

While the two can commingle practically and regulatively, he cannot directly assert or 'write' them together.

After his brief, silent nod to the possibility of God's non-exclusion, however, he again hastens to fortify his philosophical credentials by returning to a strong assertion of exclusion: "Repentance is self-sanctification ... Only man can actualize self-sanctification; no God can help him with it. God already effects much, in that he gives the commandment, and he will effect yet more. But he may not fall into the spokes of the work which the commandment demands of man."[169] Here, we return to the notion that while God gives the initial commandment, man is the one who ultimately achieves his own sanctification, an act which is now identified with that of repentance. Despite this forceful championing of man's task, Cohen appears unable to let the matter rest. A few paragraphs later, he again takes up the question of God's role, pointing out that although God is not a "co-worker" in the task, God does not disappear entirely but rather remains "the goal of self-sanctification."[170] Thus, God functions both as the source of the task, in giving the commandment, and as its aim, in that "[t]he turning should be to God."[171] God's second role as aim need not, it would seem, undermine the human being's autonomy, since, even if the human being is to turn to God, it would still be the human being who must achieve the turning.

Yet, Cohen uses the notion of God as the aim of self-sanctification to inch back toward the possibility of God's involvement in the act of repentance. As goal, he suggests, God has meaning "as an assistance [*Beistand*], although not as a collaborating helper."[172] While continuing to exclude collaboration, Cohen's admission of assistance appears to stand in direct contradiction to his insistence, just a few pages earlier, that "Any assistance [*Beistand*] ... in repentance would ... thwart the autonomous achievement and task of man."[173] Without explicitly acknowledging this contradiction, Cohen does indicate his awareness of the problematic nature of "assistance" by emphasizing that "this type of assistance must be precisely and clearly determined," so as to avoid saying 'too much' and thereby thwarting autonomy.[174]

Significantly, he does not go on to provide a strictly philosophical determination of assistance, but instead returns to Scripture. This shift may be a deliberate communicative tactic, perhaps arising from his sense that there may not actually *be* a philosophically legitimate way of introducing the notion of God's assistance.[175] Referring again to Ezekiel 18:31, Cohen writes,

Ezekiel, with his great word, "Cast off from yourselves all your sins!" had not spoken his last word; rather, he merely used this thought in order to bring the old monotheistic fundamental-thought to a new proving-true: God pardons, forgives, he "bears" the sin. Man himself must cast it off from himself, but whether his own deed succeeds, whether it leads him to the goal, he cannot know. As his task, he is concerned only with the casting off; the result and outcome of his action eludes his knowing.[176]

Here, Cohen reads Ezekiel's exhortation not as a rejection of the notion of God's forgiveness, but precisely as a restatement and reinforcement of that "old" notion.[177] As a reading of the plain sense of the biblical text, Cohen's account seems sound: *in Ezekiel's framework*, the human task does not conflict with divine involvement and pardon, and so both can be upheld at the same time. At the same time, this turn to Scripture has not resolved the initial question, which viewed God's involvement as problematic *from the philosophical perspective*. In a sense, Cohen has asked a philosophical question, but provided a scriptural answer. The contrast between the mode of the question and the mode of the answer leaves the issue with an unresolved instability.

Accordingly, when he turns again to the philosophical orientation, God's involvement in repentance raises a storm of pointed interrogations:

> If forgiveness belongs to repentance, does not a heterogenous element thereby enter into the work of repentance, in that God represents this goal and alone has to effect forgiveness?
>
> Is not the autonomy and purity of self-sanctification thus violated through forgiveness, which lies with God?
>
> The question must be sharpened: Does not, generally, the entire element of forgiveness by God constitute an external-act, which must be replaced, so that self-sanctification, and indeed precisely insofar as it always remains nothing other than an infinite task, yet contains the infinite solution within itself, would be equated with [*gleichzusetzen*] with forgiveness? Ezekiel says yes: "Cast off from yourselves all your sins, and create for yourselves a new heart." Does he not thereby make this task identical with forgiveness and does he not thereby eliminate redemption by God?[178]

Cohen's forcefulness and adamancy here is unmistakable. From the perspective of philosophy, God's involvement through forgiveness constitutes and *must* constitute a foreign and heterogenous element, just as was the case, elsewhere, with regard to the fellowman as You. Just as the presence of the You would have punctured the desired totality, so here God's involvement violates the autonomy of will that Ethics demands. While philosophy can accept the negative qualification that the human being cannot know whether his deed succeeds, it cannot accept the positive assertion that God brings about the human being's purification. In his zeal to ensure philosophical rigor, Cohen even re-reads the Ezekiel verse from the perspective of philosophy, so that Ezekiel now answers "yes" to the suggestion that forgiveness by God must be *replaced* (*ersetzt*) by self-sanctification. Not only does this restrictive reading depart from the plain sense of the verse, it also stands in contrast to the more open reading that Cohen himself had just given, wherein self-sanctification served to bolster the notion of God's forgiveness. Yet, despite this emphatic reversal, Cohen still cannot seem to close the wound of this issue. He ends the paragraph with a question, where the flow of the argument would have led us to expect a concluding proclamation, namely, that the task of self-sanctification *is* made identical with forgiveness and that redemption by God *is* thereby eliminated.

Instead, Cohen latches on to the glimmer of possibility afforded by the question; he turns around once more and embraces the notion of God's forgiveness: "It is necessary for the correlation with God, for the concept of God himself, that he and he alone be the redeemer, that he alone carry out this redemption as the pardoning, as the forgiveness of sins . . . God's being would not indicate itself conceptually in its perfection, if the forgiveness of sins were not his proper achievement."[179] Note that this pronouncement contains no response to the apparent undermining of ethical autonomy. After citing this same passage, Kenneth Seeskin comments, "Perhaps so, but this does not really answer the question. If I am worthy of being forgiven, God is only responding to what I have accomplished on my own; if I am not worthy, God cannot credit me with *self*-sanctification."[180] This is precisely the case: Cohen never explains how, despite all appearances to the contrary, God's redeeming forgiveness can be compatible with self-sanctification. Instead, he lets all the objections to God's involvement stand and says only that God as redeemer is necessary for the correlation of man and God. Thus, God *cannot* be the redeemer, yet God *must* be the redeemer. This contradictory result again underscores the fundamental paradoxicality of religious concepts. The practice of repentance—as represented in the 'rough' scriptural sources—gives rise, when reflected upon, to the notions of exclusive self-sanctification *and* of forgiveness by God. The point is not to give an explanation that could reconcile these two theoretically, but precisely to recognize that one *cannot* produce an explanation.[181] Instead, one must do one's best to avoid forms of theoretical one-sidedness that could presume to function as such an explanation. Cohen's restless reversals thus serve as an illustration and performance of the impossibility of confining the dynamic and personal concept of repentance to a static and consistent written account.[182]

After bluntly pronouncing the necessity of God's involvement in the face of its apparent elimination—a non-answer at best—Cohen turns, in the remainder of the chapter, to an extensive scriptural exploration of God's personal forgiveness. In so doing, he seems to indicate that the question which theoretical philosophy was unable to address finds its 'solution' in Scripture, which is to say, it is answered not in smooth theory but rather in practice, as represented by Scripture. Drawing heavily upon the Psalms and the major prophets, he presents a portrait of God as the good one, the one who personally shepherds the soul, the one whose grace provides redemption and liberation from sin, and the one in whom the individual human being can place her trust.[183] None of these descriptions are presented as theoretically or impersonally valid. Rather, without compromising the human task of self-sanctification, they display the way that the God-human correlation appears from the perspective of the actively striving individual.

(c) The Day of Atonement

As a final example of Cohen's fluctuating treatment of reconciliation and forgiveness, I examine a single paragraph from his chapter on "The Day of Atonement." Throughout the first part of the chapter, Cohen refers freely to God's involvement in reconciliation. For instance, drawing on the Yom Kippur liturgy's recitation of God's thirteen attributes (itself drawn from Ex. 34:6–7), he states that "God makes the sinful person pure and guiltless again."[184] Shortly thereafter, though, Cohen comments on Mishnah Yoma 8:9, raising anew the question of agency with regard to purification:

> It is understandable that Rabbi Akiva, the great Mishnah teacher and towering martyr, spoke the following word concerning the Day of Atonement: "Blessed are you, Israel; who purifies you and before whom do you yourselves purify yourselves? It is your father in heaven."[185] The father of human beings, who according the biblical *ur*-language is distinguished, through [the term] 'heaven', from earthly existence, bears witness to himself [*bezeugt sich*] in this purification of human beings. But Akiva does not stop with God; rather, he establishes his praise of Israel's blessedness in the climax, which he expresses in the phrase: "and before whom do you purify yourselves?" It is not God who purifies, as little as he expiates. The scriptural verse says only: "before the Eternal you shall be pure" [Lev. 16:30]. But since elsewhere the scriptural verse says: "you shall sanctify yourselves and you will be holy" [Lev. 11:44], Akiva thus achieves the proper climax with his phrase: you yourselves shall purify yourselves, and before your father in heaven you shall purify yourselves. No human being purifies you, and also no human being who is at the same time supposed to be a god. No son of God shall purify you, but your father only. And also you shall not purify yourselves before any other mediating being; rather, only when God is the unique and exclusive aim of your self-purification, only then can it be accomplished.[186]

In the span of a few sentences, Cohen swings back and forth between God's involvement and non-involvement. At first, after citing (his version of) the mishnaic passage, Cohen affirms God's involvement and states that God testifies to Godself through the purification of human beings. With this interpretation, he follows the plain sense of the passage, which describes both God's and Israel's activity. But then, he asserts that it is *not* God who purifies! Rather, you purify yourselves, but you do so before God. With this reading, he effectively ignores the first part ("who purifies you"), treating self-purification as the sole meaning of the passage. Subsequently, he emphasizes that self-purification also means that no other human being can purify you. This clarification, though, leads him to yet another reversal: no son of God shall purify you, but your father only. Thus, we learn that God is involved, but God is not involved, but God is involved![187] While it is possible that this paragraph represents careless editing on Cohen's part, we can also view it as a succinct representation of the paradoxicality of correlation. One must maintain both God's involvement and God's non-involvement in purification, even though these are contradictory; to prioritize either one over the other would produce an imbalance in the correlation, which in turn would result in a one-sidedness in practice and thought.

Likewise, the attempt to assign one or the other of these positions to Cohen himself is likely to result in a forced misreading and misrepresentation of his book. For example, in attempting to argue that *Religion of Reason* prioritizes self-purification over God's purifying forgiveness, Steven Schwarzschild characterizes Cohen's position as follows:

> God purifies you, but, on a higher level of truth, you purify yourself, albeit exclusively "before" God. "God purifies no more than he forgives"; you yourself do this, ethically. Cohen continues in the text by emphatically distinguishing this from Christianity and other forms of pantheism: "No man purifies you, and also no man who is supposed to be also a god. No son of God is to purify you: . . . . An unbridgeable gap must loom before [man]. . . . Truly, the Day of Atonement is the day of monotheism."[188]

In order to place self-purification "on a higher level of truth," Schwarzschild not only omits the beginning of Cohen's paragraph, which describes God's self-attesting through forgiveness, but, more strikingly, employs ellipses so that Cohen's sentence which begins "No son of God is to purify you . . ." lacks its conclusion: "but your father only"![189] The omission of this phrase occludes both Cohen's and the Mishnah's explicit reference to God's role in purification as agent and not merely as aim. The trouble with Schwarzschild's reading is not the particular interpretation that he gives—indeed, as consistent readings go, his may be as plausible as any that could be drawn from *Religion of Reason*.

Rather, Cohen's approach to purification may be such that a faithful communication should thwart *all* consistent readings: he can convey the practical concept of repentance only by giving offense to the theoretical understanding.

From Cohen's presentation of love, commandedness, and repentance, we have seen that each can be understood in two contradictory ways: as personal and as impersonal, as internal and external, as heteronomous and as autonomous, as human-centered and as centered in the God-human correlation. In addition to warding off intellectual flattening, the proper communication of the concepts requires both voices or perspectives in order to avoid the *ethical* distortion that would follow from a more 'consistent' account. For example, a one-sided account that erred on the side of self-sanctification could result in an ethically debilitating pressure of 'having to do everything yourself.' Conversely, an account that consistently asserted the involvement of God's forgiveness could lead to an equally debilitating ethical passivity. The proper ethical-correlative practice, in contrast, is such that self-sanctification and God's forgiveness would be equally valid and applicable descriptions.

The double-voicedness that results from Cohen's juxtaposition of philosophy and Scripture can thus provide a means for checking the balance of one's practice, as well as one's thought: at any given point in time, a person will require a correction in one direction or the other. This correction, furthermore, should not take the form of diminishing one tendency in order to bring it down to the level of the other. Rather, the point is to heighten both tendencies, as well as the theoretical tension between them. Each must be emphasized strongly in order to prevent the other from taking a theoretical hold, and it is precisely in emphasizing their mutual theoretical incompatibility that we create room for their practical correlative unity.

6

The Task, the Moment, and the Messianic Future

IN THE PREVIOUS chapter, we sought to account for the apparent inconsistency in Cohen's presentation of religion by raising the possibility that a theoretical contradiction could correspond to a practical unity. In this sense, certain concepts, understood as practices, can be *done* even though they cannot be consistently *thought*. This description, however, may give rise to an unwarranted fideism that asserts the legitimacy of religious claims even in the absence of philosophical grounding. An individual practitioner could proclaim, "God's love, commandments, and forgiveness represent actualities *for me*, even if the systematic theorist cannot grasp them." Here, the 'doing' seems to be easy and unproblematic; it is only the comprehending that is impossible. Cohen, in contrast, would argue that such a claim grants the sphere of religion too much immanence—if God's love and forgiveness are already 'mine,' the challenge of ethical striving can become attenuated. In this chapter, accordingly, I seek to show that Cohen's insistence on the transcendence of religious concepts may make their 'doing' appear just as impossible as their 'thinking.'

That is to say, the concepts of religion do not have practical unity simply 'for me'; rather, they achieve their practical unity *only insofar as* I am able to become an ideal, ethical self. If as, we shall see, this latter becoming constitutes an infinite task, the actual unity of the concepts would seem beyond the reach of both theoreticians *and* finite human practitioners. This reassertion of the transcendence of religious concepts, however, contains its own dangers. The infinity of the task, while certainly highlighting the need for continued striving, can also seem to render the religious concepts lifeless and overly remote. Indeed, many readers have interpreted Cohen's presentation of religious concepts in terms of a distant, asymptotic ideal that can never attain actuality.

While this reading of Cohen can serve as important corrective to overly immanentist interpretations, I argue that it neglects essential features of his paradoxical account of religion. Though he continues to uphold the infinity of the task, Cohen also raises the possibility that the task can be fulfilled in the *infinitesimal moment* of turning. This 'moment' is itself an inherently paradoxical concept; with a duration that is greater than zero yet smaller than any finite amount, it is both 'something' and 'nothing' and therefore lies 'between' actuality and non-actuality. Accordingly, because it corresponds equally to the fulfillment and to the non-fulfillment of the task, it is able to avoid the distortions of one-sided transcendence and of one-sided immanence.

By delving into the ways in which the infinitesimal moment lies at the basis of Cohen's thought, we can better understand his need for a contradictory form of communication: the paradoxicality of his style reflects and manifests the paradoxicality of his underlying idea-content. In addition, our examination of the infinitesimal moment will enable us to revisit the connection between Cohen's style in *Religion of Reason* and his earlier analysis of the style of the biblical prophets. Cohen presents his own concept of the moment as functionally equivalent to the prophetic vision of the messianic future, a linkage that indicates that the former may have originated, at least in part, from his familiarity with the logic of the prophetic texts. If, therefore, Cohen sees himself as borrowing from the prophets' messianic idea-content, it should come as no surprise that he would also have appropriated and recast crucial elements of their indirect style of communication.[1]

I. Paradox and the Infinitesimal

Before examining the details of the infinitesimal moment within *Religion of Reason*, let us first frame our study by noting the historical connections of this particular concept to questions of paradoxicality. The mathematical and philosophical concept of the infinitesimal—a number or magnitude not equal to zero, yet smaller than any finite number or magnitude—extends back to ancient Greece. For instance, Archimedes employed infinitesimals in order to arrive at solutions to a wide variety of problems in geometry and physics.[2] However, the notion of an infinitesimal quantity also gave rise to a number of philosophical quandaries, Zeno's paradox (in its different forms) being among the most famous. While the concept continued to be used heuristically—notably, in the development of the differential calculus—its unclear and seemingly inconsistent status as both 'something' and 'nothing' made it philosophically suspect, and attempts were periodically made to banish it from both philosophy and mathematics. For instance, George Berkeley famously dismissed infinitesimals as "the ghosts of departed quantities."[3] Rejecting their double-sided usage as both zero and non-zero, he maintained that "Nothing is plainer than that no just Conclusion can be directly drawn from two inconsistent Suppositions," and he ultimately concluded that infinitesimals "are in truth such shadowy Entities, so difficult to imagine or conceive distinctly, that (to say the least) they cannot be admitted as Principles or Objects of clear and accurate Science."[4] One hundred and fifty years later, their philosophical-scientific reputation was no better, as we find Georg Cantor, one of the most influential mathematicians of the nineteenth century, referring to them as "cholera bacilli of mathematics."[5] By the time Cohen began to publish, Karl Weierstrass' employment of the notion of limit was widely seen as having thankfully liberated calculus from a dependence on infinitesimals.

Notably, however, in a deliberate and defiant rejection of prevailing trends of his time, one of Cohen's early monographs—*Das Prinzip der Infinitesimal-Methode und seine Geschichte*—was devoted to an embrace and defense of this controversial concept.[6] Furthermore, this initial appropriation of the infinitesimal set the stage for its central role in Cohen's later philosophical thought. In particular, he draws upon it explicitly as a fundamental organizing principle in his *Logik der reinen Erkenntnis*, the opening volume of his *System der Philosophie*.[7] Given that Cohen's aim in his *System* was to arrive at a conceptually consistent account, we might initially be surprised that he would draw upon a notion that was rejected by many precisely for its conceptual *in*consistency.[8] As we saw in chapter 3, though, we can point to a number of key concepts assigned to the sphere of religion in *Religion of Reason* that also played a role in Cohen's earlier systematic philosophy. My contention is that while Cohen did make use of those concepts in his system, it was only later that he came to acknowledge their methodologically problematic status. Thus, we might hypothesize a similar trajectory with regard to his use of the infinitesimal: earlier, he dismissed widespread views of the infinitesimal's problematic nature in order to employ it in his system. Accordingly, he must have been convinced of its consistent systematic basis. Yet, he comes back to the same concept in *Religion of Reason*, a work in which he acknowledges a fundamental contradiction in the relationship between rational philosophy and rational religion. As such, though he does not say so explicitly, it may be that the later Cohen might very well acknowledge that the infinitesimal does contains an internal conceptual inconsistency, but that this inconsistency, far from being a deficiency or a damning feature, is precisely what gives the infinitesimal a crucial role to play in communicating the religion of reason.

However, from a certain perspective, Cohen's use of the infinitesimal in *Religion of Reason* could seem to constitute an overcoming of or a solution to the paradoxical features emphasized in my previous chapters. That is, one could say, "The infinitesimal is able to combine two seemingly contradictory aspects (namely, being both something and nothing) into *one single* concept. As such, this points to ways in which the concepts of religion are only *apparently* paradoxical, since they can in fact achieve unity through modes of reasoning modeled on the infinitesimal. Instead of having to engage in the indirect communication of stylistic oscillations, one can simply say directly: the concepts of religion are represented by the mathematical concept of the infinitesimal." Such a claim of resolving the paradox, though, turns out to be a sidestepping of the real issue, as it fails to fully appreciate the paradoxical and conceptually problematic nature of the infinitesimal itself.

That is, rather than viewing the paradoxicality of concepts of religion as merely apparent, I argue that the reverse is the case: namely, it is the ostensible *non*-paradoxicality of the infinitesimal that is merely apparent. Though the infinitesimal appears to be a single concept, it nevertheless 'splits' into a double-sided inconsistency when one attempts to provide it with a verbal conceptual definition.[9] In this sense, an attempt to explain away the paradoxical nature of religion by appealing to the infinitesimal would simply be restating the paradox in a different 'shorthand' form, without actually eliminating it.[10] Nevertheless, the above objection does show that discussion of the infinitesimal, considered in isolation, can run the risk of 'hiding' the paradox. It is for this reason that I engage in such discussion only *after* having highlighted the clearer stylistic double-voicedness in Cohen's treatment of religious love, commandedness, and atonement, in which the 'contradictions' are more visible. The present chapter, then, is intended to be read through the lens of the previous chapter, using the paradoxes uncovered there to bring out the theoretical unclarity that is present in the infinitesimal as well.

At the same time, there is an important sense in which the infinitesimal does contain a certain type of 'unity,' a unity that has a parallel in Cohen's communicative style. While the historical detractors of the infinitesimal accused it of conceptual inconsistency and theoretical ungroundedness, they nevertheless acknowledged its consistent *practical* ability to generate sound mathematical results. In other words, the infinitesimal displayed a functional-practical unity in spite of (or perhaps because of?) its theoretical-conceptual multiplicity. Likewise, the stylistic multiplicity of *Religion of Reason* serves not only to undercut any single-voiced, consistent account of religion; it also functions as the means for a positive and specific communication of the ideas of religion. The practical unity of this communicative act remains dependent on the conceptual paradoxicality of its verbal formulations—to remove the paradox would thus distort the intended communication. In the discussion that follows, I therefore aim to make Cohen's discussion of the infinite task and the infinitesimal moment 'more difficult' in one sense, in order to indicate how this same theoretical difficulty can help to further clarify the broader communicative patterns of Cohen's text.

II. The Infinity of the Task

In order to show why the concepts of religion cannot be claimed as possessions or actualities, we ought first to examine the ways in which the I of religion must always remain a task for the existing individual. As a permanent 'ought,' and never an 'is,' this ethical self cannot be treated as a static actuality or as something already-given.[11] Referring to Ezekiel's call (Ezek. 18:31) to create a new heart and a new spirit through repentance, Cohen writes, "The new heart and the new spirit are and remain *tasks* [*Aufgaben*]. The I [*das Ich*], too, can be considered as nothing other than a task. As little as one can imagine [*sich vorstellen*] that a new heart should be formed in concrete actuality [*Gegebenheit*], just as little is such a to-be-finished shape [*abzuschließende Gestalt*] the meaning of the to-be-generated I [*des zu erzeugenden Ich*]."[12] Some things may be tasks in a contingent or temporary sense; that is, something may be a task for me now, but at some later time, it will no longer be a task, since I will have completed it. In contrast, the ethical self that corresponds to the new heart and spirit is essentially and always a task: the new heart and spirit not only "are" tasks, but more specifically "are and remain" tasks. The I can never be treated as something that 'already is'; rather, it is always something that *is to be* generated. Cohen's repeated designation of the task as *unendliche* ("infinite," or, especially in the present context, "unending") underscores this notion: at *any* given point in time, the task will still not have ended. Put negatively, there can be *no point in time* at which an individual can treat the task as completed and no longer incumbent.[13]

At the same time, although the ethical self can never have static actuality, it does have 'reality,' in that it is the goal toward which the individual must strive: "[The] self-individual [*Selbst-Individuum*] does not coincide with the empirical organism; rather, the former is always only the standpoint and high-point [*der Standpunkt und der Höhepunkt*] toward which the sensual individual, insofar as he makes himself into the ethical individual, must swing upward by virtue of his task [*Aufgabe*]."[14] There is a sense in which a person is 'already' an individual, but this is true only in a sensual-empirical sense: one does not need to strive in order to become an egoistic or selfish individual.[15] In contrast, the individual as I, as ethical self, is precisely that which one is not yet. The ethical self is always 'beyond' wherever one is at any given point in time and serves to indicate the direction in which one must turn. Furthermore, it is precisely this beyond-ness, this non-coincidence with this empirical-sensual self that enables movement and change. Without an awareness of the ethical self as the distant "high-point," there would be neither impetus nor orientation for moving beyond what already is.

When presenting this idea through the categories of Scripture, Cohen identifies the task of becoming an ethical self with the commandment of Leviticus 19:2: "You shall be holy, for I the Lord your God am holy." He draws our attention to

> the difference of tense in the phrasing of holiness with regard to God and man: with God it is a be-ing [*ein Sein*]: "for I am holy." With regard to man, however, it says: "you shall be holy." Therefore one may also translate: you shall become holy. Holiness therefore means for man a *task*, whereas with regard to God it designates being.[16]

In the Hebrew text of the verse, the clause associated with man contains the imperfect verb form *tihiyu*, indicating a not-yet-ness. Conversely, the clause associated with God contains no verb form at all, indicating a constant attribute. Cohen reads this difference strongly, portraying it not simply as a call for the human being to emulate God but also as an essential contrast between the two parties: it is *God* who is holy, whereas *you*, in your current-empirical state, are *not* holy. If you already were holy, there would be no need for the imperative, future-oriented verb form. Instead, it is your task to *become* holy. In addition, the apodictic phrasing of the verse serves to bring out the infinity, the unboundedness, of the task. No limits are set on the commandment to become holy: the text does not say "you shall be holy in such-and-such a situation, or until such-and-such a time," but simply, "you shall be holy." Cohen's interpretation also seems to draw upon the verse's status as 'eternal' Scripture in order portray the unending nature of the human being's task of becoming. *Whenever* you read this verse, the term *tihiyu* will still be attached to the notion of your holiness; in other words, your holiness is always in the future, is always a task.

Beyond this particular verse, Cohen asserts that the unending task of becoming holy characterizes monotheism as a whole and distinguishes it from pantheism. In monotheism, "the harmonization with the *ur*-spirit of holiness always remains only the infinite task, whereas pantheism, in a materializing imitation of nature and its lawfulness in which there must be identity between the law and its actualization, must equate the task with its solution."[17] For Cohen, the worship of a God before whom the ideal was identified with the actual, before whom that which ought to be was equated with that which is, would no longer be worship of the unique God of monotheism.[18] Likewise, it is indeed possible for a person to view holiness as something inherent rather than as a task, but this approach will lead not to becoming the ethical self of religion but rather to a different sort of individuality. The unique God and the ethical self who worships and loves the unique God are thus both defined by the unfinalizability of the task: "If God were not the unreacheable one, my longing would have to find its end. But this end would be no conclusion for my human-ness. I remain a human being, and therefore I remain a sinner. I therefore unceasingly need God, as the one who forgives sin."[19] Just as the 'beyondness' of the ethical self provides the opportunity for the sensual individual to move beyond herself, so too the 'unreachability' of God provides the opportunity for the human being to turn longingly *to* God in repentance. If one is not to remain mired in the sensuality and sinfulness that are an intrinsic part of being human, both of these movements (which, functionally and practically speaking, are in fact a single movement[20]) must be unceasing obligations.

Likewise, while the concepts of religion are based upon the correlation between God and the human being, this correlation is itself an infinite task.[21]

Cohen states that "the carrying-out [*Durchführung*] of the correlation with God" constitutes man's "eternal task" and "eternal goal," and he refers elsewhere to the "task of intensifying, heightening, and more inwardly penetrating the correlation between the human being and God."[22] Thus, it is not the case that an individual human being 'is' in correlation with God, but rather that the individual ought to be, must be, in correlation with God. To be sure, one *can* say that 'the ethical self is in correlation with God,' but since the ethical self is itself always only an ideal and a task, so too the correlation can never be a static actuality. Instead, just as one's task is to *become* holy, to *become* the ethical self, so too the correlation between the human being and God is always that which *must come to be* through the turning of ethicality and repentance.

Consequently, *each and every concept of religion* must also be treated as an infinite task for the human being. The uniqueness of God, for instance, is an essential part of the correlation, but since the latter is always only a task, the same must be true for the former. Similarly, in relation to the ethical self, God is the creator of the world, but for the human being who is also a sensual individual, 'God as creator' can only be a task and not a given actuality.[23] 'God as commander,' 'God as revealer,' 'God as forgiver,' 'God as redeemer': all of these concepts are bound up with the correlation, and all are therefore always tasks. As Cohen writes, "Like Ethics, so also religion must always deal only with tasks, which, as such, are infinite, and can therefore also call only for infinite solutions."[24] At the same time, these various religious concepts do not necessarily correspond to determinately *separate* tasks.[25] Rather, the more that a human intensifies and inwardly penetrates the correlation through repentance, longing, and ethical self-purification, the more all of these concepts *come to be* for that individual. In this context, it is important to note that the fellowman, as part of the correlation, must also be seen as a task: the suffering individual *must become* the fellowman for me, a transformation that occurs through the power of compassion. Furthermore, this transformation cannot be a one-time event: because the fellowman can never be a static actuality, the suffering other must *always become* the fellowman for me. Hence, my obligation of compassion for the other is an *infinite* obligation.[26]

Cohen's account of infinite tasks thus helps to disclose another dimension of his contradictory style in his presentation of religious concepts. His use of two 'perspectives' or 'voices,' that of philosophy and that of Scripture, serves to underscore the difference between the actual and the ideal. Recall Cohen's assertion that the distinctive feature of religion lies in "the transformation [*Verwandlung*] of an abstraction into a person."[27] In the previous chapter, I linked 'abstraction' with the perspective of philosophy, and 'person' with that of Scripture. Here, the emphasis is on the importance of the transformation itself: the defining characteristic of religion lies not in God being statically designated as a person, but rather in the dynamic act of transform*ing* an abstraction into a person, in moving *from* the one *to* the other. This transformation is not a one-time event; rather, each individual human being must *always* transform the abstraction into a person. Thus, in Cohen's style, the presence of the voice of 'abstraction' (philosophy) serves to remind the reader that 'person' is not-yet, while the voice of 'person' (Scripture) serves as a reminder that 'abstraction' is not sufficient. In a sense, without the co-presence of the voice of 'abstraction' to serve as a contrast, the single voice of 'person' would itself become an abstraction.[28] In Cohen's presentation, by contrast, the unresolved tension between the two voices provides the impetus for movement and becoming. Together, the two voices project the existing individual's dynamic action and task onto the static sphere of writing.

III. The Infinitesimal Moment

Although the self always remains an infinite task, Cohen also emphasizes that the self *can* and *does* come to be. This coming-to-be, however, is specifically restricted to what Cohen calls "the moment" or "the moment of ascent." Describing the transition in which the sensual or sinful individual turns repentantly toward her ethical goal and toward God, he writes, "[the ethical individual] originates [*entsteht*] only in the moment of this ascent."[29] Likewise, he characterizes redemption from sin, as brought about by God's forgiveness and by self-purification, as "the ascension to the ideal moment in which the human being becomes a self [*zum Selbst wird*]."[30] Thus, it is not simply the case that the human being must strive to become a self, but also that she does become a self—yet only in "the moment."

In addition to originating (*entstehen*) only in the moment, the self also persists (*bestehen*) only in the moment. Cohen writes, "[T]he feeling of joy upon being liberated from suffering has its validity [only] as moment. Such a moment is redemption. And such a moment is also the place where the self erects itself and builds its hut [*Hütte*]. It provides it only shelter for the moment. Only for the moment does the I have duration/stability [*Bestand*]. Only for the moment can it demand and use redemption."[31] In this passage, Cohen underscores the nonpermanent and fleeting nature of the I through his emphatic repetition of moment, moment, moment. He further enhances this notion through his metaphorical presentation of the self as *sukkah*, a traditional Jewish symbol of a temporary and precarious structure. Similarly, Cohen asserts, "When [the I] is lifted up in the momentariness of an ascent, it attains to a true ethical aliveness, which admittedly can persist [*bestehen*] only in the blessedness of a moment."[32] Through the confinement of both *entstehen* and *bestehen* to the moment itself, we can see that the true ethical aliveness of the liberated self is not present *before* the moment, and it is also not present *after* the moment.

But what precisely *is* the moment? For how long does it last? Doesn't the claim of the self's persistence and duration in the moment contradict the idea that the self is always only a task, and never an actuality? As it turns out, Cohen's conception of the moment appears to be a paradoxical one, thus complementing the broader paradoxicality of his dual-voiced communicative style. If the moment were to last for any finite length of time, it *would* undermine the idea of the self as infinite task. However, as Cohen presents it, the moment is an *infinitesimal* moment, and accordingly has *no* finite duration. The moment is specifically the moment of movement, of ascent, *Aufschwung*, turning-upward. It is the moment of transition, *Durchgang, from* what already is *to* what is not yet but which ought to be.[33] This movement and transition, however, cannot be located at any point in time. One moves from 'here' (from what is) to 'not-here' (to what is not yet), so that the transition itself is after 'here' but before 'not-here.' At any point in time, though, we are either 'here' (in the same place, if movement has not yet occurred) or 'not-here' (in a different place, if movement has already occurred). That is to say, any point in time will either be prior to the transition ('here') or after the transition ('not-here').[34] Thus, if we select the *latest* possible point in time *before* the turning-upward, and the *earliest* possible point in time *after* the turning-upward, the distance between these two points—in other words, the duration of the moment of ascent, and hence the duration of the ethical self—will be infinitesimally small. Thus, while the notion of self as infinite task stipulates that there is *no* point in time at which the self can be actual, one can also say (albeit paradoxically) that there *is* 'no point in time' at which the self *can* be actual: the self *can* be actual at 'no point in time,' that is, in the infinitesimal moment, which is not a point in time.

Notably, in *Religion of Reason,* Cohen does not employ the term 'infinitesimal'; instead, he restricts himself to the term 'moment,' whose mathematical connotations are less immediately apparent. However, the association of the term 'moment' with an infinitesimally small distance or duration is no innovation on Cohen's part. Isaac Newton, for instance, in his *De Analysi*, used the Latin term *moment* to designate the infinitesimal increment on the x-axis of a curve, where the x-axis represents time.[35] (In his *Das Prinzip der Infinitesimal-Methode und seine Geschichte*, Cohen himself traces the concept of the moment back to this same text of Newton's.[36]) It is therefore noteworthy that Cohen uses this term, rather than the more usual German *Augenblick*, throughout his book. If we apply this mathematical framework to Cohen's concept of the self, we can designate the point in time prior to the transition as x_0. At any time $x_0+\alpha$, where α represents a finite increment, the transition will already have occurred. Therefore, the moment of transition must be an infinitesimal increment dx, such that for any possible subsequent point in time x_1, x_0+dx will be less than x_1. Given this notation, we can say that the self has duration in the period between x_0 and x_0+dx.[37]

However, because the moment dx is infinitesimally small, this framework can have some surprising consequences. While the concept of infinite task can and should make the self appear infinitely far away, the concept of the moment makes the self appear infinitely close. While the self is not actual at *this* point in time (i.e., 'here,' 'now'), its actuality is not *finitely separate* from this point in time: for any point in time after this point in time, the self can become actual *prior to* that point. In other words, if x_0 represents the present actuality, then the ideal is not-now; it is beyond x_0. However, the ideal is not a finite distance beyond x_0: it can be found in the moment x_0+dx, which is infinitesimally close to x_0. Because dx is like something and like nothing, x_0+dx is not the same as and yet not determinately different from x_0. Thus, while the actuality of the self is 'not at this point,' it is also 'not not at this point,' since it is (or rather, can come to be) before any point after this point. This infinite closeness can serve to emphasize the achievability of the task, since an individual is always only one moment away from becoming an ethical self.[38]

Accordingly, and in keeping with the notion that the self is not to be found *at* any point in time, we can say that the self is located *between* two points in time, between now and after-now, between now and not-now.[39] As such, to identify the self solely with not-now would be just as misleading as identifying the self with the now: while the latter makes the self too close and ignores the fact that it is also not-now, the former makes it too far away and ignores the fact that it is not determinately different from now. If one *had* to choose a static representation, one could 'come down' just as easily on one side as on the other, but each is ultimately insufficient.

This 'betweenness' of the self further clarifies Cohen's dual-voiced style. Each 'consistent' perspective corresponds to a static point in time: philosophy speaks from the perspective of the impersonal given, of present actuality, of that which already-is, while Scripture speaks from the perspective of the ideal, from the perspective of that which is not-yet. Accordingly, within the perspective of philosophy, the ideal self always appears only as a task, as a not-yet, while within the framework of Scripture, the self is presented as an actuality, as the one who speaks with and is commanded by a personal God. If the infinitesimal self of religion is to be found 'after' the already-is but 'before' the not-yet, both philosophy-alone and Scripture-alone would present a distorted picture of the self. With only philosophy, the self would appear impossibly distant, thus undermining the motivation for striving, while with only Scripture, the self would seem to be a given, thus obscuring the ethical distance that makes striving necessary. Instead, Cohen must display both perspectives together in order to convey the infinitesimal gap that lies paradoxically between the two, but which cannot itself be identified with any single static perspective.[40]

We can also approach Cohen's concept of the infinitesimal moment by focusing on its *dynamic* quality. As Cohen writes, "In religious existence, insofar as it always is regulated and developed by the guiding thread of ethicality, everything is valid only for moments of ascent and transition. There is absolutely no fixed, rigid [*starres*] existence; rather, everything is only transition."[41] Everything in religious existence is valid only for the moment, and everything is only transition. Hence, we can say that the moment—which cannot be assigned to any static point in time and which is 'between' two points in time—is itself transition, is *movement*. However, we normally think of movement as a change in state or position over time; without progression in time, there could be no movement. For this reason, the infinitesimal moment could seem like the opposite of movement: it has *no* finite duration in time, and therefore seems to allow for no amount of change. Rather than thinking of the moment as a *quantity* of change, though, we can instead view it in terms of the *quality* of change. The following illustration may be useful: we normally think of movement as involving a change over a certain distance in a certain amount of time. So, consider a situation in which an object has just traveled at a constant rate over a finite distance z in a finite time t. Before that distance was traversed, the object first had to travel half of that distance, $z/2$, in time $t/2$. But, before the distance $z/2$ was traversed, the object first had to travel half of *that* distance, $z/4$, in time $t/4$. By continuing this regress, we eventually arrive at a movement over an infinitesimal distance in an infinitesimal period of time, that is, in a moment.[42] In a certain sense, we might say that this 'movement' was not actually movement, since no finite distance was traversed; even after making this 'movement,' the object's position is not determinately different from its starting position. Yet, at the same time, it *is* movement, because the infinitesimal distance is not the same as *no* distance. We are thus left with a paradoxical concept that is both movement and non-movement.[43]

We can now apply this picture to the self and the moment. Normally, movement consists of moving *from* here *to* there. In the case of the infinitesimal moment, though, it consists simply of moving *from* here, without a determinately separate 'there.'[44] Likewise, the act of turning in repentance consists of going-beyond one's current state: the self comes to be in the act of going-beyond. The point is not 'how far' beyond one's current state one moves (this would be a finite-quantitative conception), but in the moving itself. Cohen writes, "The I can therefore mean nothing higher and absolutely nothing other than an increment [*Schritt*], a step [*Stufe*], in ascent toward the goal, which is infinite."[45] Here, the I is identified not with the result of the step, but with the step, the dynamic act of stepping, itself. Because the goal is infinite, the result of the step is not the main point; one can never be any 'closer' to the goal, since it is always infinitely far away. Rather, the focus is on the direction of movement: one moves *toward* the goal. As Cohen says elsewhere, the individual soul "is always only ascent."[46]

This statement sounds strange, since 'is' typically denotes something fixed and static, while 'ascent' refers to dynamic movement. Such strangeness is in keeping, however, with the paradoxical concept of the moment as movement and non-movement. Because the moment, and thus the self, have no finite duration, one must say that the self 'is' the act of turning itself.

The tension between the static and the dynamic is further illuminated by Cohen's assertion that "ethicality is a realm of actuality only insofar as the latter constitutes a realm of action. But as action is distinguished from the movement of nature, so too is it distinguished from all actuality of nature, from all actuality. Action establishes the realm of ethicality. But in this realm there are no other actualities than tasks to [*zu*] ever-new actualities."[47] Here, Cohen first ties actuality in ethicality (which is also to say, in religion) to dynamic action, so that the ethical self can have actuality *only insofar as* that actuality is part of the realm of action. This account accords with the idea that self's existence, its *Bestand*, is to be found only in the moment of turning. However, Cohen then insists that action must be distinguished "from all actuality": if this is the case, the "insofar as" means that ethicality is *not* a realm of actuality. He first raises the possibility of actuality, making it contingent on action, but then immediately rescinds that possibility by separating action from actuality. He seems be striving toward a notion of 'dynamic actuality,' but his attempt at direct expression is hindered by the paradoxicality of such a concept. The passage's final sentence represents a more oblique effort: the only actualities are tasks to ever-new actualities. The first part of this formulation already seems like a contradiction. If there are no actualities other than tasks, then there would seem to be no actualities at all, since a task normally means: not (yet) an actuality. The second part of the formulation, however, may reconfigure the situation. The tasks in question are not typical, finite tasks, but rather "tasks to ever-new actualities." In the case of a finite task, where the goal is a determinate actuality, the act of striving does not itself constitute a fulfillment of the task. For example, if I am given the task of going to the store and buying a loaf of bread, then the mere striving to fulfill the task is not sufficient: the task will not be fulfilled until I have actually gone to the store and purchased the bread. In the present case, though, the goal itself is not something determinate: the goal of the task is the ethical self, which must always remain an ever-new task and can never be a finalized actuality. With regard to such infinite tasks, Cohen seems to be implying, the dynamic act of striving itself constitutes the actualization of the task. The actualization does not involve 'reaching' something determinate, since there is not anything determinate to reach; rather, it is the mere *direction* of striving, the infinitesimal movement of the moment, that constitutes the fulfillment.

Thus, there seems to be an inverse relation between the fulfillment of finite and infinite tasks: a finite task *cannot* be completed in the moment, simply in the act of striving, but requires finite, determinate accomplishments in a finite amount of time. In contrast, in the case of religious concepts, the infinite task can never be completed in any finite amount of time: but this also means that—precisely because there is no finite goal—it can be fulfilled infinitesimally, in the mere act of striving. While the finite task is *neither* infinitely far away *nor* infinitely close, the infinite task is *both* infinitely far away *and* infinitely close. As such, without ever directly stating that there 'are' actualities in the realm of ethicality and religion, Cohen's somewhat strained formulations seem to leave the door open for a paradoxical fulfillment of the unfulfillable.[48] In this very straining, he models the Kierkegaardian demand that the existing subjective thinker remain just as positive as negative in his communication.

Elsewhere, drawing upon Scripture, Cohen indicates more openly that the task is dynamically fulfilled in the very act of striving. Returning to Leviticus 19:2, he writes, "[T]he holy God demands, 'You shall be holy.' This sentence, too, contains the appearance of a contradiction, for how can it be that the human being should be holy, simply because God is holy? Here too, being-holy [*das Heligsein*] can only mean becoming-holy [*das Heiligwerden*]. The task itself is the goal; the infinite task is the infinite goal."[49] In Cohen's earlier treatment of this verse,[50] he emphasized that for God, holiness is a be-ing, while for man, it is always only a task, a becoming. Thus, being-holy was contrasted to becoming-holy.[51] Here, though, he draws a different lesson. While he does not compromise the infinite and unending nature of the task, he now says that the becoming-holy is, as it were, the human being's *version of* being-holy. If the task itself is the goal, then one fulfills the task and achieves the goal simply by engaging in the task. Even though one can still never 'be' holy, one achieves the full holiness of the ethical self insofar as one engages in the act of becoming, of infinitesimally moving beyond wherever one currently is and of turning toward God and the ethical ideal.

IV. Contrast between the Moment and the Asymptote

Cohen appears to realize that the paradoxical nature of the infinitesimal self could easily lead some readers to an incomplete and one-sided understanding of his presentation. While he is able to assert the idea of the infinite task directly and straightforwardly, he can convey the 'dynamic actuality' of its fulfillment only indirectly. As a consequence, the former will stand out more clearly to a reader who expects a non-paradoxical account, while the latter is more likely to be overlooked and passed over. Thus, one could easily be left with a picture of the self and its attendant concepts in which there is only the obligation of the task, with no place for its successful fulfillment except in the far-away and distant horizon of infinity. In order to ward off such an understanding, Cohen writes,

[O]ne cannot say, one cannot have to say, that the question of success [*Gelingens*] is not at all one's concern. Although one may not make the action, which is an unconditional commandment, contingent on the fore-knowledge of success [*Erfolg*], one need not simply consider this indepen-dence from success as a lack of interest in success. This latter would be close, if not equal, to a degradation and defeat of the commandment. The view [*Hinblick*] toward the phrase "For I, your God, am holy," belongs absolutely to the entire process of self-sanctification. The view toward God belongs to the process of self-sanctification.

And this view toward God can mean nothing other than the view toward the infinite task's solution, which, although infinite, is neverthe-less actualized [*sich verwirklichende*]. The solution is infinite, since it is only a moment in the infinite task; but as this moment, it in turn signifies infinite success [*Gelingen*], the infinite result [*Erfolg*]. God can assign no task that would be only a labor of Sisyphus. Self-sanctification must arrive at infinite completion [*Abschluß*] in the forgiveness of sin by God.[52]

Here, the infinity of the task of self-sanctification, of becoming a self, does not prevent it from being actualized in the moment of turning to God.[53] The "infinite success" of the moment represents the fully successful achievement of the com-manded ideal.[54] The possibility of such success stands in contrast to a "Sisyphean" account of the task, in which, although one can come close to 'the top of the hill,' one's efforts must always fall short of the infinite ideal.

Despite his explicit opposition to this latter account, some readers have attributed to Cohen precisely such a picture of the self and the task, often couched in terms of an 'asymptotic' approximation of the ideal. For instance, according to Norbert Samuelson's account, "Cohen's ideas . . . are infinite goals, which, in a sense, exist. The way that they exist are as asymptotes (i.e., as limits that operational curves continuously approach but never reach)."[55] Such readings flatten the paradoxicality of Cohen's concepts, so that the infinity of the task rules out any full actualization. At the same time, while the model of the asymp-tote may obscure essential features of Cohen's presentation, it can also serve as a useful point of comparison and contrast. In certain key ways, Cohen's conception of the self and its task *is* similar to an asymptote. For this reason, it is important to resist the temptation to dismiss the notion of asymptote out of hand.[56] Like an asymptote, no matter where one is, and no matter how far one has previously traveled, the task of becoming a self will still always be incumbent. In this sense, the goal can be viewed as 'infinitely far away': no amount of striving can ever free a person from the obligation of further striving. Similarly, at every static point in time, the human individual will never actually be equivalent to the ideal, ethical self, just as no finite point on the curve will ever be equivalent to the asymptotic

limit. However, unlike an asymptotic limit, the self is *not only* infinitely distant
but also infinitely near.[57] Because there is no determinate, finite, separation
between the present self and the ideal, ethical self, the distance between the two
can be viewed as infinitesimally small. At any point, one is always only 'a moment
away' from perfect—though not permanent—fulfillment of the task. In contrast,
any given point on the asymptotic curve will always be a *finite* distance away from
the asymptotic limit. For this same reason, while a curve can be said to come
'closer and closer' to its asymptotic limit, one cannot be said to get 'closer' to the
goal of becoming a self—one is always the 'same' infinitesimal distance away.
Because the goal itself is not static or determinate, it does not make sense to speak
of a comparatively greater or lesser approximation of the goal. The notion of
'approximation' is a finite-quantitative concept, whereas when one achieves the
ethical self in the moment, one does so fully and infinitely. As such, while this self
may share aspects of infinity with the asymptote, the infinity of the latter seems
more akin to the spatial-objective nature of what Cohen calls the "mathematical-
physical" infinity of the natural universe, in contrast to the "ethical infinity" of
the human soul.[58]

Again, it is important to emphasize that the 'non-actual actuality' of Cohen's
concept of the self is dependent on the paradoxical, dynamic logic of the infinitesimal. If one is working within a static logic, the asymptote may very well be
the best model available for the self, especially since the alternative would be to
eliminate the infinity of the task.[59] Within a static, non-paradoxical logic, the
self must either be actual *or* not-actual, and the task must be fulfillable *or*
non-fulfillable.[60] Given these choices, the rejection of the asymptote would have
to assign static actuality to the self, an error against which Cohen warns in his
condemnation of the "popular illusion that confuses the ideal moment of a
development, which is assigned as a task, with a concrete finished shape."[61] In
contrast, Cohen's employment of the infinitesimal, which functions both as
something and as nothing, allows him to present the self as a task that is both
fulfillable *and* non-fulfillable.[62] This dynamic logic corresponds to the active, personal engagement that can encompass two contradictory perspectives at once, as
discussed in the previous chapter, whereas impersonal, non-engaged reflection
must choose between the infinity of the task and its fulfillment.

Accordingly, while the model of the asymptote does not fit Cohen's account
of religion, it *is* a fitting model for the objective-impersonal method of Ethics. As
in religion, the concepts of Ethics represent unending tasks,[63] but unlike religion,
Ethics must maintain an absolute separation between the ideal and its actualization.[64] Within the necessarily single-voiced framework of Ethics, there is no vantage point from which one could assert the fulfillment of the task without lapsing
into an egoistic concretization of the self and of God. Thus, the blanket characterization of Cohen's thought as 'asymptotic' is not wholly incorrect but rather

one-sided: while it *does* apply to his account of Ethics, it can be carried over to his paradoxical account of religion only by eliding the fundamental methodological difference between the two.

Because the ethical self's actuality is always only paradoxical, the idea of its preservation and continuity will likewise contain counterintuitive elements. Since the self's duration is infinitesimal, it may seem as though it can exist only in fleeting, fragmented, and isolated moments, with no continuity at all. Cohen emphasizes, however, that continuity of the self *is* possible, since the moment of ascent "can and should unceasingly repeat itself: it must never become old [*inveterieren*]; rather, it must and it can continually [*stets*] rejuvenate and renew itself."[65] Because the infinitesimal is paradoxically both something and nothing, the infinitesimal moment both has and does not have a distinct duration. On one hand, accordingly, to the extent that a moment 'grows old,' the ethical self drops away, so that each moment must be the result of a new movement and is therefore distinct from the previous duration. On the other hand, because each moment has no *determinate* duration, there is no determinate difference between two successive moments and thus there need be no 'gap' between moments of turning. Thus, if this turning is continuous and unceasing, the ethical self will also be continuous: the I "achieves and maintains [*gewinnt und behauptet*] its existence [*Bestand*] in the continuity [*Kontinuität*] of these moments."[66] This continuity of the self, however, must also be a lack of continuity. It is not only the moment that must be renewed for continuity of the self; rather, the self itself must also be continually renewed. Cohen writes, "[The] command of *self-sanctification* cannot be temporally limited at all. It relates to every moment of human life. And it has its eminent relation to the moment in which the I is rejuvenated to a continually new life, and it is only in this constant rejuvenation that the I can have and claim its unique constancy/existence [*Bestand*]."[67] The self is renewed in the moment, and so the continuous renewal of the moment means the continuous renewal of the self. In this sense, we can say that the ethical self must constantly change in order to remain the same, and that, conversely, if it resists renewal and attempts to remain the same, its own constancy and existence (*Bestand*) will fade away.

This situation can be likened to the relation between a function and its derivative. Because the derivative measures *change* in the function's value, a function whose value is constant will have a derivative of zero. For instance, the derivative of the function $y = 2$ is zero, because the function's value will always be the same for successive values of x.[68] For the derivative to be constantly non-zero, the function's value must be continually changing. For instance, the derivative of the function $y = x$ has a non-zero derivative of 1, since the function's value at any given value of x will always be *different* from its value at the preceding value of x.[69] Thus, as it were, the ethical self is like the derivative of the empirical individual: the ethical self can maintain its 'positive value' only by continually moving-beyond the given actuality of the empirical I.[70]

In addition, the paradoxicality of the self demands not only that the renewal be continual, but also that it be total and complete. That is, in order to maintain continuity of the self, the self that comes-to-be in each moment must be not simply different from, but completely discontinuous with the previous self, with the self that already-is. As such, the self must not only be "rejuvenated," made younger, but must undergo "rebirth [*Wiedergeburt*]," must be made *entirely* new.[71] Likewise, Cohen identifies "the continuous re-creation [*Neuschöpfung*] of the soul" as "the chief meaning and chief content of prayer."[72] Because creation marks the 'original beginning,' there can be nothing that comes before it, and so the soul that undergoes 're-creation' through turning has no continuity with any 'previous' instantiation of the soul. It would be understandable to demand such radical newness if one's sole aim were to make a break with that which came before. Yet, in Cohen's presentation, this complete discontinuity is precisely that which enables the self to maintain its continuity![73] Just as the self is limited to a non-actual actuality, it likewise can have only a strictly discontinuous continuity.

V. Other Religious Concepts in the Moment

All that I have said above concerning Cohen's conception of the self applies equally to all other concepts in the sphere of religion. As was discussed earlier, just as the self is an infinite task, so too God's roles in the correlation as unique, as creator, as redeemer, and so on, are also infinite tasks. However, as we have just seen, the self is not only infinitely far away but also infinitely near, and the same can likewise be said of these various attributes of God. For religion, writes Cohen, "the self exists [*besteht*] only in the correlation with God."[74] If the self exists and has its actuality only dynamically, in the moment of turning, then the correlation in which the self exists also gains and maintains its actuality only in the same duration of the moment. Just as the individual can fulfill the task of becoming an ethical self, so too God can truly become creator, revealer, and redeemer for that person—but only in the moment of turning and in the continuity of such moments. Thus, while the holy spirit "accomplishes [*vollzieht*] the correlation between God and man," it is also the case that "the creation of the holy spirit is a continuous re-creation," which is carried out both by God and by the human being's self-sanctification.[75] While the correlation via the holy spirit is always present ideally as a task, it can never have static actuality; rather, the task to which it corresponds can be fulfilled only in the continuous self-sanctification of turning. Likewise, "Prayer continually brings forth and fortifies anew the world of community between God and man, which the correlation demands."[76] Because it must be constantly re-actualized through prayer, the "world of community" between God and man—in which God can be addressed personally, as a You—is not a given actuality and has no *Bestand* apart from the active moment(s) of turning to God. To reiterate Cohen's general dictum, cited earlier, "In religious existence, insofar as it always is regulated and developed by the guiding thread of ethicality, *everything* is valid [*Alles gilt*] only for moments of ascent and transition."[77] For this reason, even a committed religious practitioner is unable to 'hold on' to any of the elements of the religious sphere. They are not valid simply 'for him,' but rather, more specifically, they are valid for him *only in his moments of ethical turning*. This restriction prevents 'fideistic' assertions about God's personal actuality, since the mode of making assertions *to* others *about* God is fundamentally different from the mode of turning *to* God in repentance or prayer. Furthermore, since the re-creation of the self and the correlation must be continually renewed, even the 'past experience' of a previous instance of turning does not qualify a person to put forth a static assertion of God's actuality *now*. Any such attempt could draw only upon a moment that has already 'grown old' and is consequently no longer valid. Importantly, however, these restrictions apply only to those who seek to make authoritative-sounding pronouncements concerning the supposed actuality of religious concepts. In contrast, for the individual who is concerned with her own task of ethical turning, the full actualization of these concepts is always only a moment away.

VI. *The Kingdom of God and the Messianic Future*

Cohen's account of actualization (only) in the moment applies not only to religious concepts normally thought of as having taken place 'in the past' (such as God's role as creator or revealer), but also to such concepts that are often associated with a far-distant time-to-come. In particular, he presents the messianic future as actualizable 'now.' While this approach is in keeping with Cohen's general presentation of infinite tasks, he also attempts to show that the basic underlying logic of his own practical-infinitesimal account is shared by the messianic speeches of the biblical prophets as well. Through this comparison, Cohen creates a more direct link between his own thought and his earlier description of prophetic communication in "The Style of the Prophets." Given his insistence on the direct relation between idea-content and style, it should be unsurprising that, if the substantive content of his own work shares in the logic of prophetic thought, his communicative style would also parallel the 'double-edgedness' that he finds in the prophets.

     After identifying the messianic future with "the kingdom of God" (*malchut shamayim*, i.e., the realm in which God is king),[78] Cohen argues that this latter is infinitesimally near. He writes, and I quote at length:

> Because the messianic confidence is absolutely connected with mono-
> theism, it is identical with the duty of worship. The latter, however, does
> not wait for the future; rather, it pervades my entire life and every moment

of my existence. The same must therefore be the case for the messianic future as well.

And this is the advantage of thinking of [the messianic future] as the kingdom of God. For my personal worship, the kingdom of God must not be merely future; rather, it must be a constant present/presence [*Gegenwart*]. This idea is expressed in the Jewish term "acceptance of the yoke of the kingdom of God." In old prayers the expression is found, "I prepare myself" (*hareni mitkaven*) (the Hebrew expression for devotion [*kavanah*] means, in accord with its root, establishing, thus fortifying, preparing), "to accept upon myself the yoke of the kingdom of God." I thus do not wait for the kingdom of God to come and I do not only pray for its arrival [*Erscheinen*]; rather, through my own preparing [*Rüstung*], through my own will, I bring it about.

Thus the kingdom of God becomes a present/presence [*Gegenwart*] and a personal actuality for my consciousness of duty, and this is more than it remaining merely an object of hope and confidence.[79]

Here, Cohen emphasizes the inability of normal temporal terminology to convey the status of the kingdom of God. The term 'future' normally signifies a point in time that is a finite distance away from the present. It signifies that which is-not-yet, as distinguished from that which already-is. In contrast, the infinitesimal moment lies *between* that which already-is and that which is-not-yet.[80] As such, both 'present' and 'future' are misleading, since the moment lies 'between' the two. Because the kingdom of God "must not be merely future," must not be future in a finite, non-paradoxical sense, the phrase 'messianic future' can one-sidedly color the concept, making it seem 'further away' than it truly is. However, when thought of as 'the kingdom of God,' a phrase without temporal connotations, the 'nearness' of the concept can come through more easily, in that the kingdom of God, the kingship of God, can come to be in the moment that I turn to God in prayer and thereby 'make God my king.' Whereas something that lies strictly in the future can be only "an object of hope and confidence," the paradoxicality of the infinitesimal enables the kingdom of God *also* to become "a present and a personal actuality."[81]

Importantly, though he emphasizes its nearness in this passage, Cohen does not say that the kingdom of God 'is' a present or given actuality. Rather, he consistently uses language that highlights the personal engagement that is required for its actualization. Thus, he says that the kingdom of God "must be"—not "is"—a constant present, in accord with its status as an infinite task.[82] Likewise, the constant present that is enjoined applies specifically to "my personal worship." The first-person formulation reminds the reader that it applies not to 'a person in general' but specifically to *me*. Furthermore, it is not simply 'valid for me' in a static sense; rather, it holds true only for my personal worship, only in the dynamic act of prayer. As Cohen puts it, it is only by my accepting the yoke with *kavanah*, with active devotion, that the kingdom of God is brought about.[83]

To say that the messianic future is present only in the moment of prayerful engagement is also to say that it is present only paradoxically.[84] Because "the messianic kingdom of God . . . belongs to the future [*gehört der Zukunft an*]," it can never lose its not-yet quality of futurity.[85] The ethical turning to which the moment corresponds is distorted if the absoluteness of the future is at all diminished, if the kingdom of God is afforded even the slightest trace of static actuality. After citing the Kaddish prayer—"May his kingdom come to reign in your life and in your days and in the life of all Israel"—Cohen comments, "Thus the messianic kingdom of God is prayed-in [*hineingebetet*] from the future to the present, is already made alive through the prayer of the present."[86] The messianic kingdom of God remains in the future; it never becomes 'part of' the present, let alone the past; however, it can enter into and affect the present by means of prayer. As Cohen writes, the passionate longing of prayer, so long as it continually maintains its "self-creating activity," has "the ability to anticipate [*vorwegzunehmen*] the future and to make it active [*wirksam*]."[87] At first glance, since 'anticipate' often has the connotation of 'expect' or 'look forward to,' his use of this term could create the impression that the kingdom of God is still off in the distance and remains merely an object of hope. However, Cohen seems to be drawing more literally on the word's root derivation, which in both German and English means 'to take beforehand' (*vorweg* + *nehmen*, *ante* + *capere*). Accordingly, even though the present is always 'beforehand' and 'not yet,' the act of prayer can 'take' and seize hold of the kingdom of God, making it 'active' in the moment—not only as partial effect but as infinite fulfillment.[88] Cohen thus reads the Kaddish as a performative speech-act that brings about that which it describes. To the extent that you utter the words of the Kaddish with ethical engagement, 'his kingdom' *does* comes to reign in your life and in your days; to the extent that all those who utter these words do so with ethical engagement, it also comes to reign in the life of 'all Israel.'

Cohen's account of the messianic kingdom of God, in which it can be functionally and dynamically present even while it remains future, also has implications for his understanding of 'the coming of the Messiah.' As in the case of the ethical self, the concept of the messianic kingdom is inherently and inextricably bound up with the idea of an infinite task that can have no finite conclusion or termination. As Cohen puts it, "[the Messiah's] coming is not an actual end [*ein faktischer Abschluß*]; rather, it signifies only the infinity of his coming [*die Unendlichkeit seines Kommens*]."[89] For this reason, the messianic future is different from a finite future that is not yet present but will be present at a later date. Instead, the Messiah's coming always lies in the future; there will never be a point in time at which the messianic age 'is present.' In terms of the verbal tenses involved, Steven Schwarzschild provides a fitting articulation of the Cohenian understanding when he asserts "that the Messiah not only has not come but also will never have come—that he will always be coming."[90] This "infinity of his coming," however, could easily lead some to object (in a manner akin to the rejection of Cohen's notion of 'God as idea') that such an understanding, by making the messianic future unattainable, thereby renders religious striving pointless and ineffectual. A good example of this sort of objection can be found in Franz Rosenzweig's 1927 letter to Benno Jacob, where he writes,

> I can imagine how one could object to any given present [*jeder Gegenwart*] with "You are not yet it." However, I cannot understand how one can make from this a principle for the future, and indeed for all future, without thereby undermining the future. I have no idea of how one should pray for something that one holds from the start/a priori [*von vornherein*] to be impossible. I cannot pray that two plus two should equal five. The prophets meant an earthly Zion of the future. The eternity [*Ewigkeit*], which we Jews means, lies not in infinity [*Unendlichen*], but rather "soon, in our days" . . . That which comes only in eternity, comes . . . in eternity not at all [*Was nur in Ewigkeit kommt, kommt . . . in Ewigkeit nicht*].[91]

Here, Rosenzweig contrasts "the eternity that we Jews mean" with one that lies "in infinity." In his portrayal, the notion of infinity—wherein the Messiah will always not yet have come—undermines the entire concept of the future and thus of the messianic future.[92] Rosenzweig's '2 + 2 = 5' analogy, however, indicates that he may be working with a quantitative-asymptotic understanding of 'infinity.' As we have seen, though, Cohen's understanding of the infinite task involves an ethical—not a strictly asymptotic—conception of infinity. This ethical conception is fundamentally anchored in and cannot be separated from the paradoxicality of the infinitesimal. That is to say, *if* one is confined to a non-paradoxical framework, then Rosenzweig's rejection of infinity may well be the only way to preserve the potency of the messianic future—although, as we discussed earlier, the rejection of the infinity of the task may also have deleterious ethical consequences. In contrast, Cohen's paradoxical approach allows him to preserve the active force of the Messiah's coming as well as the full responsibility of the ethical imperative.[93] While Rosenzweig claims that a Messiah who "comes only in eternity" never comes at all, Cohen might respond that a Messiah who comes only in eternity, only in ethical infinity, *can come* in the next moment. In contrast, a Messiah who does *not* "come only in eternity" is the one who never comes at all, because any Messiah that did come would not be the Messiah.[94] It is *precisely and only by* the Messiah's coming only in infinity that the Messiah is able to come in the next moment.[95]

One way of elucidating Cohen's position on this issue is to focus on the fact that the infinitesimal moment is not part of finite time. Normally, the further away something is, the less effect it has on the present. For instance, if we think of a person calling out to us, the further away the person is, the less we can hear the voice that calls us forward and the less effect it can have on us where we are. Thus, if a voice were infinitely far away, its force would be diminished essentially to nothing, and it could have no effect on us. This seems to be the sense in which an asymptotic infinity would have the effect of 'undermining' the future. In contrast, the infinity of the moment derives from the fact that it lies between two finite points in time, between 'this point' and 'the next point' in time. Thus, while the goal is 'infinitely' far away—at any subsequent point in time, it will still be not-yet-actualized—it is also infinitely close and is actualizable in the very next moment. While the combination of 'infinitely distant' and 'infinitely close' may be paradoxical, we can understand the functional 'equivalence' of the two by observing that neither of them can be identified with any point in time. 'Infinitely distant' is not part of time because it is located 'after' all subsequent finite points in time, while 'infinitely close' is not part of time because it is located after the current point in time but before the next one. Because both lie 'outside' of finite time, there is no way of determinately distinguishing between them, since the categories of before 'before' or 'after' only apply to finite temporal succession.[96] Thus, the moment of turning is the 'same' as the 'infinitely distant' future in which the messianic task is fulfilled. Along the same lines, the moment is also 'equivalent' to the original moment of creation, which is located '*before*' finite time. That is to say, the moment combines both creation and redemption within its infinitesimal duration.[97] Furthermore, this moment of redemptive re-creation is possible *only because* the task can never be fulfilled in finite time. If the Messiah's coming were *not* infinitely far away, if it were to have an end, if at some point in the future the Messiah will have come, then the Messiah's coming would be located at *that* point, a *finite* distance away from the present. In this case, because the messianic future would be finitely far away from us, it would not be equivalent to the moment of turning, and we could no longer actualize it the next moment and make it *wirksam* for us now.[98]

It is also worth commenting on the 'earthly' and 'temporal' manifestations that correspond to Cohen's conception of messianism. If the fulfillment of the task can occur only 'outside of time,' does this prevent change from coming about 'in time'? While Rosenzweig appears to think that the concept of 'infinity' (as he understands it) would undermine the earthly actualization of the ideal future, Cohen explicitly defines his understanding of messianism as "the dominion of the good *on earth*," such that "[e]thicality will be established in the *human* world."[99] Although the ideal ethical self has its *Bestand* only in the infinitesimal moment of turning, that same moment, and the continuity of such moments, will shape the ethical attitudes and actions of the existing individual.[100] Accordingly, the pull of reason and the ethical ideal on the human being provides the confidence that greater cultural self-criticism and ethical awareness will eventually (though still conditionally, not automatically or monotonically) overturn the injustice of currently existing social structures. Because this establishing of greater ethicality cannot mean the end of the infinite task, each individual must always continue to strive to become an ethical self, but such achievements *can* eliminate the basic economic oppression and political imbalances that currently hinder such striving. Similarly, in ethicality's intellectual sphere, each individual will still have to strive to avoid the one-sidedness and the urge for theoretical totality that continually tempt us with regard to ethico-religious concepts, but the tools of self-criticism can help eliminate the *conscious* and *social* promotion of irrational or one-sided doctrines and ideologies.[101] As Cohen writes, "The virtue of men will have to tread ever-new paths of unforeseen steepness, but a level of ethicality will be reached, which secures the course of human ethicality."[102] Thus, although the infinite task differs from an asymptote in that it is infinitely fulfilled in the moment, the external and social manifestations of those momentary fulfillments *do* seem to have an asymptotic shape, albeit one in which certain basic benchmarks can be outwardly achieved.[103] In this way, the paradoxical combination of 'infinitely close' and 'infinitely distant' enables the hope and the possibility of external change and growth.[104]

VII. The Infinitesimal Future and Prophetic Messianism

So far, we have discussed Cohen's 'own' conception of the messianic, which, although it draws upon traditional ideas, might seem substantially different from what one typically imagines to be the 'traditional Jewish religious understanding' of the Messiah. For this reason, it behooves us to examine more closely the ways in which Cohen explicitly links his conception to the sources of Judaism. Even though he does not claim that his philosophical constructs always correspond directly to 'the plain sense' of the biblical prophetic texts, his ways of reading uncover parallels between his own account and the basic patterns of reasoning of those texts. As such, it is possible to understand his readings as a 'deeper plain sense' interpretation of the sources. In his chapter on "The Messianic References in the Prophets," Cohen first highlights many of the 'ideal' elements of the prophetic accounts. He cites Isaiah 9:6, in which the prophet describes a coming time in which there will be "peace without end" (*Frieden ohne Ende*; *shalom ein-ketz*) and in which the government and kingdom will be upheld "through justice and righteousness from now until eternity" (*durch Recht und Gerechtigkeit von jetz und bis in Ewigkeit*; *be-mishpat u-vitzdakah me-atah ve-ad olam*). Cohen then comments, "Now the day of the Lord can no longer be thought of seriously as close at hand, for the new time is to mean a new eternity."[105] While some prophetic passages may seem like they could actually take place at a point in the finite future, Cohen reads Isaiah's declaration of infinite peace and infinite justice as an indication of the ideality of the envisioned future. Because any actual human government must, as human, be marked by finitude and therefore by shortcomings in peace and justice, such a messianic future can never have a static fulfillment; it must always be "an ideal as contrasted with actuality."[106] Likewise, Cohen cites Isaiah 25:8 and 29:18, which describe a future in which God "will swallow up death forever" and in which "the deaf will hear the words of a book, and from out of obscurity and darkness, the blind will see." He then remarks, "The miracle concerning the blind and the deaf is not much less [miraculous] than that concerning death: all of these examples are unmistakable metaphors [*Gleichnisse*]."[107] Here, he does not say merely that *we should read* these examples as metaphors, but also that the prophet *deliberately employed* metaphoric images.[108] That is, rather than describing a future event that could actually occur (e.g., "the myopic shall receive eyeglasses"), the prophet specifically describes 'impossible' happenings such as death ceasing, the blind seeing, and the deaf hearing. From Cohen's perspective, such 'impossibilities' should come as no surprise, since they dovetail neatly with the strict ideality of the messianic future. The use of metaphor must be an essential element of prophetic communication: the prophets speak in metaphor precisely because there is no literal-actual image that could correspond to the messianic future.[109] As such, the images can be designated, drawing upon Paul Ricoeur's terminology, as prime examples of "live" metaphors that cannot be translated into literal redescriptions, in contrast to "dead" metaphors, or metaphors of substitution.[110] That is to say, the prophets' ideal metaphors are not metaphors for something *for* something actual (or for something statically actualizable).[111] Accordingly, Cohen does not seek to 'explain away' the apparent miracles and impossibilities that are found throughout the prophetic speeches, since they serve to emphasize and call attention to the *type of future* (ideal and infinite, not actual or finite) that is in question.

The above readings have the benefit of showing how Cohen's dissociation of the messianic future from finite actuality can be linked to the biblical prophetic texts. However, these particular readings, with their emphasis on ideality, do not in themselves differentiate Cohen sufficiently from other approaches that he wishes to avoid. For instance, a strictly 'asymptotic' conception of the messianic future would be happy to deprive the messianic future not only of *static* actuality (as Cohen does) but of *all* actuality. Likewise, an eschatological approach could agree that static actualization is impossible in this world; it therefore posits 'another world' in which the actualization *will* come to pass. In order to combat such interpretations of the prophetic texts, Cohen must show that they display not only ideality but also the paradoxical 'dynamic actuality' of the infinitesimal moment. Thus, he argues that, if one undertakes a close reading of the entire collection of prophetic messianic references, "the understanding of messianism as eschatology reveals itself as a mistaken notion."[112] Rather,

> All of the prophets, before and after the exile, always understand 'the end of days,' even if some of them may have thought it close at hand, as a *political* future of their own people and of humanity . . . [T]he end of days is not explicitly described as an entirely distant, inconceivable future, but the more precise time-determination is left in unclarity. For the prophets, it is a matter simply of the future as opposed to the present, with its power and its unethicality, but equally as opposed to the past, with all its frissons and charms of piety. Toward the future alone do they orient their gaze, and to it do they want to direct attention, and indeed absolutely only to the earthly future with its duties, cares, and hopes.[113]

In other words, while the prophets are not speaking about a finite future, neither are they speaking about a distant future in terms of a quantitative infinity. Their emphasis is solely on the quality of 'future-ness' itself, in contrast to the already-is and the once-was, just as the infinitesimal moment stood for the quality of movement, rather than any particular quantity (whether finite or quantitatively infinite) of movement.[114]

Cohen's claim about "time-determination" likely derives from the formulations that the different prophets consistently employ to locate the messianic future. For instance, they often open their speeches with phrases such as "on that day" (*ba-yom ha-hu*), "at that time" (*ba-et ha-hi*), or "in those days" (*ba-yamim ha-hemah*). Through their use of demonstrative pronouns (that, those), these formulations give the future a definite, concrete quality that removes it from the vagueness of a distant 'someday.' At the same time, one need not interpret the *specificity* of the formulations as indicating a *finite* future. Because they lack any quantitative time-markers (i.e., they do not say, "On that day eight years from now . . ."), the deictic formulations can be understood as merely pointing out the *direction* of the messianic fulfillment. That is to say, the absence of quantitative time-markers may be a deliberate omission, if the prophets' main point is simply to emphasize the future as such (*that* day), in opposition to the present (*this* day). This structure mirrors that of the infinitesimal moment: although the moment differs from present-actuality (i.e., it is that, rather than this), one cannot assign a finite value to the amount by which it differs. In this reading, one could say that the reason that the prophets do not provide a precise time-determination is because *there can be no* precise time-determination for the infinitesimal messianic future.[115] Another common formulation (which also lacks quantitative markers) is "Behold, days are coming" (*hineh yamim ba'im*).[116] This formulation does not have the same definiteness of "in those days," but, for that same reason, it is less susceptible to being mistaken for a finite future. At the same time, the activeness of its participle indicates the nearness of the messianic future, thus distinguishing it from a far-off asymptote, while the use of *hineh* (Look here! Behold!) further heightens the sense of immediacy and of almost-here-ness. Finally, a third common locution refers to "the day of the Lord" (*yom YHVH*), and usually takes the form of "the day of the Lord is coming" (*yom YHVH ba*) or "the day of the Lord is near" (*karov yom YHVH*). Again, the emphasis is on the pressing nearness, the comingness, of the messianic future, without any finite reckonings as to *when* it is coming or *how close* it is. Under the interpretations given here, all of these types of formulations provide compelling grounds for Cohen's claim that the prophets were concerned with 'the future as such,' in a manner very much akin to his own concept of the infinitesimal messianic future.

After setting up this specific connection to his concept of the infinitesimal, Cohen engages in a series of direct comparisons between prophetic messianism and other ways of conceiving of the relationship between the ideal and the actual. These comparisons hark back to his assessment, in his introduction, of the relation between totality and plurality. There, we saw that his concept of religion was grounded in the paradoxical intersection of totality and plurality, in contrast to approaches that upheld totality alone (the method of Ethics) or plurality alone (egoism). Here, we find a similar pattern, in that the opposing approaches all seek to resolve and eliminate the tension generated by messianism's strictly dynamic conjunction of the ideal and the actual.

Having noted that the political nature of the prophets' envisioned future distances their messianism from eschatology, Cohen now adds that this distinction is further reinforced by the general *absence* of references to an afterlife, whether in the netherworld (*Unterwelt*) or in the world of heaven above (*Oberwelt*).[117] Even the prophetic phrase *be-aharit ha-yamim*—whose common translation as "in the end of days" or "in the last days" (*am Ende der Tage* in Cohen's rendering) can seem to denote the end of this (temporal, earthly) world and the transition to another (eternal, heavenly) world—may be more properly understood as meaning "in the later days," "in future days": that is, not an eschatological end, but simply the same 'future itself' (*after* in contrast to *now*) that we have seen in the other prophetic locutions.[118] However, the very success of the separation from eschatology leaves messianism susceptible to a different sort of misunderstanding. For some interpreters, the absence of other-worldly actualities and the "political," "earthly" nature of the envisioned future demonstrates that the prophets of ancient Israel, as well as the entire people of Israel, were mired in materialistic and unspiritual modes of thought and being. In this portrayal, "a people is thought to be by nature so degenerate that it had sense only for the present [*Gegenwart*] with its dominating power and opposed any interest in a supernatural [*überirdischen*] world," such that "the desires of this people are dominated by sensual actuality

[*von der sinnlichen Wirklichkeit*]."[119] In a certain way, this accusation is 'logical':
either one posits the actuality of something 'beyond' this world, or one will be left
only with the sensual-material actuality of this world. This forced option mirrors
pre-Kantian debates between dogmatists/rationalists and skeptics/empiricists:
one either asserts the existence of metaphysical objects beyond sense-data, or one
denies the reality of such objects and insists that the only truths are those that
come to us though the senses. Accordingly, given these choices, any interpretation of the prophets will either make them say too little (domination by sensual
actuality) or too much (the positing of a supernatural, eschatological world).

As Cohen presents them, however, the prophets embrace neither of these two
choices. On one hand, as shown above, they do not take refuge in a supernatural
'other world.' Yet, on the other hand, one must take into account "the almost
incomprehensible [*schier unbegreifliche*] fact that messianism defies, disparages
and condemns, annihilates mercilessly absolutely all [*gerade aller*] political
present-actuality [*Gegenwartswirklichkeit*], both its own, as well as that of
foreigners [*fremden*]."[120] At first glance, such destruction could seem to border on
nihilism: if the prophets reject all present actuality of this world, while also failing to posit an other-worldly actuality, they would seem to be left with 'nothing.'
In a sense, this is true: they place no value in any static actuality, whether it be of
this world or of a world beyond. Yet, messianism does not consist entirely of negativity; rather, it engages in its destructiveness "in order to put in the place of this
sensible present a new kind of supersensibility [*Übersinnlichkeit*], not a supernatural [*überirdische*] one, but rather that of the future. This future creates a new
earth and a new heaven, and thus a new actuality. This creation of the future, as
the true political actuality, is the great work of messianism."[121] Thus, messianism
avoids the forced option by positing a type of 'actuality' that goes beyond the
senses without going beyond this world. However, as indicated by the description
of "almost incomprehensible," this third path is one of paradox: whereas actuality
is normally associated with that which is, it is here associated with the future,
with that which is-not-yet. Furthermore, this future is not a necessary or inevitable future, but rather one that comes to be only through ethical turning. Thus,
whereas potentiality (specifically, ethical potentiality, that which ought to be) is
typically seen as the opposite of actuality, it is now designated as the true actuality! At the same time, Cohen's assertions of "a new actuality" must be qualified by
the fact that elsewhere, as we have seen, he himself describes the messianic future
as "an ideal as contrasted to actuality [*das Ideal im Gegensatz zur Wirklichkeit*]."[122]
Thus, the prophets' messianic creation of the future must be a non-actual actuality, a paradoxical concept in keeping with the 'dynamic actuality' of the infinitesimal moment of turning.

The movement that lifts the prophets beyond both eschatology and domination by the present shares a structural similarity with the Kantian movement

beyond 'other-worldly' dogmatism and 'sensual' empiricism. However, Cohen emphasizes that there are also fundamental differences between messianism and scientific philosophical Ethics. While he holds up Plato as the founder and representative figure of the latter, he also explicitly links Kant himself to this same mode of reasoning.[123] According to Cohen, Plato's understanding of the good as "beyond being" created room, through the method of scientific philosophy, for Ethical idealism. This latter shares many features with messianism, in that its "beyondness" is not a "supernatural sensibility [*überirdische Sinnlichkeit*]" and yet does consists of a "supersensibility" that creates the possibility of an ethical world by transcending mathematical, natural-scientific being.[124] Despite these similarities, Cohen argues that the contrast between the two approaches is brought out most clearly through an examination of Plato's political ideas. At first glance, Plato's "utopianism," with its "program that ostensibly turns away from the present," could appear akin to messianism's rejection of the present.[125] However, while messianism specifically rejects the present in order to put the future in its place, Plato, in his ideal state, has no notion of human growth and development.[126] Consequently, "He does not conceive of a future at all, unless it be one that is merely the unceasing repetition [*Wiederholung*] of the present. His political idealism, therefore, does not recognize a future proper [*eigentliche*], insofar as it would be a new singular [*eigenartige*] creation and development."[127] This lack of development, and thus of the future, is no mere oversight on Plato's part; rather, it is fully in keeping with and even demanded by the objective and atemporal method of Ethics through which he reasons. In his introduction, Cohen showed that this method's demand for a fully consistent, objective concept of man prevented it from recognizing the I as different from the You. For the same reason, it is also unable to account for the ethical self whose 'content' is constituted precisely by change and development, by becoming *different* from what it was at the previous point in time. Just as the method of Ethics has to wrest away the difference between particular individuals, so that the You must be simply another instance of the I, so too it must wrest away any differences over time, so that the future can only be 'another instance,' an unceasing repetition, of the present. As such, whereas the prophets find in the future "a new actuality" that takes the place of the rejected present actuality, Plato's lack of a distinct future means that he simply turns away from the present actuality *without putting any other actuality in its place*. This unfilled gap leads the method of Ethics to the verdict, sharply criticized by Cohen as by others, that the good, the ideal, can have no actuality at all.[128] The results of the method of Ethics are thus structurally equivalent to an asymptotic infinity, which, as Rosenzweig argued, has the effect of undermining the future.

In light of this shortcoming of Plato's method, Cohen details three distinct varieties of "beyond" (*Jenseits*), each of which seeks to transcend the sensible present actuality through one form or another of ideality. First, there is the escha-tological beyond, which posits a supernatural world that may be ideal and invisi-ble now, but whose actuality will one day displace the current world of temporal tasks. Secondly, there is the beyond of "scientific idealism" and the method of Ethics, which is "beyond the being of the mathematical, natural-scientific world. But it does not mean a beyond with regard to the past and present of historical experience in the development of the peoples."[129] Because it lacks a future 'beyond the past and the present,' its ideal is incapable of actualization in the temporal world. The first two beyonds also correspond the basic choices in post-Kantian philosophy: if one does not want to succumb to a positivism that recognizes only sense-data, one must either maintain the gap between the ideal and the actual (the Kantian position[130]), or one must close the gap (the Hegelian position) in a move that is functionally equivalent to the eschatological actualization of the ideal.

As we saw earlier, Rosenzweig was led by his forceful opposition to the Kantian asymptotic-infinity to argue that the ideal future will one day have become actual. In so doing, however, he slips back into the Hegelian position. In contrast, Cohen rejects *both* of these other beyonds in favor of the prophets' "messianic idealism,"[131] whose concept of the future permanently maintains the ethical gap between the actual and the ideal, while paradoxically enabling the actualization of the ideal in the dynamic moment. In other words, the messianic future posits an *infinitesimal* gap that sepa-rates the actual from the ideal: the distance between the two is both 'something'—thereby preserving the ethical task—and 'nothing'—thereby allowing the gap to be 'closed,' and the infinite task fulfilled, in the moment of turning. Cohen's description of the prophetic "supersensibility of the earthly future [*Übersinnlichkeit der irdischen Zukunft*]" thus provides a succinct form of distinguishing the messianic from other approaches.[132] Each of the other options, in order to allay the paradoxical tension, ends up eliminating one or another of this formulation's component elements. Thus, the mentality that is dominated by present actuality leaves out "supersensibility"; eschatology leaves out "earthly"; and the Platonic method of Ethics leaves out "the future." Only the messianic is able to hold all three terms together. Because Cohen considers the idea of the messianic future to be a "necessary consequence" of the prophets' idea of the unique God,[133] it stands to reason that the former should share the same resistance to 'theoretical consistency' that we have seen in the latter.

VIII. *Cohen, Messianism, and the Style of the Prophets*

Given the striking similarities between Cohen's own concept of the messianic future and the one that he draws out from the prophetic sources, we can examine anew the significance of these sources for Cohen's construction of a religion of reason. We have seen the ways in which Cohen uses Scripture for communicating his understanding of religion. Now, we can also raise the possibility that his own engagement with Scripture helped guide him to that very understanding. While some might view Cohen as reading an independently derived concept of the infinitesimal moment 'back into' Scripture, it may be that his deep familiarity with the prophetic accounts of the messianic future better enabled him to recognize the importance of the infinitesimal moment in the first place.[134] Such a process would be fully in keeping with Cohen's own account of hermeneutics as well as his account of the rabbinic-midrashic method of scriptural interpretation. In both, the details of the text *and* a reader's antecedent concepts each play an essential role in shaping the resulting interpretation. Thus, Cohen's concept of the infinitesimal future may be best understood as a hybrid product, originating from his preexisting philosophical tendencies *in conjunction with* the particular details of the prophetic sources.

We can also view Cohen's other religious concepts as stemming from this same basic notion of the messianic future: his concept of the unique God can be understood more specifically as the messianic God, the God whose conceptual paradoxicality corresponds to the paradoxicality of the messianic future. In this sense, Cohen's double-voiced account of God's love, revelation, and forgiveness— in which God's personality and agency are not 'givens' but are dependent on personal engagement in the moment—can be redescribed as a *messianic* account of those concepts.[135] Thus, while he presents messianism as a "necessary consequence" of the concept of the unique God, their order could equally have been reversed in his own experience, in that he may have been led to his understanding of the unique God via the dynamic of the infinitesimal future, as displayed in prophetic messianism.

If we now compare Cohen's reading of the prophets' messianism in *Religion of Reason* to his earlier account in "The Style of the Prophets," one difference that stands out is that the former contains little explicit treatment of the prophets' communicative style. That is, he focuses primarily on *what* their ideas consists in, rather than on *how* they convey those ideas. However, given Cohen's insistence on the general relation between idea-content and style, we should not be surprised to find that the prophets' conception of the messianic future is closely tied to their double-edged style. The messianic future, as we have seen, is linked to the infinitesimal moment. As such, it does not correspond to a finite future point in time, that is, it does *not* correspond to what we normally think of as 'the future.' Accordingly, the prophets were not soothsayers; they were not trying to 'predict' a future state of affairs. Rather, they aimed to convey to their listeners how one should be and what one should do *now*. The infinitesimal future does not lie at a distant point in time, nor does it come about inevitably; rather, it is dependent on one's ethical turning, but with that turning, it can come about in the next moment. Indeed, there is no reason to think that the prophets 'know' (or would even claim to know) what will be the case at any point in the finite future. The point of their words is not to hypothesize concerning a finite-future 'is,' but rather to convey the 'ought' that is incumbent, now and always, upon the existing individual: they are concerned not with the *will be* but with the *should be*.[136] The "supersensible actuality" that the prophets discovered would thus correspond to the infinite task that is actualized in the dynamic moment. Accordingly, those elements in their speeches that may have the surface appearance of eschatology turn out, upon closer inspection, to be nothing other than pure ethicality.[137]

We can therefore draw a connection between the prophets' 'futuristic' formulations and Cohen's account of the divine "attributes of action." According to Cohen, "The attributes of action are not so much characteristics of God; rather, they are—conceptually determined [*begrifflich bedingt*]—models for the action of human beings."[138] In this version of *imitatio dei*, God serves as the archetype of human morality, in accord with the rabbinic dictum of "As God is compassionate, so you are to be compassionate."[139] Thus, the purpose of any given biblical passage that seems be a description of God is not to make a claim about 'what God is' in any abstract sense, but rather to convey how *you* should relate, be, and act. In the same way, we can say that the purpose of a prophetic proclamation that seems to be about a future era is also to convey how you are to relate, be, and act now. Thus, for example, while Isaiah 2:4—"Nation will not lift up sword against nation, neither will they study war any more"—may seem like a prediction of a far-away time ('the end of days') in which war will somehow have ceased, the prophet's aim in speaking may be to say that *you should cease now* from "studying war," that you should eliminate your warlike ways through repentance and ethical turning in the next moment. The prophet, in other words, presents a vision of the ideal that is to have its actuality in an infinitesimal future that is, in turn, only a moment's turning away from actualization. In the case of Isaiah 2:4, the ethical-obligatory nature of the envisioned future is indicated by the immediately subsequent verse, which sharply transitions from the future tense to a call in the imperative for turning and repentance: "O house of Jacob, come and let us walk in the light of the Lord." This switching back and forth between future and imperative is found throughout the prophetic literature, indicating that the two tenses, while theoretically differentiated, may correspond practically to the same incumbent action, to the infinite task in which human beings can and must engage. The functional equivalence between the two tenses can be brought out most strikingly through a comparison of Ezekiel 18:31 and Ezekiel 36:26.[140] In the former, the prophet employs an imperative formulation in order to exhort his audience to repent: "Make yourselves a new heart and a new spirit." In the latter verse, the very same goal is presented in terms of a divine action in the messianic future: the prophet reports God as saying, "I will give you a new heart and I will put a new spirit within you." Thus, just as our previous chapter focused on the correlation of agency, such that human repentance and God's purification did not constitute determinately differentiable actions, we now see that the same practical correlation holds true with regard to tense: in prophetic speech, the task of the (human-centered) imperative is not finitely distinct from that of the (divine-centered) future. While the connection is particularly clear in these verses from Ezekiel, Cohen's basic analysis of messianism warrants us to read other instances of the prophetic 'future tense' in the same way, even in cases that lack an explicit 'imperative' parallel.

However, if words that seem to describe a time in the distant future in fact correspond to an immediately incumbent ethical task, then why do the prophets speak in terms of 'future days' at all? Since they *do* frequently express their ideas in the imperative, why not do they not simply do so in *all* instances? One important reason could stem from the irremediably paradoxical nature of the infinite task and the infinitesimal moment. On one hand, the task can be fulfilled in the very next moment—but, on the other hand, the task will still be incumbent at every future point in time, so that its fulfillment is 'infinitely far away' and therefore 'impossible.' The use of the imperative highlights the 'infinite nearness' of the messianic future: if you are exhorted, for instance, to repent and to make yourself a new heart and a new spirit, the implication is that this is something you can do now. However, if *only* the imperative were used, the 'impossibility' of the fulfillment would be lost and would not be conveyed. For this reason, the prophets must *also* present the messianic fulfillment as taking place not now but rather 'in days to come.' Thus, although the prophets' practical focus remains strictly on the ethical turning of the next moment, and *not* on any point in the finite future, they must still employ the *future tense* in their exhortative addresses. In other words, it is *precisely by* also making the task distant and impossible that they can properly convey its pressing ethical nearness and its potential for fulfillment. The 'impossibility' of the task also helps account for the fact that the agency of the 'future' fulfillment is presented as resting with God. Just as the 'infinitely distant' side of the task's infinity means that you cannot complete the task *now*, that its fulfillment lies in the future, the same infinity also means that *you*, as a finite human being, cannot complete the task, that its fulfillment must lie with God.[141] Conversely, however, just as the 'infinitely near' side of the task's infinity means that it can be fulfilled in the next moment, it likewise means that *you* are capable of fulfilling it. Again, one should not attempt to 'resolve' the contradictoriness of these two 'sides'; rather, the contradiction must remain heightened. Because the prophets intend to convey a *practice* and a *practical relation* that cannot be comprehended theoretically, their simultaneous presentation of imperative and future, as well as of human and divine agency, serves to prevent the one-sided distortion that would result if either were presented alone or as having priority over the other.

The links between the infinitesimal moment and the prophets' contradictory combination of imperative and future also enable us to revisit other aspects of their communicative style. Each of the 'strategies' that Cohen discusses in "The Style of the Prophets" can be reformulated in terms of the moment's paradoxical bringing-together of the ideal and the actual. For instance, to the extent that the infinitesimal moment and the messianic future always represent "an ideal as contrasted with actuality," a tragic style is called for, in which the human being's hope of fulfilling his task is futile. In contrast, to the extent that the task can be fulfilled in the next moment, one should employ a satiric style, wherein the challenges can be overcome and overturned with the smallest modicum of common sense.[142] Similarly, the prophetic passages of utter condemnation and destruction reflect the 'impossibility' of actualizing the ideal, while those of joy and consolation for the infinitesimal 'remnant' reflect the infinite fulfillment of the task in the infinitesimal moment. In each case, the prophets must employ two-sidedness so that their practical concepts come across as neither 'too ideal' nor 'too actual,' either of which would undermine the ethical task of turning and repentance. As such, the prophets exemplify the Kierkegaardian existing subjective thinker whose communication contains just as much of the comic as of pathos.

This concern for avoiding a de-ethicizing imbalance, either in the direction of the actual or the direction of the ideal, lies at the heart of Cohen's style as well. While Cohen does not employ combinations of tragedy and satire or of condemnation and consolation, his juxtaposition of the voices of Scripture and philosophy serves an equivalent practical purpose. From the perspective of philosophy, the various religious concepts are only ideal and infinite tasks, with no element of actuality or interpersonal relation. The perspective of Scripture, conversely, presents the correlation between the human being and God as living, personal, and actual. The conditionality of this actuality, furthermore, is underscored by the citational and interpretative element of Cohen's use of Scripture: just as the fulfillment of the task is dependent on active ethical striving, so too Cohen's presentation of Scripture as displaying the actualization of the ethical correlation is not a 'given,' but is dependent on his actively reading the source-text in that particular way. Through this combination of Scripture and philosophy, Cohen aims to communicate the same infinitesimal-ethical messianic future that he sees as the fundamental content of the biblical prophetic speeches. Since he shares both the idea-content and style of the biblical prophets, it may even be the case that Cohen considered himself to be speaking 'as' a prophet.[143] That is, the 'prophetic' ideas require a 'prophetic' communication. In this sense, the concept of 'prophet' would not, in its essence, refer to the recipient of a special revelation that is inaccessible to 'normal' people. Rather, the office of prophet would be defined by what the prophet *does*, so that a prophet would be a 'speaker' who, like Cohen, seeks to communicate and convey the practical-paradoxical vision of the unique God and the messianic future.

In this context, we should place particular emphasis on the *attempt* to communicate these ideas. Despite Cohen's efforts and those of the prophets, the opportunities for confusion and distortion remain numerous. In particular, the 'dynamic actuality' of Cohen's religious concepts risks being mistaken for a 'static actuality,' especially when expressed in the static medium of the written word. Because the concepts *can* be actual for you, in the moment of striving, it is all too easy for a person to abstract that actuality away from its personal-active conditionality and to treat religious concepts as actual 'in general.' Such abstraction, however, wrongly attempts to gain for theory that which is attainable only for practice. From the (static) perspective of impersonal thought, not only are religious concepts not inherently actual, but their actualization must be viewed as absolutely impossible. Thus, even if a person is able to *live* the full actuality of the religious concepts, that same person must still *think of* their actualization as impossible. This self-discipline is linked to the relation of religion to Ethics, wherein the former has no autonomous status, but only a paradoxical 'distinctive aspect' (*Eigenart*). Thus, when Cohen represents the actualization of the infinite task in the thought-medium of static 'is' sentences, he himself 'says too much' and compromises the requirement of austerity.[144]

For Cohen, thinking of God's personality, commandingness, and forgiveness (or even the you-ness of the fellowman) as actual or actualizable would be tantamount to a mystical concretization of what ought to be strictly regulative concepts. At the same time, in speaking of "the border-line of mysticism [*Grenzlinie der Mystik*]," Cohen writes, "[W]e have seen everywhere that the Jewish religious-teaching touches this border, but does not cross it."[145] Thus, while actualization must remain impossible, 'mere' impossibility would be saying too little. Since the proper teaching lies right at the border of mysticism, stopping short of that border would be just as erroneous as crossing it. Since any single voice, as we have seen, will fall on one side or the other of that infinitesimally narrow line, Cohen must use two voices to point indirectly to the practice that lies between the possible and the impossible. The one-sidedness of a single voice also corresponds to the one-sidedness of every individual person: at any given point in time, each person will relate to the religious concepts as either 'too actual' or 'not actual enough.' Accordingly, some people will need to think of the concepts of 'more actual' then they currently do, while others will need to think of them as 'less actual' then they currently do. As such, the 'proper' way of thinking is not a fixed point, but depends on where you currently are. It is never a question of 'actual' or 'not actual' in absolute terms; rather, the key criterion is the *direction* in which one moves. In order to achieve the proper ethical balance, one must always undermine and turn from one's present form of conceptualization, in a continuous 'repentance of thought.'

In effect, Cohen's style enacts and performs this repentance by means of its constant transitions between different voices and perspectives.[146] Though misunderstanding can still arise should any single voice be taken as a self-sufficient 'position'—a distortion to which the voice that 'says too much' may be particularly susceptible—the overall dynamic instability can help undermine the ostensibly static nature of each perspective. While different kinds of readers may be in need of different sorts of 'corrections,' Cohen's paradoxical promotion of both the ideal *and* the actual can convict both varieties in their one-sidedness. Because *Religion of Reason* resists any theoretically consistent reading, it neutralizes the interminable debate over the 'true' account of religious concepts and redirects attention to the practical ethicality that forms the basis of the religion of reason and in which alone the correlation between God and the human being can have its continual actualization.

Conclusion

MY CONCLUDING REMARKS will be somewhat brief, as my primary goal in this study—showing how best to read *Religion of Reason*—has been displayed progressively through my unfolding of Cohen's text in the foregoing chapters. His early study of prophetic style provided us with a first glimpse of the ways in which multiplicity and inconsistency can serve a practical communicative purpose. His introduction to *Religion of Reason* then demonstrated that such multiplicity applies not only to rhetorical-exhortative moral communication, but plays a crucial role in addressing a contradiction lying at the heart of the rational philosophical project. Although Cohen could not resolve that contradiction directly, Kierkegaard's account of indirect communication enabled us to view the main body of *Religion of Reason* as an attempt to convey dynamically and performatively those ideas that resist a theoretically consistent presentation and instead demand self-active engagement and appropriation. Cohen's communicative struggles and his often-strained formulations, far from indicating a lack of intellectual conviction, instead faithfully mirror the paradoxical conceptual content of the religion of reason.

While I began my introduction by discussing competing accounts of the place of *Religion of Reason* in Cohen's oeuvre, I do not attempt to place a summarizing interpretation in their stead; the indirection of Cohen's communication does not permit a single-voiced 'description' of that which his project accomplishes. Some interpreters have argued, in a directly statable position, that *Religion of Reason* broke with and went beyond Cohen's earlier philosophical system, while others have argued, equally directly, that he remained within the bounds of his previous philosophizing. In contrast, I claim that assertions of 'going-beyond' say too much, while assertions of 'staying-within' say too little; however, there is no consistent way of formulating that which lies 'between' these two. In this sense, the description of Cohen's book as a whole shares the basic characteristics of his own account, within the book, of the various correlative concepts of religion.

We can, though, revisit and reassess some of the questions raised in this study's introduction. There, we looked at some of the ways in which Cohen's thought can be placed in the context both of previous German philosophy and of Jewish religious thought. In relation to both, *Religion of Reason* stands as an implicit critique, not simply of the specific content of their claims, but more fundamentally of their method and their style. With regard to the divergences between Kant and his successors, Cohen's example implies that both camps were led astray by their desire to construct a consistent account of subject matter that stubbornly, and intrinsically, resists such theoretization. Insisting on such an account must (and indeed did) result merely in competing varieties of one-sidedness and in disputes that are incapable of resolution within the terms of the objectifying philosophical method and its corresponding style of presentation. While later recognition of the futility of these disputes led other thinkers to place this subject matter 'beyond reason,' whether through turns to positivism or existentialism, Cohen persists in affirming the fundamental rationality of the ideas of religion. Rather than rejecting the content, or the 'what,' of such ideas, he instead points to and performs a change in the 'how,' thereby producing different modes of reasoning and communication.

With regard to disputes in the Jewish religious tradition, Cohen's response is similar, although the 'indigenous' provenance of his solution stands out even more clearly. In the face of criticisms of the status of revelation, the example of *Religion of Reason* shows that other theories of Scripture suffer from a desire to clearly and directly specify its nature and origin. Rather than treating the text as straightforwardly 'divine' (and thus granting authority to 'the text itself') or as straightforwardly 'mundane' (and thus locating the source of authority in the human reader), he demonstrates, through his various readings, that source of transcendent authority lies *between* the text and the reader; it is not statically 'in' either of the two, but is accessed only through the performative act of engaged reading and interpretation. This approach, as Cohen himself points out in his introduction, has significant similarities to classical rabbinic views of oral tradition and midrashic interpretation. As such, we can view some of the modern Jewish disputes as the consequence of trying to force ideas that developed in a non-systematic, performative context into static, theoretically consistent definitions and descriptions. Against this, Cohen shows that ideas with scriptural-midrashic origins require a scriptural-midrashic form of reflection and presentation.

Yet, the midrashic thrust of Cohen's work also goes beyond this more parochial corrective. Given that *Religion of Reason* stands as a response to both Jewish and general intellectual concerns, the example of his style indicates that *philosophy itself must become scriptural*. Thus, Cohen does not simply 'happen to' adopt a rabbinic style: he insists that such a style is demanded by reason. In order to avoid a flattening of one's concepts, one must reason *from* sources, which must be displayed alongside one's interpretations. The essential 'content' of reason will not be found in one's interpretive 'results' or 'positions,' but in the dynamic vector of movement between source and interpretation. In addition, such a mode of reasoning also demands a multiplicity of 'contradictory' vectors or interpretations in order to bring out different aspects of the paradoxical concepts, since any single perspective will be deficient in one way or another.

These more radical elements of Cohen's method have direct implications for present-day readers and writers of philosophical and religious texts. For instance, the 'rationality' of a text can no longer be determined by applying the simple criteria of "Is it theoretically consistent?" Instead, the *lack* of theoretical consistency is to be an expected and necessary feature of any rational communication of religion, although, to be sure, not everything that is theoretically inconsistent is necessarily rational. In order to properly assess a text, a reader must develop the capacity to evaluate the *specific kind* of inconsistency that it displays. When applied to historical philosophico-religious texts that seem 'marred' by the co-presence of incompatible positions or voices, this approach may reveal that, like *Religion of Reason*, a practical-communicative form of rational inconsistency can be discerned in the texts of past thinkers.

Likewise, Cohen's thought, as I have presented it, places sharp demands on contemporary constructive efforts to reason more productively about religious topics. Those who seek to write about religion must follow Cohen's example by incorporating some form of 'multiple voices' into their accounts. While this paradoxical approach will admittedly make such composition more difficult, the desire to have a 'comfortable' and consistent account will lead to ill-formed concepts on the part of the writer or speaker and thus to communicative failure with regard to the audience. The current tendency of thinkers to break down into competing 'camps' on issues such as immanence versus transcendence, reason versus revelation, or divine versus human may be a direct consequence of the single-voiced and theoretically consistent style that they strive to enact. As such, a renewed attention to 'philosophical style' can play an essential role in overcoming many of these apparently interminably disputes and debates. While a writer can and should adopt a specific, definite (though not theoretically consistent) stance, that stance must be conveyed and expressed only indirectly.

It is my hope that my interpretation of *Religion of Reason*, by uncovering and presenting the fuller depth of Cohen's text and approach, can contribute to this reconfiguration of philosophical and religious reading and writing. Previous readings of his text, by presenting a truncated Cohen, have considerably obscured his originality and his significance. In contrast, the recognition of 'both sides' of his project can transform *Religion of Reason* into a highly relevant model for the 'how' of rational writing and thought: a better understanding of what Cohen is doing can enable others to go and do likewise. In this way, Cohen's juxtaposition of the voices of philosophy and Scripture would come to function—borrowing Kierkegaard's terms—as a "communication of capability" and not simply as a "communication of knowledge." Far from departing from Cohen's intentions, such a result would restore the practical-rational impulse that generated and gave rise to his 'prophetic-messianic' project of ethical and cultural repair.

Notes

INTRODUCTION

1. Cf. Hermann Cohen, *Religion of Reason Out of the Sources of Judaism* [henceforth cited as *RoR*], trans. Simon Kaplan (Atlanta: Scholars Press, 1995), 4; Hermann Cohen, *Religion der Vernunft aus den Quellen des Judentums* [1929, 2nd ed.] [henceforth cited as *RV*] (Wiesbaden: Fourier Verlag, 1978), 4–5. I should also note that my general use of the term 'Scripture' in this book is not limited strictly to the Hebrew Bible, as Cohen often draws upon rabbinic and liturgical sources as well. Rather, I use the term metonymically to encompass the broader range of the Jewish textual tradition. That is to say, Cohen's employment of 'philosophy and Scripture' refers most fundamentally to the difference between an autonomous method of analysis, on one hand, and the stubbornly particular body of historically received textual sources, on the other. At the same time, the use of the term 'Scripture' matches up well with Cohen's textual readings in *Religion of Reason*, which largely do focus on biblical sources. Furthermore, the term 'Scripture' should also call to mind the rabbinic designation of *torah she-bichtav*, the 'written' or 'enscripted' Torah, which is then expanded by means of interpretation. Cohen himself draws attention to this designation in setting out his introductory description of his own project. See *RoR* 26; *RV* 30, and Cohen's reference there to *die schriftliche Lehre*.

2. Franz Rosenzweig, "Einleitung," in *Hermann Cohens Jüdische Schriften* [henceforth cited as *JS*], ed. Bruno Strauss (New York: Arno Press, 1980), 1: xlviii–xlix, lxiv.

3. Samuel Hugo Bergman, *Faith and Reason: An Introduction to Modern Jewish Thought*, ed. and trans. Alfred Jospe (New York: Schocken Books, 1961), 38–51.

4. Nathan Rotenstreich, *Jewish Philosophy in Modern Times: From Mendelssohn to Rosenzweig* (New York: Holt, Rinehart & Winston, 1968), 62–65.

5. Alexander Altmann, "Hermann Cohens Begriff der Korrelation," in *In Zwei Welten: Siegfried Moses zum fünfundsiebzigsten Geburtstag*, ed. Hans Tramer (Tel-Aviv: Verlag Bitaon, 1962).

6. Leo Strauss, *Philosophy and Law: Essays Toward the Understanding of Maimonides and His Predecessors* [1935], trans. Fred Baumann (Philadelphia, PA: Jewish Publication Society, 1987), 28.

7. Emil Fackenheim, "Hermann Cohen—after Fifty Years," in *Jewish Philosophers and Jewish Philosophy*, ed. Michael L. Morgan (Bloomington: Indiana University Press, 1996), 49–56.

8. Julius Guttmann, *Philosophies of Judaism: The History of Jewish Philosophy from Biblical Times to Franz Rosenzweig*, trans. David W. Silverman (New York: Holt, Rinehart & Winston, 1964), 365–367.

9. Martin Buber, "The Love of God and the Idea of Deity," in *Eclipse of God* (New York: Harper & Brothers, 1952), 49–62.

10. Steven Schwarzschild, "The Title of Hermann Cohen's *Religion of Reason Out of the Sources of Judaism*," in *RoR*, 13–15. See also his "The Theologico-Political Basis of Liberal Christian-Jewish Relations in Modernity," in *Das deutsche Judentum und der Liberalismus—German Jewry and Liberalism* (Sankt Augustin: Comdok-Verlagsabteilung, 1986), 84–88.

11. Norbert M. Samuelson, *An Introduction to Modern Jewish Philosophy* (Albany: State University of New York Press, 1989), 165.

12. Peter Gordon, *Rosenzweig and Heidegger: Between Judaism and German Philosophy* (Berkeley: University of California Press, 2003), 68–70.

13. Randi Rashkover, *Revelation and Theopolitics: Barth, Rosenzweig, and the Politics of Praise* (London: T&T Clark International, 2005), 29–30; 43–44.

14. Dieter Adelmann, *Einheit des Bewußtseins als Grundproblem der Philosophie Hermann Cohens* (Heidelberg: Inaugural-Dissertation, 1968), 50–51.

15. Adelmann, *Einheit des Bewußtseins*, 50. (Here, as in all citations from Adelmann, the translation from the German is my own.)

16. Adelmann, *Einheit des Bewußtseins*, 53.

17. Adelmann points to Cohen's desire, dating to his very early writings, to give a 'scientific grounding' to religion. See Adelmann, *Einheit des Bewußtseins*, 60–63. While this desire is altered somewhat in *Religion of Reason*, Cohen nevertheless still refrains from directly asserting anything that lacks such a grounding.

18. Michael Zank, *The Idea of Atonement in the Philosophy of Hermann Cohen* (Providence, RI: Brown Judaic Studies, 2000), 165–177.

19. Zank, *Idea of Atonement*, 37–40.

20. Zank, *Idea of Atonement*, 43.

21. Zank, *Idea of Atonement*, 37.

22. Robert Gibbs, *Correlations in Rosenzweig and Levinas* (Princeton, NJ: Princeton University Press, 1992), 85.

23. Gibbs, *Correlations*, 86, 87, 187.

24. Gibbs, *Correlations*, 86.

25. Gibbs, *Correlations*, 180.

26. See Gibbs, *Correlations*, 176.

27. Andrea Poma, *The Critical Philosophy of Hermann Cohen*, trans. John Denton (Albany: State University of New York Press, 1997), 158. See also Poma's *Yearning for Form and Other Essays on Hermann Cohen's Thought* (Dordrecht: Springer, 2006).

28. Poma, *Critical Philosophy of Hermann Cohen*, 167–169.

29. The spatial metaphor of a border-relation between religion and philosophy bears a similar structure to the concept of the infinitesimal, as we shall see in chapter 6. The breadth of such a border-region ends up being infinitesimally narrow, and, as such, can have no objectively determinate status.

30. Steven Kepnes, *Jewish Liturgical Reasoning* (Oxford: Oxford University Press, 2007), 48.

31. Kepnes, *Jewish Liturgical Reasoning*, 49–77.

32. Almut Sh. Bruckstein, "Introduction," in Hermann Cohen, *Ethics of Maimonides*, trans. and commentary by Almut Sh. Bruckstein (Madison: University of Wisconsin Press, 2004), xxxii–iii.

33. Bruckstein, "Introduction," in Cohen, *Ethics of Maimonides*, xxxiv.

34. Almut Sh. Bruckstein, "Joining the Narrators: A Philosophy of Talmudic Hermeneutics," in Steven Kepnes, Peter Ochs, and Robert Gibbs, *Reasoning After Revelation: Dialogues in Postmodern Jewish Philosophy* (Boulder, CO: Westview Press, 1998), 118.

35. Pierre Hadot, "Spiritual Exercises," in *Philosophy as a Way of Life*, ed. Arnold Davidson (Oxford: Blackwell, 1995), 105.

36. Avi Bernstein-Nahar, in particular, argues that one ought to read Cohen's work as part of a tradition of "practical philosophy," in contrast to a prevailing view that tends to see him as concerned with "purely intellectual matters." See Bernstein-Nahar, "In the Name of a *Narrative* Education: Hermann Cohen and Historicism Reconsidered," in *Hermann Cohen's Ethics*, ed. Robert Gibbs (Leiden: Brill, 2006), 151–153.

 Similarly, Almut Bruckstein places Cohen's thought in the context of a Jewish philosophical tradition that displays a consciousness "of an inner gap ever at work in the process of thinking that commits itself to what is truly humane." Bruckstein refers to Shmuel Trigano's *La demeure oubliée: Genèse religieuse du politique* (Paris: Lieu Commun, 1984) as a representative example of this narrative of Jewish philosophy. See Bruckstein, "Hermann Cohen. *Ethics of Maimonides*: Residues of Jewish Philosophy—Traumatized," in Gibbs, *Hermann Cohen's Ethics*, 118.

37. On Trendelenburg and the method of science, see Klaus Christian Köhnke, *The Rise of Neo-Kantianism: German Academic Philosophy between Idealism and Positivism*, trans. R. J. Hollingdale (Cambridge: Cambridge University Press, 1991), 20–21.

38. Köhnke, *Rise of Neo-Kantianism*, 79.

39. Köhnke, *Rise of Neo-Kantianism*, 34–35. Note that Trendelenburg does make an argument for the presence of totality within the individual's *Weltanschauung*—but he denies that such totality can be captured within a theoretical system.

40. See Köhnke, *Rise of Neo-Kantianism*, 124–135.

41. See Ulrich Sieg, *Aufstieg und Niedergang des Marburger Neukantianismus: die Geschichte einer philosophischen Schulgemeinschaft* (Würzburg: Königshausen & Neumann, 1994), 100–101, and Köhnke, *Rise of Neo-Kantianism*, 161–164.

42. Sieg, *Aufstieg und Niedergang*, 104, emphasis in the original. The emphasized phrase is Sieg's citation from Lange's *Geschichte des Materialismus* (2nd ed.), 829.

43. See Köhnke, *Rise of Neo-Kantianism*, 175–178.

44. On the isolation of Cohen and the Marburg school, see Sieg, *Aufstieg und Niedergang*, 154–157, 213–214, 241, 256, 348.

45. "*[D]ie* Methode *ist alles.*" Natorp, cited in Sieg, *Aufstieg und Niedergang*, 272, emphasis in the original. See also Helmut Holzhey, "Cohen and the Marburg School in Context," in *Hermann Cohen's Critical Idealism*, ed. Reinier Munk (Dordrecht: Springer, 2005), 21.

46. See Poma, "Plato's Idea of the Good in its Different Interpretations by Cohen and Natorp," in *Yearning for Form*, 34–37. See also Judy Saltzman, *Paul Natorp's Philosophy of Religion* (Hildesheim: Georg Olms Verlag, 1981), 117–118, 175–195, and Schwarzschild, "Theologico-Political Basis," 86–87, although Schwarzschild argues that Natorp moved 'beyond method' only after Cohen's death.

47. See Michael Zank, "Between Dialogue and Disputation: Wilhelm Herrmann and Hermann Cohen on Ethics, Religion, and the Self" in *Theologie zwischen Pragmatismus und Existenzdenken*, ed. Gesche Linde, Richard Purkarthofer, Heiko Schulz, and Peter Steinacker (Marburg: N. G. Elwert Verlag, 2006), 135. The relation between Herrmann's critique and Cohen's approach in *Religion of Reason* will be further discussed in chapter 3.

48. See Köhnke, *Rise of Neo-Kantianism*, 136. Köhnke connects this same stance specifically to Cohen's thought as well; see Köhnke, 197.

49. *RoR* 7; *RV* 8.

50. *RoR* 360; *RV* 418.

51. Cohen, *Ethik des reinen Willens* [1907, 2nd ed.] (Hildesheim: Georg Olms Verlag, 2002), 331. For discussion of this passage of Cohen's, see Steven Schwarzschild, "'Germanism and Judaism'—Hermann Cohen's Normative Paradigm of the German-Jewish Symbiosis," in *Jews and Germans from 1860 to 1933: The Problematic Symbiosis*, ed. David Bronsen (Heidelberg: Winter, 1979), 140. See also Almut Bruckstein, commentary to Cohen, *Ethics of Maimonides*, 94–95.

52. See Henri Dussort, *L'école de Marbourg* (Paris: Presses universitaires de France, 1963), 66; Helmut Holzhey, *Cohen und Natorp*, vol. 1 (Basel: Schwabe, 1986), 65.

53. Indeed, in *Ethik des reinen Willens*, 331–332, Cohen himself linked the Hegelian collapse of *Sein* and *Sollen* with metaphysical theology's misguided desire for "knowledge of God" (*Erkenntnis Gottes*).

54. See *RoR* 50–51; *RV* 58–59.

55. See e.g., *RoR* 20, 26, 42, 57; *RV* 23, 30, 48, 66.

56. See *RoR* 241; *RV* 282.

57. See Maimonides, *Guide of the Perplexed*, trans. Shlomo Pines (Chicago: University of Chicago Press, 1963), and Spinoza, *Theological-Political Treatise*, ed. Jonathan Israel, trans. Michael Silverthorne and Jonathan Israel (Cambridge: Cambridge University Press, 2007). For more on the relation between Maimonides and

Spinoza, see Bruckstein's translation of and commentary on Cohen's *Ethics of Maimonides*, 86–87. For more on Spinoza and Cohen, see Leo Strauss' preface to *Spinoza's Critique of Religion* (New York: Schocken Books 1965), as well as his "Cohen's Analysis of Spinoza's Bible Science" in *Leo Strauss: The Early Writings, 1921–1932*, ed. and trans. Michael Zank (Albany: State University of New York Press, 2002), 140–172.

58. See Moses Mendelssohn, *Jerusalem: Or on Religious Power and Judaism*, trans. Allan Arkush (Hanover, NH: University Press of New England / Brandeis University Press, 1983).

59. *RoR* 357; *RV* 415.

60. Cohen, "Innere Beziehungen der Kantischen Philosophie zum Judentum," in *JS* I, 285.

61. Gershom Scholem, "Reflections on Jewish Theology," in *Jews and Judaism in Crisis* (New York: Schocken Books, 1976), 271–272.

62. For a detailed and extensive history of the *Wissenschaft des Judentums* movement, see Ismar Schorsch, *From Text to Context: The Turn to History in Modern Judaism* (Hanover, NH: University Press of New England / Brandeis University Press, 1994).

63. Christian Wiese, *Challenging Colonial Discourse: Jewish Studies and Protestant Theology in Wilhelmine Germany*, trans. Barbara Harshav and Christian Wiese (Leiden: Brill, 2005), 5. In his footnote, Wiese refers to Shulamit Volkov, "Die Erfindung einer Tradition. Zur Enstehung des modernen Judentums in Deutschland," *Historische Zeitschrift* 253, no. 3 (1991): 603–628. Volkov herself draws the phrase from *The Invention of Tradition*, ed. Eric Hobsbawm and Terence Ranger (Cambridge: Cambridge University Press, 1983), a collected volume that explores 'invented traditions' as a widespread phenomenon in nineteenth- and twentieth-century Europe.

As a counterpart to this description, Gershom Scholem notes that, especially in early *Wissenschaft des Judentums*, another tendency competed with the apologetic one: namely, the notion that one should now engage in the historical and scholarly study of Judaism precisely because the latter is no longer a living option. In the words Moritz Steinschneider, one of its chief advocates, this trend in *Wissenschaft des Judentums* sought "to give the remains of Judaism a decent burial." See Scholem, "The Science of Judaism—Then and Now," in *The Messianic Idea in Judaism and Other Essays on Jewish Spirituality* (New York: Schocken Books, 1971), 306–307. This funereal strand, however, is less directly relevant to Cohen's project in *RoR*.

64. The use of academic scholarship to justify a desired form of Jewishness was also prominent among those Jews who turned away from the quest for German-Jewish integration and instead embraced a project of separatist Jewish nationalism. See David N. Myers, *Re-Inventing the Jewish Past: European Jewish Intellectuals and the Zionist Return to History* (New York: Oxford University Press, 1995).

65. See Wiese, *Challenging Colonial Discourse*, for a very thorough and detailed discussion of this development.

66. See Zank, *Idea of Atonement*, 58–62.

67. See Cohen, *JS* II, 73–94. See also Zank, *Idea of Atonement*, 77–97.

68. "Die Nächstenliebe in Talmud" (in *JS* I, 145–174); "Die Bedeutung des Judentums für den religiösen Fortschritt der Menschheit" (in *JS* I, 18–35). For more on the former, see Zank, *Idea of Atonement*, 97–101. For more on the latter, see Wiese, *Challenging Colonial Discourse*, 314–320.

69. Christian Wiese emphasizes the connections between the emphasis on the prophets in Protestant biblical studies and the corresponding emphasis among Jewish writers (including Cohen) of the same period. See Wiese, *Challenging Colonial Discourse*, 239–248. Hans Liebeschütz points to Cohen's personal friendship with Julius Wellhausen as a chief source of the role of the prophets in Cohen's thought. Liebeschütz, "Hermann Cohen and His Historical Background," *Leo Baeck Institute Yearbook* 13 (1968): 21–23. See also David N. Myers, "Hermann Cohen and the Quest for Protestant Judaism," *Leo Baeck Institute Yearbook*, vol. 46 (2001): 207–210.

70. See below.

71. Gershom Scholem, "Science of Judaism," in *Messianic Idea*, 308–309. See also Scholem, "Reflections on Modern Jewish Studies," in *On the Possibility of Jewish Mysticism in Our Time & Other Essays* (Philadelphia, PA: Jewish Publication Society, 1997), 63–65.

72. For further elaboration, see chapter 2.

73. Schwarzschild, "'Germanism and Judaism,'" 151.

74. Schwarzschild, "'Germanism and Judaism,'" 156–157. See also his "Theologico-Political Basis," 81 fn. 47.

75. See Leo Strauss, Preface to *Spinoza's Critique of Religion*, 23–24.

76. Strauss, Preface to *Spinoza's Critique of Religion*, 25.

77. For more biographical background, see Zank, *Idea of Atonement*, 48–69.

78. See Cohen's introduction to Friedrich Albert Lange's *Geschichte des Materialismus* (Leipzig: Verlag von J. Baedeker, 1902), 518, and cf. Cohen's *Ethik des reinen Willens*, 586–587 and his "Religion und Sittlichkeit" in *JS* III, 151. See also Zank, *Idea of Atonement*, 267–272; Poma, *Critical Philosophy of Hermann Cohen*, 307.

79. See Holzhey, *Cohen und Natorp*, vol. 1, 345.

80. Cohen's concerns in this regard are similar, in certain ways, to Kant's concerns about the enthusiasm of *Schwärmerei*.

81. Cf., in this regard, Dussort's intriguing claim that it was not originally Cohen's Kantianism that made him an anti-Hegelian, but rather his anti-Hegelianism (connected to Hegel's absolutizing of Christianity and his denigration of Judaism) that made him a 'Kantian' (quotation marks Dussort's). See Dussort, *L'école de Marbourg*, 66.

82. Cohen, *Ethik des reinen Willens*, 453.

83. See Hartwig Wiedebach, "Aesthetics in Religion: Remarks on Hermann Cohen's Theory of Jewish Existence," *Journal of Jewish Thought and Philosophy* 11, no. 1 (2002): 64–65, 71–72; Andrea Poma, "Lyric Poetry and Prayer" in *Yearning for Form,* 228–230. See also Judy Saltzman, *Paul Natorp's Philosophy of Religion,* 112–116; and Irene Kajon, *Contemporary Jewish Philosophy: An Introduction* (London: Routledge, 2006), 21–22.

84. See Rosenzweig, "Einleitung," in *JS* I, xlii–xliii.

85. In this, Cohen resists a Schleiermachian trend popular among contemporary Protestant thinkers, including Cohen's Marburg colleagues Wilhelm Herrmann and Paul Natorp. See Schwarzschild, "Theologico-Political Basis," 86–88.

86. Note that while in *Religion of Reason,* Cohen argues that the method of Ethics cannot grasp the You, Cohen's own earlier *Ethik des reinen Willens* had in fact discussed the relation of the 'I' to the 'You'. See chapter 3 below for further discussion of this discrepancy.

87. See Adelmann, *Einheit des Bewußtseins,* 6–19; Steven Schwarzschild, "'Germanism and Judaism'"; and Peter Gordon's *Rosenzweig and Heidegger,* esp. his chapter on the Davos disputation, 275–304.

88. For prominent examples of this sort of criticism, see Buber, "Love of God and the Idea of Deity," in *Eclipse of God,* and Fackenheim, "Hermann Cohen—after Fifty Years," in *Jewish Philosophers and Jewish Philosophy.* One can draw an interesting link between the post-WWII criticisms of Cohen's philosophy and criticisms of his politics. Many of those who saw Cohen's philosophy as too abstract and not sufficiently grounded in the concrete particularity of Judaism also tended to view Cohen's anti-Zionism and his ideas of German-Jewish correlation as placing an insufficient emphasis on Jewish particularity. As Steven Schwarzschild has shown, however, criticisms of Cohen's "Deutschtum und Judentum" often misunderstand or distort Cohen's intentions, in a manner that may parallel the misunderstandings of *Religion of Reason* that I attempt to address here. See Schwarzschild, "'Germanism and Judaism.'"

89. In this regard, Michael Zank provides an evocative formulation of "Cohen's steering a course between the Scylla of idealistic ethics and the Charybdis of existentialism." See Zank, *Idea of Atonement,* 190.

90. On the Bakhtinian qualities of Cohen's style, see Daniel H. Weiss, "A Dialogue Between Philosophy and Scripture: Rereading Hermann Cohen through Bakhtin," *Journal of Religion* 90, no. 1 (Jan. 2010): 15–32.

91. Conversely, other thinkers may recognize the impossibility of combining the two realms. In that case, though, they tend (unlike Cohen) to prioritize one of the two above the other.

92. In his *Der Begriff der Religion,* Cohen emphasizes that the unique individual—the prime conceptual subject matter of religion—*cannot be grasped by thought,* since thought (*das Denken*) can conceive of its object only as something general (*ein Allgemeines*). (See Cohen, *Der Begriff der Religion im System der Philosophie* [1915] [Hildesheim: Georg Olms Verlag, 2002], 86–87, where this feature of religion is

contrasted to the sphere of Aesthetics within systematic philosophy—as aesthetic object, man remains only a thinkable type [*Typus*], and not a true individual. For a similar assertion, see *RoR* 161; *RV* 186.) This non-graspability by thought corresponds, in stylistic terms, to a multiplicity of voices. In contrast, to present the content of religion in a theoretically consistent manner would be to present it (wrongly) as something that *could* be grasped by thought, i.e., as something abstract and general.

In the same passage in *Der Begriff der Religion*, Cohen emphasizes that the concept of the unique individual "loses all of its theoretical interest" and thus is properly related to not through the theoretical sphere of thought but rather through the practical sphere of love (Cohen, *Der Begriff der Religion*, 86–87). Cohen will later revisit the non-theoretical status of the sphere of religion in *Religion of Reason*, where he emphasizes that one relates to the unique God not through the theoretical and dispassionate mode of knowledge (*Erkenntnis*), but rather through the engaged mode of acknowledgment (*Bekenntnis*) (*RoR* 50–51; *RV* 58–59). My general claim is that such assertions find their parallel in Cohen's inability to translate such concepts directly into the theoretical sphere of discursive writing; his scriptural-hermeneutic method, by contrast, enables him to communicate them in an indirect manner.

93. As we shall see, Cohen distinguishes the sphere of religion from the sphere of philosophy, as two distinct sub-realms within reason. In contrast to the concepts of religion, the concepts of philosophy *do* need to be theoretically consistent in order to be part of reason. For the crucial distinction in Cohen's thought between philosophy and reason, see below, "A Note on Terminology," as well as sections II–IV in chapter 2 and the section on "Religion and System" in chapter 3.

94. Cohen points to his awareness of the connection between paradox and communicative style in his observation that "the style of the greatest spirits struggles toward the light in antinomies and paradoxes." See Cohen, *Der Begriff der Religion*, 29. Cohen also indicates a similar awareness of 'rational paradox' in his other works. See, for instance, *Ethik des reinen Willens*, 266, where he states, "That is the paradox in this concept of self-consciousness. We know no I without You; thus also no self without You or We." See also *RoR* 17, 96; *RV* 19, 112; *Der Begriff der Religion*, 82, 100–101, 134; *Ästhetik des reinen Gefühls* [1912] (Hildesheim: Georg Olms Verlag, 1982), vol. 1, 341, 397; vol. 2, 21, 74, 227, 253–258; *Ethik des reinen Willens*, 102.

95. See Cohen's account of the relation between style and content in "Der Stil der Propheten," in *JS* I, 262, 265, as discussed below in chapter 1.

96. The language of the 'what' and the 'how' is drawn from Kierkegaard's/Climacus' *Concluding Unscientific Postscript*, a work whose account of indirect communication contributes significantly to the methodological thrust of this study. Just as Cohen himself insists on the connection between style ('how) and content ('what'), I will argue that Cohen's communication in *Religion of Reason* contains no autonomously assertable 'what.'

In a different context, the distinction between the 'what' and the 'how' also arises in Heidegger's thought, where he designates attention to the 'how' as constitutive of the phenomenological method. See, e.g., *Being and Time*, trans. John MacQuarrie and Edward Robinson (New York: Harper & Row, 1962), 50.

97. Cohen, *JS* I, 262–283. For a partial translation in English, see "The Style of the Prophets," in *Reason and Hope: Selections from the Jewish Writings of Hermann Cohen*, ed. and trans. Eva Jospe (New York: Norton, 1971).

A NOTE ON TERMINOLOGY

1. *RoR* 5; *RV* 6.
2. See *RoR* 13; *RV* 15.
3. Gillian Rose, "Hermann Cohen—Kant among the Prophets," in *Judaism and Modernity: Philosophical Essays* (Cambridge, MA: Blackwell, 1993), 114–115.
4. *RoR* 400; *RV* 464.
5. The same applies, more broadly, to 'philosophy': in *Religion of Reason*, as in my analysis of the book, the term designates an ideal-normative method, and different instances of actual philosophical writing—including Cohen's own *System der Philosophie*—may approximate that method to varying degrees.
6. The terms 'religion' and 'Judaism' are related thusly: Judaism represents the pattern of rational religion that is constructed through rational-constructive engagement with Jewish source-texts.
7. Andrea Poma, "Hermann Cohen: Judaism and Critical Idealism," in *The Cambridge Companion to Modern Jewish Philosophy*, ed. Michael L. Morgan and Peter Eli Gordon (Cambridge: Cambridge University Press, 2007), 92.
8. Martin Kavka, "Levinas Between Monotheism and Cosmotheism," in *Levinas Studies: An Annual Review*, vol. 2, ed. Jeffrey Bloechl (Pittsburgh: Duquesne University Press, 2007), 82, 89–90.

CHAPTER I

1. See the textual note to "The Style of the Prophets," where Cohen states, "Style is, so to speak, the objective expression for the problem whose subjective expression is genius." "Der Stil der Propheten," in *JS* I, 340.
2. Cohen, "Der Stil der Propheten," in *JS* I, 281.
3. See, e.g., Christian Wiese, "Struggling for Normality: The Apologetics of *Wissenschaft des Judentums* in Wilhelmine Germany as an Anti-colonial Intellectual Revolt against the Protestant Construction of Judaism," in *"Towards Normality?": Acculturation of Modern German Jewry*, ed. Rainer Liedtke and David Rechter (Tübingen: J.C.B. Mohr, 2003), 86–88.
4. With regard to the book of Ezekiel in particular, Michael Zank notes that the scholarly consensus of multiple authorship began to arise only toward the end of

Cohen's life and thereafter, whereas Cohen's own unified reading of the text pre-
dominated among biblical scholars at the time when Cohen first engaged Ezekiel
in depth. Zank further argues that Cohen's desire to retain the unity of the text can
be viewed as part of his broader effort to retain the unity of Judaism's legal and
moral aspects; in contrast, trends in Protestant scholarship that sharply divided the
text into prophetic (moral) and priestly (legal-ritual) sources—in order to prioritize the former—often bespoke an anti-Jewish theological attitude. See Zank, *Idea
of Atonement*, 119–123.

5. See Cohen's distinction between 'philosophy of religion' and 'history of religion'
   in his "Innere Beziehungen der Kantischen Philosophie zum Judentum," in *JS* I,
   303–304.

6. See Wiese, "Struggling for Normality," 86–88; Wiese, *Challenging Colonial Discourse*, 241, 247, 280. See also Zank, *Idea of Atonement*, 109–113, 480–487. Both
   Wiese and Zank emphasize that while Cohen affirmed the *basic methods* of biblical
   criticism, he did not always accept the *specific accounts* of Judaism and Israelite religion put forth by contemporary German Protestant scholarship.

7. See David N. Myers, *Resisting History: Historicism and its Discontents in German-
   Jewish Thought* (Princeton, NJ: Princeton University Press, 2003), 48–67. Myers
   highlights Cohen's rejection of "the dominant historicist ethos of his day" (67);
   instead, Cohen sought "to subordinate history to philosophy" (51). See also Zank,
   Idea of Atonement, 218–230, on Cohen's view of hermeneutics as a philosophically
   constructive, and not merely historical, activity.

8. See my section below on "Biblical Multiplicity," as well as my section on "*Aus*,"
   where I discuss the fact that, although Cohen's stated mode of interpretation
   may lead to 'historically implausible' results, he does not see this as a problem or
   a deficiency.

9. As Hans Liebeschütz notes, while Cohen is happy to make use of historical-critical
   scholarship on the prophets, he simultaneously emphasizes that those same biblical
   sources stand in need of rational 'idealization,' which necessarily differentiates
   Cohen's interpretive constructions from a strictly historical account. See Liebeschütz, "Hermann Cohen and his Historical Background," 22–23.

10. Franz Rosenzweig, "The Unity of the Bible," in Martin Buber and Franz Rosen-
    zweig, *Scripture and Translation*, trans. Lawrence Rosenwald with Everett Fox
    (Bloomington: Indiana University Press, 1994), 22–23.

11. Cohen, "Der Stil der Propheten," in *JS* I, 262.

12. Cohen, "Der Stil der Propheten," in *JS* I, 262.

13. Cohen's concern with *how* something is said may be compared to the rabbinic mid-
    rashic approach to the 'economy of Scripture,' which derives quite different mean-
    ings from seemingly insignificant differences in formulation.

14. Cohen, "Der Stil der Propheten," in *JS* I, 265.

15. A famous example of different types of experiment producing different results can
    be seen in the investigations that gave rise to modern quantum theory, wherein

certain experiments indicated that electrons were waves, while other experiments indicated, apparently in contradiction to the former, that they were particles. In a further connection to our discussion below of Cohen's double-voiced, oscillating style, as well as that of the prophets, we can note Werner Heisenberg's account of the light/particle dilemma: one is faced with "two pictures" which are "mutually exclusive," and the proper approach requires "playing with both pictures ... going from the one picture to the other and back again." Heisenberg, *Physics and Philosophy: The Revolution in Modern Science* (Amherst, NY: Prometheus Books, 1999 [1958]), 49.

16. Cohen, "Der Stil der Propheten," in *JS* I, 263.

17. Cohen, "Der Stil der Propheten," in *JS* I, 265.

18. Cohen, "Der Stil der Propheten," in *JS* I, 263.

19. Cohen, "Der Stil der Propheten," in *JS* I, 263.

20. Cohen, "Der Stil der Propheten," in *JS* I, 271. Note that Cohen defines "Ethics" (*Ethik*) as "the science of ethicality" (264). That is, while the prophets are deeply concerned with ethicality (*Sittlichkeit*), they are not concerned with the scientific systematization of ethicality, i.e., with Ethics (*Ethik*).

21. Cohen, "Der Stil der Propheten," in *JS* I, 271.

22. Cohen, "Der Stil der Propheten," in *JS* I, 271.

23. As will be discussed later, certain other concepts—such as the You, the unique God, and the individual as I—are also invisible to the method of scientific Ethics.

24. See Cohen, "Das soziale Ideal bei Platon und den Propheten," in *JS* I, 315–317:

> [I]t becomes clear to us that compassion alone cannot be the driving force behind the power of sociality; rather, the wellsprings of science ultimately must also be excavated and activated, if firmness, if progressive development is also to be conferred upon ethical problems. And so we must turn back again from the prophets to Plato. ... Plato's advantage lies in the principle of Knowledge. ... Without philosophy, suffering cannot come to an end among human beings. And thus knowledge becomes the cornerstone of the social world. Even suffering itself cannot be fathomed without knowledge, to say nothing of the annulment of suffering and redemption from it. The prophetic insight is merely an intuition, a vision. ... Without the unreserved acknowledgment of scientific, of philosophical knowledge of the ethical, one cannot arrive at truthfulness in the domain of religion as a whole. And here, for all time, the divine Plato remains the exhorter toward truthfulness, the guardian of scientific knowledge [considered] as the unique unfailing stronghold of truth.

25. Cf. Ludwig Wittgenstein, *Philosophical Investigations,* trans. G. E. M. Anscombe (Englewood Cliffs, NJ: Prentice Hall, 1958), §11.

26. Cohen, "Der Stil der Propheten," in *JS* I, 262–263.

27. Cohen, "Der Stil der Propheten," in *JS* I, 263. Note also that Cohen refers to Plato as "the literary founder of Ethics" (262). In other words, systematic Ethics is just as much a form of writing, a literary form, as it is a form of thinking.

28. Cohen's joining together of method, idea-content, and style thus has significant implications for projects of philosophic writing and communication. Though a thinker may explicitly claim to be putting forth ideas that go beyond systematicity, an unconscious systematizing tendency can often reveal itself in that thinker's style and way of writing. Likewise, the selection of certain styles of writing may tend to have a systematizing effect on a writer's thought, despite his or her best intentions. Accordingly, that which is ultimately conveyed to the reader may be a content of greater systematicity, which distorts ideas that are meant to be non-systematic.

29. Franz Rosenzweig later takes up this critique of Plato when he speaks against the method of traditional philosophy, in which "thinking is always solitary, even if it is happening among several 'symphilosophizing' partners: even then, the other merely raises objections which I myself would really have to raise—which is the reason why most philosophical dialogues, including most of Plato's, are so boring. In actual conversation, something happens." Rosenzweig, "The New Thinking" in *Philosophical and Theological Writings*, trans. and ed. Paul W. Franks and Michael L. Morgan (Indianapolis, IN: Hackett Publishing, 2000), 126.

    See also Luc Anckaert's contrast of Plato and Rosenzweig: "The text of Plato can be considered an immanent dialogue, while Rosenzweig's discursive manner of speaking presupposes instead a dialogue with the reader." "Language, Ethics, and the Other between Athens and Jerusalem: A Comparative Study of Plato and Rosenzweig" in *Philosophy East and West* 45, no 4 (October 1995), 545.

30. Cohen, "Der Stil der Propheten," in *JS* I, 262–263.

31. Cohen, "Der Stil der Propheten," in *JS* I, 263.

32. It should be emphasized that all of this analysis applies specifically to 'Cohen's Plato' and to 'Cohen's prophets,' rather than to their historical counterparts. Even if some of what Cohen attributes to Plato and the prophets may lack full historical or textual support, his pronouncements are still excellent sources for developing our understanding of *Cohen's* ideas and positions with regard to style, method, and communication.

33. The difficulty may also stem from the fact that while the categories of science and art can each be described directly and clearly, the category of religion is not a definite distinct category unto itself, but rather exists "between art and science." It is not science, and not art, but neither is it something completely different from them. In a sense, it partakes of both categories even though they are mutually exclusive of one another.

34. Cohen, "Der Stil der Propheten," in *JS* I, 263.

35. Cohen, "Der Stil der Propheten," in *JS* I, 265, emphasis added.

36. Cohen, "Der Stil der Propheten," in *JS* I, 282. Cf. Kant's *Critique of the Power of Judgment*, ed. Paul Guyer, trans. Paul Guyer and Eric Matthews (Cambridge: Cambridge University Press, 2000), 90 (5:204–205): a palace can be judged as beautiful even if it was built by unethical or wasteful means—a pure judgment of taste [i.e., of beauty] must be free of all interest, which would include questions of moral worth or usefulness.

In contrast, delight in the *good* is always coupled with interest (*Critique of the Power of Judgment*, 93 [5:207]). See also 115 (5:231): A *judgment* of taste is pure only if the person judging has abstracted from any end that the object under consideration might have. Accordingly, having ethicality as an end prevents the prophetic addresses from being pure art and the prophets from being absolute artists.

37. To use Kierkegaardian terminology, they are engaged in a communication of capability, and not simply a communication of knowledge. See Kierkegaard, *Søren Kierkegaard's Journals and Papers*, ed. and trans. Howard V. Hong and Edna H. Hong (Bloomington: Indiana University Press, 1975), 1:303–308.

38. The prophets do not oppose either art or science/philosophy per se, but only their absolute, pure forms. Because they create a border-area between art and science, their method and style are thus 'impure.' They are artists, but not mere or absolute artists. Similarly, they "concern themselves . . . with the scientificality [*Wissenschaftlichkeit*] of their ethical teaching" (Cohen, "Der Stil der Propheten," in *JS* I, 263), but their productions are not science in a strict sense, because they do not confine themselves to science's systematic methodology.

39. Cohen, "Der Stil der Propheten," in *JS* I, 278.

40. Cohen, "Der Stil der Propheten," in *JS* I, 277, emphasis in the original. Cf. Kant, *Critique of the Power of Judgment*, 190 (5:312): "Fine art shows its superiority precisely in this, that it describes things beautifully that in nature we would dislike or find ugly. The Furies, diseases, devastations of war, and so on are all harmful; and yet they can be described, or even presented in a painting, very beautifully."

41. Cohen, "Der Stil der Propheten," in *JS* I, 278.

42. Cohen clearly emphasizes, though, that not all art is absolute art, and that there is a type of artist "in whom [the] spirit of the prophets streams, the spirit that guards the ethical ideal of humanity." Cohen points to Michelangelo as an example of this type of artist ("Der Stil der Propheten," in *JS* I, 283).

43. Cf. Søren Kierkegaard, *Concluding Unscientific Postscript to Philosophical Fragments* [henceforth cited as *CUP*], ed. and trans. Howard V. Hong and Edna H. Hong (Princeton, NJ: Princeton University Press, 1992), 35n, where Climacus similarly condemns the desire to have something firm and fixed that can exclude the dialectical.

It should also be noted that the structure of Cohen's criticism of art's one-sidedness can be equally applied to forms of philosophizing. Cohen's disciple Franz Rosenzweig opens the first pages of his *Star of Redemption* with a salvo against 'one-sided' philosophers who ignore the reality of the death of the individual, just as the prophets' aesthetic opponents ignore the reality of the death and suffering of the poor. See Rosenzweig, *The Star of Redemption*, trans. William W. Hallo (Notre Dame, IN: Notre Dame Press, 1985).

44. Cohen, "Der Stil der Propheten," in *JS* I, 277.

45. In at least one other essay, Cohen does say that certain apparent contradictions regarding God's nature are *aufgehoben*. See Michael Zank, *Idea of Atonement*, 132.

However, this occurs in a different context from the present one. Here, there is no mention of an *aufhebung* of the prophetic contradictions.

46. Cohen, "Der Stil der Propheten," in *JS* I, 267.

47. Cohen, "Der Stil der Propheten," in *JS* I, 267.

48. Cohen, "Der Stil der Propheten," in *JS* I, 267. Cohen's rendition departs slightly from the biblical text.

49. Cohen also highlights the satirical nature of the prophet's portrayal of idolatry as adulterous unfaithfulness to God ("Der Stil der Propheten," in *JS* I, 267). Idolatry is thus no more excusable than adultery, which, from the perspective of the prophets, is by no means unavoidable.

50. Cohen, "Der Stil der Propheten," in *JS* I, 267.

51. Cf. Kant's account of regulative principles in his *Critique of Pure Reason*, trans. Paul Guyer and Allen W. Wood (Cambridge: Cambridge University Press, 1998): "If merely regulative principles are considered as constitutive, then as objective principles they can be in conflict; but if one considers them merely as *maxims*, then it is not a true conflict, but it is merely a different interest of reason that causes a divorce between ways of thinking" (B694–695, emphasis in the original). Here, although it is not a true conflict practically/regulatively, the conflict is unavoidable if the principles are viewed theoretically/constitutively.

52. Cohen, "Der Stil der Propheten," in *JS* I, 274.

53. Cohen seems to be borrowing this phrase from the New Testament (Mark 13:31; Matt. 24:35; Luke 21:33): "Heaven and earth will pass away, but my word will not pass away." However, the general trope of "heaven and earth passing away" can also be found in the Talmud, e.g., Babylonian Talmud [henceforth BT] Berachot 32a. The basic concept is drawn from Is. 65:17.

54. Cohen, "Der Stil der Propheten," in *JS* I, 274.

55. Rosenzweig also makes use of the concept of the remnant, and in one place, explicitly connects it to Isaiah's "remnant of Israel." See Rosenzweig, *Star of Redemption*, 404. Eric Santner treats the concept of the infinitesimal remnant as a key to understanding Rosenzweig's philosophy as a whole. See Santner, *On the Psychotheology of Everyday Life: Reflections on Freud and Rosenzweig* (Chicago: University of Chicago Press, 2001), 32, 65, 70, 113, 121. See also Santner, 145, where he links Rosenzweig's ideas to Cohen's "logic of the remnant."

56. As such, it is im-possible.

57. NRSV translation.

58. Other translations of verse 13 accentuate the 'nothingness' of the holy seed even further: "And though a tenth remains in the land, it will again be laid waste. But as the terebinth and oak leave stumps when they are cut down, so the holy seed will be the stump in the land" (NIV); "And if there be yet a tenth in it, it shall again be eaten up; as a terebinth, and as an oak, whose stock remaineth, when they cast their leaves, so the holy seed shall be the stock thereof" (JPS 1917 edition). The NRSV seems to equate the tenth with the stump, and then equates the stump with the holy

seed, which could make it seem like the holy seed is part of the tenth and is therefore finite. In contrast, the NIV and the 1917 JPS implies that the tenth itself will be also fully destroyed. The stump is thus that which is left after the *entire* tree is felled.

By way of contrast, it should be noted that the 1999 JPS edition gives a quite different translation: "But while a tenth part yet remains in it, it shall repent. It shall be ravaged like the terebinth and the oak, of which stumps are left even when they are felled: its stump shall be a holy seed." Here, the tenth part that "repents" appears to be the holy seed, and thus the destruction would not have reached everyone and everything. Such a rendering of the text differs notably from Cohen's description of the destruction of "the entire people."

59. One can also draw connections between the logic applied here to the idea of the "holy seed" and that displayed in Cohen's presentation of the infinitesimal ethical self in *Religion of Reason* (see chapter 6 of this book).

60. Cohen, "Der Stil der Propheten," in *JS* I, 279.

61. Cohen, "Der Stil der Propheten," in *JS* I, 274.

62. Cohen, "Der Stil der Propheten," in *JS* I, 272.

63. Indeed, Cohen's own position, that God is distanced from all actuality (see e.g., *RoR* 160; *RV* 185), has likewise been subject to great misunderstanding.

64. Cohen, "Der Stil der Propheten," in *JS* I, 273.

65. Note that the present, performative tense can turn the act of creating into a continual action: whenever the text is read, one hears, "I create," "I am hereby creating." In this sense, each successive moment in time can be viewed not simply as a continuation from the moment before, but as a new creation without a 'natural' link to the previous moment.

66. In this regard, we call also recall the creation account of the first chapter of Genesis, which employs the same Hebrew verb and in which the creating quite explicitly takes the form of a performative 'speech-act.' Likewise, rabbinic literature repeatedly refers to God as "the one who spoke and the world came into being," *mi she-amar ve-hayah ha-olam*.

67. It is true that the complete dissociation from the present precludes a finite distance between present and future, but this non-finite distance need not be infinitely large; it can also be infinitely small.

68. A link can also be drawn between the odd temporal status of the hoped-for future and Cohen's repeated use of the term *einst / einstig* ("Der Stil der Propheten," in *JS* I, 272, 279). In German, this term has a dual usage: it can be used to indicate the past (in the sense of "in times past," "long ago") as well as the future (in the sense of "some day," "in times to come"). While no point in finite time can be both in the past and in the future, the term *einst* designates both of them 'simultaneously.' Thus, Cohen's very phrasing of *die einstige Zukunft* serves to distinguish the meaning of the prophetic future that of a normal temporal future.

69. Cf. BT Sanhedrin 98a, in which the prophet Elijah tells R. Yehoshua that the Messiah will come "Today, if you hearken to his [i.e., God's] voice."

70. The significance of this messianic-temporal tension, as it appears in *Religion of Reason*, will be discussed in greater detail in chapter 6 of this book.
71. Cohen, "Der Stil der Propheten," in *JS* I, 280–282.
72. Cohen, "Der Stil der Propheten," in *JS* I, 275.
73. Cohen, "Der Stil der Propheten," in *JS* I, 275.
74. Cohen, "Der Stil der Propheten," in *JS* I, 275.
75. Cohen, "Der Stil der Propheten," in *JS* I, 275.
76. Importantly, though all static and objectified features are destroyed, the self, like Israel, is not *absolutely* destroyed: a remnant—the name and the infinitesimal self—remains, out of which the ethical self grows. Cohen's account here thus differs the method of Ethics (as portrayed in *Religion of Reason*), which completely tears away individuality and leaves nothing at all of the individual self behind.
77. Cohen, "Der Stil der Propheten," in *JS* I, 268, emphasis in the original.
78. Cohen, "Der Stil der Propheten," in *JS* I, 282, emphasis in the original.
79. It is also interesting to note that, since the prophetic style in general has a dual and 'mixed' quality, Ezekiel generates the individual through a mixing of mixed styles. One can draw comparisons with Cohen himself, who also draws upon earlier sources and who presents his ideas via a mixing of philosophy and Scripture.
80. Cohen, "Der Stil der Propheten," in *JS* I, 270.
81. Compare this to the ways in which Cohen's ideas contain a duality of the ideal/transcendence/philosophy (justice), on one hand, and actuality/immediacy/immanence/Scripture (love), on the other. In expressing these ideas, Cohen likewise requires a dual-edged style.
82. Cohen, "Der Stil der Propheten," in *JS* I, 274. From a strictly historical-critical perspective, such stylistic 'leaps' would likely be viewed not as indicating internal contradictions within a single author's self-consciousness, but rather as pointing to a multiplicity of different source-documents. As such, there would be less motivation in seeking conceptual significance in those inconsistencies. However, from the perspective of Cohen's approach, which treats the text as a functional unity, the leaps can point crucial elements of religious concepts and their communication. In this, Cohen parallels the approach of the classical midrashic readers of Scripture, who noticed many of the same 'fault lines' in the text as did historical-critical scholars, but who assigned a quite different significance to those gaps.
83. Elsewhere in the essay, Cohen also praises R. Yochanan's "very fine style-comment [*Stilbemerkung*]" (drawn from BT Megillah 31a): "Wherever in the Bible one finds the greatness of God, there is his humility praised at the same time" (276). Here (as in the prophetic oscillation), when communication of God's character is in danger of becoming one-sided, an opposite attribute must also be mentioned.

    One can again draw a comparison to Cohen's later work, in which there are sudden shifts from philosophical utterances to scripturally-saturated passages. Both modes are necessary, yet they are 'incompatible,' and neither can be reduced to the other.

84. Cohen, "Der Stil der Propheten," in *JS* I, 281.

85. Cohen, "Der Stil der Propheten," in *JS* I, 281.

86. See, e.g., Is. 13:1; Is. 14:28; Lam. 2:14; Jer. 23:33; Ezek. 12:10; Nah. 9:1; Mal. 1:1, etc.

87. Cohen, "Der Stil der Propheten," in *JS* I, 281.

88. This lack of ownership of the idea of the unique God can be contrasted to Cohen's description of the Greek gods: "Their poets could have invented them" ("Der Stil der Propheten," in *JS* I, 271). The implication that the unique God could not have been "invented" seems to lie in the conceptual paradox that such an idea contains. A concept can only be said to come from within an empirical individual if that concept can also be grasped by an individual consciousness.

89. Thus, just as the prophets felt that their words were given to them by God, so too ordinary people can receive the prophetic ideas only if they receive them 'from God.' The prophet himself can only be an occasion. For this reason, he must make sure that he does not directly convey a determinate idea; instead, he must convey something dual and contradictory, and let God unify it for the other person (although it will still remain contradictory to the receiver's understanding). Cf. *CUP* 101, where Climacus criticizes Jacobi for forgetting "that in his God-relationship one human being is not the equal of another, which makes the presumed teacher a learner who attends to himself and makes all teaching a divine jest, because every human being is essentially taught solely by God."

90. Cohen, "Der Stil der Propheten," in *JS* I, 280.

91. Cohen, "Der Stil der Propheten," in *JS* I, 280.

92. Cohen, "Der Stil der Propheten," in *JS* I, 280.

93. Thus, Ezekiel rejects a binary hermeneutic, wherein X means Y ("The sacrifice *is* good" or "The sacrifice *is* bad"), and instead employs a triadic hermeneutic, wherein X means Y to Z ("The sacrifice *can be* positive if interpreted in this way").

94. Michael Zank notes an apologetic element in Cohen's defense of Ezekiel, which mirrors Ezekiel's defense of the sacrificial institution. I do not deny that Cohen (or his counterpart and namesake Ezekiel) may be partially motivated by apologetics; however, there is *also* a methodological basis for his retention and reinterpretation of received tradition. See Michael Zank, *Idea of Atonement*, 130 fn. 235.

95. One can say that while Ezekiel's reading of the individual out of the sacrifice may not be a 'plain sense' reading *tout court*, it can be characterized as a 'deeper plain sense' reading. One can also describe Ezekiel's movement from the sacrifice to the individual as abductive, rather than deductive, reasoning. For more on abduction, see chapter 2 of this book.

96. Elizabeth Napier notes that Goethe used this term, with its alchemical origins, to describe psychological separating-out as analogous to chemical separating-out. Cohen may thus be drawing upon such earlier analogies in making his ethical metaphor. See Elizabeth R. Napier, "Aylmer as 'Scheidekünstler': The Pattern of Union and Separation in Hawthorne's 'The Birthmark,'" *South Atlantic Bulletin* (1976): 32.

97. Cohen, "Der Stil der Propheten," in *JS* I, 282.

98. One can profitably compare the use of the term *aus* in the previous citation to the use of the term in the title of Cohen's *Religion der Vernunft aus den Quellen des Judentums*.

99. This account of the prophetic methods corresponds to Cohen's own approach in *Religion of Reason*. Just as Ezekiel draws upon the ethically ambiguous institution of sacrifice, so Cohen draws the religion of reason out of the 'philosophically unrefined' sources of Judaism. There are elements of baseness in these sources, but Cohen is able to uncover underlying patterns as part of the 'deeper plain sense.' While some would reject these sources because of their baseness or vagueness, Cohen insists that the base material is necessary for drawing out the ideals of the unique God, the Thou, the individual as I, and ethical humanity. If one confines oneself to the pure and elevated realm of systematic philosophy, these ideals will remain undiscoverable. Additionally, in presenting these ideas, he must express them through and alongside the scriptural sources from which he drew them.

100. Note that this lack of unity in the theoretical sphere does not mean that a person must 'feel divided' in the practical sphere. Rather, the duality arises when the person *reflects on* the ideas cognitively or speculatively. Again, this recalls Kant's account of regulative principles, wherein conflict arises only when they are considered constitutively (*Critique of Pure Reason*, B694).

101. Cohen, "Der Stil der Propheten," in *JS* I, 269, emphasis in the original: "Zunächst bricht sich der Pessimismus nicht am Optimismus, sondern am *tragischen Pathos*."

102. Cohen, "Der Stil der Propheten," in *JS* I, 272.

103. Likewise, saying that love is God's essence (and not simply part of God's essence) indicates the absence of cognitively accessible qualities or predicates; there are only relationally accessible ones.

104. Cohen, "Der Stil der Propheten," in *JS* I, 281.

105. NRSV translation. Alternatively, ". . . they hear your words, but they will not do them" (*ve-sham'u et-devarekha ve-osim einam otam*).

106. Cf. Kant's *Critique of the Power of Judgment*, 95 (5:209): for matters of the good, it is not only the object itself, but its existence (i.e., its actualization) that pleases—it is a "pure practical" pleasing. In contrast, aesthetic *judgment*s are indifferent to the existence of the object.

107. Cohen, "Der Stil der Propheten," in *JS* I, 276–277. The translation of the verse from Jeremiah is based on Cohen's own German rendition.

108. In addition, knowledge of God is not portrayed here as involving any 'thinking about God,' but rather as pertaining to acting toward other humans. This does not rule out the possibility of direct relation to God, but emphasizes that the prophets' 'knowledge of God' need not involve conscious or determinate conceptions of God.

109. Cohen, "Der Stil der Propheten," in *JS* I, 273.

110. Cohen, "Der Stil der Propheten," in *JS* I, 276.

111. Cohen, "Der Stil der Propheten," in *JS* I, 264.

112. Cf. *CUP* 198: "[A]ll ethical and ethical-religious knowing is essentially a relating to the existing of the knower."

113. Cohen, "Der Stil der Propheten," in *JS* I, 271.

114. Note that in this context, Cohen does not have to provide 'his own opinion' regarding the nature of God. He does not have to say whether God should be characterized as 'an idea,' as 'a person,' or as both. Here, he merely presents the outlook of the prophets, who *do* appear to think in terms of a personal relationship to God.

115. Cohen, "Der Stil der Propheten," in *JS* I, 271.

116. Cohen, "Der Stil der Propheten," in *JS* I, 272.

CHAPTER 2

1. According to Andrea Poma, Cohen saw historicism's strict inductivism as an understandable, though ultimately misguided, reaction to the "opposite, equally unilateral deductivism" of a metaphysical variety that characterized previous research in philosophy of religion. See Poma, "Religion of Reason and Judaism in Hermann Cohen," in *Yearning for Form*, 116–117.

2. *RoR* 2; *RV* 2. Cohen uses the phrase "so-called religion" (*angeblichen Religion*), to register his protest against the application of the term 'religion' to historical cults, sects, and denominations. He considers 'religion' (like 'Judaism,' as we shall see) to be a transcendental concept, not an empirical-historical one. In this, he may be registering awareness of the fact that the empirical use of the term is largely a modern development, while the earlier use of the term was indeed more transcendental, in the sense of an ideal. See, for example, Wilfred Cantwell Smith, *The Meaning and End of Religion* (Minneapolis, MN: Fortress Press, 1991).

3. *RoR* 2; *RV* 2.

4. *RoR* 2; *RV* 2.

5. For more on Cohen's criticism of the historical method, see David N. Myers's chapter on Cohen in *Resisting History*, 35–67. In light of my use of Kierkegaard later in this study, it is interesting to note that Myers uses a citation from the *Concluding Unscientific Postscript* as the epigraph of his Cohen chapter: "How can something of a historical nature be decisive for an eternal happiness?" (See Myers, 35; *CUP* 94).

6. *RoR* 2; *RV* 2–3: "Der Begriff wird hier durchaus als das Fazit der Entwicklung gedacht: während er vielmehr ihr Vorbild, ihre Vorzeichnung sein müßte."

7. *RoR* 3; *RV* 3.

8. *RoR* 3; *RV* 3. Cohen does not say that this anticipatory approach is necessary for all readings of all texts. It may be that the inductive approach of historical science is valid for certain topics, but not with regard to 'rational' concepts such as religion.

9. In taking this position, Cohen may be intentionally opposing Spinoza's approach to Scripture. In his preface to his *Theological-Political Treatise*, Spinoza rejects those readers of Scripture (chief among them Maimonides) who, prior to engaging the actual details of the text, "take it as a fundamental principle (for the purpose of understanding Scripture and bringing out its true meaning) that Scripture is true and divine throughout. But of course this is the very thing that should emerge from a critical examination and understanding of Scripture. It would be much better to derive it from Scripture itself, which has no need of human fabrications, but they assume it at the very beginning as a rule of interpretation." See Spinoza, *Theological-Political Treatise*, 8. Spinoza wants a reader to be taught purely by "Scripture itself." In contrast, Cohen *does* seem to assume a principle for interpretation "at the very beginning." However, Cohen does not claim that the text 'is' divine; instead, he says that *we* must deliberately *read it as* divine/ideal for the purpose of constructing an ideal religion of reason. As such, he might agree with Spinoza's criticism of Maimonides' 'dogmatism,' while also rejecting Spinoza's alternative 'empiricist' hermeneutic.

10. *RoR* 3; *RV* 4. While Cohen's assertion that "reason must rule everywhere in history" (*RoR* 3; *RV* 3) has a Hegelian ring to it, a closer look reveals that Cohen takes an opposite stance to fundamental Hegelian views of reason and history. Rather than claiming that the events of history have inherent necessity because they are all the product of reason's development and self-unfolding, he argues that history only gains necessity when judged by the standards of reason, that it is only in the wrestling to actualize reason that "history becomes the history of reason" (*RoR* 8; *RV* 9). Thus, while a Hegelian position might claim that "that which is actual, is rational," Cohen argues that only those historical developments that meet the criteria of reason are to be judged as rational. In other words, if one approaches history with the concept of reason, one can find traces of reason in history, but there are many things that are actual without being rational.

11. *RoR* 3; *RV* 4.

12. *RoR* 3; *RV* 4.

13. Cf. Climacus' critique of history in *Philosophical Fragments* and in *Concluding Unscientific Postscript*.

14. *RoR* 3–4; *RV* 4.

15. Cf. Kant's *Critique of Pure Reason*, B xviii.

16. *RoR* 4; *RV* 4–5. Again, cf. Kant, *Critique of Pure Reason*, A51/B75.

17. *RoR* 4; *RV* 4–5. In actuality, according to Cohen's account, it would be impossible for someone to arrive at a concept of Judaism by being "simply conducted by the literary sources' authority," since the literary sources in themselves are mute and blind. Rather, what *can* happen is that an interpreter may be conducted by an unconscious concept, in which case the interpreter may *feel* that 'the text alone' is doing the conducting. In contrast, being "instructed" by the sources occurs when the interpreter has greater awareness of his or her guiding concept.

18. Cf. Kant's account of cognition, wherein judgments result neither from intuition alone nor from the concept alone. See, e.g., *Critique of Pure Reason*, A51–52/B75–76.

19. *RoR* 3; *RV* 3.

20. For an account of abduction (which he also calls retroduction) in comparison to deduction and induction, see Charles S. Peirce, *Pragmatism as a Principle and Method of Right Thinking*, ed. Patricia Ann Turrisi (Albany: State University of New York Press, 1997), 229–230, 245–246, and his "A Neglected Argument for the Reality of God," in *Charles S. Peirce: Selected Writings*, ed. Philip P. Wiener (New York: Dover, 1966), 368–371. The basic differences in the modes of reasoning can be seen in the following three arguments, one from each mode:

    DEDUCTION: All P are Q. S is P. *Deductive conclusion*: S is Q.
    INDUCTION: S is P. S is Q. *Inductive conclusion* (assuming multiple iterations): it is likely that all P are Q.
    ABDUCTION: S is Q. All P are Q. *Abductive conclusion*: perhaps S is P.

21. See, e.g., Leo Strauss's argument in his preface to *Spinoza's Critique of Religion*, 25. However, against this, Cohen explicitly states that "history of religion," because it does not (and should not) employ idealization, cannot properly construe the essence of religion, a task that can be accomplished only by "philosophy of religion," which *does* employ idealization. Thus, whatever failings the method of idealization may have, it is also an indispensible method for certain projects and tasks. See Cohen, "Innere Beziehungen der Kantischen Philosophie zum Judentum" in *JS* I, 303–304.

22. Cohen thus follows Kant's opposition to both empiricism/skepticism and rationalism/dogmatism.

23. See *RoR* 6–7; *RV* 7–8.

24. See, for example, G. W. F. Hegel, "Introductory Lecture on the Philosophy of Religion," in *On Art, Religion, and the History of Philosophy: Introductory Lectures*, ed. J. Glenn Gray (Indianapolis: Hackett Publishing Company, 1997), 145: "Thus religion and philosophy come to be one. Philosophy is itself, in fact, worship; it is religion, for in the same way it renounces subjective notions and opinions in order to occupy itself with God."

25. *RoR* 7; *RV* 8.

26. *RoR* 7; *RV* 8.

27. Irene Kajon, *Contemporary Jewish Philosophy: An Introduction* (London: Routledge, 2006), 27.

28. *RoR* 7; *RV* 8.

29. *RoR* 7–8; *RV* 9.

30. *RoR* 7; *RV* 8.

31. *RoR* 7; *RV* 8. Cohen's claim that no particular people's consciousness can exhaustively capture the religion of reason parallels his earlier claim that, generally, only reason, and not consciousness (*Bewußtsein*), can be the source for religion (*RoR* 4; *RV* 5). Thus, just as the religion of reason transcends any particular collective consciousness, so too does it transcend any particular individual consciousness. This

limitation of consciousness will also affect the way in which an account of the religion of reason must be communicated. Because consciousness relates to the unity
of the mind, it can grasp only that which can be comprehended as a unity. The
sphere of religion, in contrast, corresponds to ideas that cannot be fully unified in
the static form of comprehension. Therefore, a faithful presentation of religion
must avoid the communication of 'results' that could be grasped in a unified manner by the reader's consciousness.

32. Such intellectual pluralism on Cohen's part may have parallels in his own personal
self-identification as both a Jew *and* a German. A thinker of 'purely German' or
'purely Jewish' allegiance might feel less of a need to uphold such pluralism, and
could be more comfortable in asserting, "German culture is *the* superior culture" or
"Jewish culture is *the* superior culture." In contrast, Cohen upholds both the Jewish
and the German sides of his identity, and refuses to prioritize one over the other.
(See Steven Schwarzschild, "'Germanism and Judaism.'") To claim that reason can
be embodied most fully only in a single culture would be to undermine his own
identity.

This is not to say that Cohen's biography should be viewed as the exclusive
generating force of his philosophy. A pluralistic philosophy could also be put forth
by someone with a more homogenous self-identity. We can say, though, that
Cohen's self-identity was at the very least not a hindrance to a pluralistic philosophy. In addition, even if his biography played a role in leading him to his philosophy, this fact would not in itself detract (nor add to) the rationality and truth of the
ideas at which he arrived.

On a related note, the ways in which Cohen straddles a 'cultural border'
between multiple identities can also be linked to the repeated emphasis that he
places on the philosophical-conceptual idea of borderlines. For instance, he says
that the prophets create a style in the border-area (*Grenzgebiet*) between art and
science ("Der Stil der Propheten," in *JS* I, 263). He also speaks of the inextinguish-
able battle that continually and fruitfully rages in monotheism at the border
(*Grenze*) of religion and philosophy (*RoR* 30; *RV* 34). The motifs of 'both-and,' of
'neither alone,' and of 'the between' that are fundamental to Cohen's philosophy
might thus have something in common with the 'both-and' of his self-identity and
of the modern Jewish experience more generally.

33. *RoR* 7–8; *RV* 8–9.

34. *RoR* 8; *RV* 9. One should not be misled by Cohen's use of the term "scientific." This
term does not refer primarily to technological or industrial development, but
rather to cultural self-criticism. A culture can display technological complexity and
yet be completely enthralled by its dominant myths and ideologies. Indeed, such a
culture may actually manifest a *lower* overall level of reason in comparison with 'less
developed' cultures.

35. Likewise, even if Judaism may appear to some to be less scientifically and philosophically advanced than European Christian culture, this would not indicate its

inherent inferiority. Instead, it would simply indicate that its scientific potential has not yet been fully developed. Rather than abandoning Judaism for Christianity, the proper response is to raise up the Jewish cultural tradition through self-criticism—in other words, to draw the religion of reason out of the sources of Judaism.

36. For instance, Norbert Samuelson writes of Cohen: "In *Religion [of Reason]* he attempted to demonstrate that the only actual religion of reason is Judaism." See Samuelson, *An Introduction to Modern Jewish Philosophy*, 175. Later in his introduction, Cohen himself warns against such an understanding of his book: "I do not assert that Judaism is uniquely and alone the religion of reason" (*RoR* 34; *RV* 39).

37. *RoR* 8; *RV* 9.

38. *RoR* 8; *RV* 9.

39. As Wendell Dietrich points out, Cohen had to contend with sharp opposition to his account of Judaism, and he was thus well aware that the same sources can also give rise to other constructions of 'Judaism' if approached differently. See Dietrich, *Cohen and Troeltsch: Ethical Monotheistic Religion and Theory of Culture* (Atlanta, GA: Scholars Press, 1986), 35–36, 58.

40. From today's vantage point, we can note that Cohen's approach may help him avoid some of the pitfalls of modernist philosophy. The recognition that so-called 'universal principles' may not actually be universal has led some to give up entirely on the idea of a universal philosophy. That is, under the assumption that the universal can only come from the universal, the lack of universal principles precludes the possibility of a universal philosophy. If our supposedly universal principles actually turn out to be particular, then our philosophy must be particular as well. Such a conclusion can give rise to both relativism (all particular philosophies are equally legitimate) or fundamentalism (my particular philosophy is superior, simply on my say-so). In contrast, Cohen's hypothesis, that one arrives at the universal through the particular, can provide a way out of the impasse created by the untenability of universal starting principles.

41. Cohen does claim that the Jewish sources are unique in their role as an "original source" for other sources of the religion of reason (*RoR* 8; *RV* 9). Presumably, he has in mind the development of Christian sources from out of the Hebrew Bible. Cohen argues that this status as an original source gives "an undeniable spiritual and psychological advantage" to the Jewish sources (*RoR* 8; *RV* 10). He makes a similar claim towards the end of the introduction (*RoR* 34; *RV* 39–40). Technically, this does not compromise the criterion of universality, since he maintains that one can derive the religion of reason from other sources. As such, however, it is not clear what this "advantage" of the Jewish sources consists in—does Cohen thinks that one can derive the religion of reason more easily from the Jewish sources than from other sources? Perhaps he is primarily motivated by apologetic defensiveness, trying to ward off the accusation that the Jewish sources are less suited to the project of a religion of reason than are Christian ones.

42. *RoR* 9; *RV* 10. Elsewhere, Cohen reiterates his insistence that the Jewish biblical sources do not contain philosophy in the strict, scientific sense of term. See *RoR* 22; *RV* 26; *RoR* 106; *RV* 123; "Das soziale Ideal bei Platon und den Propheten," in *JS* I, 310; "Der Stil der Propheten," in *JS* I, 264, 265.

43. *RoR* 9; *RV* 10, emphases in the original.

44. *RoR* 9; *RV* 10.

45. *RoR* 5; *RV* 6.

46. *RoR* 9; *RV* 11.

47. Andrea Poma argues that Cohen's previous system equated critical thought with scientific thought, whereas in *Religion of Reason* he separates the two. This separation enables him to find critical-rational elements in the Jewish sources, even though they lack a scientific-objective methodology. See Poma, "Correlation in Hermann Cohen's Philosophy of Religion: A Method and More Than a Method," in *Yearning for Form*, 76.

48. *RoR* 9–10; *RV* 11.

49. *RoR* 9; *RV* 11.

50. *RoR* 9; *RV* 11. My presentation of Cohen thus differs slightly from that of Irene Kajon, who maintains that Cohen presents two subdivisions of philosophy, such that "the philosophical doctrine of man seems to be divided between the point of view held by an ethics based on scientific philosophy, and a point of view oriented by ethics expressed by religion." However, in order to make this argument, she translates Cohen's "*entstellt*" in the above quotation not as "distorted," but rather as the less pejorative "rendered precarious." In contrast, I argue that, to understand Cohen's subsequent arguments regarding the status of religion, it is important to maintain the strict sense of 'philosophy,' such that applying the term to a non-scientific form of reasoning would indeed be a distortion. As such, religion, as well the Jewish sources, would contribute to the *rational* doctrine of man, but not to the *philosophical* doctrine of man. See Kajon, *Contemporary Jewish Philosophy*, 27–28.

51. *RoR* 11; *RV* 13.

52. *RoR* 11–12; *RV* 13.

53. Thus, Cohen's opposition may have been directed not so much at *them* personally but rather at the basic methodological presupposition (the exclusive primacy of the philosophical method) that they all share.

54. *RoR* 12; *RV* 14.

55. See my introductory chapter.

56. *RoR* 12; *RV* 14.

57. *RoR* 12; *RV* 14.

58. *RoR* 13; *RV* 14–15. Note Cohen's use of the term "self-sufficient" (*selbständigen*) here. While there cannot be two self-sufficient methods, Cohen will later assert that religion is *not* self-sufficient.

59. In contrast, if they *were* to provide the same content, then they would no longer be methodologically distinguishable, and religion would be again collapsed into Ethics.

60. Cohen's rejection of the two "disastrous" options corresponds to Michael Zank's assertion that Cohen "avoids subordination as well as coordination of philosophy and religion." Subordination of religion to philosophy would be equivalent to the first option, while coordination of religion and philosophy would be equivalent to the second option. See Zank, *Idea of Atonement*, 32.

61. As Michael Zank points out, Cohen employs the term "sources of Judaism" in a quite restricted manner, and he fails to include many of the textual sources that historical scholars would call 'Jewish.' However, these omissions are less significant for my analysis here, since Cohen's primary concern in *Religion of Reason* is not to draw a sharp line between Jewish and not-Jewish, but rather to show the rational resources in the texts on which he does focus. See Zank, "Hermann Cohen und der rabbinische Literatur," in *Hermann Cohen's Philosophy of Religion: International Conference in Jerusalem 1996*, ed. Stéphane Moses and Hartwig Wiedebach (Hildesheim: Georg Olms Verlag, 1997), 265.

62. *RoR* 24; *RV* 28.

63. Recent literary approaches to the biblical text have been more amenable to the idea of multiplicity. See Robert Alter's account of "composite artistry" in the opening chapters of Genesis in his *The Art of Biblical Narrative* (New York: Basic Books, 1981), 141–147. See also Carol Newsom's chapter on "The Book of Job as Polyphonic Text" in her *The Book of Job: A Contest in Moral Imaginations* (New York: Oxford University Press, 2003), 3–31, as well as her "Bakhtin, The Bible, and Dialogic Truth," *Journal of Religion* 76, no.2 (Apr. 1996), 290–306.

64. The attempt to reconcile the two creation narratives thus parallels scholarly attempts to 'reconcile' the different 'voices' in *Religion of Reason*.

65. *RoR* 25; *RV* 28–29.

66. It should be noted that the double-character of theory and practice that Cohen attributes to Deuteronomy is not identical to the 'contradictoriness' that he discerns in doubled creation narratives of Genesis. However, both forms of 'twoness' serve to prevent the 'oneness' that a realm of autonomous theory would demand.

67. *RoR* 26; *RV* 30. Cohen's description of the prophets as lifting Moses' veil may be an allusion to Paul's description in 2 Cor. 3. There, referring to the account of Moses' veil in Ex. 34:33–35, Paul asserts, "to this very day, when [the people of Israel] hear the reading of the old covenant, that same veil is there, since only in Christ is it set aside. Indeed, to this very day, whenever Moses is read, a veil lies over their minds; but when one turns to the Lord, the veil is removed." In contrast, Cohen asserts that the "old covenant" prophets had *already* lifted Moses' veil.

68. This logic parallels the logic of the infinitesimal, in which $x + dx$ is not the same as x, but neither is it objectively different. The continuity of a curve is built up by a continuous series of such infinitesimal "exceptions." Later in the book, Cohen will apply this logic of continuous origination and renewal to the ideas of creation, prayer, and repentance.

69. See especially Michael Fishbane's *Biblical Interpretation in Ancient Israel* (New York: Oxford University Press, 1985), from which I have borrowed the terms *traditio* and *traditum*.

70. *RoR* 26; *RV* 30.

71. On the orality of scribal culture, see Martin Jaffee, *Torah in the Mouth: Writing and Oral Tradition in Palestinian Judaism, 200 BCE–400 CE* (New York: Oxford University Press, 2001), 15–27. Additionally, Cohen's linking of the scribes to 'singers of old' anticipates later twentieth-century studies of orality, the most well-known of which is Albert Lord's *The Singer of Tales* (Cambridge, MA: Harvard University Press, 1960).

72. *RoR* 26; *RV* 30. Cohen uses the phrase *mündliche Lehre*. Though I translate it here as "oral teaching," it is clear that he refers to the Hebrew phrase *torah she-be-al peh*, the "oral Torah."

73. *RoR* 26; *RV* 30.

74. In a manner strikingly similar to Cohen's account, Jaffee speaks of the continuous re-origination of the transmitted texts: "[T]he 'original' text did not mean the 'first' version that came from the mouth or the pen of the author. In functional terms, the 'original' text meant the version whose words reached the audience at a given performative reading" (*Torah in the Mouth*, 18). Thus, we could say that Cohen's logic of origin is closely linked to the logic of orality.

75. Cohen also states that the Torah "would only have had temporal value" if the oral teaching had not been recognized a legitimate continuation of the original teaching (*RoR* 26; *RV* 30). In making this assertion, Cohen is most likely thinking of Spinoza, who famously argued that the Torah had value only as the law-code of the ancient state of Israel and lost its validity with the destruction of that state (see chapter 5 of his *Theological-Political Treatise*, 68). While Cohen ultimately disagrees with Spinoza, he indicates that Spinoza's judgment would be correct *if* one were to equate the Torah only with its written form.

76. *RoR* 28; *RV* 32.

77. In a Hebrew essay of 1917, Hayyim Bialik also describes the interrelation between the halakhah and aggadah. See his "Halakhah and Aggadah, or Lore and Love," translated into English in *Contemporary Jewish Record* 7, no. 6 (Dec. 1944): 662–680. In very correlative language, Bialik writes, "Like ice and water, Halakha and Aggadah are really two things in one, two facets of a single entity" (663). However, as Gordon Tucker points out, Bialik views halakhah as the nourishing "fruit" and aggadah as the beautiful "flower." Thus, aggadah comes across as more of a luxury than does halakhah. In opposition to this view (and more in line with Cohen's description of two parallel branches growing out of the same tree), Abraham Joshua Heschel argues that aggadah is just as nourishing and essential as halakhah. See Heschel, *Heavenly Torah: As Refracted by the Generations*, trans. Gordon Tucker (New York: Continuum, 2005), 7 and Tucker's notes to that same page.

78. In his literary analysis of talmudic stories, Jeffrey Rubinstein similarly argues that the "halakhic context" of an embedded story contributes significantly to our understanding of it. See his *Talmudic Stories: Narrative Art, Composition, and Culture* (Baltimore: Johns Hopkins University Press, 1999), 15.

79. *RoR* 28; *RV* 32.

80. See, e.g., BT Berachot 34b, as well as Rashi on Ex. 7:1 and Rashbam on Gen. 20:7.

81. Cohen's description here also seems indebted to Kant's account of spontaneity. See, for example, *Critique of Pure Reason* B130, where Kant identifies the synthesis of a manifold as an act of spontaneity and B132, where he links spontaneity with original (*ursprüngliche*), in contrast to empirical, apperception. The oral teaching's connection to the primary origin (*Ursprung*) is what allows it to be spontaneous, unmediated, and a new synthetic creation.

82. *RoR* 28; *RV* 32–33. In describing the oral teaching as "not closed" (*nicht abgeschlossenes*) and "unceasing" (*unaufhörlich*), Cohen may have in mind the midrashic interpretation of Deut. 5:19, *kol gadol ve-lo yasaf,* as "a great voice that did not cease." See Exodus Rabbah 28:6.

83. Cohen later discusses other ways in which the Jewish conception of revelation breaks with the idea of revelation having occurred only at a single historical point in time. See *RoR* 72–74; *RV* 84–86.

    It should also be noted that Cohen's interpretation of the phrase *halakhah le-moshe mi-sinai* may differ from its use in the classical rabbinic texts themselves. While Cohen views it in terms of an exegetical freedom that allows for ever-new rational re-originations of the oral teaching, David Weiss Halivni argues that the rising prevalence of the phrase in the Amoraic period actually signified a movement *away from* reasoned exegesis. See his *Revelation Restored* (Boulder, CO: Westview Press, 1997), 54–74. However, the modes of reasoning that Cohen attaches to *halakhah le-moshe mi-sinai are* prominent in rabbinic literature, even if they were not associated with that particular phrase.

84. In commenting on "halakhah to Moses from Sinai," Cohen probably has in mind BT Menachot 29b, in which Moses is transported to Rabbi Akiva's classroom, but cannot understand what is being taught. However, he is reassured when Akiva tells his students that his teaching is *halakhah le-moshe mi-sinai.* Paradoxically, Moses received the teaching 'then' (at Sinai) yet did not receive it until 'now' (when it is taught by Akiva).

85. A famous expression of the notion that all future manifestations of the oral teaching were given at Sinai can be found in Exodus Rabbah 28:6, where it is stated that "not only did the prophets receive their prophecy from Sinai, but also the sages who will arise in every generation: each and every one of them received his [portion] from Sinai [*kibel et shelo mi-sinai*]."

86. Cf. Climacus' discussion of "The Follower at Second Hand" in the fifth chapter of *Philosophical Fragments.*

87. In this sense, the rabbinic prohibition against writing down the oral Torah (see, e.g., BT Gittin 60b, BT Temurah 14b) may have stemmed from the *impossibility* of truly writing down the oral Torah.

88. *RoR* 28; *RV* 33. Cohen goes on to link the inward nature of the Torah with its portability: the Torah, along with the national spirit "is not localized in Palestine"; rather, "wherever the Talmud is taught, there the Torah is alive." The idea that the Torah cannot be identified with any place outside of the individual shares the same logic as the idea that it cannot be identified with any particular geographic location. It may be no coincidence that the verses in Deut. 30 preceding "it is in your heart" portray an exilic setting: being told that the Torah is in your heart is most applicable to someone who is far away from the geographic location where the Torah might otherwise be *thought* to reside. In this sense, Deut. 30 may display an inwardness that is aided or initiated by circumstance, analogous to the replacement of sacrifice with prayer and repentance after the destruction of the temple.

89. *RoR* 28; *RV* 33, emphasis added.

90. *RoR* 29; *RV* 33.

91. *RoR* 29; *RV* 33.

92. For an account of ways in which rabbinic midrash rhetorically represents the act of interpretation so as to make it *appear* that Scripture is self-interpreting and that the reader engages the text merely as a passive hearer, see Azzan Yadin, *Scripture as Logos: Rabbi Ishmael and the Origins of Scripture* (Philadelphia: University of Pennsylvania Press, 2004), 34, 80. Yadin further argues that the rabbis adopt such rhetorical strategies as a result of "a tension born of the commentators' need to be at once identical with the biblical text and other than it" (137). The logic of 'both the same and different' is very similar to Cohen's notions of re-origination and correlation.

93. *RoR* 29; *RV* 33.

94. Daniel Boyarin criticizes both of these approaches of midrash for basing themselves on a strict dichotomy between "objective" readings (the 'formalistic' account) and "subjective" readings (the 'prooftext' account). See his *Intertextuality and the Reading of Midrash* (Bloomington: Indiana University Press, 1990), 1–11.

95. *RoR* 29; *RV* 33.

96. See *RoR* 392; *RV* 455–456.

97. Boyarin's account of midrash is similar to Cohen's: the biblical verses cited are not prooftexts but rather the "generating force" behind the interpretation (*Intertextuality*, 22), though the interpretations also display the rabbis' own specific perspectives: "Ideology affected their reading but their ideology was also affected by their reading" (19).

98. *RoR* 29; *RV* 33. Cohen's description of "the word" as "alive" may be drawing upon BT Hagigah 3b, which interprets *netu'im* in Ecclesiastes 12:11 ("The words of the wise are like goads, and like well-planted [*netu'im*] nails are those of the masters of

assemblies, given by one shepherd") to mean: "Just as a plant is fruitful and increases, so the words of the Torah are fruitful and increase." (According to Leo Rosenzweig's annotations to *Religion of Reason,* Cohen also alludes to this passage when discussing the relation between the oral teaching and the "imperishable national fruitfulness" of Jewish culture. See *RoR* 28/463, note 3; *RV* 28/535.)

Additionally, as Azzan Yadin points out, the classical rabbinic texts personify treat the written Torah and describe it as "speaking," using phrases such as *amrah torah* (Torah said) or *ha-katuv medabber* (the Scripture speaks). See his *Scripture as Logos,* 10–33. While *torah* is usually described as speaking or acting in the past tense, *ha-katuv* is portrayed as acting and speaking in the present tense, underscoring the fact that the word is still 'alive' (33).

99. *RoR* 29; *RV* 33–4.

100. Almut Bruckstein argues for the fundamental similarity between Cohen's modes of reasoning and "traditional interpretative methods of the Jewish oral tradition." See her "Introduction," in Cohen, *Ethics of Maimonides,* xxxvii. See also Bruckstein, "Joining the Narrators: A Philosophy of Talmudic Hermeneutics," in Kepnes et al., *Reasoning After Revelation,* 107–108.

Michael Zank (though without referring to Cohen's own account of midrash) also describes Cohen's general neo-Kantian approach to transcendental philosophy as "midrashic," precisely because it employs this same abductive logic in relation to the sources that it analyzes and rationally idealizes. See Zank, "The Ethics in Hermann Cohen's Philosophical System," in Gibbs, *Hermann Cohen's Ethics,* 4–5.

101. Cf. Daniel Boyarin, who argues midrash is made possible precisely *because* of the Bible's textual heterogeneity (*Intertextuality,* 39).

102. *RoR* 29; *RV* 34.

103. Ibn Ezra on Gen. 22:4.

104. Cf. Kant's *Critique of Pure Reason,* B694–5, where he discusses the conflict that arises from wrongly taking constituitively principles that should be taken regulatively.

105. *RoR* 29–30; *RV* 34.

106. *RoR* 30; *RV* 34.

107. *RoR* 30; *RV* 34.

108. This characterization of the history of Jewish philosophy accords with Steven Schwarzschild's subsequent account of the "Jewish twist," wherein he claims that Jewish philosophers consistently tweaked the intellectual systems in which they worked by maintaining the primacy of practical reason. See Schwarzschild, "An Agenda for Jewish Philosophy in the 1980's," in *Studies in Jewish Philosophy: Collected Essays of the Academy for Jewish Philosophy 1980–1985,* ed. Norbert Samuelson (Lanham, MD: University Press of America, 1987), 101–125. See also Schwarzschild, "The Lure of Immanence," in *The Pursuit of the Ideal: Jewish Writings of Steven Schwarzschild,* ed. Menachem Kellner (Albany: State University of New York Press, 1990), 63–64.

109. *RoR* 31; *RV* 36. Steven Schwarzschild also discusses the "re-convergence" of "mysticism and rationalism" despite their outward "divergence." He sees this phenomenon as particularly prevalent in Jewish philosophy, and he links it to the practical-ethical volitionism that he identifies as a common thread running through the former. See Schwarzschild, "An Introduction to the Thought of R. Isaac Hutner," in *Modern Judaism* 5, no. 3 (Oct. 1985), 257–261.

110. Cf. Cohen's "Die Lyrik der Psalmen," in *JS* I, 237–239, where the apparent multiplicity of psalmic perspectives have their unity in the praying individual.

111. A number of scholars have presented Cohen as standing firmly opposed to mysticism (e.g., Andrea Poma, *The Critical Philosophy of Hermann Cohen*, 69; Almut Bruckstein, commentary to Cohen, *Ethics of Maimonides*, 102; Ze'ev Levy, "Hermann Cohen and Emmanuel Levinas," in Moses and Wiedebach, *Hermann Cohen's Philosophy of Religion*, 133). While Cohen does repeatedly criticize mysticism for its ethics-undermining tendencies (e.g., *RoR* 108–109, 386, 414; *RV* 125–126, 449, 480), the present passage seems to indicate that Cohen does have respect for at least some representatives of what he calls 'mysticism.' It may be that his negative attitude is directed primarily at those forms of mysticism that are not 'fruitfully counterbalanced' by ethical-intellectual principles—in other words, against a mysticism that becomes a self-sufficient 'ism' unto itself.

112. *RoR* 32; *RV* 37.

113. *RoR* 32, 33; *RV* 37, 38.

114. *RoR* 32–33; *RV* 38.

115. In this, Cohen follows Kant, who also denies that there can be special duties to God. See *Religion Within the Limits of Reason Alone*, trans. Theodore M. Greene and Hoyt H. Hudson (New York: Harper Torchbooks, 1960), 142.

116. *RoR* 33; *RV* 39.

117. *RoR* 34; *RV* 39, emphasis in the original.

118. *RoR* 34; *RV* 39.

119. Thus, Cohen asserts that other religions "establish their right as religions" not on the basis of universally shared propositions, but only "insofar as they prove themselves as religions of reason *from out of their sources*" (*RoR* 34; *RV* 39, emphasis added). In addition, while all religious traditions have the duty to construct a religion of reason from out of their sources, this task may prove comparatively more difficult for some traditions, depending on the ways in which their received sources are bound up with certain types of mythological thinking.

120. *RoR* 34; *RV* 39. Andrea Poma views Cohen's use of the term 'philosophy of religion' as inappropriate for describing the religion of reason, since, as Cohen has already stated, the religion of reason goes beyond philosophy proper. However, I do not think that Cohen means to equate 'philosophy of religion' with 'the religion of reason.' Rather, the former designates a conscious, reflective attempt to communicate the latter through the use of philosophical analysis. Poma's hesitancy is justified, though, since 'philosophy of religion' is a peculiar notion that

would have to differ stylistically from other types of philosophy: whereas other types seek to clarify their subject matter through a fully consistent presentation, a philosophy of religion can 'clarify' (i.e., clear up confusions about) its subject matter only by refraining from a fully consistent presentation. See Poma, "Religion of Reason and Judaism in Hermann Cohen," in *Yearning for Form*, 112, 123–124.

121. One can draw a parallel between Cohen's modeling his own style on that of the Jewish sources and Rosenzweig's later statement that "the Jewish is my method, not my subject matter." See Rosenzweig, *Briefe und Tagebücher: Der Mensch und sein Werk: Gesammelte Schriften*, vol. 1.2, ed. Rachel Rosenzweig and Edith Rosenzweig-Schienmann (The Hague: Martinus Nijhoff, 1979), 720. Gesine Palmer attempts to connect Rosenzweig's dictum to Cohen's work in her "Judaism as a 'Method' with Hermann Cohen and Franz Rosenzweig," in Gibbs, *Hermann Cohen's Ethics*, 38–39.

CHAPTER 3

1. *RoR* 13; *RV* 15: "If we now, to begin with, leave aside objections concerning method...." While Cohen's qualification of "to begin with" may seem to indicate that he will return to the question or refute the objections later on, this never occurs, and the objections still remain.
2. *RoR* 9; *RV* 11.
3. Adelmann, *Einheit des Bewußtseins*, 25–27.
4. Adelmann, *Einheit des Bewußtseins*, 26, 55–57. This role of religion can also be discerned in the basic chapter-structure of Cohen's *Der Begriff der Religion*.
5. Adelmann, *Einheit des Bewußtseins*, 73–78.
6. Adelmann, *Einheit des Bewußtseins*, 60–61, 70.
7. Andrea Poma notes that in Cohen's earlier system, he still equated the scientific method with reason *tout court*, and that he largely maintains this stance in *Der Begriff der Religion*. It is only in *Religion of Reason* that he is able to assert religion as a sphere that does *not* fall within the scientific method, and yet *is* part of reason. See Poma, "Correlation in Hermann Cohen's Philosophy of Religion: A Method and More than a Method," in *Yearning for Form*, 75–79.
8. In this regard, Poma's description—religion "is placed outside the scientific method, not in opposition to it, however"—overly softens the tension inherent in Cohen's approach, since, in an important sense, Cohen holds that for religion to be outside the scientific method of philosophy *is* to be in 'opposition' to it. See Poma, "Correlation," in *Yearning for Form*, 78.
9. See Zank, *Idea of Atonement*, 107–151.
10. Zank, *Idea of Atonement*, 189–192, 285–286. See also Gibbs, *Correlations*, 178–181. Note that the You appears not only once, but multiple times through the *Ethik*. See Cohen, *Ethik des reinen Willens*, 248–249, 258, 266, 274–275, 493.
11. *RoR* 178; *RV* 208–209.

12. Peter Gordon also highlights this passage, describing it as "a moment of dissonance in Cohen's argument"; in his reading, it indicates that "[r]eligion and ethics are not only incompatible, they are locked in opposition." See Gordon, *Rosenzweig and Heidegger*, 68.

13. *RoR* 15; *RV* 17.

14. As Zank points out, the rhetoric of Cohen's argument in *Religion of Reason* makes it seem as though the You was a new and surprising discovery, as though he had not already treated the concept in depth in his *Ethik*. See Zank, *Idea of Atonement*, 189. Such 'rhetoric of surprise' fits in well with my argument below that Cohen adopts a deliberately ironic presentation of the method of philosophy. Both stylistic moves point to Cohen's attempt to mark out the concepts of religion as both commensurate and incommensurate with his earlier system.

To be clear, Cohen does not mention his own *Ethik* when discussing the incompatibility of the You with the totalizing 'method of Ethics,' and so the question of an explicit revisionism on this point cannot be answered conclusively. That is to say, he indicates that the You is incompatible with the method of Ethics without explicitly indicating whether the You is incompatible with the *Ethik*. However, since the approach of the *Ethik*, with its goal of totality, seems to fit the description in *Religion of Reason* of 'the method of Ethics,' it seems reasonable to view *Religion of Reason* as critiquing the presence of the You in Cohen's own earlier *System*. (Cf. Cohen's assessment of the way that the concept of God appeared in his *Ethik*; see *RoR* 20; *RV* 23.) However, the precise ways in which the *Ethik* might stand in need of revision would require a separate study.

15. As we shall see in chapter 6, this can also serve as a fitting description of Cohen's use of the infinitesimal.

16. See, for example, Cohen, *Ethik des reinen Willens*, 54, 218, 298–299, 556.

17. See, for instance, Robert Gibbs's claim that "the concerns and modes of argumentation in *The Ethics* also appear in Cohen's more explicitly Jewish writings." Gibbs, "Hermann Cohen's *Ethics*," in Gibbs, *Hermann Cohen's Ethics*, viii.

18. This observation can shed light on Rosenzweig's account of the relation between Cohen's *Religion* and Cohen's *System*. While this account has rightly been criticized for overstating the 'break' between the two and for overlooking their continuities, Rosenzweig's presentation does correspond more closely to the way that this relation is portrayed within *Religion of Reason*; it may simply be that this latter portrayal is itself misleading.

19. Accordingly, one cannot come to a full understanding of *Religion of Reason* unless one studies it alongside and in relation to Cohen's earlier *System*, discerning precisely where the similarities and the dissimilarities lie.

20. Well before *Der Begriff der Religion*, the debate between Cohen and Herrmann on the question of religion already had an extensive history. Dietrich Korsch traces through these exchanges, which began as early as 1879. See Korsch, "Hermann Cohen und die protestantische Theologie seiner Zeit," *Zeitschrift für Neuere Theologiegeschichte* 1 (1994): 80–85.

21. Poma, *Critical Philosophy of Hermann Cohen*, 162, maintains that Cohen accepted Herrmann's criticism, but still wanted to fit religion and the individual into the system. See also Michael Zank, "Between Dialogue and Disputation," 143–144.

22. Zank, "Between Dialogue and Disputation," 145, discussing Cohen, *Der Begriff der Religion*, 52.

23. Cohen, *Der Begriff der Religion*, 53.

24. Cohen, *Der Begriff der Religion*, 58; see Zank, "Between Dialogue and Disputation," 146–148.

25. *RoR* 13–15, 178; *RV* 15–18, 208–209. One shortcoming of Zank's otherwise-thorough account is that he does not address this key difference between *Der Begriff der Religion* and *Religion of Reason*. Instead, he maintains that "[t]here is no conceptual tension between the two books," and that the difference between them is simply one of genre rather than of intellectual substance. Zank, *Idea of Atonement*, 37.

26. *RoR* 16–17; *RV* 18–19.

27. *RoR* 13; *RV* 15. Note that while Cohen sometimes uses the term 'ethical' (*ethisch*) in a more general sense, he here seeks specifically to highlight the concept of man within systematic Ethics, the concept that is generated through the use of Ethics' distinctive method.

28. *RoR*, 13; *RV* 15, emphasis in original.

29. Cf. Climacus' derisive description of the attempt to achieve "objective thinking," in which "the existing subjectivity evaporates more and more" (*CUP* 123).

30. Cohen's exaggerated praise of 'purity' here may very well be an ironic allusion to the three volumes of his *System*, each of which—*Logik der reinen Erkenntnis*, *Ethik des reinen Willens*, and *Ästhetik des reinen Gefühls*—emphasized 'purity' in their titles. The purity that his systematic method previously sought to achieve is now lightly mocked—yet without being determinately rejected.

31. *RoR* 13; *RV* 15.

32. Cf. Kant's distinction between the law of homogeneity and the law of specification. The former attempts to group multiple species into overarching encompassing classes, while the latter seeks to break down larger groupings into different species. In Cohen's terms, we might call these the law of totality and the law of plurality. As such, the method of Ethics can be described as a method that employs the law of homogeneity/totality exclusively. However, Kant emphasizes that while the two laws are 'opposed' to one another in theory, one can in practice profitably employ both for different purposes. Thus, while the method of Ethics cannot be responsive to both totality and plurality, human beings *can* do so. See Kant, *Critique of Pure Reason*, B682–B692.

33. One can profitably draw comparisons here with the use of pseudonyms in Kierkegaard's authorship.

34. *RoR* 13; *RV* 15–16. Cohen's ironic description of the "true individuality" conferred by the method of Ethics is strikingly similar to Climacus' description of the consequences of speculative thought's systematizing attempts: "To be a human being has been abolished, and every speculative thinker confuses himself with humankind, whereby he becomes something infinitely great and nothing at all" (*CUP* 124).

35. In a slightly different sense, Adam Zachary Newton also highlights parallels between the interpretation of texts and the ethical 'interpretation' of persons. See his *Narrative Ethics* (Cambridge, MA: Harvard University Press, 1995).

36. If we can link the method of Ethics to a certain mode of reading, it may be that the sphere of religion will likewise correspond to another, different, approach to the particularity of texts.

37. *RoR* 13–14; *RV* 16.

38. *RoR* 14; *RV* 16.

39. *RoR* 14; *RV* 16. Steven Schwarzschild points to this passage in order to express concern that Cohen praises the state too highly and that he appears to ignore the dangerous and threatening elements of the state-structure. However, while Schwarzschild takes this passage at face value, I maintain that Cohen's seeming 'praise' of the state is in fact highly ironized here, and that it is precisely through such irony that he points toward the state's destructive tendencies. See Schwarzschild, "The Democratic Socialism of Hermann Cohen," *Hebrew Union College Annual* 27 (1956): 438.

40. Later in *Religion of Reason*, Cohen reiterates that the "dissolution of the individual is the highest triumph of Ethics. The ethical individual perishes [*geht unter*] as an isolated single being that has its life-basis in its metabolism, and his resurrection is accomplished in the I of the state and, by means of the federation of states, in humanity." *RoR* 178; *RV* 208–209.

41. *RoR* 14; *RV* 16.

42. For the federation of states, see, for example, *RoR* 254, 361–363; *RV* 296–297, 420–421. Cohen's favorable references to humanity are too numerous to list; one of the longest chapters in *Religion of Reason* is entitled "The Idea of the Messiah and Humanity [*Menschheit*]."

43. As late as 1915, Cohen approvingly formulates Kant's categorical imperative as: do *not* regard yourself as an I in the empirical sense, but *only* as the I of humanity. See Cohen's "Deutschtum and Judentum" in *JS* II, 263.

    Regarding the continued upholding of Ethics in *Religion of Reason*, Gabriel Motzkin suggests that Cohen may have been responding to irrationalist trends in the "wartime culture" of Germany—trends that could easily manifest themselves in the enthusiasm of nationalism and *sacro egoismo*. Motzkin writes, "I believe Cohen 'discovered' religious experience as *singular* experience because he wanted to *preserve* science as general experience. *He developed his religious thought not because he wanted to save religion in an age of science, but because he wanted to save science in an age of religion*" (emphases in the original). See Motzkin, "The Problem of Knowledge in Cohen's Philosophy of Religion," in Moses and Wiedebach, *Hermann Cohen's Philosophy of Religion*, 153.

44. This reading of Cohen stands in contrast to Leo Strauss's general hermeneutic, which tends to correlate the apparent presence of two perspectives in a text with exoteric and esoteric positions. See his *Persecution and the Art of Writing* (Glencoe, IL: The Free Press, 1952).

45. *RoR* 14; *RV* 17.

46. This perspective is strikingly exemplified by the famous passage from Kant's *Foundations of the Metaphysics of Morals*, where he presents one of his varied formulations of the categorical imperative: "Handle so, daß du die Menschheit sowohl in deiner Person als in der Person eines jeden anderen, jederzeit zugleich als Zweck, niemals bloß als Mittel brauchst"; "Act so that you treat humanity [*Menschheit*], whether in your own person or in that of another, always as an end and never as a means only" (Kant, *Foundations of the Metaphysics of Morals*, trans. Lewis White Beck [New York: Macmillan, 1959], 4:429). Here, the object of one's ethical treatment is not "the other person"; Kant does not say that one should treat *the other person* as an end and not merely as a means. Rather, that which one treats as an end is *humanity*, an abstract concept which can be found "in"—and is thus distinct from—an individual person. The individual person as such does not enter into the maxim of Ethics and is present only as a bearer of humanity. Likewise, no distinction is made between "your person" and "the person of any other": both are interchangeable vessels for the one significant factor, humanity.

   Interestingly, when Cohen cites Kant's passage in his *Ethik*, he changes the wording slightly; he omits humanity, so that the statement stipulates the treatment of *your person* and the *person* of another: "Handle so, dass Du Deine Person, wie die Person eines jeden Ändern jederzeit zugleich als Zweck, niemals bloss als Mittel brauchst." In this, we can already see Cohen beginning to move toward the individual person and away from 'humanity in general.' See Cohen, *Ethik des reinen Willens*, 320. When Cohen cites this passage in *Religion of Reason*, however, he does in the context of a discussion of "humanity" and so retains Kant's use of the term. See *RoR* 241; *RV* 282.

47. *RoR* 14; *RV* 17. Although Cohen does not focus explicitly on the concept of speech in the main body of his book, his pointing to speech as the source of the You indicates that his mode of reasoning may prefigure the 'linguistic turn' of Rosenzweig's later *Sprachdenken*. Robert Gibbs explores some of the ways in which *Religion of Reason* may have influenced Rosenzweig's account of speech; see his *Correlations in Rosenzweig and Levinas*, 85–88. However, perhaps because he largely follows Altmann's rejection of Rosenzweig's account of Cohen, he does not discuss this passage. This is an unfortunate omission, because the passage would lend support to his broader claim of Cohen's influence on Rosenzweig—but it would also call Altmann's account into question, in that Cohen seems to agree with Rosenzweig that speech can go where autonomous philosophy cannot.

   Almut Bruckstein, on the other hand, finds sources for Rosenzweig's *Sprachdenken* in Cohen's prioritization of oral tradition, although she, like Gibbs, does not discuss the present passage that links the You with speech. See Bruckstein, "Joining the Narrators," in Kepnes et al., *Reasoning After Revelation*, 114–117; also Bruckstein, "Introduction," in Cohen, *Ethics of Maimonides*, xxxvii–xxxviii.

254 Notes to Pages 104–105

In another connection, Eveline Goodman-Thau emphasizes the importance of speech for Cohen's presentation of prayer. See her "Das Gebet zwischen Erkenntnis und Handlung," in *"Religion der Vernunft aus den Quellen des Judentums": Tradition und Ursprungsdenken in Hermann Cohens Spätwerk: Internationale Konferenz in Zürich 1998*, ed. Helmut Holzhey, Gabriel Motzkin, and Hartwig Wiedebach (Hildesheim: Georg Olms Verlag, 2000), 166–174.

48. *RoR* 15; *RV* 17: "[O]nly the You, the discovery of the You, is able to bring me myself to consciousness of my I, to the ethical [*sittlichen*] knowledge of my I."

49. Ketil Bonaunet argues that the inability of Ethics to grasp the individual also reflects the inability of "thinking" to grasp the individual. He directs us in particular to Cohen's statement (in *Der Begriff der Religion*, 86), that "Thought [*Das Denken*] grasps its object only as something general [*als ein Allgemeines*]." This principle will be very important for chapter 5 of this book, where I argue that the concepts of religion correspond to practices that can be *done*, but not *thought* in a consistent manner. See Bonaunet, *Hermann Cohen's Kantian Philosophy of Religion* (Bern: Peter Lang, 2004), 46.

50. *RoR* 15; *RV* 17, emphasis in the original.

51. *RoR* 15–16; *RV* 18. This dilemma seems strikingly related to Gödel's Incompleteness Theorem, which states that for any consistent formal system, there will be a statement that is true but which cannot be proven within that system. Here, the You amounts to the 'statement' that is a true classification within humanity yet cannot be grasped ('proved') by the system of Ethics founded on humanity.

52. *RoR* 16; *RV* 18.

53. Cf. Cohen's statement in his earlier "Ethics of Maimonides" regarding "philosophy's impotence" vis-à-vis the problem of divine attributes. Bruckstein, in her commentary, maintains that this impotence involves philosophy's inability to account for or to ground "ethical thinking as such." See Bruckstein, commentary to Cohen, *Ethics of Maimonides*, 68–70.

Cohen's upholding of the You, as a concept which Ethics and philosophy cannot access, also calls into question Leo Strauss's account of Cohen in the former's introductory essay to *Religion of Reason*. There, Strauss notes, "The Jewish religion might be understood as revealed religion." As such, although a philosopher may still attempt to engage revelation, such an endeavor would itself "not be philosophic since it rests on an assumption that the philosopher as philosopher cannot make." He then states: "Cohen excludes this manner of understanding the relation between philosophy and Judaism by speaking of the religion of reason." In light of what has been discussed here, it seems that Strauss mischaracterizes Cohen, since the concept of the 'You' rests precisely on "an assumption that the philosopher as philosopher cannot make." To be sure, Cohen's account of religion may differ in outward form from more traditional doctrines of revelation. However, it need not be the case that Cohen's speaking of the religion of reason excludes revelation, especially since his definition of reason explicitly goes beyond philosophy. See Strauss, "Introductory Essay," in Cohen, *Religion of Reason*, xxiii.

Interestingly, my account of Cohen sounds very much like Leora Batnitzky's description of Strauss's own position, namely, that "the possibility of philosophical, religious, and political rationalism depends on the *analytical separation* and subsequent *practical coordination* of philosophy and revelation," and that "the relation between revealed religion and philosophy is *philosophically*, thought not politically, irreconcilable." See Leora Batnitzky, *Leo Strauss and Emmanuel Levinas: Philosophy and the Politics of Revelation* (New York: Cambridge University Press, 2006), 14, xxi, emphases in the original. However, Cohen's conception of what such 'practical coordination' entails may differ significantly from Strauss's.

54. Compare the opening pages of Rosenzweig's *Star of Redemption*. There, he mocks the philosophers who claim to overcome the fear of death by abstracting away from the particular individual and by seeking solace in the All (cf. Cohen's *Allheit*, totality). But, Rosenzweig argues, the actual existing human being *still* remains afraid of death, despite the arguments of the philosophers. The appeal of Rosenzweig's assertion lies not in its objective validity, but in what one might call its subjective appeal: the reader identifies and empathizes with Rosenzweig's portrayal of the fragility and precariousness of existence. In contrast, the philosophers themselves would not view Rosenzweig's observation as a successful refutation of their claims; they would argue: if someone is still afraid of death, this is not because death is actually significant, but because that person has not fully wrested away his individuality!

55. *RoR* 16; *RV* 18.

56. I therefore depart slightly, but significantly, from Irene Kajon's account of the relation between religion and Ethics. With regard to the project of making the two consistent, she admits that "it is hard for such an attempt to be successful." However, she then goes on to say, "One can only, then, keep both points of view without, however, renouncing research on the possibility of unifying them." I argue, conversely, that the project of unifying them is not simply difficult, but impossible; one should acknowledge and uphold the paradox, rather than trying to unify them through (theoretical) research. See Kajon, *Contemporary Jewish Philosophy*, 28.

57. Looking at post-Cohenian Jewish thought, Martin Buber's *I and Thou* stands out as a good example of this style of language and writing. Abraham Joshua Heschel also tends in this direction, emphasizing the difference between "descriptive" language, which describes literally and directly, and "indicative" language, which merely points indirectly to ineffable meaning. See Heschel's *God in Search of Man* (New York: Farrar, Straus & Giroux, 1955), 181–182 and his *Man is Not Alone* (Philadelphia: Jewish Publication Society of America, 1951), 21. This style is also often characteristic of mystical compositions that claim that their subject matter cannot be directly conveyed in 'objective' language.

58. Kierkegaard's pseudonymous works (e.g., those authored by Climacus and by anti-Climacus) could serve as an example of this approach.

59. Cf. Climacus' mocking of the philosophers who perpetually claim that "the sys-
    tem" is on the verge of being completed—there are still a few small holes left to fix,
    but it will certainly be finished by "next Sunday." See *CUP* 106–109. The idea of
    holes in an ostensibly self-consistent text also seems akin to a Derridean notion of
    deconstruction.

60. *RoR* 16; *RV* 19 (the Greek appears in Cohen's original text).

61. In Cohen's account of the self which is constituted by and dependent on compas-
    sion for the suffering other, we can see an important precursor to Levinas' account
    of the self that is 'held hostage' by the face of the other. For further comparisons
    between Cohen and Levinas see Edith Wyschogrod, "The Moral Self: Emmanuel
    Levinas and Hermann Cohen," *Daat* 4 (Winter, 1980), 35–58; and Ze'ev Levy,
    "Hermann Cohen and Emmanuel Levinas," in Moses and Wiedebach, *Hermann
    Cohen's Philosophy of Religion*, 133–143.

62. *RoR* 17; *RV* 20.

63. *RoR* 17; *RV* 20. Compassion becomes an "illusion," not only because there is
    there no room in Ethics for passion and compassion, but also because one relates
    to the other as an object, and compassion cannot properly apply to objects. Fur-
    thermore, portraying compassion as illusory can make it harder to actually *be*
    compassionate. It is difficult to pretend to be compassionate if compassion is not
    something real. In a sense, the method of Ethics creates a schizophrenic outlook,
    in that it turns personal relation into something unreal, into a mere role that one
    plays yet is distanced from. See R. D. Laing's *The Divided Self* (New York: Pan-
    theon Books, 1960), in which his contrast of sanity with schizophrenia (influ-
    enced by Buber) shares many features with Cohen's criticism of the method of
    Ethics.

    In contrast to the approach that turns compassion and relationality into an
    illusion, Cohen argues that compassion is precisely that which is *most* real, in that
    it is constitutive of the human self. Compassion even makes possible the reality of
    other objects: without compassion, one would be unable to judge *anything* as
    real, since one would not actually be a human self (who is capable of making such
    judgments).

64. *RoR* 18; *RV* 20.

65. *RoR* 19; *RV* 22.

66. Cohen's non-dualism has parallels in the sources of Judaism: in biblical sources, for
    example, *nefesh* and *neshamah* refer to the living, breathing person as a whole. They
    are not identical to the body (since they are not present in a dead body), but neither
    do they have existence apart from the body. Likewise, according to Daniel Boyarin,
    in classical rabbinic Judaism, "the human being was defined as a body—animated,
    to be sure, by a soul—while for Hellenistic Jews . . . the essence of a human being
    was a soul housed in a body." Boyarin further links these differing views of embod-
    iment to differing methods of interpretation: "[Paul and Philo's] allegorical read-
    ing practice and that of their intellectual descendants is founded on a binary

opposition in which meaning exists as a disembodied substance prior to its incarnation in language, that is, in a dualistic system in which spirit precedes and is primary over body. Midrash, the hermeneutic system of rabbinic Judaism, seems precisely to refuse that dualism, eschewing the inner-outer, visible-invisible, body-soul dichotomies of allegorical reading. Midrash and platonic allegory are alternate techniques of the body." See Boyarin, *Carnal Israel: Reading Sex in Talmudic Culture* (Berkeley: University of California Press, 1993), 5, 9.

Thus, it may be no coincidence that Cohen's criticism of the method of Ethics—which he associates with Plato (see "Der Stil der Propheten," in *JS* I, 263)—and his recovery of the embodied self go hand and hand with his appropriation of midrashic-abductive hermeneutics.

67. In asserting that the concept of sin is applicable only to myself, Cohen can be viewed as extending Kant's 'Copernican revolution.' Kant asserted that we cannot make assertions about things considered 'in themselves,' apart from our human categories of judgment. While Cohen would agree with this basic approach, he would draw further distinctions. While Kant's account applies to certain concepts—namely, objective ones—there are other concepts whose application is restricted even further. With regard to concepts in the sphere of religion, not only can one not make judgments about them considered 'in themselves,' but one also cannot make judgments about them from the general human perspective. One can talk about them only from the perspective of the particular individual, or more precisely, *I* can talk about them only from the perspective of *myself* as an individual.

68. *RoR* 22; *RV* 25.

69. Here, we can draw connections between Cohen's account and Levinas' *non-reciprocal* relation between self and other. There are things that I can say or demand of myself that I cannot say or demand of the other.

Ketil Bonaunet, commenting on this concept of Cohen's, argues that its "asymmetry" is "problematical," in that it appears to eliminate the possibility of attributing accountability and responsibility to others. While this observation seems valid, it may be that the problematic or paradoxical nature of this concept is precisely that which characterizes the sphere of religion as a whole. As such, its appearance here is not necessarily something that should be given a 'solution.' See Bonaunet, *Hermann Cohen's Kantian Philosophy of Religion*, 77–79.

70. Buber also remarks on the significance of Cohen's tendency to slip into the first person. See "Love of God and the Idea of Deity," in *Eclipse of God*, 56.

71. *RoR* 20; *RV* 23, emphasis added.

72. Siegfried Ucko argues, in his *Der Gottesbegriff in der Philosophie Hermann Cohens* (Berlin-Schöneberg: Siegfried Scholem, 1927), that it is specifically uniqueness (*Einzigkeit*) that characterizes God in *Religion of Reason* and that although Cohen uses the term *Einzigkeit* in his *Ethik,* it appears there only as a functional synonym for *Einheit* (unity) and thus lacks the non-totalized particularity of its use in

Religion of Reason (Ucko, 32). Notably, Ucko points to "Der Stil der Propheten" as Cohen's first anticipatory formulation of this later sense of God's uniqueness (Ucko, 30–31, citing Cohen, "Der Stil der Propheten," in *JS* I, 265).

In addition, however, Ucko argues that the concept of God's uniqueness not only moves beyond Ethics, but that it also points beyond Cohen's long-held commitment to "rationalism," toward "the sphere of an irrational being [*die Sphäre eines irrationalen Seins*]" (Ucko, 33). This assessment seems to neglect Cohen's broader sense of reason; while the concept of uniqueness does point beyond reason in its philosophical form, it need not be seen as going beyond the conception of reason that *also*—albeit problematically—includes religion.

73. As noted above, however, Cohen's *Ethik des reinen Willens* does discuss the relationship between I and You. This indicates that, in that book, Cohen may not have fully applied the method of Ethics (as presented in *Religion of Reason*), since the You ought to have been wrested away by its objectifying-abstracting method. Apparently, though, Cohen *was* able to apply it consistently enough so as to preclude the personality of God (cf. *Ethik des reinen Willens*, 453).

74. *RoR* 19; *RV* 22. Cohen's use of 'border' or 'limit' calls to mind Wittgenstein's *Tractatus Logico-Philosophicus*, trans. D. F. Pears and B. F. McGuinness (London: Routledge & Kegan Paul, 1961): "What can be said at all can be said clearly" (preface); "The world is everything that is the case" (1); "The limits [*grenzen*] of language mean the limits [*grenzen*] of my world" (5.6); "Logic pervades the world: the limits of the world are also its limits" (5.61); "So too it is impossible for there to be propositions of ethics. Propositions can express nothing that is higher" (6.42); "It is clear that ethics cannot be put into words. Ethics is transcendental" (6.421); "There are, indeed, things that cannot be put into words. They make themselves manifest. They are what is mystical" (6.522); "What we cannot speak about we must pass over in silence" (7). In this portrayal, only that which can be put into clear propositions can be said to have significance. This criterion mirrors that of the method of Ethics. Yet, there are things at the limits of language, of logic, of the world that cannot be put into propositional form—as Cohen says of the You. What Wittgenstein calls 'ethics' and 'the mystical' appears similar to what Cohen calls 'religion.' However, Cohen and Wittgenstein differ in that the latter (at least in the rhetoric of the *Tractatus*) insists that one must remain silent about such non-propositional matters. While Cohen might agree that we cannot 'speak about' the You, he does not restrict his communication only to the options of direct propositional description and silence. Thus, Cohen might say: what we cannot speak about directly, we must speak about indirectly; what we cannot speak about in a single voice, we must speak about with multiple voices.

75. *RoR* 19; *RV* 22. Here, notably, Cohen's uses the term 'ethical' (*ethische*) not to designate the method of Ethics, but rather to highlight a practical-relational concept (that of compassion) that the method of Ethics cannot access.

76. That is to say, even though the *subject matter* of Ethics may involve practical action, it still gives a *theoretical account* of that non-theoretical subject matter.

77. *RoR* 22; *RV* 26.

78. For instance, the method of Ethics enables one to make the general statement that God is the guarantor of humanity. Here, we should distinguish Cohen's description of the non-theoretical nature of the concept of the God of religion from Kant's account of the theoretical and practical uses of reason. For Kant, the concept of God (which corresponds to what Cohen calls the God of Ethics) belongs to the realm of practical reason, but it is still a theoretical-general concept, since it is produced and legitimated by the objectifying method of philosophy and of Ethics.

CHAPTER 4

1. Other sources for Kierkegaard's views of indirect communication include his "The Point of View for My Work as an Author," (in *The Point of View*, ed. and trans. Howard V. Hong and Edna H. Hong [Princeton, NJ: Princeton University Press, 1998]), as well as the entries grouped under the heading "Communication" in *Søren Kierkegaard's Journals and Papers*, 1:252–319.

    For a recent book-length study that presents Kierkegaard's indirect communication in a manner congenial to my account here, see Genia Schönbaumsfeld, *A Confusion of the Spheres: Kierkegaard and Wittgenstein on Philosophy and Religion* (New York: Oxford University Press, 2007).

2. Even (or especially) if they generally represent 'opposite' points of view, the fact that both of them agree on *this* matter may indicate that what they say in this regard could also be attributed to 'Kierkegaard himself.' However, their usefulness for elucidating Cohen remains independent of this conjecture.

3. Michael Zank, "First Critical Edition of the Writings of Hermann Cohen," *European Association for Jewish Studies Newsletter* 16 (Spring 2005): 52.

4. Steven Schwarzschild, "The Lure of Immanence" in *Pursuit of the Ideal*, 71.

5. Eugene Borowitz, *Choices in Modern Jewish Thought: A Partisan Guide*, 2nd ed. (New York: Behrman House, 1995), 227. Other Cohen-Kierkegaard contrasts include Martin Buber, who writes, "Rosenzweig did not remove himself so far from Kierkegaard as Cohen did" ("Afterword," in *Between Man and Man*, trans. Ronald Gregor-Smith [London: Routledge, 2002], 252). Almut Bruckstein notes that, although Cohen distinguishes between 'the God of Aristotle' and 'the God of Israel,' "in Pascal and Kierkegaard this distinction attains a radically different meaning" (commentary to Cohen, *Ethics of Maimonides*, 50). Irene Kajon asserts that, in *Religion of Reason*, Cohen "is able . . . to establish deep relationships between" such conceptual pairs as "man and God, individuality and humanity," whereas Kierkegaard "radically split[s]" these elements ("Hermann Cohen's Concept of Revelation as a Response to Hegelianism" in Moses and Wiedebach, *Hermann Cohen's Philosophy of Religion*, 116).

6. See, e.g., *RoR* 93; *RV* 108, where Cohen contrasts "the mere realm of theoretical knowledge" with "that of the ethical." See also *RoR* 411; *RV* 477, where "the ethical" is presented as equivalent to "the subjectivity of personality."

7. *CUP* 134.

8. To take one example, Astrid Deuber-Mankowsky employs a Kierkegaardian phrase, "the suspension of the ethical" (*die Suspension des Ethischen*), in order to describe a position that Cohen opposes. While Deuber-Mankowsky is correct in arguing that Cohen does oppose a certain type of "suspension of the ethical," the implicit allusion to Kierkegaard is misleading. Likewise, in arguing for Cohen's preservation of the ethical, she speaks interchangeably of "the ethical" and "Ethics." Thus, she describes "the connection of the ethical and the I" (*die Verbindung von Ethischem und Ich*) alongside "Cohen's grounding of Ethics in the I" (*Cohens Grundlegung der Ethik im Ich*). While the first corresponds with Cohen's usage, the second obscures Cohen's assertion that Ethics (in the strict sense) does not and cannot recognize the individual I. Of course, the fact that Cohen himself does not explicitly emphasize the difference between these terms could be partly to blame for this blurring. See Astrid Deuber-Mankowsky, "Das Gesetz und die Suspension des Ethischen: Jacob Taubes und Hermann Cohen," in *Torah-Nomos-Ius: Abendländischer Antinomismus und der Traum vom herrschaftsfreien Raum*, ed. Gesine Palmer et al. (Berlin: Vorwerk 8, 1999), 257, 260.

9. Similarly, while many of Kierkegaard's pseudonyms might denigrate 'reason' in an Hegelian sense, there are no obvious grounds for asserting that they would oppose Cohen's conception of reason, which "does not exhaust itself in science and philosophy" (*RoR* 7; *RV* 8).

10. Along similar lines, one might also call into question the perceived opposition between Kierkegaard and 'rabbinic Judaism' more generally. A common strain of thought sees Kierkegaard's conception of 'faith' as incompatible with Jewish conceptions; see, for example, Marvin Fox, "Kierkegaard and Rabbinic Judaism," *Judaism* 2, no. 2 (Spring 1953): 160–169 and Milton Steinberg, "Kierkegaard and Judaism," in *Modern Jewish Thought: Selected Issues, 1889–1966* (New York: Arno Press, 1973), 161–180.

Jacob L. Halevi argues, however, that the portrayal of Abraham in *Fear and Trembling* corresponds quite closely to many accounts of the *akedah* in classical rabbinic midrash. See his "Kierkegaard and the Midrash," *Judaism* 4, no. 1 (Winter 1954): 13–28 and "Kierkegaard's Teleological Suspension of the Ethical—Is It Jewish?" *Judaism* 8, no. 4 (Fall 1959): 291–302. Halevi further contends that a key factor in convincing many Jewish interpreters of Kierkegaard's incompatibility of Judaism was Martin Buber's essay "The Question to the Single One." According to Halevi, Buber drastically misrepresents Kierkegaard's account of the ethical and of one's duties to God and to human 'others.' See Halevi, *A Critique of Martin Buber's Interpretation of Soren Kierkegaard* (Ph.D. diss., Hebrew Union College–Jewish Institute of Religion, 1959) and Buber, "The Question to the Single One," in *Between Man and Man*.

Other comparisons of Kierkegaard with pre-Cohenian Jewish religious thought include Abraham Joshua Heschel, *A Passion For Truth* (Woodstock, VT: Jewish Lights Publishing, 1995); Jerome Gellman, *The Fear, the Trembling, and the Fire: Kierkegaard and the Hasidic Masters on the Binding of Isaac* (Lanham, MD: University Press of America, 1994); Jerome Gellman, *Abraham! Abraham! Kierkegaard and the Hasidim on the Binding of Isaac* (Aldershot: Ashgate, 2003).

11. Martin Yaffe, "An Unsung Appreciation of the Musical-Erotic in Mozart's *Don Giovanni*: Hermann Cohen's Nod Toward Kierkegaard's *Either/Or*," in *International Kierkegaard Commentary on Either/Or I*, ed. Robert L. Perkins (Macon, GA.: Mercer University Press, 1995), 73–89. Yaffe's essay is the only article-length piece that I have encountered that is devoted to a sustained comparison between Cohen and Kierkegaard. Alfred Schutz's "Mozart and the Philosophers" (which Yaffe himself draws upon) also contains discussion of Cohen, Kierkegaard, and Dilthey's views of Mozart. See Schutz, *Collected Papers*, vol. 2: *Studies in Social Theory*, ed. Arvid Brodersen (The Hague: Martinus Nijhoff, 1964).

12. Sylvain Zac, *La philosophie religieuse de Hermann Cohen* (Paris: J. Vrin, 1984), 127, my translation.

13. Robert Jan Van Pelt and Carroll William Westfall, *Architectural Principles in the Age of Historicism* (New Haven, CT: Yale University Press, 1991), 79.

14. Pierfrancesco Fiorato, *Geschichtliche Ewigkeit: Ursprung und Zeitlichkeit in der Philosophie Hermann Cohens* (Würzburg: Königshausen & Neumann, 1993), 168.

15. Bonaunet, *Hermann Cohen's Kantian Philosophy of Religion*, 94, 117. Bonaunet also argues, however, that Cohen opposes the idea of a teleological suspension of the ethical (118). As indicated above, it seems to me that Cohen's de-absolutizing of Ethics can be viewed as very much analogous to de Silentio's teleological suspension of the ethical.

16. Samuel Hugo Bergman, "Hermann Cohen" in *Between East and West: Essays Dedicated to the Memory of Bela Horovitz*, ed. A. Altmann (London: East and West Library, 1958), 43. While some details of Bergman's account of Cohen might stand in need of correction by more recent scholarship, his sense of the general parallels between Cohen and Kierkegaard still seems valid. Bergman reiterates Cohen's similarity to Kierkegaard in his *Dialogical Philosophy from Kierkegaard to Buber*, trans. Arnold Gerstein (Albany: State University of New York Press, 1991), 153.

17. In addition to Bergman, "Hermann Cohen," 43, see also Steven Schwarzschild, "Democratic Socialism of Hermann Cohen," 421–425; Schwarzschild, "Modern Jewish Philosophy," in *The Pursuit of the Ideal*, 230–231; Dussort, *L'école de Marbourg*, 66.

18. Cohen, *Ethik des reinen Willens*, 331–332. At the same time, it is noteworthy that this opposition to Hegelian closure is located within Cohen's *Ethik*—the central volume in Cohen's project of constructing a totalizing system of knowledge! Thus, there are certainly Hegelian tendencies in Cohen's thought that stand alongside his anti-Hegelian proclamations. (For more in this regard, see Poma, *Critical Philosophy*

of Hermann Cohen, 287–289.) However, it is the anti-Hegelian and anti-totalizing modes that come to the fore most strongly in *Religion of Reason* and that are most relevant to my analysis of Cohen's style.

19. *CUP* 118.

20. See Ronald Green, *Kierkegaard and Kant: The Hidden Debt* (Albany: State University of New York Press, 1992).

21. Ulrich Knappe, *Theory and Practice in Kant and Kierkegaard* (Berlin: Walter de Gruyter, 2004).

22. Moses Mendelssohn, *Philosophical Writings*, ed. Daniel O. Dahlstrom (Cambridge: Cambridge University Press, 1997), 141–142. As we will see in subsequent chapters, there are suggestive parallels between the 'mixedness' of Mendelssohn's conception and the 'mixedness' of Cohen's double-voiced style, as well the internal conceptual 'mixedness' of the infinitesimal.

23. Willi Goetschel, *Spinoza's Modernity: Mendelssohn, Lessing, and Heine* (Madison: University of Wisconson Press, 2004), 98.

24. Goetschel, *Spinoza's Modernity*, 98.

25. Goetschel, *Spinoza's Modernity*, 94. Cohen also explicitly differentiates affects from the passions; see *RoR* 451; *RV* 520.

26. Goetschel, *Spinoza's Modernity*, 103.

27. Goetschel, *Spinoza's Modernity*, 105.

28. See Mendelssohn, *Philosophical Writings*, 150–151, on the subordination of sentiment to rational analysis, and cf. *RoR* 160; *RV* 186, where Cohen emphasizes the importance of uniting intellect, feeling, and will under the governance of the rational unity of consciousness.

29. Cohen, *Ästhetik des reinen Gefühls*, vol. 1, 94.

30. Cohen, *Ästhetik des reinen Gefühls*, vol. 1, 95.

31. Cohen, *Ästhetik des reinen Gefühls*, vol. 1, 97–98. Cohen echoes this notion in *Religion of Reason*, where he describes pure aesthetic feeling, identified with love, as "a new power of consciousness." See *RoR* 160; *RV* 186.

32. Cohen, *Ästhetik des reinen Gefühls*, vol. 1, 92.

33. See *RoR* 17; *RV* 19. Cohen repeatedly emphasizes the connection of affects to the sphere of religion: see, for example, *RoR* 139–142, 150, 160–162, 236, 374, 404, 451; *RV* 161–164, 174, 186–188, 276, 434–435, 468–469, 520.

34. See *RoR* 17–18, 132, 136, 140; *RV* 20–21, 153, 158, 162.

35. See *CUP* 61–125. For a recent overview of Kierkegaard's relation to Lessing, as well as an extensive bibliography of previous scholarship linking the two, see Curtis L. Thompson, "Gotthold Ephraim Lessing: Appropriating the Testimony of a Theological Naturalist," in *Kierkegaard and the Renaissance and Modern Traditions. Tome 1: Philosophy*, ed. Jon Stewart (Surrey, UK: Ashgate, 2009), 77–112. Gérard Vallée, in his study of Lessing's relation to religion, has also emphasized the double-sided "oscillating" of Lessing's style and approach, with striking parallels to my presentation of Cohen's style. See Vallée, *Soundings in G. E. Lessing's Philosophy of*

Religion (Lanham, MD: University Press of America, 2000), esp. 102–103, 107–109, 117–118.

36. Michael Zank also points to some key intermediate links in a chain of thought running from Mendelssohn to Cohen, including Wilhelm von Humboldt, Friedrich Schleiermacher, August Boeckh, and Cohen's own teacher Heymann Steinthal. Of particular import for the question of style and communication, Zank maintains that Cohen's concern for hermeneutics, aesthetics, and theory of language can be traced to this intellectual heritage. See Zank, *Idea of Atonement*, 11, as well as 213–214, 218–30. Dieter Adelmann provides further details to some of these links in his "H. Steinthal und Hermann Cohen," in Moses and Wiedebach, *Hermann Cohen's Philosophy of Religion*. In beginning to map some of these connections onto Kierkegaard, we could point to the possible influence of Schleiermacher on Kierkegaard's multi-persona literary style, as argued by Richard Crouter in his *Friedrich Schleiermacher: Between Enlightenment and Romanticism* (Cambridge: Cambridge University Press, 2005), esp. 109–119, in a chapter entitled, "Kierkegaard's Not So Hidden Debt to Schleiermacher."

37. Karl Barth, *Epistle to the Romans*, trans. from the sixth edition by Edwyn C. Hoskins (New York: Oxford University Press, 1968), 22. For more on Barth's connection to Cohen, see Simon Fisher, *Revelatory Positivism? Barth's Earliest Theology and the Marburg School* (Oxford: Oxford University Press, 1988) and John Lyden, "The Influence of Hermann Cohen on Karl Barth's Dialectical Theology" in *Modern Judaism* 12, no. 2 (May 1992): 167–183.

38. Bergman states, "I do not think Cohen read Kierkegaard, even though it was not impossible at the time" (*Dialogical Philosophy*, 153). He offers the same assessment in "Hermann Cohen," 39. Schutz, however, argues that Cohen's analysis of Mozart indicates that he was familiar with Kierkegaard's writings, especially *Either/Or* ("Mozart and the Philosophers," 186). Yaffe concurs with Schutz on this point ("Unsung Appreciation," 74–75). Both Schutz and Yaffe acknowledge, though, that Cohen never mentions Kierkegaard by name, and so their claim remains an unverified, though intriguing, conjecture. It seems possible, for instance, that Cohen could have been familiar with a 'Kierkegaardian' interpretation of *Don Giovanni* without having actually read Kierkegaard's text. One piece of evidence for this latter possibility is indicated by the presence in Cohen's personal library of Georg Brandes' *Sören Kierkegaard: Ein literarisches Charakterbild* (Leipzig: Johann Ambrosius Barth, 1879). Brandes' book was the first academic study in German of Kierkegaard's philosophy and life. Among other topics, it includes a chapter on "Don Juan," which expounds Kierkegaard's view of Mozart's opera as put forth in *Either/Or* (see Brandes, 116–125). Additionally, Cohen's copy of Brandes' book is inscribed "Herrn Prof. Steinthal ergebnest vom Verfasser [To Prof. Steinthal, sincerely, from the author]." See Hartwig Wiedebach, *Die Hermann-Cohen Bibliothek* (Hildesheim: Georg Olms Verlag, 2000), 69. "Steinthal" presumably refers to Heymann Steinthal, one of Cohen's earliest academic mentors. (Interestingly, Brandes

cites Steinthal in a footnote on page 177 of his Kierkegaard book.) Thus, it appears that Cohen received the book from Steinthal, who had himself received it from Brandes. Brandes' book could have provided Cohen with the basic outline of Kierkegaard's interpretation of *Don Giovanni*, without Cohen having read *Either/Or* itself. Although it is not clear when Cohen first received or read Brandes' book, it may be the case that Cohen also learned from it about other aspects of Kierkegaard's philosophy. In particular, chapter 21 treats of "das Paradoxe" and discusses the *Concluding Unscientific Postscript* (see Brandes, 166–182).

39. Kierkegaard's texts became increasingly prominent in German culture beginning around the last decade of Cohen's life. See Habib C. Malik, *Receiving Søren Kierkegaard: The Early Impact and Transmission of His Thought* (Washington, DC: Catholic University of America Press, 1997). Judging from Malik's account, Jews (among them Georg Brandes) appear to comprise a strikingly high proportion of the earliest German-language intellectuals to take note of Kierkegaard, although Malik himself does not remark on this trend. If this represented a general pattern in German-Jewish intellectual circles, the likelihood of Cohen's indirect exposure to Kierkegaard is further increased, as his own intellectual milieu, especially in his Berlin years, was probably largely Jewish.

40. See *CUP* 197–199.

41. *CUP* 80. See also *CUP* 357: "The subjective *thinker's form*, the form of his communication, is his *style*. His form must be just as manifold as are the opposites that he holds together" (emphasis in the original).

42. *CUP* 85.

43. See *CUP* 475: "True religiousness ... is distinguished by invisibility."

44. *CUP* 87. Climacus treats Socrates as a prime example of an existing subjective thinker who thus combines pathos with the comic (*CUP* 87–89). Notably, Cohen also identifies Socrates as one for whom the negative, in the form of irony, is inextricably linked to the positive, in the form of truthfulness. See Cohen, *Ethik des reinen Willens*, 530–531.

45. *CUP* 87.

46. *CUP* 89–90.

47. Elsewhere, Climacus contrasts one-sided pathos with "pathos in the form of contrast," which "remains with the communicator even when expressed, and cannot be appropriated directly except through the other's *self*-activity" (*CUP* 242, emphasis in the original). The form of contrast makes passive appropriation by consciousness and by the understanding impossible, and demands the active engagement of the existential individual self.

48. Even if a given interpretation lay 'midway between' the two poles, it would still be halfway vague, as well as halfway depersonalized.

49. The *equal* importance of each perspective must be especially emphasized. One must avoid the temptation to say, "Yes, I can see how one *could* view God in impersonal terms, but in the end, God is *really* a person."

50. Cf. Climacus' conception of "the dialectical." He writes, "In a human being there is always a desire, at once comfortable and concerned, to have something really firm and fixed that can exclude the dialectical, but this is cowardliness and fraudulence toward the divine. Even the most certain of all, a revelation, *eo ipso* [precisely thereby] becomes dialectical when I am to appropriate it; even the most fixed of all, an infinite negative resolution, which is the individuality's infinite form of God's being within him, promptly becomes dialectical. As soon as I take away the dialectical, I am superstitious and defraud God of the moment's strenuous acquisition of what was once acquired. It is, however, far more comfortable to be objective and superstitious, boasting about it and proclaiming thoughtlessness" (*CUP* 35n). Note that the dialectical nature arises precisely when appropriation is to take place. Thus, it is not the case that the concepts are dialectical until personal appropriation occurs or that such appropriation will remove the dialectical. Rather, the more a person is able to appropriate the concepts, the more dialectical and thus destabilized they should seem to that person.
51. *CUP* 65.
52. *CUP* 65.
53. *CUP* 141–142, emphasis in the original.
54. *CUP* 167, emphasis in the original.
55. *CUP* 173.
56. *CUP* 171.
57. As Climacus later states, "the language of abstraction really does not allow the difficulty of existence and of the existing person to come up" (*CUP* 304).
58. Climacus indicates that verbalization of any form poses a risk of objectification; one is faced with "the inadequacy of language, because, compared with existing in actuality, language is very abstract" (*CUP* 465).
59. Cf. *RoR* 378; *RV* 440, and Cohen's *Der Begriff der Religion*, 116.
60. See *RoR* 22; *RV* 25.
61. Kierkegaard, *Practice in Christianity*, ed. and trans. Howard V. Hong and Edna H. Hong (Princeton, NJ: Princeton University Press, 1992), 125.
62. Kierkegaard, *Practice in Christianity*, 125. Anti-Climacus' emphasis on the unity of jest and earnestness is very similar to Climacus' account of the way in which the subjective existing thinker has just as much of the comic as of pathos.
63. Kierkegaard, *Practice in Christianity*, 125.
64. Kierkegaard, *Practice in Christianity*, 133.
65. Kierkegaard, *Practice in Christianity*, 133. It also seems that such a communication could produce the opposite result: the atheist sees it as a defense of the faith and the most orthodox sees it as an attack.
66. Kierkegaard, *Practice in Christianity*, 134.
67. Here, it is important to distinguish between two types of consistent, impersonal hypotheses. In one type, the reader seeks, in Anti-Climacus' words, to "form a judgment about what is presented." I argue that a hypothesis of this sort will be unable

to account for that which Cohen seeks to communicate. However, another type of hypothesis seeks to form a judgment not about *what* is communicated, but about the act of communicating. This is the kind of hypothesis that is put forth in the present book: while one cannot impersonally comprehend the religious concepts themselves, one can assess, in a more objective and impersonal manner, what Cohen is *doing*, i.e., how he uses Scripture and philosophy in an attempt to communicate.

68. Recall *RoR* 31; *RV* 36 (discussed in the previous chapter), where Cohen raises the idea of "a contradiction in principles" that need not be "a contradiction in the consciousness of the persons."

69. See *RoR* 95; *RV* 110.

70. Kierkegaard, *Practice in Christianity*, 133.

71. See Michael Fishbane, *Biblical Myth and Rabbinic Mythmaking* (New York: Oxford University Press, 2003), 110 and Appendix II, 325–401. See also Moshe Halbertal, "If it were not a written verse, it could not be said" (Hebrew), *Tarbiz* 68 (1998), 39–59.

72. Both Climacus (*CUP* 73) and Anti-Climacus (*Practice in Christianity*, 133) use the term "double-reflection" to describe the individual's inherently personal and non-general relation to such concepts.

73. See *CUP* 74–77, where Climacus gives several examples of ideas whose inherently personal nature is distorted through direct communication.

74. *CUP* 74.

75. See *RoR* 11–13; *RV* 12–15.

76. Recall that Cohen, in his introduction, links his methodological stringency with his efforts to avoid the notion of a conflict between duties to man and duties to God. See the last section in my chapter 2, and *RoR* 32–33; *RV* 37–39.

77. See *RoR* 213; *RV* 249.

78. Which is also to say: as personal and as subjective, in Climacus' sense of the word.

79. BT Sanhedrin 34a. After the passage cited above, the Talmud goes on to say, "In the school of Rabbi Ishamel it was taught: '[Is not my word like fire, declares the Lord,] and like a hammer that shatters the rock?' [Jer. 23:29]. Just as the hammer produces many sparks [when it strikes the rock], so one verse produces multiple meanings."

80. The juxtaposition of multiple interpretations is a common feature of classical rabbinic midrash. After one interpretation is given, the midrashic text will say, *davar aher*, "another interpretation," before offering a different reading of the same verse. Steven Fraade argues that the redactors of midrashic collections deliberately present multiple interpretations for specific pedagogical-communicative purposes. See his *From Tradition to Commentary: Torah and Its Interpretation in the Midrash Sifre to Deuteronomy* (Albany: State University of New York Press, 1991). In this sense, then, the communicative multiplicity of Cohen's text may have a precedent in the rabbinic modes of reasoning that he approvingly presents in his introduction to *Religion of Reason*.

81. Cf. *CUP* 85–86, where Climacus describes the existing subjective thinker who is "continually striving" and "continually in the process of becoming," and who consequently is "never finished" and has no "results."

82. In chapter 6, I develop the ways in which Cohen presents religious ideas as having a type of *dynamic* actuality, or actuality in the infinitesimal moment. Here, I am primarily concerned to emphasize the ways in which their lack of *static* actuality prevents Cohen from speaking in his own voice.

83. Climacus frequently contrasts the perspective of an existing human being to the way matters would appear *sub specie aeterni*, from the perspective of eternity. Many religio-philosophic assertions go astray by forgetting that human beings are existing, and not purely eternal. As such, that which they assert "is indeed actually that way for God, but it is not that way for any existing spirit, because this spirit, itself existing, is in the process of becoming" (*CUP* 190). Likewise, Cohen emphasizes that it is necessary "to distinguish God's being from all the temporality of *becoming*" (*RoR* 46; *RV* 53, emphasis in the original). With man, however, the situation is the opposite: while God's holiness is bound up with God's being, man's holiness is a task that "can have no termination, therefore cannot be a permanent rest, but only infinite striving and becoming" (*RoR* 111; *RV* 129). Thus, in relation to Cohen's project, Scripture (as God's word) can present things as they are "for God" in a way that existing human beings cannot.

84. *CUP* 358.

85. See *CUP* 195.

86. Cf. *CUP* 243: "No anonymous author can more slyly hide himself, and no maieutic can more carefully recede from a direct relation than God can. He is in the creation, everywhere in the creation, but he is not there directly, and only when the single individual turns inward into himself (consequently only in the inwardness of self-activity) does he become aware and capable of seeing God." See also *CUP* 138: "In fables and fairy tales there is a lamp called the wonderful lamp; when it is rubbed, the spirit appears. Jest! But freedom, that is the wonderful lamp. When a person rubs it with ethical passion, God comes into existence for him." Here, the implication is that if a person does not rub the lamp of freedom, then God, as it were does not exist. A similar dynamic is displayed in Sifre Deuteronomy, Piska 346: "'You are my witnesses, declares the Lord, and I am God' [Is. 43:12]—when you are my witnesses, I am God, and when you are not my witnesses, as it were, I am not God. Likewise, 'I lift up my eyes to you, the one who is enthroned in the heavens' [Ps. 123:1]—if not for me [lifting up my eyes], as it were, you would not be enthroned in the heavens."

87. Again, even this 'content' is only of a practical, and not a theoretical, nature.

88. *CUP* 196.

89. *CUP* 190.

90. *CUP* 156.

91. *CUP* 305.

92. See *CUP* 388: "The point here as everywhere is to keep the specific spheres separated from one another, to respect the qualitative dialectic, the tug of decision that changes everything, so that what was the highest in another sphere must be absolutely rejected in this."

93. *CUP* 305.

94. *CUP* 305.

95. *CUP* 305.

96. Irene Kajon sees *Religion of Reason* as motivated by a similar opposition to Hegel: "Cohen establishes connections not only between God and human beings, but also beyond the individual and humanity in general, life in time and life beyond time, human beings and history or nature. Instead of Hegelian mediation which unifies these elements until they lose their identity in a third element, there is in *Religion of Reason* the meeting of these different elements in a spiritual force or feeling which never transforms itself into a substance." See Kajon, "Hermann Cohen's Concept of Revelation as a Response to Hegelianism," in Moses and Wiedebach, *Hermann Cohen's Philosophy of Religion*, 112.

97. Climacus states that if a person employs "direct utterance" in an attempt to communicate existential truth, "the form of the communication interferes, just as when the tongue of an epileptic utters the wrong word, although the speaker may not notice it as clearly as the epileptic" (*CUP* 82).

98. *CUP* 136, 162.

99. *CUP* 242.

100. It is important to emphasize that Climacus does not reject objective thinking entirely, but only when it is misapplied to properly subjective ethico-religious concepts. As he states, "It is always to be borne in mind that I am speaking of the religious, in which objective thinking, if it is supposed to be supreme, is downright irreligiousness. But wherever objective thinking is within its rights, its direct communication is also in order, precisely because it is not supposed to deal with subjectivity" (*CUP* 76). See also *CUP* 93: "That objective thinking has its reality [*Realitet*] is not denied, but in relation to all thinking in which precisely subjectivity must be accentuated it is a misunderstanding."

101. See *CUP* 275n.

102. *CUP* 228.

103. Cohen explicitly refers to the biblical root *y-d-'a*. See *RoR* 51; *RV* 59.

104. *RoR* 51; *RV* 59. In some places, it appears as though Climacus uses the term "knowledge" unqualifiedly to designate theoretical, objective knowledge. Thus, he states that ethico-religious matters must not be "communicated as knowledge" (*CUP* 249). However, he refers elsewhere to "essential knowing," which he describes as "knowing whose relation to existence is essential" and which stands in contrast to objective knowing (*CUP* 197). Thus, it is not "knowledge" per se that that distorts ethico-religious matters, but only impersonal, indifferent knowledge.

As such, we need not view Cohen's emphasis on the knowledge of God as putting him in conflict with Climacus' account.

105. Cf. *CUP* 380, where Climacus warns against the mistake of thinking that "Christianity is empty of content because it is not a doctrine," i.e., because it is not something with directly assertable content.

106. Referring to his earlier book, *Philosophical Fragments*, Climacus notes that "[r]eligiously, there is no pupil and no teacher" and that "the teacher is only the occasion." See *CUP* 573n and *Philosophical Fragments*, 14–18; 23–36.

107. *RoR* 34; *RV* 39.

108. See, e.g., *RoR* 106; *RV* 123: "Judaism in its biblical sources does not philosophize."

109. *RoR* 37–38; *RV* 44. Eliezer Schweid emphasizes that for Cohen, a key element of the Bible's naïveté lay in the fact that it presented different strata of tradition alongside one another—such that "the earliest layers at times express religious and ethical ideas incompatible with those expressed in the later strata"—without feeling the compulsion to smooth out those incompatibilities. Instead, it is in seeing the difference between the ideas that one can discern their dynamic development. See Schweid, "Hermann Cohen's Biblical Exegesis" in Holzhey et al., *"Religion der Vernunft aus den Quellen des Judentums": Tradition und Ursprungsdenken in Hermann Cohens Spätwerk*, 361.

In a similar manner, the communicative value of Cohen's multiple 'incompatible' voices is not found in any one of them, but in the relation and dynamic movement between them.

110. For example, the biblical text frequently employs the term 'You' in relation to God, and does not, as a rule, talk about 'God in Godself,' as an object separate from God's relation to human beings or to creation. Cf. Cohen's observation that the psalms "sing neither of God alone, nor of man alone" (*RoR* 58; *RV* 67).

111. In terms of the various dangers Cohen discusses in his introduction, it might be easier to de-egoize/de-mythify potentially egoistic or mythical concepts than to re-personalize/de-objectify totalized concepts.

112. See *CUP* 293. It may also be the case that there are certain concepts that caused confusion in other cultures but that do *not* cause confusion in our own.

113. *CUP* 160.

CHAPTER 5

1. *RoR* 79; *RV* 91, emphasis in the original.

2. *RoR* 127; *RV* 147.

3. *RoR* 419; 486–487. Again, Cohen's description is largely borrowed directly from Scripture. The "tears" description alludes to Ps. 6:7, while "intestines burn" draws upon Lam. 1:20.

4. *RoR* 405; *RV* 470.

5. *RoR* 294; *RV* 343.

6. *RoR* 442; *RV* 510. While Cohen does not explicitly connect the notion of God-human friendship to any specific scriptural verses, he may have in mind such passages as Ex. 33:11: "The Lord spoke to Moses face to face, as a man speaks to his friend [*re'ehu*]"; Is. 41:8, in which God describes Abraham as "my friend/lover [*ohavi*]"; and Jer. 3:4, where Israel is said to call God "the friend [*aluf*] of my youth."

7. *RoR* 41, 42; *RV* 48. See also "Einheit oder Einzigkeit Gottes" (*JS* I, 90–91), where Cohen, reasoning from God's self-revelation in Ex. 3:14, comments, "Thus it is already characteristic that this Being is designated not in the neuter, but as an I."

8. *RoR* 41; *RV* 48.

9. Rosenzweig's "A Note on Anthropomorphisms," in *God, Man, and the World*, ed. and trans. Barbara Galli (Syracuse, NY: Syracuse University Press, 1998), distinguishes between 'anthropomorphism' (with quotation marks) and anthropomorphism (without quotation marks) (143). He uses the former to designate the forms of biblical language that have raised rationalistic hackles among some philosophers, who have therefore tried to explain them away. In opposition to this, Rosenzweig argues that the Bible's language should not be viewed as problematic, since it describes only "meetings between God and man," (138) in contrast to genuine anthropomorphism (without quotation marks), which attempts to describe God Godself, apart from man. According to Leora Batnitzky (*Idolatry and Representation* [Princeton, NJ: Princeton University Press, 2000], 21), Cohen and Maimonides, as exemplars of rationalism, are the chief targets of Rosenzweig's criticisms. However, Rosenzweig's essay never mentions Cohen (or Maimonides, for that matter) by name. I would argue, furthermore, that Cohen is *not* averse to biblical language in the manner of Rosenzweig's 'rationalists,' as evidenced by his own use of strongly personal language, drawn from the biblical text, when speaking of the individual's relation to God. Rather, Cohen's opposition to anthropomorphism applies primarily to what Rosenzweig calls "genuine" anthropomorphism. At the same time, Cohen does retain a concern (which Rosenzweig does not seem to share) that even the biblical language *can lead* to anthropomorphism if it is approached wrongly. Thus, Cohen is careful to balance his biblically inflected statements with a 'contradictory' philosophical perspective, so that concepts that should be strictly regulative and relational are not treated as constitutive.

10. Later in the same paragraph, Cohen refers to "the danger that is indeed linked with the [notion of] person" (*RoR* 42; *RV* 49). Thus, the danger is linked to (and may even follow inevitably from), but is not identical with, the notion of person.

11. *RoR* 144; *RV* 167.

12. *RoR* 145; *RV* 168.

13. *RoR* 144; *RV* 168. See also *RoR* 51, 295; *RV* 59, 343.

14. *RoR* 145; *RV* 168.

15. Cohen, "Der Stil der Propheten," in *JS* I, 263.

16. Notably, the apparent impossibility of such religious love in relation to God also applies to religious love in relation to the fellowman. The idea of a personal yet non-erotic love of another human raises a baffled response from Cohen's imaginary interlocutor: "How is the selfish man able to love another, the same selfish man who can supposedly only love the woman, the flesh of his flesh? Is it not an illusion, this transference, this metaphor of sexual love?" This skeptical attitude corresponds to Cohen's observation in his introduction, that the concept of the 'You' seems impossible from the perspective of the method of philosophy and Ethics. As in his introduction, he points to compassion as the solution to this apparent impossibility. Must such non-selfish love be illusion or metaphor? "No—as compassion, this love ceases to carry the suspicion of being a metaphor" (*RoR* 146; *RV* 170). In the case of both man and God, however, the problem of religious love does ultimately lack a *theoretical* solution and remains an offense to a purely philosophical and objective approach.

17. *RoR* 44; *RV* 51.

18. *RoR* 33; *RV* 38. Cf. *CUP* 332: "God does not exist [*existere*]; he is eternal."

19. *RoR* 159–160; *RV* 185. Cohen also denies that God has any "biological life" and that God "is living in the sense of living creatures" (*RoR* 160, 413; *RV* 185, 480).

20. Thus, Steven Schwarzschild ("The Title of Hermann Cohen's 'Religion of Reason out of the Sources of Judaism'" in *RoR*, 17) renders Cohen's "Gott ist nicht wirklich" (*RoR* 413; *RV* 480) as "God is not real."

21. Pierfrancesco Fiorato describes Cohen's "theology of the 'in'-existence of God" as "the most scandalous face of Cohen's loyalty to anti-ontologism." See Fiorato, "Notes on Future and History in Hermann Cohen's Anti-Eschatological Messianism," in Munk, *Hermann Cohen's Critical Idealism*, 145.

22. *RoR* 44; *RV* 51.

23. *RoR* 160; *RV* 185.

24. *RoR* 160; *RV* 185. Note that, according to Cohen, the Bible itself is not free of anthropomorphism. However, the type of anthropomorphism that Cohen wants to combat relates specifically to God's sensibility, and not to God's personality or relationality. In addition, Cohen's general interpretive attitude requires us to clarify what it means to talk about anthropomorphism 'in' the Bible. A text can use anthropomorph*ic* language, but anthropomorph*ism* is an error that applies specifically to a conceptualization or interpretation, which can be found only in an individual human being. In other words, there are elements in the Bible that, if interpreted sensually, can lead a reader to anthropomorphism. Those same elements, though, if interpreted in a personal-relational (yet non-sensual) way, need not result in anthropomorphism. Thus, anthropomorphism would not be strictly 'in' the Bible itself, but rather *between* the biblical text and its reader. In general, Cohen's approach to the Bible in *Religion of Reason* displays this latter conception (see especially *RoR* 4; *RV* 4–5). In this regard, his approach seems more hermeneutically attuned than that displayed by Rosenzweig in "A Note on Anthropomorphism," who, reacting to the claim that biblical language constitutes anthropomorphism, argues that the Bible

does *not* contain anthropomorphisms. In contrast, Cohen might say that the biblical formulations neither 'are' nor 'are not' anthropomorphisms, but that they *can be* anthropomorphisms, depending on whether they are *taken* relationally or sensually, regulatively or constitutively.

25. *RoR* 160–161; *RV* 185.

26. See, e.g., Buber, who, drawing upon Pascal, characterizes 'God as idea' as representative of "the God of the philosophers," in contrast to "the God of Abraham." Likewise, Emil Fackenheim contrasts "Cohen's God-idea" with "the existing God of Judaism." See Buber, "Love of God and the Idea of Deity," in *Eclipse of God*, 49; "Die Liebe zu Gott und die Gottesidee" in *Gottesfinsternis* (Gerlingen: Lambert Schneider, 1994), 51. See also Emil Fackenheim, "Hermann Cohen—after Fifty Years" in his *Jewish Philosophers and Jewish Philosophy*, 52.

27. A similar distinction is made by Kant in his critique of the ontological argument, when he notes that while my financial assets may be aided by a hundred actual dollars, they are not similarly aided by the mere concept of a hundred dollars. (In that instance, however, he uses this distinction to *oppose* those who want to argue that God is 'more than an idea.') See Kant, *Critique of Pure Reason*, B627.

28. Kant, *Critique of Pure Reason*, B383.

29. *RoR* 160; *RV* 185.

30. Buber, "Love of God and the Idea of Deity," in *Eclipse of God*, 59; "Die Liebe zu Gott und die Gottesidee," in *Gottesfinsternis*, 61: "Aber wäre es sogar richtig, daß man in der »sinnlichen« Liebe (vielmehr: in der sinnlichkeitsumfassenden Liebe) nur die idealisierte Person liebe, so wäre damit keineswegs gesagt, daß man da nur die Idee der Person liebe: auch die idealisierte Person bleibt eine Person und wird nicht zur Idee."

31. In Gabriel Motzkin's reading of this passage, "love is taken here to be differentiating the physical person from some other ideal aspect, and therefore in some way reconstituting the person. This conception cannot help but be much like the Platonic notion of idea." While this has similarities to my reading, it can also create an impression of a (Platonic) physical-spiritual dualism. In accord with Cohen's embrace of the embodiment of the self, I would argue that Cohen does differentiate the ideal 'You' from every specific physical attribute, but not from the physical person as such. That is, the 'You' can be described as not not-physical. See Motzkin, "Love and Knowledge in Cohen's 'Religion of Reason,'" in Holzhey et al., *"Religion der Vernunft aus den Quellen des Judentums": Tradition und Ursprungsdenken in Hermann Cohens Spätwerk*, 98.

32. Kenneth Seeskin also explicates Cohen's position by arguing for the equivalence of loving God as an idea and loving God as a person. However, he does so by *redefining* 'person' in terms of normativity (rather than in terms of particularity and individuality) in order to make it philosophically and theoretically compatible with 'idea.' In contrast, I argue that 'God as person' and 'God as idea' should remain theoretically incompatible, and that their 'equivalence' is strictly a practical-functional one.

See Seeskin, *Jewish Philosophy in a Secular Age* (Albany: State University of New York Press, 1990), 115.

33. Similarly, Cohen's description of God as "an archetype of ethicality" and as "the ethical ideal" (see *RoR* 160–162; *RV* 186–188) can also be understood as intimately connected with a personal love and relation. While 'archetype' and 'ideal' may sound impersonal, Cohen also describes them as a model for emulation, alluding to the tradition of *imitatio dei*, and citing the rabbinic formulation (BT Shabbat 133b) of "As God is compassionate, so you are to be compassionate" (*RoR* 162; *RV* 188). Thus, Cohen never explicitly denies that the archetype is personal, and the closer he gets to source-texts, the more he is able to use personal language himself.

    Note too that Kant refers to the ethical archetype in personal terms, associating it with the figure of Christ. While Kant's presentation of the archetype, in comparison to Cohen's, might be more humanized (as distinguished from 'personalized'), it corroborates the idea that 'archetype' need not be impersonal. See Kant, *Religion Within the Limits of Reason Alone*, 54–72.

34. For example, Buber writes, "It is only because the person whom I idealize actually exists that I can love the idealized one." Here, "actually" designates precisely one of the chief attributes that, because of its connection to sensuality, Cohen explicitly denies to God. "Love of God and the Idea of Deity," in *Eclipse of God*, 59; "Die Liebe zu Gott und die Gottesidee," in *Gottesfinsternis*, 61: "nur weil es die Person, die ich idealisiere, wirklich gibt, kann ich die idealisierte lieben."

35. Cohen himself recognizes this concern when he writes, "It is as if [*als ob*] God's being were actual [*aktuell*] in man's knowledge only, so powerful is the effect of the correlation. Man is no longer merely the creature of God, but his reason, by virtue of his knowledge and also for the sake of it, makes him at least subjectively, as it were [*gleichsam*], the discoverer of God." (*RoR* 88; *RV* 103). Here, Cohen emphasizes that because God is not *objectively or theoretically separate* from the human being, it can *appear* as if God had no independence apart from the human being's act of conceiving. However, with his use of "as if" and "as it were," he indicates that one should not mistake that appearance for a constitutive determination of the God-human relationship.

    Cohen's use of "as if" in this instance may also be an ironic allusion to Hans Vaihinger's well-known *Die Philosophie des Als Ob*, first published in 1911. Vaihinger, claiming to be drawing upon Kant, proposes that one should view God (as well as other notions that experience cannot verify) as a useful fiction: one should act and believe 'as if' there were a God, even though there are no rational grounds for such an assertion. Cohen reverses this proposal, maintaining that the fictive 'as if' applies instead to the notion that God is nothing but a useful fiction! (Cohen may also have Vaihinger in mind when his discusses the "pragmatism" that views compassion only as a "useful illusion" [*förderliche Illusion*] [*RoR* 17; *RV* 20]). It should be noted that Cohen does agree with Vaihinger that the ideas of religion have no objective grounding; however, his concept of correlation prevents him from having to conclude that they must for that reason be merely subjective fictions. See Vaihinger, *The Philosophy of 'As if': A System of the Theoretical, Practical and Religious Fictions of Mankind*, trans. C. K. Ogden (London: Routledge & Kegan Paul, 1968).

In an intriguing juxtaposition, Steven Schwarzschild links the rabbinic trope of *kivyachol* ("as it were") to a Kantian and Cohenian conception of 'as if.' Further research on this connection could prove fruitful, especially in light of similarities between *kivyachol* and "Were it not written in Scripture, it would be impossible to say it," the latter of which, as we saw in the previous chapter, has analogies to Cohen's communicative style. See Schwarzschild, "An Introduction to the Thought of R. Isaac Hutner," 255.

36. *RoR* 74; *RV* 86, emphasis added. Here, the notion that the dividing wall is "subjective" does not mean that God is 'merely subjective' in the sense of lacking reality apart from man's imagination. Rather, Cohen's emphasis is on the lack of strictly objective elements in the God-human correlation.

   Cohen's use of "subjective" in this context is similar to Climacus' use of the term in the *Concluding Unscientific Postscript*. Interpreters of that work, frequently working in categories of a binary dichotomy, have often wrongly understood Climacus' "subjectivity is truth" in terms of the 'mere subjectivity' of an individual's finite imagination, even though Climacus explicitly rejects this identification (see *CUP* 194). Climacus, like Cohen, emphasizes that there are no objective factors in the relation between God and the individual, and he criticizes the person who "does not want to understand that there is nothing between him and God but the ethical" (*CUP* 137; see also *CUP* 246, 600).

37. One may compare Cohen's approach here to the Kantian opposition to both empiricism (objects are external to and separate from us) and idealism (objects are internal to and dependent on us).

38. Buber, "Love of God and the Idea of Deity," in *Eclipse of God*, 59; "Die Liebe zu Gott und die Gottesidee," in *Gottesfinsternis*, 61: "Und ich wage zu sagen: auch Cohen hat Gott zwar also Idee gedacht, aber geliebt hat auch er ihn als—Gott."

39. Emil Fackenheim states that "what must be sought by a postidealistic philosophy of Judaism is not the God-Idea but, beyond it, the absolute Person." In my reading of Cohen, a *philosophy* of Judaism should not seek the absolute Person; rather, it is the existing individual (the individual Jew, or the Jewish community composed of existing individuals) who should do so. In contrast, Cohen's *Religion of Reason*, as a written-theoretical philosophy of Judaism, is right to retain 'God as idea,' since 'God as person' cannot be directly asserted in a theoretical medium. See Fackenheim, "Hermann Cohen—after Fifty Years" in *Jewish Philosophers and Jewish Philosophy*, 55.

   Likewise, although Eliezer Berkovits' assertion that "Cohen would have shuddered intellectually at the thought of an I-Thou relation with God" misunderstands Cohen in important ways, there is nevertheless a sense in which the notion of relating to God as a You ought properly to produce a certain type of 'intellectual shuddering,' if 'intellectual' is taken in the sense of theoretical-philosophical thought. See Berkovits, *Major Themes in the Philosophy of Judaism* (New York: KTAV, 1974), 16.

40. Andrea Poma provides a helpful take on the Buber-Cohen dispute. He argues, like Buber, for the inadequacy of Cohen's concept of God as idea, but he then asserts that Buber's "personalist-existentialist" view of God is *also* inadequate. Poma argues that no concept can be adequate to God, since God constitutes "the limit problem of philosophy and human thought in general." As such, Cohen's concept is no more inadequate than Buber's, and it has the advantage of avoiding anthropomorphic dangers that lurk in the latter. See Poma, *The Critical Philosophy of Hermann Cohen*, 232–233. I depart slightly from Poma in arguing that Cohen presents God not only as idea, but also as person: both perspectives are, to be sure, inadequate on their own, but the alternation between them can enable an 'adequate' form of practical communication, beyond the limitations in the theoretical realm of "philosophy and human thought in general."

41. *RoR* 375; *RV* 435.

42. See my chapter 1 and Cohen, "Der Stil der Propheten," in *JS* I, 262.

43. *RoR* 372; *RV* 432.

44. In addition to literary manifestations, differences in idea-content will also manifest themselves in differing actions and practices. Thus, the examination of source-texts is one way of indirectly approaching concepts; one could also approach them through the analysis of ritual, daily habits, and social politics.

45. *RoR* 372; *RV* 433.

46. *RoR* 213; *RV* 248.

47. See *RoR* 163, 212; *RV* 189, 248.

48. *RoR* 163; *RV* 189.

49. Conversely, if one is currently positioned at a notion of union, then one needs *less* immanence and closeness.

50. *RoR* 373; *RV* 433.

51. *RoR* 372; *RV* 433, emphasis added.

52. *RoR* 371; *RV* 431.

53. *RoR* 372; *RV* 433.

54. *RoR* 373; *RV* 433.

55. David Novak argues that for Cohen, unlike Buber, the I-You relation is limited to the relation between human beings and does not apply to relations between human beings and God. While it is true that 'God as You' is a paradoxical idea that cannot be asserted directly, Cohen's description of the psalm as a lyric address demonstrates that Cohen's account does include 'saying You to God.' See Novak, *The Election of Israel: The Idea of A Chosen People* (Cambridge: Cambridge University Press, 1995), 62–63.

Gabriel Motzkin, in maintaining that Cohen does conceive of God as a You, argues that such a conception follows naturally and automatically from Cohen's

assertion that the I as individual is constituted through a unique other. See Motzkin, "The Problem of Knowledge in Cohen's Philosophy of Religion," in Moses and
Wiedebach, *Hermann Cohen's Philosophy of Religion*, 158–159.

56. In this regard, even psalms such as Psalm 29, which do not explicit employ a second-
person form of address, are transformed from the viewpoint of prayer: from this
viewpoint, one cannot utter such lines as "ascribe unto the Lord glory and strength,"
without first inwardly bringing forth one's ethical-individual I, and the nature of
such terms as 'glory' and 'strength' will likewise be transformed in the context of
a personal, and no longer objective, relation.

57. Just as to speak of man is implicitly to speak of God, and vice versa (see my chapter 2 and *RoR* 32–33; *RV* 37–39), so to strive for God also requires a striving to
become an I.

58. *RoR* 58; *RV* 67.

59. *RoR* 373; *RV* 433. Pierre Bouretz remarks upon the "paradoxical appearance" (*allure
paradoxale*) of this last sentence. However, he does not remain with the paradox, but
instead removes it by arguing that Cohen, despite the fact that he "gestures toward the
idea of an interpersonal relation with between the human being and God," ultimately
restricts the you-relation to other human beings, such that "God is not a second person." Here, Bouretz prioritizes Cohen's (admittedly important) anti-anthropomorphic tendency in order to create a more consistent, non-paradoxical account of
Cohen's thought. See Bouretz, *Témoins du future: philosophie et messianisme* (Paris:
Gallimard, 2003), 104–105.

60. In connection with the notion of speech bringing forth the I, Cohen's statement in
his essay "Die Lyrik der Psalmen" is noteworthy: "Nur wenn die Seele *spricht*,
spricht die *Seele*" (Only when the soul *speaks*, does the *soul* speak; emphases in the
original). The significance of the self or soul being constituted by speech is brought
out even more strongly when one contrasts Cohen's statement to that of Schiller's
epigram "Sprache," to which Cohen presumably alludes: "Warum kann der leben-
dige Geist dem Geist nicht erscheinen? / *Spricht* die Seele, so spricht ach! schon die
Seele nicht mehr" (Why can't the living spirit manifest itself to the spirit? / If the
soul *speaks*, it is, alas, no longer the *soul* that speaks.) See Cohen, "Die Lyrik der
Psalmen," in *JS* I, 246. See also *RoR* 471; *RV* 431: "Speech is the proper expression
of reason."

61. Cohen's notion of unearthing one's inward self through dialogue has a very Freud-
ian ring to it.

62. The notion of directing oneself beyond oneself to an addressee that has no objective existence beyond oneself parallels Cohen's account of the relation between
religion and Ethics. One must go beyond Ethics, beyond that which is objectively
systematizable, and yet that which one aims at, i.e., religion, has no independent
standing apart from Ethics.

63. *RoR* 373; *RV* 433.

64. *RoR* 212; *RV* 247.

65. Again, Cohen's descriptions should not be taken as historical-objective descriptions of the biblical text. Just as the psalm's differentiation from the hymn of praise was not to be found 'externally' but only with regard to the personal-practical viewpoint of prayer, so too his claim that the psalm is free of all sensuality is not an 'empirical' observation. That is, there may be psalms whose passionate longing *can* outwardly appear to be sensually inflected. Instead, we should understand Cohen's claim as an abduction: he *reads* the psalms in accord with a preconceived idea, which in turn leads to a rejection of sensuality in his interpretations. Thus, strictly speaking, 'the psalm' as manifestation of religious love does not exist apart from Cohen's own personal engagement of the sources.

66. *RoR* 373; *RV* 433.

67. *RoR* 373; *RV* 433.

68. *RoR* 212; *RV* 248, emphasis added.

69. *RoR* 162; *RV* 188, emphasis added.

70. *RoR* 373; *RV* 433–434.

71. In this regard, we can note the difference between Cohen's insistence here on man's love for God, and his more reductive description of the biblical psalms in his *Ästhetik des reinen Gefühls*: in the latter's systematic-philosophical account, the psalms' description of God's love for man and man's love for God are to be understood merely as a poetic simile (*Gleichnis*), while in *Religion of Reason* that distancing term no longer appears in the analysis of psalmic love. See Cohen, *Ästhetik des reinen Gefühls*, vol. 2, 36.

72. In Kant's account, which Cohen largely follows, 'nature' corresponds to "the sum total of all objects of experience [*der Inbegriff aller Gegenstände der Erfahrung*]" (*Prolegomena to Any Future Metaphysics*, trans. and ed. Gary Hatfield [Cambridge: Cambridge University Press, 1997], sec. 16 [4:295]). Because God and the soul have no empirical-sensual qualities, they cannot be objects of experience and would therefore not be included in 'nature.' As such, the soul's love of God would have to be a super-natural "miracle."

73. In this regard, Steven Schwarzschild notes Cohen's fondness for the line from the end of Goethe's *Faust*: "The indescribable—here is it done" ("Das Unbeschreibliche, Hier ist's getan"). See Schwarzschild, "On Jewish Eschatology," in *Pursuit of the Ideal*, 224. The line is cited by Cohen in his *Ethik des reinen Willens* (637) as well as in his *Ästhetik des reinen Gefühls* (vol. 1, 209; vol. 2, 96).

74. *RoR* 373; *RV* 434.

75. *RoR* 375; *RV* 436.

76. Cf. Cohen's "Die Lyrik der Psalmen" in *JS* I, 246.

77. To be sure, in some cases, the prophet speaks not in his own voice, but from the perspective of God's own words, so that God is, in a sense, the first person, rather than the third person. However, the involvement of the prophet, as a third party in addition to the hearer and God, still runs the risk of representing the love and service of God as something general and hence theoretical, rather than as individually personal and regulative.

78. *CUP* 77.

79. *RoR* 162; *RV* 188–189.

80. Cf. Climacus' designation of the "passion of infinity" as the true criteria of prayer, and his corresponding assertion that "objective knowledge is suspended." He links this to an emphasis on the "how" in contradistinction to an emphasis on the "what." See *CUP* 201–204.

81. In a typical lyric poem, moreover, description is not only possible but also necessary: without defining descriptive characteristics, the singer's beloved would remain undefined. In contrast, even though the psalm lacks description of the beloved, the beloved is still distinctively characterized—as the one who can be uniquely identified precisely by the absence and impossibility of description. Compare Climacus' remark: "[A] person, just by describing the 'how' of his inwardness, can indirectly indicate that he is a Christian without mentioning Christ's name . . . With regard to [inter-human] loving . . . it holds true that a person cannot say what or whom he loves by defining his 'how.' All lovers have the 'how' of erotic love in common, and now the particular individual must add the name of his beloved. But with regard to having faith (*sensu strictissimo* [in the strictest sense]), it holds true that this 'how' fits only one object" (*CUP* 613–614n). That which Climacus says about faith corresponds to what Cohen says about religious love: the lover's longing, i.e., his 'how', is enough to uniquely identify the object of his love; direct description (naming) of the beloved is neither necessary nor possible.

82. *RoR* 373; *RV* 433–434.

83. See *RoR* 190, 229; *RV* 222, 267–268.

84. For an overview of the different connotations of *Erfahrung* and *Erlebnis* in German intellectual history, see Scott Lash, "Experience," in *Theory, Culture & Society* 23, nos. 2–3 (2006): 335–341.

     Cohen's use of *Erlebnis* calls into question Steven Schwarzschild's assertion that Cohen "rejects all rest and reliance on alleged experience (*Erlebnis*), of 'life,' self, and God." However, it remains true that Cohen's account of religion does not rest or rely, theoretically-assertionally, on *Erlebnis*; rather, he retains the practical-paradoxical tension that preserves the infinity and normativity of the ethical task and does not collapse the gap between the ideal and the actual. In this sense, it is significant that while Cohen speaks of "the soul's experience," he does not speak in terms of a substantive object of that experience, i.e., he does not say "the soul's experience *of God.*" See Schwarzschild, "Theologico-Political Basis," 88.

85. *RoR* 373; *RV* 433–434.

86. *RoR* 50; *RV* 58. This same shift also mirrors religion's "transformation of the neuter into a person" (*RoR* 41; *RV* 48).

87. *RoR* 162; *RV* 188.

88. *RoR* 51; *RV* 59, emphasis in the original.

89. See *RoR* 50; *RV* 58: "*Bekenntnis* surpasses *Erkenntnis*, as the action of the will surpasses the thinking of the understanding." Cf. *CUP* 160: "But the ethical is not only a knowing; it is also a doing that is related to a knowing."

90. Cf. J. L. Austin's analysis of performative utterances in his *How To Do Things with Words*, 2nd ed., ed. J. O. Urmson and Marina Sbisà (Cambridge, MA: Harvard University Press, 1975).

   Ketil Bonaunet also analyzes Cohen's concept of confession as a type of speech-act, and points out that Cohen himself uses the term *Sprachhandlung* to describe prayer (*RoR* 399; *RV* 463). Cohen also discusses the significance of *Sprachhandlung* in his *Ethik des reinen Willens* (194, 196). See Bonaunet, *Hermann Cohen's Kantian Philosophy of Religion*, 109–110.

91. Rosenzweig's approach to the story of Balaam's ass displays a similar logic: "Not that doing necessarily results in hearing and understanding. But one hears differently when one hears in the doing. All the days of the year Balaam's talking ass may be a mere fairy tale, but not on the Sabbath wherein this portion is read in the synagogue, when it speaks to me out of the open Torah. But if it is not a fairy tale, what then? I cannot say right now; if I should think about it today, when it is past, and try to say what it is, I should probably only utter the platitude that it is a fairy tale. But on that day, in that very hour, it is—well, certainly not a fairy tale, but that which is communicated to me provided I am able to fulfill the command of the hour, namely, to open my ears." See Nahum N. Glatzer, ed., *Franz Rosenzweig: His Life and Thought* (New York: Schocken Books, 1953), 246. For Cohen, that which Rosenzweig says about Balaam's ass is true of *all* concepts of religion: apart from the doing, one cannot assert their actuality.

92. *RoR* 378; *RV* 440.

93. *CUP* 203.

94. The notion of an antinomy that cannot be overcome in thought but only through passionate action recalls Johannes de Silentio's account of faith in *Fear and Trembling*, as well as Johannes Climacus' meditations on Lessing's refusal of Jacobi's proposed leap in the *Concluding Unscientific Protest*. See, in the latter, *CUP* 93–106. In this context, Climacus even echoes Cohen's emphasis on the lyric psalm when he refers to "the lyrical culmination of thinking in the leap . . . in lyrically seeking to surpass itself, thinking wills to discover the paradoxical" (*CUP* 104).

95. In the last sentence of the paragraph, Cohen's use of the deictic terms "now" and "this prayer" further emphasizes the temporal particularity of the love of God, in additional to the personal particularity of "my." Such temporal particularity will be examined in detail in the next chapter.

96. Cohen, *Der Begriff der Religion*, 116: "Die Allheit, als welche die Menschheit zu denken ist, verbürgt nicht die Individualität, *als solche*. Dazu bedarf ich Gottes, als *meines* Gottes. *Mein eigener Gott ist der Gott der Religion*" (emphases in the original).

97. *RoR* 373–374; *RV* 434.

98. *RoR* 387; *RV* 450.

99. For a good example of a typical presentation of the problem, see Kenneth Seeskin, *Autonomy in Jewish Philosophy* (Cambridge: Cambridge University Press, 2001), chapter 1, 1–27.

100. Cf. Kant's famous formulation in his *Critique of Practical Reason*, trans. Lewis White Beck (New York: Macmillan, 1993): "Two things fill the mind with ever new and increasing admiration and awe, the more often and steadily we reflect upon them: the starry heavens above and the moral law within me" (5:161). Note, however, that Kant contrasts the internal moral law not with an external divine command, but with an external natural phenomenon.

101. *RoR* 158; *RV* 183.

102. Note that the personal language of Cohen's "God has awakened in *us* through his commandments" parallels Deuteronomy's "God commanded *you*."

103. *RoR* 19; *RV* 22.

104. *RoR* 202; *RV* 236. Kaplan's translation has: ". . . is in the heart of man and has been elucidated in the spirit of man's holiness."

105. One wonders whether Kant had this verse in mind when he contrasted "the starry heavens above" with "the moral law within me" (*Critique of Practical Reason*, 5:161).

106. *RoR* 81; *RV* 94.

107. *RoR* 81; *RV* 94.

108. See *RoR* 163–164, 212; *RV* 189–190, 248.

109. At the most, one could perhaps say that the commandment is not not internal.

110. *RoR* 202; *RV* 236.

111. Steven Schwarzschild comes close to this view when he states, with regard to Cohen's *Ethik*, "Indeed, even 'theonomy' is not incompatible with but is conducive to Kantian autonomy properly understood—if, that is, the God who is regarded as issuing imperatives is understood as the 'God of Truth', i.e., the God of philosophical reason." However, while autonomy is compatible with theonomy in one sense, Schwarzschild may also underemphasize the fact that the permanent *in*compatibility between the two remains equally important for Cohen in *Religion of Reason*. See Schwarzschild, "Introduction," in Hermann Cohen, *Ethik des reinen Willens* (Hildesheim: Georg Olms Verlag, 1981), xvi–xvii.

112. The biblical verse can itself be seen as opposing the theoretization of the commandment. Even in opposing a too-external understanding, Deut. 30:14 does not say that the word "is in your heart" as a categorical, static state of affairs; rather, it is in your heart specifically *la'asoto*, "to do it," "for doing it": practically, when you do it, that which is commanded by God ought also to appear as an internal command.

113. *RoR* 83–84; *RV* 97.

114. In his chapter on "Creation," Cohen writes, "[T]he problem of creation crosses over from the realm of causality to that of teleology" (*RoR* 70; *RV* 81). Because of this, the concept of God as creator of bread is not in 'competition' with the causal-natural explanations of bread's origin. Though he does not repeat the specific

terms "teleology" and "causality," he seems to be applying a similar distinction to the giving of the Torah, so that God's command does not compete with the inward imperative of autonomy. Later, he employs the same distinction in relation to God's forgiveness, in order to ward off questions as to *how* (i.e., by what means) God forgives: "God's entire relation to man is assigned to the domain of *teleology*, which is distinguished from all causality and from the metaphysics that is bound up with causality. Therefore there cannot be any question of the mechanism through which God effects forgiveness, or of the mediation through which it is infused in man. Rather, the teleological meaning of this relation is deflected from all of these would-be [*vermeintlich*] theoretical interests" (*RoR* 214; *RV* 250, emphasis in the original). For Cohen, the teleological nature of the God-human relation is inherently tied up with the non-theoretical nature of its concepts and thus with the need for non-direct forms of communication.

115. *RoR* 202; *RV* 235–236. This sounds very much like Kant's definition of religion: "Religion is (subjectively regarded) the recognition of all duties as divine commands" (*Religion Within the Limits of Reason Alone*, 142).

116. *RoR* 339; *RV* 395.

117. See *RoR* 11–12; *RV* 13–15; and my chapter 3 above.

118. *RoR* 178; *RV* 208.

119. *RoR* 202; *RV* 235–236.

120. Randi Rashkover suggests that Cohen's account of revelation, which she links to his concept of acknowledgement, betrays a "tension between Jewish sources and Cohen's notion of autonomous ethics. One may argue in fact that rather than successfully bind Jewish life to ethical idealism, Cohen's notion of acknowledgement reveals a strain between the two approaches to religious life." While this description rings true, the "tension" and "strain" may in fact be part and parcel of Cohen's communicative style. See Rashkover, *Revelation and Theopolitics*, 27.

121. *RoR* 323–324; *RV* 376.

122. Indeed, one account put forth in the Talmudic passage indicates precisely such a situation of heteronomous coercion: "'And they stood under/at the base of [*be-tachtit*] the mountain' (Ex. 19:17). R. Abdimi bar Hama bar Hasa said: this teaches that the Holy One, blessed be He, overturned the mountain over them like a cask and said to them, 'If you accept the Torah, well and good. If not, there will be your grave'" (BT Shabbat 88a). However, the other accounts in the passage lack the element of violent threat.

123. Cf. *CUP* 220: "Thus God is a supreme conception that cannot be explained by anything else but is explainable only by immersing oneself in the conception itself."

124. In this regard, Cohen's interpretation is similar to that implied by Buber and Rosenzweig's translation of the book of Exodus. They render *na'aseh ve-nishma* as "wir tuns, wir hörens," "we do, we hear/understand." The conjunctive *vav* becomes

a comma, so that the two actions are not separated: rather, the second is equivalent to the first. See *Die Fünf Bücher der Weisung* (Berlin: Lambert Schneider, 1930), 243.

Emmanuel Levinas takes Buber and Rosenzweig's translation to mean, "We will do *in order to* understand," "Nous allons faire *afin de* comprendre" (emphasis in the original). He describes this account as "transform[ing] action into a mode of understanding," a move that he decries as lacking in depth. However, it seems to me that he has misrepresented Buber and Rosenzweig's intentions, which, if anything, would be better described as a transformation of understanding into action. See Levinas, *Nine Talmudic Readings*, trans. Annette Aronowicz (Bloomington: Indiana University Press, 1990), 42; *Quatre lecture talmudiques* (Paris: Éditions de Minuit, 1968), 93.

125. *RoR* 74; *RV* 86.
126. BT Shabbat 88a.
127. See, e.g., BT Hagigah 16a; Sifre Numbers *Korah* 119.
128. *RoR* 164; *RV* 190.
129. *RoR* 77; *RV* 90.
130. A similar understanding is expressed by Franz Rosenzweig, who, in response to Martin Buber's assertion that "God is not a Law-giver," responded, "For me, too, God is not a Law-giver. But he commands." 'Law' has an objective, impersonal sense, while 'command' implies personality and direct relation. Thus, God commands but does *not* do so in an objective or objectively recognizable manner. See Rosenzweig, *On Jewish Learning*, ed. N. N. Glazer (New York: Schocken Books, 1955), 115, 116.
131. *RoR* 324; *RV* 377.
132. BT Bava Kamma 38a, translation based on Cohen's formulation.
133. *RoR* 324; *RV* 377.
134. See Kant, *Foundations of the Metaphysics of Morals*, trans. Lewis White Beck (New York: Macmillan, 1959), 4:397.
135. *RoR* 345; *RV* 401. See Kant, *Critique of Practical Reason*, 5:82.
136. As Cohen writes, "The ethical-law is the autonomous law of my reason, insofar as I am able to certify my will as the will of reason through my subjugation, through the taking-on of the law as my duty" (*RoR* 324–325; *RV* 377–378). *Insofar* as I subjugate myself, the ethical-law is the law of *my* reason; but insofar as I do not subjugate myself, the ethical-law is imposed from 'outside myself.'
137. *RoR* 28; *RV* 32–33.
138. Cf. Climacus: "[F]or a long time it was deemed possible to exclude dialectics from faith by saying that its conviction was upheld by virtue of authority. Then if someone wanted to question the believer, that is, to speak dialectically with him, with a certain *unbefangen* [uninhibited] frankness he would turn the matter this way: I am not able and should not be able to account for it, because I rest in a confidence in others, in the authority of the saints, etc. This is an illusion, because dialectics

merely turns and asks, that is, speaks dialectically with him about what authority is then and why he now regards these as authorities. Consequently it speaks dialectically with him not about *the faith* he has *out of confidence in them* but about *the faith* he has *in them*" (*CUP* 24, emphases in the original).

139. While the above description may sound in some ways like a Hegelian dialectic, Martin Kavka argues that Cohen's concept of correlation "stands against a model of dialectic as the 'exchange [*Wechsel*]' of apparent opposites. Rather, correlation is described as a 'preservation [*Erhaltung*]' of the apparent opposites." See Kavka, *Jewish Messianism and the History of Philosophy* (Cambridge: Cambridge University Press, 2004), 104, referring to Cohen's *Logik der reinen Erkenntnis*, 60–62.

   However, even though the opposites are both preserved in the practical appropriation, it may be that the correlative ideas may take on a dialectical *appearance* when projected onto the realm of theoretical conceptualization for the purposes of communication. That is, the presentation of one side of the correlation may subsequently call forth a counterbalancing presentation of the other side. However, there is still never any theoretical *Aufhebung* of the opposites. In this sense, one could call Cohen's presentation 'dialectical,' but in the specifically Kierkegaardian sense of the term (see *CUP* 35n).

140. This last phase misquotes Psalm 51:11, which actually reads, "Hide your face from my sins." However, the main point (namely, that the speaker is asking God for forgiveness) is unaffected.

141. *RoR* 102; *RV* 118–119.

142. *RoR* 103; *RV* 119.

143. Indeed, even my use of terms such as 'the particular individual' and 'God' has already crossed over into third-person language, whereas Cohen, echoing the psalmist, instead speaks simply of 'my' relation to 'you.'

144. Strictly speaking, one could also describe the psalm as human-centered, since it focuses on the pleas of the psalmist, but the implied agency for forgiveness still lies with the divine addressee.

145. See *RoR* 103; *RV* 120. The same phrase ("I, the Lord, sanctify you") also occurs in Lev. 20:8 and Lev. 21:8. Cohen cites and refers to the phrase through an abbreviated "I sanctify you," although he does not include the chapter and verse for the source of his reference. However, he does include the chapter and verse when, earlier in the section, he refers to the first half of Lev. 22:32, "And I will be sanctified in the midst of Israel."

   In his essay "Der Heilige Geist" (in *JS* III, 187), Cohen *does* note the sources of the phrase "I, the Lord, sanctify you" as Ex. 31:13, Lev. 20:8, and Lev. 21:8. When incorporating this essay into *Religion of Reason*, he seems (presumably accidentally) to have omitted this reference.

146. *RoR* 103; *RV* 119–120, emphasis in the original. This rendition of Lev. 11:44 is based on Cohen's own German translation, as is the emphasis on 'yourself.'

147. *RoR* 103; *RV* 120.

148. In proposing this correspondence, Cohen may be influenced by Lev. 20:7–8, in which the command "sanctify yourselves" is followed in the very next verse by "I, the Lord, sanctify you." Even the plain sense of the verses can seem to indicate a correlative process of sanctification.

149. *RoR* 103; *RV* 120.

150. See Lev. 20:7–8, as well as Sifre Numbers *Shalah* 115 and Sifra *Kedoshim* 10:2 (to which Cohen alludes on *RoR* 103; *RV* 120). In addition, the standard blessing-formulation states: *asher kidshanu be-mitzvotav*, "who has sanctified us with his commandments."

151. *RoR* 105; *RV* 121.

152. *RoR* 105; *RV* 122.

153. *RoR* 105; *RV* 122.

154. The same dynamic is displayed in Cohen's theoretically contradictory notion of plurality within totality: he opposes egoism (associated with plurality), which creates too much distance between individuals, as well as the universalizing-generalizing method of Ethics (associated with totality), which does not provide enough distance.

155. *RoR* 105; *RV* 122.

156. *RoR* 105; *RV* 121.

157. *RoR* 189; *RV* 220–221.

158. Cohen does not cite specific verses from Jeremiah. His assertion is most likely formed from a melding-together of Jer. 31:30–33 (in which God promises to make a new covenant with the house of Israel, and to write it in their hearts, so that they will all know God and sin no more), Jer. 24:7 (in which God says, "I will give them a heart to know me"), and Jer. 32:39 (in which God says, "I will give them one heart/unity of heart [*lev echad*] . . . so that they will fear me). However, Jeremiah never uses the specific phrases "new heart" or "new spirit."

159. *RoR* 194; *RV* 226, emphases in the original.

160. *RoR* 194; *RV* 226. Cohen's contrast between Jeremiah and Ezekiel may be a bit contrived. Jeremiah also calls for a turning from sin through alteration of the heart, exhorting his audience to "take away the foreskin of your heart" (4:4) and to "wash your heart from wickedness, so that you may be saved" (4:14). Conversely, Ezekiel reports God as saying, "I will give you a new heart and I will put a new spirit within you" (36:26, see also 11:19). Thus, the notion that Jeremiah thinks that God will give the new heart and spirit, while Ezekiel excels him by turning this into a task for man, does not seem to hold up categorically—indeed, Cohen himself later refers to Ezek. 36:26 and 11:19, acknowledging their difference from Ezek. 18:31 (*RoR* 280–281; *RV* 326–327). This does not, however, invalidate Cohen's general linking of Ezekiel's call here with the notion of self-renewal and turning.

161. *RoR* 194; *RV* 226.

162. *RoR* 199; *RV* 232. Cf. Climacus' emphasis on the importance of "comprehend[ing] inwardly that the God-relationship of the individual human being is the main point, that the meddling busyness of a third person is a lack of inwardness and a superfluity of amiable obtuseness" (*CUP* 77).

163. *RoR* 199; *RV* 232.

164. *RoR* 201; *RV* 235.

165. *RoR* 200; *RV* 233.

166. *RoR* 201–202; *RV* 235.

167. *RoR* 202; *RV* 236.

168. *RoR* 202–203; *RV* 237.

169. *RoR* 205; *RV* 239–240.

170. *RoR* 206; *RV* 241

171. *RoR* 206; *RV* 241.

172. *RoR* 206; *RV* 241.

173. *RoR* 202; *RV* 236.

174. *RoR* 206; *RV* 241.

175. Randi Rashkover compares Cohen's treatment of repentance and forgiveness with Kant's account in *Religion Within the Limits of Reason Alone*. She notes that while Cohen and Kant both have similar concerns regarding the philosophical legitimacy of divine assistance, Cohen "boldly and unabashedly asserts the reality of the forgiving God," whereas Kant is more reticent and merely mentions the possibility that "some supernatural cooperation may be necessary." To the extent that Cohen is more forthcoming on this topic, I maintain that this is because he avails himself of the voice of Scripture, whereas Kant limits himself to the single-voiced, autonomous method of philosophy, and thus (rightly) refrains from direct assertions of forgiveness. See Rashkover, *Revelation and Theopolitics*, 34–35, and Kant, *Religion Within the Limits of Reason Alone*, 40.

176. *RoR* 206; *RV* 241.

177. In other words, Ezekiel's meaning was not "You must cast off your sins, for God is not involved in the process," but rather "You must cast off your sins, for your father's sins (and the power of fate more generally) are not involved."

178. *RoR* 207; *RV* 242.

179. *RoR* 207–208; *RV* 242–243. While arguing that Cohen "rigorously maintained" his exclusion of God's forgiveness in *Religion of Reason*, Andrea Poma does remark on Cohen's description of God as redeemer. Poma maintains that in this "'new sense' of correlation . . . the religion of reason is stretched to the limits of its methodological meaning" and he cites, in a footnote, Cohen's insistence that God, as redeemer, must be the forgiver of sins. However, Poma does not fully address the fact of the theoretical incompatibility in Cohen's different formulations. See Poma, "Correlation in Hermann Cohen's Philosophy of Religion: A Method and More Than a Method," in *Yearning for Form*, 82–85. Poma addresses this question in a similar fashion in *Critical Philosophy of Hermann Cohen*, 230–232.

180. Kenneth Seeskin, *Searching for a Distant God: The Legacy of Maimonides* (New York: Oxford University Press, 2000), 115.

181. In *Religion Within the Limits of Reason Alone*, Kant also recognizes the impossibility of such an explanation and describes the notion of divine aid as "incomprehensible" (49) and a "mystery" (134). Cohen differs from Kant, however, in incorporating the radicalness of this non-comprehensibility into his style and form of communication.

182. Randi Rashkover provides a good description of the difficulties inherent in Cohen's account of repentance. She writes, "Like his account of the love of God, Cohen's account of divine forgiveness and repentance reveals a tension within his application of critical idealism to the sources of Judaism. Cohen attempts to navigate between moral autonomy and divine forgiveness through his account of the relation between the self who repents and her need for a God who guarantees the success of her repentant action. Nonetheless, Cohen cannot render self-sanctification and divine forgiveness simultaneously meaningful without betraying either the language of the Jewish tradition or the categories of critical idealism." My reading of Cohen is fully compatible with this description, though I would adjust the valuations associated with it. As noted earlier, Cohen's account does indeed reveal a "tension," but this tension is rational and beneficial, and should be preserved and heightened rather than overcome. Likewise, it is true that he cannot render the two perspectives "simultaneously meaningful," for this would entail a form of semantic consistency that would flatten the personal-practical concept. Thus, he attempts to maintain the language of the Jewish tradition alongside the categories of critical idealism, yet without granting priority to either of these two 'incompatible' perspectives. In this way, the two are neither 'simultaneously' meaningful nor 'successively' meaningful, but rather correlatively meaningful. See Rashkover, *Revelation and Theopolitics*, 10; see also 30–46, where she repeatedly notes that Cohen "contradicts" himself regarding repentance and forgiveness, putting forth different claims that "conflict" with one another.

183. *RoR* 208–212; *RV* 243–248.

184. *RoR* 222; *RV* 259.

185. Cohen reverses the order of the phrases from the mishnaic passage, which actually reads: "Blessed are you, Israel; before whom do you purify yourselves and who purifies you? It is your father in heaven." Michael Zank argues that Cohen reverses the phrases in order to put climatic stress on self-purification. See Zank, *Idea of Atonement*, 147.

186. *RoR* 223–224; *RV* 260–261.

187. Without attaching too high a degree of significance to Cohen's word choice, we may also note that while "God" (a non-relational term) does not purify, "your father" (a relational term that explicitly draws upon the mishnaic source) does purify. This may correspond to the notion that it is only from a personal-relation

perspective that one can speak of God purifying; one cannot say this in general-impersonal language.

188. Steven Schwarzschild, "The Title of Hermann Cohen's 'Religion of Reason out of the Sources of Judaism,'" in *RoR*, 19. The ellipses and brackets are Schwarzschild's.

189. Elsewhere, Schwarzschild approvingly acknowledges the "paradoxical" view in classical rabbinic Judaism that forges an "integral, dialectical unity" out of the seemingly contradictory factors of human action and divine response. However, he seems not to apply this observation to his reading of Cohen. See Schwarzschild, "The Theology of Jewish Survival," in *Pursuit of the Ideal*, 85. Schwarzschild also discusses "the dialectic of works and grace" in his "On Jewish Eschatology," in *Pursuit of the Ideal*, 225.

CHAPTER 6

1. Note that in this chapter, when I talk about "ethical turning," I refer to an action, a practice, which, as we saw in the last chapter, can be described in terms of both human-centered and God-centered agency. So, although I discuss the fulfillment of this practical task primarily in connection to human repentance and striving for self-sanctification, this same action could, in each instance, also be described in terms of God's forgiveness.

2. See John L. Bell, *The Continuous and the Infinitesimal in Mathematics and Philosophy* (Milano: Polimetrica, 2005), 28.

3. Berkeley, *The Analyst*, §15, in George Berkeley, *De Motu; and, The Analyst: A Modern Edition with Introductions and Commentary*, ed. and trans. Douglas M. Jesseph (Dordrecht: Kluwer Academic Publishers, 1992). See also Bell, *Continuous and the Infinitesimal*, 116.

4. Berkeley, *Analyst*, §15, §49.

5. See Bell, *Continuous and the Infinitesimal*, 166.

6. For the relation between Cohen's positive employment of the infinitesimal and his intellectual and cultural context, see Gregory B. Moynahan, "Hermann Cohen's *Das Prinzip der Infinitesimalmethod*, Ernst Cassirer, and the Politics of Science in Wilhelmine Germany," *Perspectives on Science* 11, no. 1 (2003): 35–75.

7. For the significance of the concept of the infinitesimal for Cohen's thought, see Samuelson, *Introduction to Modern Jewish Philosophy*, 169–175; Kavka, *Jewish Messianism*, 98–110; Gibbs, *Correlations*, 47–52. In general, though, these accounts do not emphasize the paradoxical aspects of the infinitesimal.

8. Indeed, many other thinkers criticized Cohen's philosophy precisely because of its positive employment of the 'dubious' infinitesimal. See Marco Giovanelli, *Reality and Negation—Kant's Principle of Anticipation of Perception: An Investigation of Its Impact on the Post-Kantian Debate* (Dordrecht: Springer, 2010), 178–198, and see also Bell, *Continuous and the Infinitesimal*, 176–179.

9. It should be noted that in the twentieth century, mathematicians such as Abraham Robinson were able to develop a more rigorous basis for the infinitesimal, thus rehabilitating the long-maligned concept. See Bell, *Continuous and the Infinitesimal*, 18, 259–264, 283–321. At the same time, although it may be possible to give the infinitesimal a formal grounding in symbolic mathematical terms, this still does not mean that it can be directly translated into verbal propositions in non-symbolic language or grasped as a conceptual unity in conscious thought. In this regard, see Alba Papa-Grimaldi, "Why Mathematical Solutions of Zeno's Paradoxes Miss the Point: Zeno's One and Many Relation and Parmenides' Prohibition," *Review of Metaphysics* 50 (Dec. 1996): 299–314.

10. Thus, instead of removing the paradox from *Religion of Reason*, Cohen's use of the infinitesimal can be seen as inserting an ultimately paradoxical concept into the very core of his earlier *System*.

11. Throughout this discussion, the phrases "the ethical individual" or "the ethical self" refer not to the individual of the method of Ethics, but rather to the individual or self of religion. See my "Note on Terminology" for discussion of my translation of Cohen's *sittliche* as "ethical" rather than as "moral."

12. *RoR* 204; *RV* 238, emphasis in the original.

13. Cf. *CUP* 91: "That the existing subjective thinker is continually striving does not mean, however, that in a finite sense he has a goal toward which he is striving, where he would be finished when he reached it. No, he is striving infinitely, is continually in the process of becoming."

14. *RoR* 305; *RV* 355.

15. Cf. *CUP* 132: "[W]e are all so-called subjects of sorts. And yet piety is rooted precisely in subjectivity; one does not become pious objectively."

16. *RoR* 96; *RV* 111, emphasis in the original.

17. *RoR* 223; *RV* 260.

18. Cf. Cohen's account of the prophets' critique of the actuality of the present in "Der Stil der Propheten," in *JS* I, 279.

19. *RoR* 212; *RV* 248.

20. For Cohen, one cannot turn to God without becoming an ethical self, and vice versa. See *RoR* 313; *RV* 364, where God's nearness is my good only if it is also self-nearing, i.e., becoming an ethical self. See also *RoR* 375; *RV* 436, where the longing for God corresponds to the human being's desire not to despair of himself, i.e., his desire to retain his commitment to becoming an I.

21. For some observations regarding connections between Cohen's understanding of God and his understanding of infinity, see Steven Schwarzschild, "The Religious Stake in Modern Philosophy of Infinity," *Bar Ilan* 22/23 (1987): 75–77.

22. *RoR* 111, 335; *RV* 129, 390.

23. Cf. Climacus' claim that the individual can come to see nature as God's work only through the inwardness of self-activity (*CUP* 243, 246).

24. *RoR* 204; *RV* 238.

25. I.e., it is *not* the case that the task that corresponds to 'God as commander' is determinately separable from the task that corresponds to 'God as forgiver.'

26. Cf. Levinas' discussion (in *Otherwise Than Being*, trans. Alphonso Lingis [The Hague: Martinus Nijhoff, 1981], 9–11, 124–129) of my "unlimited responsibility" for the other.

27. *RoR* 42; *RV* 48.

28. In addition, Cohen further heightens the notion of task by presenting the perspective of 'person' not 'in his own voice' but rather by *citing* Scripture. His use of formal citation underscores the fact that the perspective of 'person' belongs to Scripture, and is not (yet) his own; instead, it must *become* his own through engagement of the task of turning. Thus, he produces the movement-enabling 'distance' both through the contrast of the perspective of 'abstraction' to that of 'person' and through the contrast of his own voice to that of Scripture.

29. *RoR* 305; *RV* 355. Cf. *CUP* 197: "Only momentarily can a particular individual, existing, be in a unity of the infinite and the finite that transcends existing. This instant is the moment of passion." See also *CUP* 35n; 203.

30. *RoR* 235; *RV* 274.

31. *RoR* 230; *RV* 269.

32. *RoR* 204; *RV* 238. See also *RoR* 376, 305; *RV* 437, 355.

33. Cf. *RoR* 230; *RV* 269: "In religious existence . . . everything is valid only for moments of ascent [*Aufschwungs*] and of transition [*Durchgangs*]."

34. Conversely, we could say that the transition is after 'here' but before 'not-here.'

35. Bell, *Continuous and the Infinitesimal*, 83.

36. Cohen, *Das Prinzip der Infinitesimal-Methode und seine Geschichte* [1883] (Hildesheim: Georg Olms Verlag, 2005), 80–81 (§63, '*Das Moment*').

37. The use of the notation *dx* to represent the infinitesimal increment was initially developed by Leibniz, not Newton. See Bell, *Continuous and the Infinitesimal*, 95.

38. While I present the ethical self as located in the infinitesimal moment of the differential *dx*, Martin Kavka's different but related analogy draws upon another aspect of differential calculus in explicating Cohen's ethical-religious thought. In Kavka's account, the ethical act in which the I binds itself to the You represents an 'integration' of these two 'infinitesimal' elements and creates a relation akin to that of two continuous points on a curve. See Kavka, *Jewish Messianism*, 113, 119–120.

39. Pierfrancesco Fiorato argues that Cohen's conception of time is derived from the Kantian notion, in which moments are themselves not part of time, but rather designate borders/limits between which time lies. See Fiorato, *Geschichtliche Ewigkeit*, 136; and Kant, "Inaugural Dissertation: On the Form and Principles of the Sensible and the Intelligible World," in Kant, *Theoretical Philosophy, 1755–1770*, trans. and ed. David Walford (New York: Cambridge University Press, 1992), sec. 14 (2:399), and *Critique of Pure Reason*, B211. Interestingly, Kant's *Dissertation*, composed in Latin, uses the term *momenta* for 'moments,' thus forging a terminological link to

Newton's mathematical use of the term. For my purposes here, the notion that points in time lie between moments is functionally equivalent to the notion that moments lie between points in time.

40. As noted above, the paradoxicality of Cohen's infinitesimal self parallels the fact that, historically, many mathematicians viewed the infinitesimal itself as a contradictory concept and therefore sought to eliminate it from their analysis. See Bell, *Continuous and the Infinitesimal*, esp. ch. 4, "The Reduction of the Continuous to the Discrete in the 19th and Early 20th Centuries," 139–187. We can thus draw a parallel to those readers of Cohen who, in an attempt to construct a 'consistent' reading of his book, have attempted to eliminate the apparent contradictions contained in *Religion of Reason*. In contrast to this approach, the fact that Cohen grounds his thought in the 'contradictory' concept of the infinitesimal can provide support to the hypothesis that his book as a whole ought to be read in a contradictory, non-consistent manner.

41. *RoR* 230; *RV* 269.

42. This regress is similar to Zeno's 'dichotomy' paradox. However, whereas that paradox uses the regress to conclude that finite motion is impossible, we here begin with the fact of the finite movement and use the regress to conclude that the movement must have begun with an infinitesimal 'movement.'

43. Again, this presentation is consistent with the notation of dx as representing an infinitesimal change in x. As such, dx is a change, and yet not a change, in the sense that $x+dx$ is not determinately different from x.

44. Cohen points to the difference between typical movement and the 'movement' of the moment when he distinguishes the "action" (*Handlung*) of ethicality from "the motion of nature" (*der Bewegung der Natur*) (*RoR* 160).

45. *RoR* 204; *RV* 238, emphasis in the original.

46. *RoR* 308; *RV* 358.

47. *RoR* 160; *RV* 186.

48. Almut Bruckstein notes that this same dynamic of 'fulfillment in the moment' applies to midrashic hermeneutics: in the infinitesimal moment (and only in the moment) in which the scriptural text is cited, the interpreter can overcome the apparently mythical character of the text and can use that momentary citation to ground ethicality at the point where autonomous reasoning fails. See Bruckstein, "Introduction," in Cohen, *Ethics of Maimonides*, xxxv.

49. *RoR* 204; *RV* 239. Cf. also *RoR* 322; *RV* 375: "For the individual, the reward [which Cohen identifies in the next sentence with 'the goal'] consists only in the action itself," and *RoR* 374; *RV* 435: "The quest [of drawing near to God in prayer] is the end in itself [*Selbstzweck*] of the religious soul." Note that the *Selbstzweck* here is a dynamic action; this parallels the condemnation, in "Der Stil Der Propheten," of those who would treat a merely static object as a *Selbstzweck*.

50. *RoR* 96; *RV* 111.

51. Even when Cohen asserts that that holiness is a be-ing for God, he does not thereby indicate a static attribute. Rather, "this designation of be-ing with regard to God involves not his metaphysical causality, but rather his purposive acting, which is the model for the purposive action of the human being" (*RoR* 96; *RV* 111–112). Thus, the being-holy of God and the becoming-holy of the human being are both active and dynamic.

52. *RoR* 206–207; *RV* 241–242.

53. Pierfrancesco Fiorato notes that Cohen had already, in his *Ethik des reinen Willens*, distinguished between the fulfillment (*Erfüllung*) and the conclusion (*Erledigung*) of a task. See Fiorato, *Geschichtliche Ewigkeit*, 172, and Cohen, *Ethik des reinen Willens*, 144.

54. For a discussion of the different ways in which Kant, Kierkegaard, and Levinas also argue for the fulfillability of an infinite task, see M. Jamie Ferreira, *Love's Grateful Striving* (New York: Oxford University Press, 2001), 124–127.

55. Norbert Samuelson, *Introduction to Modern Jewish Philosophy*, 173. See also Edith Wyschogrod, "The Moral Self: Emmanuel Levinas and Hermann Cohen," 54: "For Cohen this unique 'I' is neither a substance bearing qualities nor a functional concept but a regulative idea: the moral self is conceived as an infinite task. The will's efforts at actualization approach asymptotically but never attain the moral perfection of the ideal."

    Steven Schwarzschild also describes Cohen's thought as asymptotic. While Schwarzschild viewed this notion in a negative light in his earlier work, he eventually reversed this valuation and affirmed the asymptotic nature of the ideal in his later writings. In those later writings, however, he also explicitly rejects the notion that the infinity of the task makes it Sisyphean. See Schwarzschild, "Democratic Socialism of Hermann Cohen," 436–437; "The Personal Messiah—Toward the Restoration of a Discarded Doctrine," 19–20, "On Jewish Eschatology," 218, "Afterword," 254, all three in *Pursuit of the Ideal*.

56. For a defense, in the context of Cohenian thought, of the concept of asymptote against common misunderstandings, see Norbert Samuelson, "A Critique of Borowitz's Postmodern Jewish Theology," *Zygon* 28, no. 2 (June 1993): 273–277.

57. Simon Rawidowicz notes that Maimonides similarly combined nearness and distance, envisaging both "the maximum of remoteness and the infinite nearness between God and man." Furthermore, he attributes Maimonides' double-conception to his commitment to both philosophical purity and to traditional conceptions of God, leading to "perpetual endeavors to hold the balance between these two conflicting doctrines." See Rawidowicz, "Knowledge of God: A Study in Maimonides' Philosophy of Religion," in *Studies in Jewish Thought*, ed. Nahum Glatzer (Philadelphia: Jewish Publication Society, 1974), 271–272. Martin Kavka contends that these observations also apply to Cohen's thought: "For Cohen . . . there appears to be a conflation between the infinite and the infinitesimal, similar to that which

Rawidowicz observed in Maimonides." Kavka, *Jewish Messianism and the History of Philosophy*, 103 (see also 79).

58. *RoR* 323; *RV* 375. In this connection, Robert Gibbs highlights a passage in Cohen's *Ethik des reinen Willens*, in which the infinity of space can be subsumed in a totality. In contrast, the infinity that characterizes time cannot be thus subsumed, and is not to be equated simply with an "and-so-on." Gibbs links this non-totalizability of time to Cohen's messianism, in which the future is always something not-yet and therefore new, and which stands in contrast to the "bad infinite" of space. See Gibbs, "Hermann Cohen's Messianism: The History of the Future," in Holzhey et al., *"Religion der Vernunft aus den Quellen des Judentums": Tradition und Ursprungsdenken in Hermann Cohens Spätwerk*, 338, and Cohen, *Ethik des reinen Willens*, 400.

   Cohen's contrast, in the present passage, of the infinity of space with the ethical infinity of the soul, may indicate that the infinity of the soul is analogous to the non-totalizable infinity of time. This conclusion would accord well with Cohen's emphasis on the temporal nature of the soul and the self, which come-to-be only in the infinitesimal moment.

59. While a standard asymptotic graph conveys a misleading picture of Cohen's account of the self, it may be that any other static picture or graph would be equally misleading. That is, a representative graph would have to display have to display the following characteristics: (a) at every finite point, the function is not equal to the ideal ('asymptotic') value, yet, at each of those points, is only an infinitesimal distance away from that value; and (b) the function *is* equal to the ideal value at the infinitesimal space 'between' every pair of consecutive finite points. Such a function does not seem to be visually representable on the coordinate plane.

60. Note that this non-paradoxical logic corresponds to expression in subject-predicate sentences whose concepts are clear and distinct. That is to say, *if* one insists on expressing the concepts in verbal-sentential form, they will give rise to paradox and contradiction. However, if one works within a non-propositional context, the concepts can be analyzed without giving rise to direct contradiction, even though the results of this process still cannot be translated into consistent 'thought.' In this regard, we can be fruitfully instructed by differences between Wittgenstein's earlier *Tractatus Logico-Philosophicus* and his later *Philosophical Investigations*, as well as by C. S. Peirce's different varieties of existential graphs.

61. *RoR* 204; *RV* 238. Climacus similarly condemns those speculative philosophers who neglect the task of existence and instead posit a "fantastical I-I." In contrast to this illusion, Climacus insists: "Only momentarily can a particular individual, existing, be in a unity of the infinite and the finite that transcends existing. This instant is the moment of passion" (*CUP* 197). See also *CUP* 203.

62. The notion of the infinitesimal as both something and nothing can also be applied to the relation between Ethics and religion. Religion is not objectively or autonomously

separable from Ethics, but neither is religion subsumed by Ethics. Thus, the 'difference' between the two is both 'something' and 'nothing.' As such, we can speak of an 'infinitesimal gap' between Ethics and religion. As applied to Cohen's own work, we can posit an infinitesimal relation between his *Ethik* and his *Religion*, in that his thought in the latter neither 'breaks with' nor 'is consistent with' his thought in the former.

63. *RoR* 204; *RV* 238.

64. *RoR* 20–21; *RV* 24.

65. *RoR* 204; *RV* 238.

66. *RoR* 204; *RV* 239.

67. *RoR* 205; *RV* 239, emphasis in the original.

68. When $x = 0$, $y = 2$; when $x = 1$, $y = 2$; when $x = 2$, $y = 2$; when $x = 3$, $y = 2$, and so on.

69. When $x = 0$, $y = 0$; when $x = 1$, $y = 1$; when $x = 2$, $y = 2$; when $x = 3$, $y = 3$, and so on.

70. On a related point, just as the function itself must be continuous in order for it to be differentiable (i.e., in order for the derivative to exist), so too the empirical self is a necessary and valuable foundation of the ethical self. Because the ethical self originates in moving-beyond the empirical self, a neglect of the empirical self would leave nothing to move-beyond, and hence the ethical self could not come to be. As Cohen emphasizes, "the ascent to religious being must begin from sensual being" (*RoR* 231; *RV* 269); see also *RoR* 376; *RV* 437: "The soul of man needs the biological individual, and on account of the latter [*auf Grund*], the historical individual. Thus the religious I demands as its negative condition the empirical substratum [*Unterlagen*] of the I."

71. *RoR* 302–303; *RV* 351–352: "The human being has the task and the power of repentance, and thus of self-renewal and *rebirth*," emphasis in the original. See also *RoR* 223; *RV* 260: "The human being is born anew [*neu geboren*]."

72. *RoR* 381; *RV* 443.

73. One reason that continuity of the self requires discontinuity is that the 'normal' concept of continuity involves constancy over time. However, each infinitesimal moment is *not part of finite time*. Thus, if the self were to have any continuity with previous instantiations, this would mean that the moment and the self had 'grown old,' had absorbed some aspect of finite temporality. Thus, there must be absolute discontinuity in time so that there can be 'continuity' with regard to the infinitesimal moment that lies 'outside of' time.

74. *RoR* 226; *RV* 264.

75. *RoR* 104; *RV* 120–121.

76. *RoR* 399; *RV* 463.

77. *RoR* 230; *RV* 269, emphasis added.

78. *RoR* 309; *RV* 360.

79. *RoR* 310; *RV* 360–361, parenthetical and bracketed Hebrew terms in the original.

80. Almut Bruckstein notes similarities between Cohen's conception of the messianic, non-finite future and Maimonides' account of 'the world to come,' *olam ha-ba*. See Bruckstein, commentary to Cohen, *Ethics of Maimonides*, 174–175.

81. Cf. *RoR* 235; *RV* 274: "Redemption does not at all need to be deferred to the end of days; rather, it already adheres to each moment of suffering."

82. This combination of nearness and conditionality is also reflected in the narrative of BT Sanhedrin 98a, which midrashically interprets Psalm 95:7 so as to signify that the Messiah will come "today—*if* you hearken to [God's] voice."

83. Interestingly, the Hebrew term for 'accept' in this instance comes from the root *k-b-l* (see, e.g., Mishnah Berachot 2:2), whose connation encompasses both active and passive elements. On one hand, the receiver actively takes the yoke upon himself, but, on the other hand, the acceptance can be seen a passive submission to the one who imposes the yoke. Thus, the acceptance of the yoke has the same dual structure that we saw in the apparent contradiction between forgiveness by God and self-purification and between God's command and ethical autonomy. In each case, while the concept may have a practical unity and may correspond to a distinct practice, there can be no determinate answer to the pseudo-theoretical question of agency.

84. It is over this notion of paradox that my reading departs from Martin Kavka's interpretation of Cohen. In many ways, his reading is very similar to my own. He highlights the unresolved tensions in Cohen's account of messianism: on one hand, the messianic future "is relegated to the far-off distance," but, on the other hand, "it exists in the present moment of my ethical act" (127). In addition, he views this tension as representative of the "doubled descriptions of concepts in the Religion" (125).

    However, whereas I argue that this unresolved tension corresponds to the paradoxicality of religious concepts themselves and therefore plays a crucial role in Cohen's communication, Kavka describes it as "confusion" and as a "philosophical problem" that is to be given "an answer" through phenomenological analysis (127). Likewise, he says that "it is never clear in the Religion what the relation is between the figure of the Messiah and its actualization in history" (122). Kavka's use of the term "clear" indicates that he views the situation as undesirable, whereas it may be that Cohen's 'unclarity' is a deliberate and necessary feature of his writing. Importantly, though, Kavka does not blame the unclarity simply on Cohen himself, but rather emphasizes that the concepts themselves resist straightforward formulation: "Cohen's language becomes complex because this situation—intimacy without identity—cannot be easily expressed" (122). Again, while this account is close to my own, I would say that Cohen's language is not merely complex, but contradictory, and that the situation cannot be directly 'expressed' at all. See Kavka, *Jewish Messianism and the History of Philosophy*.

85. *RoR* 385; *RV* 448.

86. *RoR* 386; *RV* 448.

87. *RoR* 375; *RV* 435.

88. Lawrence Kaplan observes a related sort of anticipation in *Religion of Reason*: "Of course, peace, precisely as 'the principle of finality or the end,' is a regulative, asymptotic ideal that may only be approached and never achieved. But the joy that the individual experiences in the present serves as 'the proof of the living power of peace' [*RoR* 456; *RV* 527]. It is as if the ideal of peace, despite its being 'the most inward, the most hidden, and therefore the least revealed power of human, of historical consciousness,' demonstrates its 'forceful magical power' [*RoR* 458; *RV* 529] precisely by radiating joy from the future into the present." However, Kaplan's description of peace as an "asymptotic" ideal, and his use of the phrase "as if," indicates that he may still be working with a non-paradoxical understanding Cohen's approach to the ideal future. See Kaplan, "Suffering and Joy in the Thought of Hermann Cohen," *Modern Judaism* 21, no. 1 (2001): 19.

    Pierfrancesco Fiorato's account of Cohen's messianism, however, is very similar to my own. He repeatedly describes Cohen's conception of the future as a paradox (169, 171, 175), and he argues that, for Cohen, the ideal future can be made present through anticipation while still always remaining future (171). Likewise, he maintains that Cohen's concept of the ideal "leads to no metaphysical solution to the antinomy, but only to a settlement of the dispute, in which the tension of opposing terms neither can nor should be dissolved" (175). See Fiorato, *Geschichtliche Ewigkeit*, particularly 166–176.

89. *RoR* 314; *RV* 366.

90. Steven Schwarzschild, "On Jewish Eschatology," in *Pursuit of the Ideal*, 211.

91. Franz Rosenzweig, letter to Benno Jacob, dated May 23, 1927, in *Briefe und Tagebücher*, 1150. An English translation of this letter can be found in Glatzer, *Franz Rosenzweig: His Life and Thought*, 356–358. While Rosenzweig clearly opposes the notion of "infinity of the Messiah's coming," it is unclear whether his intention in this citation is to attribute this notion to Cohen himself. Paul Mendes-Flohr argues that this is the case, referring to this passage as "Franz Rosenzweig's criticism of Hermann Cohen's asymptotic theology" ("'To Brush History against the Grain': The Eschatology of the Frankfurt School and Ernst Bloch" in *Divided Passions: Jewish Intellectuals and the Experience of Modernity* (Detroit, MI: Wayne State University Press, 1991), 388n74. See also Mendes-Flohr, "'The Stronger and the Better Jews': Jewish Theological Messianism in the Weimar Republic," in *Jews and Messianism in the Modern Era: Metaphor and Meaning*, ed. Jonathan Frankel (New York: Oxford University Press, 1991), 168, and "Franz Rosenzweig and the Crisis of Historicism," in *Divided Passions*, 336n104. In contrast, Robert Gibbs maintains that Rosenzweig saw (the later) Cohen as in agreement with himself, precisely on this issue of the messianic future. That is, Rosenzweig associated "infinity" with Cohen's earlier *System*, but saw *Religion of Reason* as having broken with this notion and as having achieved the 'proper' (i.e., Rosenzweig's) understanding of the coming kingdom. See Gibbs, "Lines, Circles, Points: Messianic Epistemology in Cohen,

Rosenzweig and Benjamin," in *Toward the Millennium: Messianic Expectations from the Bible to Waco*, ed. Peter Schäfer and Mark Cohen (Leiden: Brill, 1998), 370. Steven Schwarzschild, pointing to Rosenzweig's introduction to Cohen's *Jüdische Schriften*, similarly argues that Rosenzweig associates the idea of "infinity" specifically with the 'earlier' Cohen. See Schwarzschild, "Franz Rosenzweig's Anecdotes about Hermann Cohen," in *Gegenwart im Rückblick*, ed. Herbert Arthur Strauss and Kurt R. Grossmann (Heidelberg: L. Stiehm, 1970), 210. While Gibbs's and Schwarzschild's accounts of Rosenzweig's distinction between the early and the later Cohen seem valid, Mendes-Flohr may also be correct that Rosenzweig continued to associate Cohen with the notion of "infinite progress." For instance, in his *Jehuda Halevi*, Rosenzweig refers to Cohen as "a believer in the false messiah of the nineteenth century." See Rosenzweig, *Jehuda Halevi: Der Mensch und sein Werk: Gesammelte Schriften*, vol. 4.1, ed. Rafael N. Rosenzweig (The Hague: Martinus Nijhoff, 1983), 203. It therefore appears that Rosenzweig's view of Cohen may not have been entirely consistent. However, as we shall see, it may be that Rosenzweig was unable to recognize that Cohen's rational conception of the messianic future may itself have been structurally 'inconsistent' in this regard.

92. See also Rosenzweig's introduction to Cohen's *Jüdische Schriften*, where he similarly argues that the traditional Jewish eternity of "soon, in our days" is incompatible with the notion of "infinity." See *JS* I, xxxv.

93. In defending Cohen against Rosenzweig's criticism, Schwarzschild similarly argues (though without the emphasis on paradoxicality) that the 'infinity' of Cohen's position is crucial for the preservation of ethical responsibility. See Steven Schwarzschild, "On Jewish Eschatology," in *Pursuit of the Ideal*, 211–212.

94. Cf. Schwarzschild, "On Jewish Eschatology," in *Pursuit of the Ideal*, 357.

95. In some ways, Rosenzweig's own position, as expressed in his *Star of Redemption*, may appear similar to the one he rejects in the above citation from his letter to Benno Jacob. For instance, he writes that the messianic kingdom of eternity "comes from the beginning, it is always coming. So its growth is necessary. It is always in the future—but in the future it is always. It is always just as much already-here as in the future. It is not yet there once and for all. It comes eternally ... Eternity is a future that, without ceasing to be future, is nevertheless present" (*Stern der Erlösung: Der Mensch und sein Werk: Gesammelte Schriften*, vol. 2 [The Hague: Martinus Nijhoff, 1976], 250; *Star of Redemption*, 224). Here, one could easily read Rosenzweig as asserting that the kingdom "comes only in eternity." For example, Norbert Samuelson describes Rosenzweig's concepts of both creation and redemption as "asymptotes." See Norbert Samuelson, *Judaism and the Doctrine of Creation* (Cambridge: Cambridge University Press, 1994), 222; see also 32–33, 80, 238.

However, we can already note a number of differences from Cohen. First of all, Rosenzweig says that the eternity of the messianic kingdom "*is* present [*gegenwärtig ist*]," without any qualifications regarding its conditionality or its personal-individual nature, whereas Cohen would say that it *can be* present *for me* in the moment of turning. Likewise, while Rosenzweig says that it "is" just as much already-here as in the future, Cohen would say that it *can be* just as much already-here as in the future.

In addition, while Rosenzweig's description here might sound like an 'endless' process of eternal growth and development, he specifically rejects the concept of infinity and contrasts it to that of eternity: "infinite is not eternal [*unendlich ist nicht ewig*]" (*Stern*, 253; *Star*, 226). For Rosenzweig, that which is eternal can be present "in the next moment," whereas that which is "infinite" cannot (*Stern*, 253; *Star*, 227). Because he feels compelled to reject infinity—as he says in his letter to Jacob, "I have no idea of how one should pray for something that one holds from the start/a priori [*von vornherein*] to be impossible"—he is drawn to the seemingly inescapable conclusion that the Messiah one day 'will have come.' Thus, while the current present is to look toward the future with hope and anticipation, there will come a day when "the task of those who hope comes to an end" (*Jehuda Halevi*, 203).

In contrast, Cohen's paradoxical logic enables him to avoid this dilemma. The task of the messianic future is infinite and has no end, yet it can also be present in the next moment. Rosenzweig's opposition to the idea of praying for something impossible indicates that he may not fully appreciate the paradoxicality of the situation. From Cohen's perspective, one *should* hold it to be impossible 'a priori,' since it gains actuality only in the active moment of turning. That is to say, from within the perspective of the a priori, it *is* impossible. However, in the case of the messianic future, it is precisely by praying for 'something that can never be' that that something *does* come to be, in the moment.

96. Cf. the rabbinic dictum that "there is no before and after in the Torah" (*ein mukdam u-me'uchar ba-torah*), BT Pesachim 6b. In the rabbinic context, this may be related to the notion that the Torah preceded creation and is eternal—hence, it is not subject to the normal rules of temporal order. In Cohen's context, we can link this same idea to the fact that Scripture represents the ideal correlation as an actuality. Since such actuality is impossible in time, Scripture must be outside of time would therefore not be subject to the 'before and after' of finite temporality.

97. Cf. Cohen's interpretation of Is. 65:17, wherein *redemption* is designated by a *re-creation* of the heaven and the earth, both of which occur in the performative moment of "I am hereby creating." See "Der Stil der Propheten," in *JS* I, 273.

Since Cohen designates "the proper meaning" of revelation as "God comes into relation with the human being," (*RoR* 71; *RV* 82), the moment of turning can also be linked to revelation: it is precisely in the ethical moment that the correlation between man and God is (re-)actualized. This re-origination of revelation parallels Cohen's assertion, in his introduction, that each 'new' instance of oral Torah is a re-creation of the 'original' teaching at Sinai. See my chapter 2; *RoR* 28; *RV* 32–33.

98. In connection with the debate over messianism between Rosenzweig and Cohen, it is important to emphasize that it is not merely an intra-Jewish parochial dispute. Rather, as Peter Schmid emphasizes, Cohen's concept of messianism is "a universal principle of reason" and is thus directly relevant to philosophical thought more broadly. See Schmid, *Ethik als Hermeneutik: Systematische Untersuchungen zu Hermann Cohens Rechts- und Tugendlehre* (Würzburg, 1995), 197, cited in Pierfrancesco Fiorato, "Notes on Future and History in Hermann Cohen's Anti-Eschatological Messianism," in Munk, *Hermann Cohen's Critical Idealism*, 142.

99. *RoR* 21; *RV* 24, emphasis added.

100. See *RoR* 307; *RV* 357, where Cohen describes the ability of messianism to cultivate the proper ethical "dispositions of the soul [*Seelenanlagen*]."

101. Cohen's hope for the establishment of ethicality in the human world also allows us to revisit one of Rosenzweig's anecdotes about Hermann Cohen. According to Steven Schwarzschild's skeptical analysis of the anecdote, Rosenzweig claims that Cohen first asked, "When do you think the Messiah will come?" and then, misunderstanding Rosenzweig's response as "a hundred years," replied, "Oh please, make it fifty!" Schwarzschild maintains that it is impossible to "believe that the event could have happened the way it is described." Because Cohen held firmly to the infinity of the messianic task, Schwarzschild argues, it is absurd to think that he would have spoken of any finite delimitation for the messianic age. See Schwarzschild, "Franz Rosenzweig's Anecdotes about Hermann Cohen," 210–211.

    While Schwarzschild is correct that Cohen never abandoned the infinity of the messianic future, there may potentially be more truth to Rosenzweig's anecdote than Schwarzschild allows. If we look at the text of the Rosenzweig's anecdote itself, we find that he does *not* claim that Cohen asked, "When do you think the Messiah will come?" Rather, what Cohen supposedly said is: "I am still hoping to see the advent of the messianic era." Rosenzweig then comments, "By this he meant . . . the conversion of the Christians to the 'pure monotheism' of his Judaism, which he believed he saw spreading [*sich verbereiten*] in liberal Protestant theology" (*Jehuda Halevi*, 203). (Similarly, referring to the same incident in his introduction to Cohen's *Jüdische Schriften*, Rosenzweig claims that Cohen "had faith that he would yet live to see the advent of the messianic federation of religions [*Religionenvereinigung*]" [xxxv].)

    Thus, according to Rosenzweig, it was specifically the spread of rational religion, of the religion of reason, that Cohen hoped to live to see. Such a hope would not contradict Cohen's commitment to the infinity of the messianic task: even if a commitment to rational religion were widespread, the task of self-criticism and ethical turning would be no less incumbent. Thus, it is entirely possible that Cohen hoped to see this benchmark achieved within the next hundred, or even fifty, years. Even though Cohen was wrong about its specific timing, his general hope for such a development would be fully in keeping with his understanding of the messianic future. At the same time, it is also likely that Rosenzweig partially misunderstood Cohen: because Rosenzweig viewed the actualization of the messianic future as incompatible with the notion of infinity, he assumed that Cohen's fervent hope of "in our days" meant that he had broken away from the notion of infinite task, and this in turn may have colored his telling of the anecdote. In contrast, I argue that while Cohen may have hoped to see certain 'messianic' developments, he would not have associated these developments with the end of the (infinite) messianic task.

102. *RoR* 21; *RV* 25.

103. Similarly, with regard to the self, one can say that the sensual individual can undergo 'asymptotic' development and growth through ethical striving and prayer, even though the ideal self is still 'fully achieved' in each moment of turning. The task can never have an end, even though one can achieve increasing levels of ethical self-control, compassion, and truthfulness.

104. It should also be emphasized that while Cohen's messianism creates the possibility for such 'progress,' the actuality of 'progress' is wholly dependent on the ethical turning. That is to say, 'progress' toward the ideal is not inevitable, but occurs only as the result of ethical means. For this reason, no unethical means can be justified by laying claim to the pursuit of 'progress,' since 'progress' is not measured externally but is defined strictly as that which results from ethical turning.

105. *RoR* 272; *RV* 318.

106. *RoR* 249; *RV* 291. Note that Cohen's is not the only possible reading of the text: one could understand Isaiah's vision as a future actuality, either by treating his 'infinite' language as hyperbole, so that he is simply referring to a government that embodies justice to a significant, though finite, degree; or by a change in human nature, such that humans lose their finite qualities and thereby become capable of participation in an infinitely just government. However, Cohen's reading of Isaiah's future as ideal seems to be the only way to preserve both the ostensive infinity of his vision and the finite (i.e., 'human') nature of humanity.

107. *RoR* 274–275; *RV* 320.

108. That is, in his reading, the metaphor-structure is part of the plain sense of the text. Cf. Maimonides' assertion that the prophets' visionary proclamations were intended as parables and should be read as such (e.g., *Guide of the Perplexed* 2:43, 2:47, 3:9).

109. Again, it is also possible to interpret Isaiah's imagery differently. (a) One could understand the images as 'poetic' descriptions of actually-possible events, such as the end of war (Cohen notes the possibility of this reading in *RoR* 274; *RV* 320, though he does not lay claim to it himself). In this case, since a literal image *could* have been employed, Isaiah's description of the future would be merely *contingently* metaphorical. In contrast, in Cohen's reading, Isaiah's vision is *essentially and necessarily* metaphorical. (b) One could also understand Isaiah as referring to a future occurrence in which death will actually cease, the blind will actually see,

and the deaf will actually hear. In this case, however, Isaiah's envisioned future would be eschatological, rather than messianic (cf. *RoR* 289; *RV* 336).

110. See Paul Ricoeur, *Interpretation Theory* (Fort Worth: Texas Christian University Press, 1976), 51–52. For an overview of the relation between religious topics and Ricoeur's account of metaphor, see Dan R. Stiver, *Theology after Ricoeur: New Directions in Hermeneutical Theology* (Louisville, KY: Westminster John Knox Press, 2001), 105–113.

111. In other words, one cannot explain the prophets' use of metaphor simply by claiming that they were 'unsophisticated' and lacked the proper philosophical concepts for a clear, non-metaphoric account. Rather, for philosophers as well as for prophets, the paradoxical concept of messianic future itself is *inherently* unrepresentable in consistent 'literal' terms. In this regard, Cohen differs from Maimonides: while the latter did view the prophets as employing metaphors (parables), he held further that they did so only as a concession to the unsophistication of their audience and that their parables in fact corresponded to theoretical philosophical truths. See *Guide of the Perplexed*, Introduction, 9–12; also 1:33. Thus, while Maimonides endeavors to translate the prophetic metaphors into philosophical propositions, Cohen holds that they can only be 'translated' into ethical-practical *deeds* that have no consistent theoretical correlate.

That Maimonides' account of prophetic metaphors conforms to a 'substitution' model is not surprising, since this view of metaphor was dominant in philosophical circles from ancient Greek thought up to the modern period. In particular, Aristotle (upon whom Maimonides draws heavily) played a major role in laying the groundwork for this view. See Mark Johnson, "Introduction: Metaphor in the Philosophical Tradition," in *Philosophical Perspectives on Metaphor*, ed. Mark Johnson (Minneapolis: University of Minnesota Press, 1981), 4–16.

112. Pierfrancesco Fiorato argues that "the elimination of any eschatological value from messianism" is characteristic of Cohen's writings as a whole. See his "Notes on Future and History in Hermann Cohen's Anti-Eschatological Messianism," 136.

113. *RoR* 289; *RV* 337.

114. Cf. Kant's assertion that one cannot talk about the world's extension in space or time as either finite or as infinite. Instead, he holds that the proper description is that of an indefinite magnitude (Critique of Pure Reason, B547–548). Such a notion may have fruitful intersections with Cohen's of a prophetic future that is also neither finite nor infinite, that is "not . . . entirely distant" yet whose time-determination "is left in unclarity."

Similarly, Kant distinguishes between different determinate magnitudes of time and time itself as an a priori "pure form of sensible intuition" that grounds all particular representations (*Critique of Pure Reason*, B46–48). In other words, there is a difference between a judgment about a time five minutes from now, and the more basic 'pure intuition' of time itself which makes the first judgment possible.

This distinction parallels the distinction made above between particular determinate points in the future and the prophetic notion of 'future-ness as such.'

115. That is, it is not that they *lack knowledge of* the precise time-determination, but that *there is no* precise time-determination to be given, even if one could 'see into the future.'

116. This formulation (which always includes *hineh*) is found primarily in Jeremiah (15 occurrences), but also appears in Amos (8:11, 9:8), 1 Samuel (2:31), 2 Kings (20:17), and Isaiah (39:6). Note that the Kings verse and the Isaiah verse are identical to one another. In Malachi 4:1, we find a slight variation: "behold, the day is coming" (*hineh ha-yom ba*).

117. *RoR* 290; *RV* 337.

118. In addition to the use of the phrase in the classical prophetic books, the phrase also appears in Genesis 49:1, where Jacob's dying blessing does not seem at all eschatological, but simply describes what will happen to his sons' tribes *in the future*. Other more clearly non-eschatological uses of the phrase include Numbers 24:14, Deuteronomy 4:30, and Deuteronomy 31:29. For more on the non-eschatological nature of *be-aharit ha-yamim*, see Marc Brettler, "Cyclical and Teleological Time in the Hebrew Bible," in Time and Temporality in the Ancient World, ed. Ralph Mark Rosen (Philadelphia: University of Pennsylvania Museum of Archaeology and Anthropology, 2004), 120–122.

119. *RoR* 290–291; *RV* 338.

120. *RoR* 291; *RV* 338. For a similar presentation by Cohen of the prophetic rejection of the present, see "Der Stil der Propheten," in *JS* I, 279. Robert Gibbs argues that this employment of the future to criticize the present and past also characterizes a "family" of other modern Jewish thinkers after Cohen, including Rosenzweig, Buber, Benjamin, Scholem, Levinas, and Derrida. See Gibbs, "Messianic Epistemology," in *Derrida and Religion*, ed. Yvonne Sherwood and Kevin Hart (New York: Routledge, 2005), 120.

121. *RoR* 291; *RV* 338–339. Regarding the prophets' replacement of a supernatural afterlife with the future, cf. Climacus' question: "For an existing person, is not eternity not eternity but the future?" (*CUP* 306).

122. *RoR* 249; *RV* 291.

123. *RoR* 291; *RV* 339: "From [Plato's] Ethics, a straight road leads, crossing over millennia, to Kant."

124. *RoR* 291; *RV* 339.

125. *RoR* 292; *RV* 340.

126. Cf. *RoR* 289; *RV* 337: "Messianism alone affirms [*behauptet*] development of humankind." Note, however, that this development takes place through *discontinuity*, since the current present actuality is *completely* rejected. This accords with both with Cohen's statements on 'complete destruction' in "Der Stil der Propheten" (in *JS* I, 274, 279) as well as with his account of the ethical self that must undergo rebirth and re-creation at each moment. As such, the development of

humankind consists as much in revolution as in evolution, or rather in the paradoxical conjunction of the two.

127. *RoR* 292; *RV* 340.

128. *RoR* 20–21; *RV* 23–24.

129. *RoR* 292; *RV* 340.

130. In designating this position as "Kantian," we should note that although Kant did connect the striving for holiness and blessedness with an "infinite progress" toward a goal that "is never fully reached by any creature," he also argues that, in God's eyes, such progress toward the goal is deemed to be "possession [*Besitz*]" and attainment of the goal. Thus, although he does not go into great detail on the subject, we can say Kant viewed the goal as attained—at least from a certain perspective—in the very act of striving toward the goal. He may therefore come closer to Cohen's practical-paradoxical account of infinite fulfillment in the moment of turning. As such, the "Kantian" position may be more applicable to Kant's successors than to Kant himself. See Kant, *Critique of Practical Reason*, 5:122–124.

131. *RoR* 292; *RV* 340.

132. *RoR* 293; *RV* 341.

133. *RoR* 293; *RV* 341.

134. In this connection, Almut Bruckstein notes Ernst Cassirer's claim that all of Cohen's earlier systematic philosophy, and not just *Religion of Reason*, had its origin in Cohen's commitment to the idea of monotheism as formulated by the prophets. See Bruckstein, "Practicing 'Intertextuality': Ernst Cassirer and Hermann Cohen on Myth and Monotheism," in *The Symbolic Construction of Reality: The Legacy of Ernst Cassirer*, ed. Jeffrey Andrew Barash (Chicago, IL: University of Chicago Press, 2008), 178.

135. Note that this redescription does not 'resolve' the paradoxicality of the concepts, nor does it remove the need for double-voicedness in their communication.

136. However, one can also say that they are concerned with a paradoxical combination of 'will be' and 'should be': not with what will be automatically, but with what will be if/when you turn. The slash between 'if' and 'when' cannot be removed.

137. Cf. Steven Schwarzschild's section heading, "Eschatology as Ethics," in his "On Jewish Eschatology," in *Pursuit of the Ideal*, 218.

138. *RoR* 95; *RV* 110.

139. BT Shabbat 133b; *RoR* 162; *RV* 187–188.

140. S. H. Bergman also notes the significance for Cohen's thought of the juxtaposition of these two verses. However, Bergman focuses primarily on the correlation between God's agency and human agency, while I emphasize, in addition, the grammatical correlation between the future tense and the imperative mood. See Bergman, *Faith and Reason*, 50–51.

141. This 'impossibility' also shows how Cohen's account of the messianic future can be viewed as being in keeping with 'traditional Jewish conceptions.' Cohen need

not reject the traditional description of the messianic future as "divine intercession at the end-point of history" (to use Steven Schwarzschild's phrase in "The Personal Messiah" in *Pursuit of the Ideal*, 20). He would simply add that the *practical significance of* those traditional conceptions is functionally equivalent to the ethical task of turning in the next moment, and has nothing to do with theoretical or metaphysical hypotheses concerning 'future events.'

142. However, this connection of the tragic with the ideal and the satiric with the actual does not precisely correspond to Kierkegaard's motif (discussed in chapter 4) of 'pathos and the comic.' Although pathos may 'sound like' the tragic, and the comic like the satiric, it is in fact pathos (in which one can address God personally, as 'you') that corresponds to the nearness and the actualization of the infinite goal, while the comic (in which a personal address to God seems ludicrous) that corresponds the goal's ideality and its infinite distance.

143. Cf. Eliezer Schweid, who argues that *Religion of Reason*, in addition to engaging in a philosophical analysis of the character of biblical prophecy, is itself written as a philosophical form of prophecy. See Schweid, "Hermann Cohen's Philosophical Prophecy" (Hebrew), *Daat* 35 (Summer 1995), 67–68, 75.

144. Even though he qualifies this actualization by confining it to an infinitesimal moment, the reader is still likely to over-actualize this idea, since reflective thought cannot conceive of an infinitesimal duration. Instead, a reader is likely to think of the ideal as actualizable for a 'very short' duration, thus eroding the fundamental impossibility of fulfilling the infinite task. Ironically, by abrogating the infinity of the task, this mitigation of impossibility can distract one from the necessity of continuous ethical striving and thereby prevent the dynamic actualization that is possible in the moment.

Steven Schwarzschild notes some of the communicative dangers inherent in Cohen's tendency to use 'is' language when discussing subjects that Cohen himself insists should be regarded only as ideal tasks with no static actuality. See Schwarzschild, "'Germanism and Judaism,'" 153–157.

145. *RoR* 335; *RV* 390. It must also be noted that Cohen states elsewhere that "the boundary of mysticism is never touched" (*RoR* 212; *RV* 248). In the latter statement, however, he uses the term *Schranke*, rather than the more correlatively significant term *Grenz*.

146. I thank Asher Biemann for suggesting the metaphoric connection between the concept of repentance and Cohen's stylistic oscillations.

Bibliography

Adelmann, Dieter. *Einheit des Bewußtseins als Grundproblem der Philosophie Hermann Cohens*. Heidelberg: Inaugural-Dissertation, 1968.

———. "H. Steinthal und Hermann Cohen." In *Hermann Cohen's Philosophy of Religion: International Conference in Jerusalem, 1996*, edited by Stéphane Moses and Hartwig Wiedebach, 1–33. Hildesheim: Georg Olms Verlag, 1997.

Alter, Robert. *The Art of Biblical Narrative*. New York: Basic Books, 1981.

Altmann, Alexander. "Hermann Cohens Begriff der Korrelation." In *In Zwei Welten: Siegfried Moses zum fünfundsiebzigsten Geburtstag*, edited by Hans Tramer, 377–399. Tel-Aviv: Verlag Bitaon, 1962.

Anckaert, Luc. "Language, Ethics, and the Other between Athens and Jerusalem: A Comparative Study of Plato and Rosenzweig." *Philosophy East and West* 45, no. 4 (October 1995): 545–567.

Austin, John L. *How To Do Things with Words*. 2nd ed. Edited by J. O. Urmson and Marina Sbisà. Cambridge, MA: Harvard University Press, 1975.

Barth, Karl. *Epistle to the Romans*. Translated from the sixth edition by Edwyn C. Hoskins. New York: Oxford University Press, 1968.

Batnitzky, Leora. *Idolatry and Representation: The Philosophy of Franz Rosenzweig Reconsidered*. Princeton, NJ: Princeton University Press, 2000.

———. *Leo Strauss and Emmanuel Levinas: Philosophy and the Politics of Revelation*. New York: Cambridge University Press, 2006.

Bell, John L. *The Continuous and the Infinitesimal in Mathematics and Philosophy*. Milano: Polimetrica, 2005.

Bergman, Samuel Hugo. "Hermann Cohen." In *Between East and West: Essays Dedicated to the Memory of Bela Horovitz*, edited by Alexander Altmann, 22–47. London: East and West Library, 1958.

———. *Faith and Reason: An Introduction to Modern Jewish Thought*. Edited and translated by Alfred Jospe. New York: Schocken Books, 1961.

———. *Dialogical Philosophy from Kierkegaard to Buber*. Translated by Arnold Gerstein. Albany: State University of New York Press, 1991.

Berkeley, George. *De Motu; and, The Analyst: A Modern Edition with Introductions and Commentary*. Edited and translated by Douglas M. Jesseph. Dordrecht: Kluwer Academic Publishers, 1992.

Berkovits, Eliezer. *Major Themes in the Philosophy of Judaism*. New York: KTAV, 1974.

Bernstein-Nahar, Avi. "In the Name of a *Narrative* Education: Hermann Cohen and Historicism Reconsidered." In *Hermann Cohen's Ethics*, edited by Robert Gibbs, 147–185. Leiden: Brill, 2006.

Bialik, Hayyim. "Halakhah and Aggadah, or Lore and Love" [1917]. *Contemporary Jewish Record* 7, no. 6 (December 1944): 662–680.

Bonaunet, Ketil. *Hermann Cohen's Kantian Philosophy of Religion*. Bern: Peter Lang, 2004.

Borowitz, Eugene. *Choices in Modern Jewish Thought: A Partisan Guide*. 2nd ed. New York: Behrman House, 1995.

Bouretz, Pierre. *Témoins du future: philosophie et messianisme*. Paris: Gallimard, 2003.

Boyarin, Daniel. *Intertextuality and the Reading of Midrash*. Bloomington: Indiana University Press, 1990.

———. *Carnal Israel: Reading Sex in Talmudic Culture*. Berkeley: University of California Press, 1993.

Brandes, Georg. *Sören Kierkegaard: Ein literarisches Charakterbild*. Leipzig: Johann Ambrosius Barth, 1879.

Brettler, Marc. "Cyclical and Teleological Time in the Hebrew Bible." In *Time and Temporality in the Ancient World*, edited by Ralph Mark Rosen, 111–128. Philadelphia: University of Pennsylvania Museum of Archaeology and Anthropology, 2004.

Bruckstein, Almut Sh. "Joining the Narrators: A Philosophy of Talmudic Hermeneutics." In Steven Kepnes, Peter Ochs, and Robert Gibbs, *Reasoning After Revelation: Dialogues in Postmodern Jewish Philosophy*, 105–121. Boulder, CO: Westview Press, 1998.

———. "Introduction," in Hermann Cohen, *Ethics of Maimonides*. Translated and with commentary by Almut Sh. Bruckstein, xxi–xliii. Madison: University of Wisconsin Press, 2004.

———. "Hermann Cohen. *Ethics of Maimonides*: Residues of Jewish Philosophy—Traumatized." In *Hermann Cohen's Ethics*, edited by Robert Gibbs, 115–125. Leiden: Brill, 2006.

———. "Practicing 'Intertextuality': Ernst Cassirer and Hermann Cohen on Myth and Monotheism." In *The Symbolic Construction of Reality: The Legacy of Ernst Cassirer*, edited by Jeffrey Andrew Barash, 174–188. Chicago: University of Chicago Press, 2008.

Buber, Martin. *Eclipse of God*. New York: Harper & Brothers, 1952.

———. *Gottesfinsternis*. Gerlingen: Lambert Schneider, 1994.

———. *I and Thou*. Translated by Walter Kaufmann. New York, NY: Touchstone, 1996.

———. *Between Man and Man*. Translated by Ronald Gregor-Smith. London: Routledge, 2002.

Buber, Martin, and Franz Rosenzweig. *Die Fünf Bücher der Weisung*. Berlin: Lambert Schneider, 1930.

Buber, Martin, and Franz Rosenzweig. *Scripture and Translation*. Translated by Lawrence Rosenwald with Everett Fox. Bloomington: Indiana University Press, 1994.

Cohen, Hermann. *Religion der Vernunft aus den Quellen des Judentums* [1929, 2nd ed.]. Wiesbaden: Fourier Verlag, 1978.

———. *Hermann Cohens Jüdische Schriften*. 3 vols. Edited by Bruno Strauss. New York: Arno Press, 1980.

———. *Ästhetik des reinen Gefühls* [1912]. 2 vols. Hildesheim: Georg Olms Verlag, 1982.

———. *Religion of Reason Out of the Sources of Judaism*. Translated by Simon Kaplan. Atlanta, GA: Scholars Press, 1995.

———. *Ethik des reinen Willens* [1907, 2nd ed.]. Hildesheim: Georg Olms Verlag, 2002.

———. *Der Begriff der Religion im System der Philosophie* [1915]. Hildesheim: Georg Olms Verlag, 2002.

———. *Ethics of Maimonides*. Translated and with commentary by Almut Sh. Bruckstein. Madison: University of Wisconsin Press, 2004.

———. *Das Prinzip der Infinitesimal-Methode und seine Geschichte* [1883]. Hildesheim: Georg Olms Verlag, 2005.

———. *Logik der reinen Erkenntnis* [1914, 2nd ed.]. Hildesheim: Georg Olms Verlag, 2005.

Crouter, Richard. *Friedrich Schleiermacher: Between Enlightenment and Romanticism*. Cambridge: Cambridge University Press, 2005.

Deuber-Mankowsky, Astrid. "Das Gesetz und die Suspension des Ethischen: Jacob Taubes und Hermann Cohen." In *Torah-Nomos-Ius: Abendländischer Antinomismus und der Traum vom herrschaftsfreien Raum*, edited by Gesine Palmer et al., 243–262. Berlin: Vorwerk 8, 1999.

Dietrich, Wendell. *Cohen and Troeltsch: Ethical Monotheistic Religion and Theory of Culture*. Atlanta, GA: Scholars Press, 1986.

Dussort, Henri. *L'école de Marbourg*. Paris: Presses universitaires de France, 1963.

Fackenheim, Emil. *Jewish Philosophers and Jewish Philosophy*. Edited by Michael L. Morgan. Bloomington: Indiana University Press, 1996.

Ferreira, M. Jamie. *Love's Grateful Striving*. New York: Oxford University Press, 2001.

Fiorato, Pierfrancesco. *Geschichtliche Ewigkeit: Ursprung und Zeitlichkeit in der Philosophie Hermann Cohens*. Würzburg: Königshausen & Neumann, 1993.

———. "Notes on Future and History in Hermann Cohen's Anti-Eschatological Messianism." In *Hermann Cohen's Critical Idealism*, edited by Reinier Munk, 133–160. Dordrecht: Springer, 2005.

Fishbane, Michael. *Biblical Interpretation in Ancient Israel*. New York: Oxford University Press, 1985.

———. *Biblical Myth and Rabbinic Mythmaking*. New York: Oxford University Press, 2003.

Fisher, Simon. *Revelatory Positivism? Barth's Earliest Theology and the Marburg School.* Oxford: Oxford University Press, 1988.

Fox, Marvin. "Kierkegaard and Rabbinic Judaism." *Judaism* 2, no. 2 (Spring 1953): 160–169.

Fraade, Steven. *From Tradition to Commentary: Torah and Its Interpretation in the Midrash Sifre to Deuteronomy*. Albany: State University of New York Press, 1991.

Gellman, Jerome. *The Fear, the Trembling, and the Fire: Kierkegaard and the Hasidic Masters on the Binding of Isaac*. Lanham, MD: University Press of America, 1994.

———. *Abraham! Abraham! Kierkegaard and the Hasidim on the Binding of Isaac*. Aldershot: Ashgate, 2003.

Gibbs, Robert. *Correlations in Rosenzweig and Levinas*. Princeton, NJ: Princeton University Press, 1992.

———. "Lines, Circles, Points: Messianic Epistemology in Cohen, Rosenzweig and Benjamin." In *Toward the Millennium: Messianic Expectations from the Bible to Waco*, edited by Peter Schäfer and Mark Cohen, 363–382. Leiden: Brill, 1998.

———. "Hermann Cohen's Messianism: The History of the Future." In *"Religion der Vernunft aus den Quellen des Judentums": Tradition und Ursprungsdenken in Hermann Cohens Spätwerk: Internationale Konferenz in Zürich 1998*, edited by Helmut Holzhey, Gabriel Motzkin, and Hartwig Wiedebach, 331–349. Hildesheim: Georg Olms Verlag, 2000.

———. "Messianic Epistemology." In *Derrida and Religion*, edited by Yvonne Sherwood and Kevin Hart, 119–129. New York: Routledge, 2005.

———. "Hermann Cohen's *Ethics*." In *Hermann Cohen's Ethics*, edited by Robert Gibbs, vii–xi. Leiden: Brill, 2006.

———, ed. *Hermann Cohen's Ethics*. Leiden: Brill, 2006.

Giovanelli, Marco. *Reality and Negation—Kant's Principle of Anticipation of Perception: An Investigation of Its Impact on the Post-Kantian Debate*. Dordrecht: Springer, 2010.

Glatzer, Nahum N., ed. *Franz Rosenzweig: His Life and Thought*. New York: Schocken Books, 1953.

Goetschel, Willi. *Spinoza's Modernity: Mendelssohn, Lessing, and Heine*. Madison: University of Wisconson Press, 2004.

Goodman-Thau, Eveline. "Das Gebet zwischen Erkenntnis und Handlung." In *"Religion der Vernunft aus den Quellen des Judentums": Tradition und Ursprungsdenken in Hermann Cohens Spätwerk: Internationale Konferenz in Zürich 1998*, edited by Helmut Holzhey, Gabriel Motzkin, and Hartwig Wiedebach, 147–174. Hildesheim: Georg Olms Verlag, 2000.

Gordon, Peter Eli. *Rosenzweig and Heidegger: Between Judaism and German Philosophy*. Berkeley: University of California Press, 2003.

Green, Ronald. *Kierkegaard and Kant: The Hidden Debt*. Albany: State University of New York Press, 1992.

Guttmann, Julius. *Philosophies of Judaism: The History of Jewish Philosophy from Biblical Times to Franz Rosenzweig* [1933]. Translated by David W. Silverman. New York: Holt, Rinehart & Winston, 1964.

Hadot, Pierre. *Philosophy as a Way of Life*. Edited by Arnold Davidson. Oxford: Blackwell, 1995.

Halbertal, Moshe. "If it were not a written verse, it could not be said" (Hebrew). *Tarbiz* 68 (1998): 39–59.

Halevi, Jacob L. "Kierkegaard and the Midrash." *Judaism* 4, no. 1 (Winter 1954): 13–28.

———. "Kierkegaard's Teleological Suspension of the Ethical—Is It Jewish?" *Judaism* 8, no. 4 (Fall 1959): 291–302.

———. *A Critique of Martin Buber's Interpretation of Soren Kierkegaard*. Ph.D. dissertation, Hebrew Union College–Jewish Institute of Religion, 1959.

Halivni, David Weiss. *Revelation Restored*. Boulder, CO: Westview Press, 1997.

Heidegger, Martin. *Being and Time*. Translated by John MacQuarrie and Edward Robinson. New York: Harper & Row, 1962.

Hegel, G. W. F. *On Art, Religion, and the History of Philosophy: Introductory Lectures*. Edited by J. Glenn Gray. Indianapolis, IN: Hackett Publishing Company, 1997.

Heisenberg, Werner. *Physics and Philosophy: The Revolution in Modern Science* [1958]. Amherst, NY: Prometheus Books, 1999.

Heschel, Abraham Joshua. *Man is Not Alone: A Philosophy of Religion*. Philadelphia, PA: Jewish Publication Society of America, 1951.

———. *God in Search of Man: A Philosophy of Judaism*. New York: Farrar, Straus & Giroux, 1955.

———. *A Passion For Truth*. Woodstock, VT: Jewish Lights Publishing, 1995.

———. *Heavenly Torah: As Refracted by the Generations*. Translated by Gordon Tucker. New York: Continuum, 2005.

Hobsbawm, Eric, and Terence Ranger, eds. *The Invention of Tradition*. Cambridge: Cambridge University Press, 1983.

Holzhey, Helmut. *Cohen und Natorp*. 2 vols. Basel: Schwabe, 1986.

———. "Cohen and the Marburg School in Context." In *Hermann Cohen's Critical Idealism*, edited by Reinier Munk, 3–37. Dordrecht: Springer, 2005.

Holzhey, Helmut, Gabriel Motzkin, and Hartwig Wiedebach, eds. *"Religion der Vernunft aus den Quellen des Judentums": Tradition und Ursprungsdenken in Hermann Cohens Spätwerk: Internationale Konferenz in Zürich 1998*. Hildesheim: Georg Olms Verlag, 2000.

Jaffee, Martin. *Torah in the Mouth: Writing and Oral Tradition in Palestinian Judaism, 200 BCE–400 CE*. New York: Oxford University Press, 2001.

Johnson, Mark. "Introduction: Metaphor in the Philosophical Tradition." In *Philosophical Perspectives on Metaphor*, edited by Mark Johnson, 3–47. Minneapolis: University of Minnesota Press, 1981.

Kajon, Irene. "Hermann Cohen's Concept of Revelation as a Response to Hegelianism." In *Hermann Cohen's Philosophy of Religion: International Conference in Jerusalem, 1996*, edited by Stéphane Moses and Hartwig Wiedebach, 105–119. Hildesheim: Georg Olms Verlag, 1997.

———. *Contemporary Jewish Philosophy: An Introduction*. London: Routledge, 2006.

Kant, Immanuel. *Foundations of the Metaphysics of Morals*. Translated by Lewis White Beck. New York: Macmillan, 1959.

———. *Religion Within the Limits of Reason Alone*. Translated by Theodore M. Greene and Hoyt H. Hudson. New York: Harper Torchbooks, 1960.

———. "Inaugural Dissertation: On the Form and Principles of the Sensible and the Intelligible World." In Kant, *Theoretical Philosophy, 1755–1770*. Translated and edited by David Walford. New York: Cambridge University Press, 1992.

———. *Critique of Practical Reason*. Translated by Lewis White Beck. New York: Macmillan, 1993.

———. *Prolegomena to Any Future Metaphysics*. Translated and edited by Gary Hatfield. Cambridge: Cambridge University Press, 1997.

———. *Critique of Pure Reason*. Translated by Paul Guyer and Allen W. Wood. Cambridge: Cambridge University Press, 1998.

———. *Critique of the Power of Judgment*. Translated by Paul Guyer and Eric Matthews. Cambridge: Cambridge University Press, 2000.

Kaplan, Lawrence. "Suffering and Joy in the Thought of Hermann Cohen." *Modern Judaism* 21, no. 1 (2001): 15–22.

Kavka, Martin. *Jewish Messianism and the History of Philosophy*. Cambridge: Cambridge University Press, 2004.

———. "Levinas between Monotheism and Cosmotheism." In *Levinas Studies: An Annual Review*, vol. 2, edited by Jeffrey Bloechl, 79–103. Pittsburgh, PA: Duquesne University Press, 2007.

Kepnes, Steven. *Jewish Liturgical Reasoning*. Oxford: Oxford University Press, 2007.

———, Peter Ochs, and Robert Gibbs. *Reasoning After Revelation: Dialogues in Postmodern Jewish Philosophy*. Boulder, CO: Westview Press, 1998.

Kierkegaard, Søren. *Søren Kierkegaard's Journals and Papers*. Edited and translated by Howard V. Hong and Edna H. Hong. Bloomington: Indiana University Press, 1975.

———. *Fear and Trembling; Repetition*. Edited and translated by Howard V. Hong and Edna H. Hong. Princeton, NJ: Princeton University Press, 1983.

———. *Philosophical Fragments; Johannes Climacus*. Edited and translated by Howard V. Hong and Edna H. Hong. Princeton, NJ: Princeton University Press, 1985.

———. *Practice in Christianity*. Edited and translated by Howard V. Hong and Edna H. Hong. Princeton, NJ: Princeton University Press, 1992.

———. *Concluding Unscientific Postscript to Philosophical Fragments*. Edited and translated by Howard V. Hong and Edna H. Hong. Princeton, NJ: Princeton University Press, 1992.

————. *The Point of View*. Edited and translated by Howard V. Hong and Edna H. Hong. Princeton, NJ: Princeton University Press, 1998.

Knappe, Ulrich. *Theory and Practice in Kant and Kierkegaard*. Berlin: Walter de Gruyter, 2004.

Köhnke, Klaus Christian. *The Rise of Neo-Kantianism: German Academic Philosophy between Idealism and Positivism*. Translated by R. J. Hollingdale. Cambridge: Cambridge University Press, 1991.

Korsch, Dietrich. "Hermann Cohen und die protestantische Theologie seiner Zeit." *Zeitschrift für Neuere Theologiegeschichte* 1 (1994): 66–96.

Laing, R.D. *The Divided Self*. New York: Pantheon Books, 1960.

Lange, Friedrich Albert. *Geschichte des Materialismus und Kritik seiner Bedeutung in der Gegenwart*. Introduction by Hermann Cohen. Leipzig: Verlag von J. Baedeker, 1902.

Lash, Scott. "Experience." *Theory, Culture & Society* 23, nos. 2–3 (2006): 335–341.

Levinas, Emmanuel. *Quatre lecture talmudiques* (Paris: Éditions de Minuit, 1968).

————. *Otherwise Than Being, or Beyond Essence*. Translated by Alphonso Lingis. The Hague: M. Nijhoff, 1981.

————. *Nine Talmudic Readings*. Translated by Annette Aronowicz. Bloomington: Indiana University Press, 1990.

Levy, Ze'ev. "Hermann Cohen and Emmanuel Levinas." In *Hermann Cohen's Philosophy of Religion: International Conference in Jerusalem, 1996*, edited by Stéphane Moses and Hartwig Wiedebach, 133–143. Hildesheim: Georg Olms Verlag, 1997.

Liebeschütz, Hans. "Hermann Cohen and His Historical Background." *Leo Baeck Institute Yearbook* 13 (1968): 3–33.

Lord, Albert. *The Singer of Tales*. Cambridge, MA: Harvard University Press, 1960.

Lyden, John. "The Influence of Hermann Cohen on Karl Barth's Dialectical Theology." *Modern Judaism* 12, no. 2 (May 1992): 167–183.

Maimonides, Moses. *Guide of the Perplexed*. Translated by Shlomo Pines. Chicago: University of Chicago Press, 1963.

Malik, Habib C. *Receiving Søren Kierkegaard: The Early Impact and Transmission of His Thought*. Washington, DC: Catholic University of America Press, 1997.

Mendelssohn, Moses. *Jerusalem: Or on Religious Power and Judaism*. Translated by Allan Arkush. Hanover, NH: University Press of New England / Brandeis University Press, 1983.

————. *Philosophical Writings*. Edited by Daniel O. Dahlstrom. Cambridge: Cambridge University Press, 1997.

Mendes-Flohr, Paul. "'The Stronger and the Better Jews': Jewish Theological Messianism in the Weimar Republic." In *Jews and Messianism in the Modern Era: Metaphor and Meaning*, edited by Jonathan Frankel, 159–185. New York: Oxford University Press, 1991.

————. *Divided Passions: Jewish Intellectuals and the Experience of Modernity*. Detroit, MI: Wayne State University Press, 1991.

Moses, Stéphane, and Hartwig Wiedebach, eds. *Hermann Cohen's Philosophy of Religion: International Conference in Jerusalem, 1996*. Hildesheim: Georg Olms Verlag, 1997.

Motzkin, Gabriel. "The Problem of Knowledge in Cohen's Philosophy of Religion." In *Hermann Cohen's Philosophy of Religion: International Conference in Jerusalem, 1996*, edited by Stéphane Moses and Hartwig Wiedebach, 145–159. Hildesheim: Georg Olms Verlag, 1997.

———. "Love and Knowledge in Cohen's 'Religion of Reason.'" In *"Religion der Vernunft aus den Quellen des Judentums": Tradition und Ursprungsdenken in Hermann Cohens Spätwerk: Internationale Konferenz in Zürich 1998*, edited by Helmut Holzhey, Gabriel Motzkin, and Hartwig Wiedebach, 89–104. Hildesheim: Georg Olms Verlag, 2000.

Moynahan, Gregory B. "Hermann Cohen's *Das Prinzip der Infinitesimalmethod*, Ernst Cassirer, and the Politics of Science in Wilhelmine Germany." *Perspectives on Science* 11, no. 1 (2003): 35–75.

Munk, Reinier, ed. *Hermann Cohen's Critical Idealism*. Dordrecht: Springer, 2005.

Myers, David N. *Re-Inventing the Jewish Past: European Jewish Intellectuals and the Zionist Return to History*. New York: Oxford University Press, 1995.

———. "Hermann Cohen and the Quest for Protestant Judaism." *Leo Baeck Institute Yearbook* 46 (2001): 195–214.

———. *Resisting History: Historicism and its Discontents in German-Jewish Thought*. Princeton, NJ: Princeton University Press, 2003.

Napier, Elizabeth R. "Aylmer as 'Scheidekünstler': The Pattern of Union and Separation in Hawthorne's 'The Birthmark.'" *South Atlantic Bulletin* (1976): 32–35.

Newsom, Carol. "Bakhtin, The Bible, and Dialogic Truth." *Journal of Religion* 76, no.2 (April 1996): 290–306.

———. *The Book of Job: A Contest in Moral Imaginations*. New York: Oxford University Press, 2003.

Newton, Adam Zachary. *Narrative Ethics*. Cambridge, MA: Harvard University Press, 1995.

Novak, David. *The Election of Israel: The Idea of a Chosen People*. Cambridge: Cambridge University Press, 1995.

Palmer, Gesine. "Judaism as a 'Method' with Hermann Cohen and Franz Rosenzweig." In *Hermann Cohen's Ethics*, edited by Robert Gibbs, 37–63. Leiden: Brill, 2006.

Papa-Grimaldi, Alba. "Why Mathematical Solutions of Zeno's Paradoxes Miss the Point: Zeno's One and Many Relation and Parmenides' Prohibition." *Review of Metaphysics* 50 (December 1996): 299–314.

Peirce, Charles S. *Charles S. Peirce: Selected Writings*. Edited by Philip P. Wiener. New York: Dover, 1966.

———. *Pragmatism as a Principle and Method of Right Thinking*. Edited by Patricia Ann Turrisi. Albany: State University of New York Press, 1997.

Poma, Andrea. *The Critical Philosophy of Hermann Cohen*. Translated by John Denton. Albany: State University of New York Press, 1997.

———. *Yearning for Form and Other Essays on Hermann Cohen's Thought*. Dordrecht: Springer, 2006.

———. "Hermann Cohen: Judaism and Critical Idealism." In *The Cambridge Companion to Modern Jewish Philosophy*, edited by Michael L. Morgan and Peter Eli Gordon, 80–101. Cambridge: Cambridge University Press, 2007.

Rashkover, Randi. *Revelation and Theopolitics: Barth, Rosenzweig, and the Politics of Praise*. London: T&T Clark International, 2005.

Rawidowicz, Simon. *Studies in Jewish Thought*. Edited by Nahum Glatzer. Philadelphia: Jewish Publication Society, 1974.

Ricoeur, Paul. *Interpretation Theory*. Fort Worth: Texas Christian University Press, 1976.

Rose, Gillian. *Judaism and Modernity: Philosophical Essays*. Cambridge, MA: Blackwell, 1993.

Rosenzweig, Franz. *On Jewish Learning*. Edited by N. N. Glazer. New York: Schocken Books, 1955.

———. *Der Stern der Erlösung: Der Mensch und sein Werk: Gesammelte Schriften*, vol. 2. The Hague: Martinus Nijhoff, 1976.

———. *Briefe und Tagebücher: Der Mensch und sein Werk: Gesammelte Schriften*, vol. 1.2. Edited by Rachel Rosenzweig and Edith Rosenzweig-Schienmann. The Hague: Martinus Nijhoff, 1979.

———. "Einleitung." In *Hermann Cohens Jüdische Schriften*, vol. 1, edited by Bruno Strauss, xiii–lxiv. New York: Arno Press, 1980.

———. *Jehuda Halevi: Der Mensch und sein Werk: Gesammelte Schriften*, vol. 4.1. Edited by Rafael N. Rosenzweig. The Hague: Martinus Nijhoff, 1983.

———. *The Star of Redemption*. Translated by William W. Hallo. Notre Dame, IN: University of Notre Dame Press, 1985.

———. *God, Man, and the World*. Edited and translated by Barbara Galli. Syracuse, NY: Syracuse University Press, 1998.

———. *Philosophical and Theological Writings*. Translated by Paul W. Franks and Michael L. Morgan. Indianapolis, IN: Hackett Pub., 2000.

Rotenstreich, Nathan. *Jewish Philosophy in Modern Times: From Mendelssohn to Rosenzweig*. New York: Holt, Rinehart & Winston, 1968.

Rubinstein, Jeffrey. *Talmudic Stories: Narrative Art, Composition, and Culture*. Baltimore, MD: Johns Hopkins University Press, 1999.

Saltzman, Judy. *Paul Natorp's Philosophy of Religion*. Hildesheim: Georg Olms Verlag, 1981.

Samuelson, Norbert M. *An Introduction to Modern Jewish Philosophy*. Albany: State University of New York Press, 1989.

———. "A Critique of Borowitz's Postmodern Jewish Theology." *Zygon* 28, no.2 (June 1993): 267–282.

——. *Judaism and the Doctrine of Creation.* Cambridge: Cambridge University Press, 1994.

Santner, Eric L. *On the Psychotheology of Everyday Life: Reflections on Freud and Rosenzweig.* Chicago: University of Chicago Press, 2001.

Scholem, Gershom. *The Messianic Idea in Judaism and Other Essays on Jewish Spirituality.* New York: Schocken Books, 1971.

——. *Jews and Judaism in Crisis.* New York: Schocken Books, 1976.

——. *On the Possibility of Jewish Mysticism in Our Time & Other Essays.* Philadelphia, PA: Jewish Publication Society, 1997.

Schönbaumsfeld, Genia. *A Confusion of the Spheres: Kierkegaard and Wittgenstein on Philosophy and Religion.* New York: Oxford University Press, 2007.

Schorsch, Ismar. *From Text to Context: The Turn to History in Modern Judaism.* Hanover, NH: University Press of New England / Brandeis University Press, 1994.

Schutz, Alfred, *Collected Papers,* Volume 2: *Studies in Social Theory.* Edited by Arvid Brodersen. The Hague: Martinus Nijhoff, 1964.

Schwarzschild, Steven. "The Democratic Socialism of Hermann Cohen." *Hebrew Union College Annual* 27 (1956): 417–438.

——. "Franz Rosenzweig's Anecdotes about Hermann Cohen." In *Gegenwart im Rückblick,* edited by Herbert Arthur Strauss and Kurt R. Grossmann, 209–218. Heidelberg: L. Stiehm, 1970.

——. "'Germanism and Judaism'—Hermann Cohen's Normative Paradigm of the German-Jewish Symbiosis." In *Jews and Germans from 1860 to 1933: The Problematic Symbiosis,* edited by David Bronsen, 129–172. Heidelberg: Winter, 1979.

——. "Introduction." In Hermann Cohen, *Ethik des reinen Willens,* vii–xxxv. Hildesheim: Georg Olms Verlag, 1981.

——. "An Introduction to the Thought of R. Isaac Hutner." *Modern Judaism* 5, no. 3 (October 1985): 235–277.

——. "The Theologico-Political Basis of Liberal Christian-Jewish Relations in Modernity." In *Das deutsche Judentum und der Liberalismus—German Jewry and Liberalism,* 70–95. Sankt Augustin: Comdok-Verlagsabteilung, 1986.

——. "An Agenda for Jewish Philosophy in the 1980's." In *Studies in Jewish Philosophy: Collected Essays of the Academy for Jewish Philosophy 1980–1985,* edited by Norbert Samuelson, 101–125. Lanham, MD: University Press of America, 1987.

——. "The Religious Stake in Modern Philosophy of Infinity." *Bar Ilan* 22/23 (1987): 63–83.

——. *The Pursuit of the Ideal: Jewish Writings of Steven Schwarzschild.* Edited by Menachem Kellner. Albany, NY: State University of New York Press, 1990.

——. "The Title of Hermann Cohen's 'Religion of Reason Out of the Sources of Judaism.'" In Hermann Cohen, *Religion of Reason Out of the Sources of Judaism,* translated by Simon Kaplan, 7–20. Atlanta, GA: Scholars Press, 1995.

Schweid, Eliezer. "Hermann Cohen's Philosophical Prophecy" (Hebrew). *Daat* 35 (Summer 1995): 67–85.

———. "Hermann Cohen's Biblical Exegesis." In *"Religion der Vernunft aus den Quellen des Judentums": Tradition und Ursprungsdenken in Hermann Cohens Spätwerk: Internationale Konferenz in Zürich 1998*, edited by Helmut Holzhey, Gabriel Motzkin, and Hartwig Wiedebach, 353–379. Hildesheim: Georg Olms Verlag, 2000.

Seeskin, Kenneth. *Jewish Philosophy in a Secular Age*. Albany: State University of New York Press, 1990.

———. *Searching for a Distant God: The Legacy of Maimonides*. New York: Oxford University Press, 2000.

———. *Autonomy in Jewish Philosophy*. Cambridge: Cambridge University Press, 2001.

Sieg, Ulrich. *Aufstieg und Niedergang des Marburger Neukantianismus: die Geschichte einer philosophischen Schulgemeinschaft*. Würzburg: Königshausen & Neumann, 1994.

Smith, Wilfred Cantwell. *The Meaning and End of Religion*. Minneapolis, MN: Fortress Press, 1991.

Spinoza, Benedict. *Theological-Political Treatise*. Edited by Jonathan Israel. Translated by Michael Silverthorne and Jonathan Israel. Cambridge: Cambridge University Press, 2007.

Steinberg, Milton. "Kierkegaard and Judaism." In *Modern Jewish Thought: Selected Issues, 1889–1966*, 161–180. New York: Arno Press, 1973.

Stiver, Dan R. *Theology after Ricoeur: New Directions in Hermeneutical Theology*. Louisville, KY: Westminster John Knox Press, 2001.

Strauss, Leo. *Persecution and the Art of Writing*. Glencoe, IL: The Free Press, 1952.

———. *Spinoza's Critique of Religion*. Translated by E. M. Sinclair. New York: Schocken Books, 1965.

———. *Philosophy and Law: Essays Toward the Understanding of Maimonides and his Predecessors* [1935]. Translated by Fred Baumann. Philadelphia, PA: Jewish Publication Society, 1987.

———. "Introductory Essay." In Hermann Cohen, *Religion of Reason Out of the Sources of Judaism*, translated by Simon Kaplan, xxiii–xxxviii. Atlanta, GA: Scholars Press, 1995.

———. *Leo Strauss: The Early Writings, 1921–1932*. Edited and translated by Michael Zank. Albany: State University of New York Press, 2002.

Thompson, Curtis L. "Gotthold Ephraim Lessing: Appropriating the Testimony of a Theological Naturalist." In *Kierkegaard and the Renaissance and Modern Traditions. Tome 1: Philosophy*, edited by Jon Stewart, 77–112. Surrey, UK: Ashgate, 2009.

Trigano, Shmuel. *La demeure oubliée: Genèse religieuse du politique*. Paris: Lieu Commun, 1984.

Ucko, Siegfried. *Der Gottesbegriff in der Philosophie Hermann Cohens*. Berlin-Schöneberg: Siegfried Scholem, 1927.

Vaihinger, Hans. *The Philosophy of 'As if': A System of the Theoretical, Practical and Religious Fictions of Mankind*. Translated by C. K. Ogden. London: Routledge & Kegan Paul, 1968.

Vallée, Gérard. *Soundings in G. E. Lessing's Philosophy of Religion*. Lanham, MD: University Press of America, 2000.

Van Pelt, Robert Jan, and Carroll William Westfall. *Architectural Principles in the Age of Historicism*. New Haven, CT: Yale University Press, 1991.

Volkov, Shulamit. "Die Erfindung einer Tradition. Zur Enstehung des modernen Judentums in Deutschland." *Historische Zeitschrift* 253, no. 3 (1991): 603–628.

Weiss, Daniel H. "A Dialogue between Philosophy and Scripture: Rereading Hermann Cohen through Bakhtin." *Journal of Religion* 90, no. 1 (January 2010): 15–32.

Wiedebach, Hartwig. *Die Hermann-Cohen Bibliothek*. Hildesheim: Georg Olms Verlag, 2000.

———. "Aesthetics in Religion: Remarks on Hermann Cohen's Theory of Jewish Existence." *Journal of Jewish Thought and Philosophy* 11, no. 1 (2002): 63–73.

Wiese, Christian. "Struggling for Normality: The Apologetics of *Wissenschaft des Judentums* in Wilhelmine Germany as an Anti-colonial Intellectual Revolt against the Protestant Construction of Judaism." In *"Towards Normality?": Acculturation of Modern German Jewry*, edited by Rainer Liedtke and David Rechter, 77–101. Tübingen: J.C.B. Mohr, 2003.

———. *Challenging Colonial Discourse: Jewish Studies and Protestant Theology in Wilhelmine Germany*. Translated by Barbara Harshav and Christian Wiese. Leiden: Brill, 2005.

Wittgenstein, Ludwig. *Philosophical Investigations*. Translated by G. E. M. Anscombe. Englewood Cliffs, NJ: Prentice Hall, 1958.

———. *Tractatus Logico-Philosophicus*. Translated by D. F. Pears and B. F. McGuinness. London: Routledge & Kegan Paul, 1961.

Wyschogrod, Edith. "The Moral Self: Emmanuel Levinas and Hermann Cohen." *Daat* 4 (Winter 1980): 35–58.

Yadin, Azzan. *Scripture as Logos: Rabbi Ishmael and the Origins of Scripture*. Philadelphia: University of Pennsylvania Press, 2004.

Yaffe, Martin. "An Unsung Appreciation of the Musical-Erotic in Mozart's *Don Giovanni*: Hermann Cohen's Nod Toward Kierkegaard's *Either/Or*." In *International Kierkegaard Commentary on Either/Or I*, edited by Robert L. Perkins, 73–89. Macon, GA.: Mercer University Press, 1995.

Zac, Sylvain. *La philosophie religieuse de Hermann Cohen*. Paris: J. Vrin, 1984.

Zank, Michael. "Hermann Cohen und der rabbinische Literatur." In *Hermann Cohen's Philosophy of Religion: International Conference in Jerusalem, 1996*, edited by Stéphane Moses and Hartwig Wiedebach, 263–291. Hildesheim: Georg Olms Verlag, 1997.

———. *The Idea of Atonement in the Philosophy of Hermann Cohen*. Providence, RI: Brown Judaic Studies, 2000.

———. "First Critical Edition of the Writings of Hermann Cohen." *European Association for Jewish Studies Newsletter* 16 (Spring 2005): 48–58.

———. "The Ethics in Hermann Cohen's Philosophical System." In *Hermann Cohen's Ethics*, edited by Robert Gibbs, 1–15. Leiden: Brill, 2006.

———. "Between Dialogue and Disputation: Wilhelm Herrmann and Hermann Cohen on Ethics, Religion, and the Self." In *Theologie zwischen Pragmatismus und Existenzdenken*, edited by Gesche Linde, Richard Purkarthofer, Heiko Schulz, and Peter Steinacker, 131–148. Marburg: N. G. Elwert Verlag, 2006.

Author and Subject Index

abstraction
    in contrast to personal engagement,
        125–126, 198, 213, 265n57, 266n72
    as contrasted to God as person,
        142–143, 289n28
    and faculty of thought, 225–226n92
    and language, 265n58
    and method of philosophy,
        134–135, 186–187. *See also* method;
        humanity
actuality
    of God, 144–146, 197, 271nn20–21
    and the ideal, 16, 59, 116, 132–133, 203,
        208, 210–213, 234n81, 238n10
    and the infinitesimal, 181
    of the messianic future, 198–200,
        203–208
    of religious concepts, 26, 132–133,
        183–192, 196, 267n82. *See also*
        future, messianic; task
Adelmann, Dieter, 6, 92–93, 220n17,
    263n36
aesthetic sphere
    connections to sphere of religion, 24,
        117–118, 152, 262n31
    contrast to prophetic/religious
        concepts, 47–49, 61, 144, 226n92,
        230–231n36
    and style, 42–43
Alter, Robert, 243n63

Altmann, Alexander, 5–9, 253n47
Anckaert, Luc, 230n29
Archimedes, 181
Aristotle, 259n5, 300n111
Ästhetik des reinen Gefühls, 24, 118,
    277n71, 251n30
asymptote
    Cohen's thought and, 291nn55–56
    contrast to moment, 192–195
    infinite task as, 180, 200–203,
        292n59, 295n88, 296n95,
        299n103
atonement. *See* redemption; repentance
audience
    communication and, 120–125, 132–133,
        216, 235n89, 269n106
    of prophets, 47–48
Austin, J. L., 279n90
autonomy. *See* revelation; repentance

Bakhtin, Mikhail, 27
Barth, Karl, 119, 263n37
Batnitzky, Leora, 255n53, 270n9
*Begriff der Religion im System der
    Philosophie*
    and the particular individual, 14, 96,
        157, 225–226n92
    relation to philosophy, 92, 249n4
    relation to *Religion of Reason*, 7, 25,
        249n7, 251n25

Weiss, Daniel H., 225n90
Wellhausen, Julius, 224n69
Westfall, Carroll William, 115
Wiedebach, Hartwig, 225n83
Wiese, Christian, 20, 224n65, 224n68–69,
227n3, 228n6
Wittgenstein, Ludwig, 10, 229n25,
258n74, 292n60
writing
and orality, 78–83, 166, 219n1,
244n71–75, 245n82, 246n87
and its relation to ideas, 187, 226n92,
229–230nn27–28
Wyschogrod, Edith, 256n61, 291n55

Yadin, Azzan, 246n92, 247n98
Yaffe, Martin, 115, 261n11, 263n38
You
as address to God, 121–122, 130–131,
151, 154, 269n110, 274n39,
275–276n55, 303n142
and ethical responsibility,
141–142, 159–160, 163,
253n46, 256n61, 257n69,
289n38
and ethical selfhood, 56, 125, 226n94,
254n48

and love of fellowman, 146–147, 175,
186, 217n16
as non-graspable by Ethics, 24, 38,
94–95, 104–108, 207, 225n86,
249n10, 250n14, 253n47, 254n51,
254n53, 258nn73–74
as non-objective, 17, 83
and physical embodiment, 108–109,
256–257n66, 272n31

Zac, Sylvain, 115
Zank, Michael
on continuities in Cohen's thought,
6–7, 93–94, 250n14
on Cohen and Herrmann, 222n47,
251n21, 251nn24–25
on Cohen and Jewish texts,
224nn66–68, 227–228n4,
228nn6–7, 235n94, 243n61,
247n100, 286n185
on Cohen and Kierkegaard, 114
on Cohen's intellectual background,
224nn77–78, 225n89, 231n45,
263n36
on religion and philosophy in Cohen,
243n60
Zeno, 181, 288n9, 290n42

Scripture Index